D0918103

The Shadow Side of Fieldwork

Athena McLean dedicates this book to Thea Helen McLean and Trevor Jakob McLean, who have been ongoing sources of inspiration and support.

Annette Leibing dedicates it to Valesca von Usslar and Nellie Leibing.

The Shadow Side of Fieldwork

Exploring the Blurred Borders between Ethnography and Life

Edited by Athena McLean and Annette Leibing

Blackwell
Publishing

Barry University Library
11300 NE Second Avenue
Miami Shores, FL 33161

© 2007 by Blackwell Publishing Ltd

BLACKWELL PUBLISHING
350 Main Street, Malden, MA 02148-5020, USA
9600 Garsington Road, Oxford OX4 2DQ, UK
550 Swanston Street, Carlton, Victoria 3053, Australia

The right of Athena McLean and Annette Leibing to be identified as
the Authors of the Editorial Material in this Work has been asserted
in accordance with the UK Copyright, Designs, and Patents Act 1988.

All rights reserved. No part of this publication may be reproduced,
stored in a retrieval system, or transmitted, in any form or by any
means, electronic, mechanical, photocopying, recording or otherwise,
except as permitted by the UK Copyright, Designs, and Patents
Act 1988, without the prior permission of the publisher.

First published 2007 by Blackwell Publishing Ltd

1   2007

Library of Congress Cataloging-in-Publication Data

The shadow side of fieldwork : exploring the blurred borders between
ethnography and life / edited by Athena McLean and Annette Leibing.
        p. cm.
    Includes bibliographical references and index.
     ISBN 978-1-4051-6130-5 (hardcover : alk. paper)—ISBN 978-
1-4051-6981-3 (pbk. : alk. paper)   1. Ethnology—Field work.
2. Ethnology—Moral and ethical aspects.   I. McLean, Athena.
II. Leibing, Annette.
GN346.S33 2007
305.80072′3—dc22

                                                    2006034732

A catalogue record for this title is available from the British Library.

Set in 11.5/13.5pt Bembo
by Graphicraft Typesetters Ltd

The publisher's policy is to use permanent paper from mills
that operate a sustainable forestry policy, and which has been
manufactured from pulp processed using acid-free and elementary
chlorine-free practices. Furthermore, the publisher ensures that the
text paper and cover board used have met acceptable environmental
accreditation standards.

For further information on
Blackwell Publishing, visit our website:
www.blackwellpublishing.com

Contents

Contributors

Rose-Marie Chierici is Associate Professor in the Department of Anthropology, SUNY Geneseo, and Executive Director of Haiti Outreach-Pwoje Espwa (H.O.P.E), an NGO that supports community development initiatives in Borgne, Haiti, a subject in which she has conducted extensive fieldwork. She is author of *Denele: Making It, Migration and Adaptation among Haitian Boat People in the United States* and *Caribbean Migration in the Age of Globalization: Transnationalism, Race and Ethnic Identity*.

Ellen Corin is Professor at the Departments of Anthropology and Psychiatry, McGill University, Researcher at the Douglas Hospital Research Centre, and Psychoanalyst, member of the Canadian Psychoanalytic Society. Her publications include *Beyond Textuality. Asceticism and Violence in Anthropological Interpretation*, 1995, with G. Bibeau, and chapters in *Schizophrenia, Culture and Subjectivity* (Jenkins and Barrett, 2004) and *Subjectivity, Ethnographic Investigations* (Biehl, Good, and Kleinman, 2006).

Vincent Crapanzano is Distinguished Professor of Anthropology and Comparative Literature at the Graduate Center of the City University of New York. Among his most recent books are *Serving the Word: Literalism in America from the Pulpit to the Bench* (New Press, 2000) and *Imaginative Horizons: An Essay in Literary-Philosophical Anthropology* (University of Chicago Press, 2004).

Thomas J. Csordas is Professor of Anthropology at the University of California, San Diego. His publications include *The Sacred Self: A Cultural Phenomenology of Charismatic Healing* (University of California Press, 1994); *Embodiment and Experience: the Existential Ground of Culture and Self*, ed. (Cambridge University Press, 1994); *Language, Charisma and Creativity: Ritual Life in the Catholic Charismatic Renewal* (University of California Press, 1997); *Body/Meaning/Healing* (Palgrave, 2002).

Gelya Frank is Professor, Division of Occupational Science and Occupational Therapy at the School of Dentistry and Department of Anthropology, University of Southern California. Her publications focus on micro- and macro-histories and narratives in a range of social and cultural contexts. She is author of *Venus on Wheels: Two Decades of Dialogue on Disability, Biography and Being Female in America* (University of California Press, 2000), which was awarded the Basker Prize by the Society for Medical Anthropology. Also included in her publications are Gelya Frank and Carole Goldberg, *Defying the Odds: One California Tribe's Struggle for Sovereignty in Three Centuries* (Yale University Press, forthcoming), and L. L. Langness and Gelya Frank, *Lives; An Anthropological Approach to Biography* (Chandler and Sharp, 1981).

Gillian Goslinga is an anthropologist and graduate of the History of Consciousness Program at the University of California, Santa Cruz. Her work on gender, reproductive technologies, and "traditional" virgin birth beliefs in Tamil Nadu, South India, explores the interfaces of religion, science, and modernity in the lives of women. She has published in Feminist Studies on gestational surrogacy in the US, and directed/produced an ethnographic video on the subject, *The Child The Stork Brought Home*. Dr. Goslinga teaches at San Francisco State University. She is working on her next ethnographic video, *The Priest's Daughter* (forthcoming 2008).

Annette Leibing is an anthropologist with research interests in psychiatry, aging (esp. Alzheimer), medications, and new medical technologies (such as stem cells). She has taught anthropology at the Institute of Psychiatry, Federal University of Rio de Janeiro and been a visiting professor in Social Studies of Medicine, McGill (2002–05). She is now an associate professor for medical anthropology at the Faculty of Nursing, Université de Montréal. Her latest book, co-edited with Lawrence Cohen, is entitled *Thinking about Dementia – Culture, Loss, and the Anthropology of Senility* (Rutgers, 2006).

Anne M. Lovell, an anthropologist, is Senior Research Scientist at INSERM, the French national institute of health and medical research in Marseilles, France. Among her publications are "The City is My Mother," *American Anthropologist*, 1997. Most recently, she edited *Santé Mentale et Société* and co-edited *La Maladie Mentale en Mutation*. Dr. Lovell has conducted research in the injection drug use and risk, violence, homelessness, and the anthropology of disaster.

Athena McLean is Professor of Anthropology, the Department of Sociology, Anthropology and Social Work, Central Michigan University. Dr. McLean's research interests concern the production of clinical knowledge and practices regarding aging and psychiatry. She has particular interests in dementia care and advocacy movements in mental health and aging. Her writings include "Contradictions in the Social Production of Clinical Knowledge: the Case of Schizophrenia," *Social Science and Medicine*, 1990, and *The Person in Dementia: A Study of Nursing Home Care in the U.S.* (Broadview, 2007).

Dimitris Papageorgiou is Assistant Professor in the Department of Cultural Technology and Communication, University of the Aegean, Mytilini, Lesvos, Greece. He completed his B.A. in Biology at the University of Athens and his Ph.D. in Social Anthropology in the University of the Aegean, Mytilini. His research interests focus on hermeneutical approaches to performative practices and representational forms organizing promotion and management of cultural data in "real" (analogical) or digital contexts of interaction.

Barbara Rylko-Bauer is a medical anthropologist whose areas of research interest include applied anthropology, narrative, various facets of health inequities, health and human rights, violence, and the Holocaust. Recent publications include "Reclaiming Applied Anthropology: Its Past, Present, and Future" (with Merrill Singer and John van Willigen), *American Anthropologist*, 2006 and "Lessons about Humanity and Survival from My Mother and the Holocaust," *Anthropological Quarterly*, 2005.

Nancy Scheper-Hughes is Professor of Medical Anthropology at the UC Berkeley, where she directs the doctoral program in Critical Studies in Medicine, Science and the Body and is Director of Organs Watch, a medical human rights project. Her most recent books are *Commodifying Bodies* (co-edited with Loïc Waquant), 2002, Sage; *Violence in War and Peace: an Anthology* (co-edited with Philippe Bourgois), 2003, Blackwell Publishing; and *The Ends of the Body: the Global Traffic in Organs*, forthcoming, Farrar, Straus & Giroux.

Since completing his residency in 1991, **Jason Szabo** has been actively involved in HIV care and clinical research at McGill University. In 2004 he received a Ph.D. from McGill University in history and was a post-doctoral fellow in the Department of the History of Science, Harvard University from 2003–05. Dr. Szabo's main research interests are the history of chronic disease, disability, and terminal care. His book on the cultural history of incurable illness will appear in 2007. He was recently awarded a CIHR post-doctoral fellowship to work at the University of Paris (Paris 13) on a history of the AIDS epidemic.

Alisse Waterston is Associate Professor, Department of Anthropology, John Jay College of Criminal Justice with interests in political-economic and psychological aspects of dispossession and structural violence, and urban poverty and policy issues in the U.S. related to destitution, homelessness, and substance abuse. Her publications include *Love, Sorry and Rage: Destitute Women in a Manhattan Residence* and *Street Addicts in the Political Economy*, both with Temple University Press, and "Are Latinos Becoming 'White' Folk? And What that Still Says about Race in America," *Transforming Anthropology*, 2006.

Meira Weiss is Chair, Medical Sociology and Anthropology, The Hebrew University of Jerusalem. Professor Weiss has studied parents' selection of their children, testing and screening of soldiers, the commemoration and bereavement of fallen soldiers, media coverage of terrorist bombings, and women living under the masculine script of soldiering. Her publications include *The Chosen Body: The Politics of the Body in Israeli Society* (2002, Stanford University Press), and *Finger-printing the Collectivity: Power and Knowledge at the Israeli National Institute of Forensic Medicine* (forthcoming, Princeton University Press).

Foreword
In the Shadows:
Anthropological Encounters
with Modernity

Gillian Goslinga and Gelya Frank

In this path-breaking volume, editors Athena McLean and Annette Leibing turn our attention to the shadowy areas that anthropologists sometimes unexpectedly enter when performing ethnographic fieldwork. They issued a call for colleagues to write about "situations where the borders of personal life and formal ethnography begin to blur and the research field loses its boundedness." Interestingly, McLean and Leibing did not provide much more in the way of defining these shadows, nor did they need to. The theme drew an immediate and resounding response, first in a panel of papers at the annual meeting of the American Anthropological Association in 2003, and now with the publication of this book. Some of contemporary anthropology's most prominent figures are included here alongside scholars less well known outside their specialized research areas. The challenge to explore the "shadow side of fieldwork" has proven to be a great leveler, however.

Each essay displays unique authority as it draws us into territories where conventional professional comportment and methodological truisms fail as guides to action. We are faced with vivid ethnographic-style accounts of encounters that were disturbing for the fieldworker and that presented an intellectual and, almost as often, a moral challenge. The accounts are, at first glance, disarmingly singular and incommensurable. We might fear that taken together they have little to say to core issues in anthropology because what the authors find in the shadows is specific to each situation. Yet something important must be at stake here, where intuitively the authors converge so readily on this elusive shadow phenomenon. What is this phenomenon? And what is at stake for the discipline? These essays, in our view, address the very foundations of the production of knowledge under conditions of modernity. Readers should not be fooled, then, into thinking that this volume is simply a collection of "personal accounts" of fieldwork. Much more is going on here.

Our foreword aims to lay out some of the most salient theoretical and historical conditions that, we think, produce the shadows that the essays address. It should surprise no one familiar with anthropology that tensions between professional and personal dimensions of experience arise in field-work. Fieldwork, after all, has been defined precisely as the use of a person as the research instrument. Consequently, we can view this volume in contemporary methodological terms as a "multi-sited ethnography" of the shadows that emerge when the personal fails to fit within the framework of professionalism. The shadows can then be examined as locations where the sensory, imaginary, emotional, moral, and intellectual dimensions of actual experience provide knowledge that is incompatible with public knowledge. The residue, which these essays attempt to restore to public consideration, the editors and authors insist, is not merely private. The question the volume raises is: *Must we accept the dichotomy of "life" and "work" that constitutes, yet also confounds, the experience of fieldwork?* This question is important to answer because the split between "life" and "work" is precisely where public knowledge and private knowledge have been ripped apart.

A Brief Genealogy: Splits in the Modern Subject . . . And, Thereby, in the Anthropologist

By the 19th century, specific historical forces under capitalism effectively split "work" (remunerative occupations in the public sphere) from the rest of "life" (non-remunerative occupations in the domestic or private sphere). This split in European history was gendered, with the consequence that reparation has also been often gendered and stigmatized as "female." Most forms of feminist critique have tried to re-engage private worlds and the domestic domain with knowledge in the public sphere, but even its greatest victories cannot effectively challenge the positivist bent of know-ledge production at large. McLean and Leibing, and the authors of the essays, push up against this stigma and marginalization when they examine the shadows in fieldwork. This is because the shadows described in this volume present problems that are never strictly public or intellectual. These shadows arise when, paradoxically, "work" and "life" come together as they do, for example, in fieldwork. The contributors show that this coming together of "life" and "work" belongs not just to a feminist critique (e.g., "the personal is political") or to the specific province of a sub-method or subgenre within anthropology (e.g., reflexivity or "auto-ethnography"), but instead carries possibilities for anthropology at large. As their point of departure, the essays present the lives of professional researchers in ways that recognize the person as agent across personal and professional sites of activity, challenging what has been this false and counterproductive wall between "life" and "work." That wall has remained standing, despite anthropology's reflexive turn. These essays open novel routes and passages, and invite us to explore the long shadows this split has cast in two directions: on the privatized experience of fieldwork and on the published text.

The separation of "work" and "life" marks a politicized and disciplined border in the very constitution of the modern subject, his relationship to the living world, and what he can know about it. We deliberately gender this modern subject as male ("he") because this split mode of being emerged among male elites of Europe in the 17th and 18th centuries, later becoming generalized and hegemonic by the 19th century through the expansion of disciplinary institutions, including the academy. Philosopher Michel Foucault's work began to richly document the modern episteme in *The Order of Things* (*Les mots et les choses*) and postcolonial scholars have further detailed and historicized modernity as well. Ironically, the impulses of 20th-century anthropology, with its craftsman-like ideal of knowledge production based on prolonged face-to-face experience in pre-capitalist, non-literate, and non-Western communities, ran counter to this Western European episteme, which solicits universal classifications and theoretizations that can be captured – and exchanged as commodities – through text. But even though we anthropologists are trained to pay close attention to local particularities, and to avoid seemingly old-fashioned generalizations about Western (or non-Western) cultures, the modern episteme nevertheless compromises our profession's ways of encountering reality.

Why are we still steeped in this way of knowing? In Foucault's terms, the character of the modern episteme is distinctively "anthropological," presupposing that all things be classified and categorized by means of representation, and calling forth a space for Man to do the naming and ordering. These acts of representation depend on writing, if they are to be known to all, an idea that has been elaborated by Michel De Certeau. The episteme also demands that knowledge conform to a shared public standard that contrasts with and reinforces the existence of Man's private interiority ("the self," "experience"). This configuration naturalizes in our thinking an ontology of exteriorities and interiorities, of public and private realms, and of general, ubiquitous categories of experience presumed to be shared by all. Postcolonial scholar Dipesh Chakrabarty has called this last feature "the generalizing impulse of the sociological imagination."

Concepts such as "culture," "the social," "history," "nature," become so theoretically persuasive as to behave in our texts as a universal ontology, and not the historical intellectual constructs that they are. Consequently, a manner of categorizing and relating to the living world that emerged historically has doubled back to appear as literal maps of life; the manner is distinctly "anthropological" in so far as these maps are Man-made and yet, they mark off Man as merely their scribe.

These "doubling" processes clarify why, in our epoch, and in this volume, blurring the sharp distinction between "life" and "work" can seem at once transgressive and threatening. These essays will dislodge our categories: Do they convey real generalizable knowledge or merely personal reflections on methodology? Are they more than footnotes or asides to the discipline's agenda? The dilemma signals precisely why we must push on, and be careful not to dismiss these accounts from the frontlines.

The subject that knows

Foucault arrived at his characterization of modern knowledge as "anthropological" by tracing the history of representation from the Middle Ages to the near-contemporary period. The transformation was profound. In the episteme of the Middle Ages, signification and representation were not securely fixed in the hands of men. Meanings of things emerged according to principles of "resemblance" among propinquities, analogies, and associations of visible and salient marks of the surfaces of things. To know meant to divine the "signatures" of the "prose of the world"; wherein the meaning of things was ordered and reordered apart from human control and had to be read constantly anew. To know was to practice a hermeneutic in which the terms were not textual but close to the living world, and the world's own teeming manner of unfolding.

To this order of things, the Classical period from the 16th century to the close of the 18th introduced a profound break that coincided with the start of the colonial expansion, a public culture of print and graphics, and the enclosure of the commons – coincidences that were no accident since one could say that knowledge also was "privatized" during this period. As anthropologist Marilyn Strathern elaborates in her most recent work, texts began to be treated legally and conceptually as the "children" and "intellectual property" of authors. Representation was no longer a play of signs in the living world, hinting at meanings established by Divine intention or natural history since the beginning of time, but instead a heuristic that increasingly began to dominate encounters with the world. Classical representation – such as the ambitious projects of the *Taxinomia* or the *Mathesis* tables – called forth what Foucault describes as "a subject that knows." This subject was endowed with "the power to present himself with representations" and thus could stand as sovereign in his own right – as "author." The subject's power drew from his separate interiority in the Classical Age, a process for which Descartes's famous Cogito ("I think, therefore I am") has become an emblem.

By the 19th century, Man would appear to himself and to others as both an object of knowledge and a subject that knows – or, in Foucault's words, "an enslaved sovereign, observed spectator." The relationship between words and things had radically altered: Things no longer manifested their identity in representation, but instead, as Foucault explains, in their external relation to the human being. This method of encountering the world inscribed a set of public and standardized categories onto the nature of things – thereby also differentiating the sovereignty of the knowers with respect to the things themselves. The "subject that knows" now thinks of himself as separate from the world and its manifold possibilities. Glimpses of pre-modern epistemes are pushed to the margins of private experience. Some scholars have tried to redirect our attention toward the living world – "the blooming, buzzing confusion" of the infant's mind (William James), surprising encounters with the "bumptious, non-literal world" for which our texts fail to prepare us (Donna Haraway), and even the floating signifier of Derridean deconstruction. Our habits of textual representation from the Classical and Modern periods make it extremely difficult to deal with these breakthroughs except by reinscribing familiar categories, thus sustaining the sovereignty and authority of "the subject that knows." Anthropology's recent embrace of narrative theory, interpretative approaches ("thick description"), and the "poetics and politics of representation" may be seen as a rearguard struggle to illuminate but also to control unsettling encounters with an unruly and all-too-material world.

An awareness of the historical artifice of our knowledge-making practices opens to inquiry both "representation" and the "subject that knows." While "representation" has been the focus of analysis in anthropology in recent years, the "subject that knows" remains somewhat shadowed still. Because our very methods require that we use our experiences, our encounters, our one-on-one relationships with informants as our primary research instruments, we anthropologists during fieldwork are confronted almost daily with the ambiguities and limitations of the public/private split in the "subject that knows." Our trademark method of "participant observation" captures in its name this tension and the contradiction. On the one hand, we are called to maintain critical distance and, on the other, to plunge again and again into the living world. It is no wonder then that the "crisis of representation" has been so acute for anthropologists and the discipline, or so productive of enlightening critiques of modern knowledge and its metaphysical conceits at large. It is no wonder, either, that perplexity, excitement, and tentativeness characterize many of the essays in this volume, as they make public these tensions. For, generally speaking, in the rift between "life" and "work," all forms of embodied and living knowledges are policed in order to uphold the purity of the representation and the sovereignty of the "subject that knows": emotions, aesthetics, affinities, moral feelings and urges, and, when contrary to national and institutional regimes, political commitments and actions.

Toward New Ethical Epistemontologies

The crises, desires, explorations, and risk-takings of the authors speak, then, to a specifically European knot of culture, history, and power – a knot that, as Bruno Latour put it (*We Have Never Been Modern*), has gripped "all critical positions" of knowledge. The most salient consequences for our experiences as anthropologists have been that, despite our seemingly prolonged engagement in the field, we may have been forced too quickly to judge the meaning of things, obligated as we are to produce texts in conversation with ongoing intellectual debates and literature. We may have treated our representations as all too definite and literally real. As a result, we may become impatient for knowledge and generally resistant to the unfolding of the living world. Possible dimensions of understanding that do not conform to existing categories or that expediently result in them thus might have eluded us. Anthropologists such as Michael Jackson, Paul Stoller, Frédérique Apffel-Marglin, and Edith Turner have suggested as much, and we feel, like them, that there is a great deal at stake. The "shadows" the writers speak of here concern these elided dimensions.

Finally, our knowledge risks remaining anthropocentric in the sense that all order is imposed from a modern human point of view. This is a point that critics from a number of directions have been making, including indigenous peoples, environmentalists, and, more recently, animal studies scholars. Often, these distinctly non-modern or even nonhuman experiences are passed over in public accounts of fieldwork and the writing of knowledge precisely because they do not conform but in fact sometimes outright defy existing categories. Though there may be outlets in "alternative" culture to represent these nonhuman-centered dimensions, they are rarely objects of serious critical inquiry. Rather they are dismissed as fringe or private matters. These essays powerfully, if cautiously, challenge us to make public knowledge out of those experiences.

New approaches that might be called "epistemontologies" following Karen Barad will be needed if subjects are to be respectful of what they do not know, what they cannot fully and clearly name, and what exists in relationships beyond a certain narrow range of anthropocentric experience. Anthropology has perhaps never been challenged more to fulfill its radical promise to apprehend other ways of being. The bringing together of life with work is imperative. Without even having to abandon the subject's centrality in Western tradition, it *is* possible to found knowledge on premises other than modern epistemology. As Emmanuel Levinas proposes (*Otherwise than Being* (*Autrement qu'être*)), the world is quite different if founded ethically face-to-face with Others as living beings. Several of the writers articulate fieldwork challenges that echo Levinas's call for ethics first in our manner of relating with the living world. These writers disclose unsettling moral rumblings in the act of conducting research, as well as experiences outside conventional ontology that provoke different knowledges. These writers' very embodiment – feelings, intuitions, gut reactions – becomes a moral and intellectual compass.

When the "subjects that know" are not tethered to a particular manner of making knowledge, or to a particular professional public persona in a disciplinary context, or to a particular body of knowledge, the production of knowledge then becomes dynamic, tentative, relational. This is why the editors readily acknowledge that they find it premature to theorize the shadows definitively. Perhaps our own theorization of the split between "life" and "work" as an adequate explanation of the shadows in fieldwork may require amendment. To theorize these shadows prematurely would be to force narrative closure on a mode of encountering the world that is necessarily embodied and therefore complex, emergent, and heterogeneous. To allow for the world to unfold requires time and respect for things as they show themselves to be, not necessarily as they are represented to be.

To achieve this manner of encounter, however, the "subject that knows" must risk giving up his or her sovereignty. When the need is to be sovereign, other voices and sources of signification have to be repressed or, if not repressed, then muted or "inappropriate/d" for other ends, as feminist Donna Haraway has suggested (*Ecce Homo*). The authors in this volume begin methodologically with an "I" that does not claim to be in textual possession of the living world. This more humble "I" troubles the border of privacy that guarantees the professional authority of the public representation, and allows other voices and sources of signification into the production of knowledge. The willingness of each author to describe moments of perceived failure or dissonance, or of intense identification and gut reaction, or of uncomfortable feedback or silence from their subjects, enables them to engage with something beyond the representational

veneer of the "successful" ethnography. Such choices are not just methodological and political, but also theoretical. They counter "the generalizing
impulse of the sociological imagination" by resisting it. Resisting this impulse
means slowing down and becoming comfortable with ambiguity, contradictions, heterogeneity, and the real consequences, in James Clifford's terms,
of knowing that we have only "partial knowledges."

To venture out invites a predictable backlash: a loss of authority because
of the imputation of a loss of objectivity. Some readers may take away an
impression that the knowledge produced here is too small in scope or
too concrete, that is under-theorized or, worse, plainly untheoretical. The
authors, each in his or her own way, do in fact wrestle with the problem
of preserving professional integrity. And they ask us to seek with them
the theoretical value of the knowledges they acquired in their field
experiences. We have tried in this Foreword to suggest something of the
theoretical value of their efforts to bring together "life" and "work." This
important volume helps to clear a path through shadows that our discipline
cannot afford to leave unexplored.

Acknowledgments

The authors wish to thank Barbara Rylko-Bauer for her thoughtful comments throughout this project, and editors at Blackwell (Jane Huber, Steve Smith, and Rosalie Robertson) for their support in bringing this project to fruition.

We also acknowledge permissions to reprint the following materials:

Chapter 1 by Alisse Waterston and Barbara Rylko-Bauer is an adaptation of "Out of the Shadows of History and Memory: Personal Family Narratives in Ethnographies of Rediscovery," which appeared in *American Ethnologist* 33(3):397–412, © 2006, American Anthropological Association. Used with permission. All rights reserved.

Chapter 3, "The Scene: Shadowing The Real," by Vincent Crapanzano appeared under the same title in *Theoretical Anthropology* 6(4), © 2006, Sage Press. Used with permission. All rights reserved.

"Learn to Value Your Shadow!" An Introduction to the Margins of Fieldwork

Annette Leibing and Athena McLean

The advice "learn to value your shadow" is the moral of "The Wonderful History of Peter Schlemihl" (von Chamisso 1814), a story about a man who, like Goethe's Faust, sold his shadow to the devil.[1] *The Shadow Side of Fieldwork* follows Schlemihl's advice, since its aim is to value and increase awareness of what generally remains hidden in fieldwork productions: that which is unspoken or unspeakable, invisible, mysterious, or not immediately perceivable to the ethnographer, the interlocutor, or the reader. These deal with the twilight of the obvious, the backgrounded (cf. Douglas 1999:3–5), the taken for granted, the allowed, and the imposed. These issues are most apparent in situations where the borders of personal life and formal ethnography begin to blur and the research "field" loses its boundedness. However, shadows are present in all fieldwork.[2] In the Jewish tradition, Schlemihl (*Schlemiel* in Yiddish) is a clumsy and unfortunate figure, but in von Chamisso's story Schlemihl became unfortunate because he did not take his shadow seriously. In contrast to von Chamisso's unlucky character who never received his shadow back, the authors of this volume point to different ways of at least getting closer to what is being overshadowed in fieldwork.

As the chapters in this volume illustrate, shadow and light exist in relation to each other. The question we ask is, "How can we approach and describe this relation of light and shadow?" – while keeping in mind that some issues should perhaps be kept in the dark (cf. Strathern 2000; Star and Strauss 1999:23). There may be manifold reasons why something may be hidden and we do not pretend to cover the full range of possibilities. However, it is worth challenging the borders and the margins of the commonly perceivable and observable in research not only because new knowledge and understandings may be revealed, but also because the shadow might directly trouble or "overshadow" what lies in the light.

We do not suggest that by doing this we will be able to achieve wholeness or transparency (Latour 2005), or presume that this would be desirable or even possible (cf. Frankenberg 2005). Our aim is rather to initiate a discussion about the different levels and layers of fieldwork processes and of social and cultural phenomena, which are overshadowed and sometimes completely out of sight in our research and texts. In doing so, we call attention to the possibility of play of light and shadow in order to achieve a fuller, more critical, and nuanced picture (cf. Strathern 2004). However, we do not intend to offer an ultimate theory regarding the shadow. Our theoretical discussion will be more tentative, framing, than providing a final conception or recipe. In the most general terms, paying attention to the shadow means "seeing what frames our seeing" (Davies et al. 2004:364).

There are many motivations for exploring the shadow. The researcher may be driven by a curiosity about the mysterious, hidden, or uncanny side of reality. The exploration may be provoked by the need to engage the painful, protected, or secretive elements that, to some extent, are part of all fieldwork. The researcher may also seek to examine a troubling, perhaps unequal relationship (e.g., Lambek 1997), or bring attention to the power differentials under which prior knowledge was constructed. Writing about such shadows, however, should not be mistaken for common voyeuristic revelations.[3] In fact, as many of the chapters show, the shadows confronted by the writers often extend beyond observable phenomena to sensory, affective, and experiential perceptions and reflections.

The chapters in this volume examine the research experiences and dilemmas as well as personal and political challenges of scholars who have questioned the source, or acknowledged the hidden or paradoxical nature of their ethnographic findings and insights. They ask, for example, about their ongoing positioning and repositioning in the field in relation to their interlocutors. Some wonder as well how a researcher who is part of, or involved with, a research setting, an organization, a reference group, or even a relationship can legitimately study it (Labaree 2002). The contributors, however, go beyond postmodern assertions of "locating" themselves (cf. Simpson 2002) or getting "involved with the field" – shifting the focus of analysis from only Schlemihl's soul to the devil itself.

Dia-Ethnography of the Shadow

By describing and theorizing the "beyondness" of anthropological research, we do not use "the shadow" only as a metaphor; but as an approximation of the very real, though less perceivable relations, practices, and field experiences dealt with by the authors. Nevertheless, the shadow is rich in its imagery, its degrees of revealing and hiding – *umbra* and *penumbra* – and its polyvocality in relation to various levels of anthropological theorizing. Technically, a shadow is caused by the interception of radiation by an opaque object (Jenkins and White 2001). The position of the source of radiation, its angle to the object, plays an important role in the shaping of the shadow and, more importantly, in one's capacity to notice it. As all the articles of this volume show, changing position is an important tool for throwing additional light on the object under study.

But there is rarely only one source of radiation, and often multiple sources of obfuscation produce many shadows over the course of fieldwork. Confronting them requires moving back and forth between areas of light and shade during research – before, during, and after being "in the field." This kind of movement is captured in ethnographic practices that Paul Rabinow (1996) calls "dia-ethnography": "In Greek, *dia* . . . denotes relation and/or motion" (p. ix). Rabinow emphasizes that ethnographies are active, processual, and made up of "situated curiosity."

Every ethnographer's relation with hidden, mysterious, evasive, or forbidden phenomena in fieldwork (whether at the intrapsychic, intersubjective, or more broadly social and political levels) is unique, varying with the nature of the shadows and the intersection(s) among them. Although some of the authors in this volume emphasize the processual, diachronic aspects of ethnographies, many pay attention more to the relational elements of fieldwork, privileged somewhat by the title of our book. Nevertheless, the processual is implicit in most texts (e.g., the historical situatedness of the category "Holocaust survivor" in Waterston and Rylko-Bauer's article).

Some of the writers in this volume focus mainly on their personal struggles (the self of the ethnographer in relation to her *internal* shadows) as a means for understanding their social world. Others focus more on *external* phenomena or shadows they encounter in the field and their relation to them. Most of the essays address both to some extent, at least implicitly in their work.

Taking a closer look at the relational aspects of dia-ethnographies – which cannot be perceived independently from the processual – we might tentatively frame the different approaches to the shadow in this volume as relying on a continuum between two poles. One pole focuses on the author herself (and her personal shadows) as a means of better understanding social phenomena. The other pole focuses toward social phenomena and the ethnographer's negotiations with the social world and the shadows encountered there. These may range from immediate intersubjective relations to more globally remote social and political phenomena. The elements, which occupy these two poles, or lie between them, are combined and juxtaposed in a different way by each author, as she confronts various shadows, or formulates her specific approaches to them.

The dynamic quality of dia-ethnography captures each writer's movement back and forth between the two poles (or points along it) both during the process of conducting research and in subsequent reflections on it. Although such movement between the ethnographer and her or his data is part of any reflexive process of ethnography, it is even more vital in the critical reflexive work that occurs when examining shadows. This is because when working in these elusive, typically neglected, and possibly unsanctioned areas, the researcher is likely to feel especially vulnerable: this realm of the ambiguous would be safer left alone.

These dia-ethnographies are necessarily *processual*, with the researcher actively engaging with points present, past, and future over the course of research and later reflection. Movement in time cannot be separated from movement between the two poles, however, as each researcher uniquely juxtaposes memories and past data, present experiences and observations, and vision for future praxis. The processual, when approaching the shadow, involves two different, though complementary, approaches for the editors. One editor (McLean) emphasizes the impact of the researcher (and her personal shadows) on the research and the interpenetration between research and private life. The second editor (Leibing) stresses more the historical embeddedness of research data (and the researcher herself) and its concomitant shadows.

Carl Gustav Jung was among the earliest to relate the concept "shadow" to the self, exploring intra-psychic aspects as related to the social world. Writing early last century, he discussed personal shadows as the ignored and troublesome parts of a person, in direct opposition to the conscious ego: "Taking it in its deepest sense, the shadow is the invisible saurian tail that man still drags behind him. Carefully amputated, it becomes the healing serpent of the mysteries. Only monkeys parade with it" (Jung 1973 [1939]:217).

For Jung, integrating the shadows of the intra-psychic world into one's consciousness was a moral obligation of the person, because failing to do so would result in their negative projection into the social world, as with xenophobia or wars (cf. Kast 2001): "Such a man knows that whatever is wrong in the world is in himself, and if he only learns to deal with his own shadow he has done something real for the world . . . shouldering . . . part of the gigantic, unsolved social problems of our day" (Jung 1938:140).

Identifying intra-psychic ills as the direct cause of social ailments is no longer theoretically or political supportable.[4] Still, the importance Jung gave to first resolving the *situatedness of the personal* in order to be able to come to terms with social phenomena is an important insight relevant to the ethnographic encounter. Furthermore, not doing so may cast additional shadows on the researcher, the research process, and the findings.

The second pole, which approaches shadow phenomena as primarily social, may be illustrated by Mary Douglas's (1999; see also Douglas 1995) efforts to "examine the implicit" (which approximates what we would call "the shadow"). The implicit is information "pushed out of sight" (p. 3), or "backgrounded" when, for example, something is being called untrue or even "too true" to be questioned. She recommends, for example, study-ing "the classifications by which people decide if an action has been done well or badly, whether it is right or wrong" (p. vi) in order to get closer to implicit meaning.

Douglas, without doubt, perceives these (implicit) shadows as linked to the researcher. In one of her essays, for example, she writes about the role of animals in the daily life of the Lele, a group she studied at the end of the 1940s. Looking back, she laments her initial, superficial gaze when doing fieldwork: "If my fieldwork had been more thorough I would have been able to understand better the meaning this scaly ant-eater had for them. *Their knowledge was not explicit; it was based on shared, unspoken assumptions*" (p. xi; emphasis added). Thus, while dealing primarily with manifesta-tions in the social world, Douglas acknowledges the importance of the researcher in helping to unearth that which is implicit. But she does so not by looking at her personal or intrapsychic shadows, but rather by confronting how cultural institutions work to mark what they value.

By drawing attention to processes of "backgrounding" social phenomena into the shadows – as invisible or forgotten – she echoes work in other critical studies that confront or "make visible" the self-evident (see Rabinow 2003:41). This becomes important for addressing the *political* dimension of "backgrounding" that determines which phenomena will be made visible or invisible and which voices will be heard or silenced (cf. Achino-Loeb 2006:2–3).

Other contemporary ethnographers have also used the shadow – as an image (e.g., Stoller and Olkes 1987; Liu 2000; Bluebond-Langner 2000) or tool (e.g., Das and Poole 2004:30; Frank 2000; Behar 1993; Crapanzano 1992) – to write about less perceivable issues. Like most of them, we use the shadow to trouble the topic under study, and not necessarily to dig out something to be found under the surface of appearances.

The notion of the shadow brings attention to field experiences and some-times troubling field relationships of which the author and researcher is an important part. These may involve the ethnographer herself as a source of illumination, or unwittingly, of obstruction to knowledge. They may address the partial or complete "blindness" of the observer, as many of the articles in this volume do. Like Schlemihl with his shadow, ethnographers of this volume are inextricably tied to their research, their own shadows inevitably infusing the subjects they study. This delicate matter of bringing the author/observer into the analysis – as a source of light but not as the light itself (as sometimes happens in autoethnographies), as directly related to the object under study but not the object itself – forms the blurred borders between ethnography and life.

The Blurred Borders between Ethnography and the Ethnographer's Life

This volume was inspired by the quandary one of us (Athena McLean) faced when studying a topic (nursing home care) that mirrored events in her own life with her mother. She found it increasingly difficult to separate personal sentiments and experiences from her research, and gradually came to value not doing so. Her personal involvement gave her privileged access to some data, while simultaneously blinding her to other data – and inflected her findings, questions, and interpretations. Delicate matters such as shame, fear, or mourning had to be dealt with as "rationalized emotions" (cf. Miceli 2004).

McLean invited Annette Leibing to join her in exploring similar epistemological challenges in the work of other scholars. Leibing suggested extending our scope to yet broader shadows. Together we invited several anthropologists and one historian of medicine to consider examining the shadow sides of their own research. We were surprised by the enthusiastic answers we received, although some colleagues showed hesitation, fearing implications on their professional lives: the margins of fieldwork seem to trouble a number of people, but for very different reasons, as the essays in this volume show. As Michel Foucault (2000) observed:

> Every time I have tried to do a piece of theoretical work it has been on the basis of elements of my own experience: always in connection with processes I saw unfolding around me. It was always because I thought I identified cracks, silent tremors, and dysfunctions in things I saw, institutions I was dealing with, of my relations with others, that I set out to do a piece of work, and each time was partly a fragment of autobiography. [p. 458; quoted in Davies et al. 2004]

Why not, we wondered, address these "cracks" and "dysfunctions" directly? The resulting contributions, though varied in subject matter and theoretical focus, bring the personal to bear on epistemological and ethical challenges in fieldwork. Many of the writers recognize the elusive character of some of their field encounters. Several admit uncertainties about the phenomena they encounter, or acknowledge possible distortions or misrepresentations in their interpretations. All the writers appreciate the complexity of the world as a source of potentially renewable understanding that their shadows may hold, as well as the "partial nature" of what can be known (Achino-Loeb 2006:14). Part of what we have called "relational" in fieldwork is the product of dialogue and intersubjective encounters. Various degrees of intimacy, empathy, intuition, reflexivity, and self-disclosure are at stake, problematizing the researcher in relation to her ethnographic data. These issues, faced by the contributors of this volume, have a long history in anthropology. Before discussing the articles, let's turn to that history.

Anthropologists' Selves in the Field

British social anthropology was fashioned as a social science that sought generalizable truth. Anthropologists sorted through their collected data to find regularities and cohesion in the confusion wrought by colonialism, and reported these in finished texts, undisturbed by personal sentiment. By the early part of the 20th century in the United States, however, anthropology had borne a distinctively Boasian appreciation for uniqueness and historical complexity. Drawing from his training in German romantic idealism and materialism (Stocking 1974), Boas's science had antipositivist leanings that permitted, even sometimes encouraged, personal reflection in his students (Frank 2000:95).[5]

However, after World War II, and especially after the 1950s, demands for a neutral, value-free research in the social sciences had strengthened (Callaway 1992:38) also in the United States. It was now incumbent upon the anthropologist to remain a neutral detached observer, all while coming to terms with the very sentient, intersubjective demands of her or his practice. Renegade outlets for creative expressions, such as Laura Bohannan's legendary novel, *Return to Laughter* (1954, *nom de plume*, Eleanor S. Bowen), conveyed suppressed sentiments and personal anecdotes that were disallowed as messy, too soft and "feminine" (Bruner 1993:5), or ambiguous (Callaway 1992:39) for the largely male-fashioned, acceptable, academic venue. It was no wonder that only toward the end of her career did Hortense Powdermaker (1967) venture to incorporate autobiographical material in her writing. The strictures were such that even a deeply reflective researcher like Barbara Myerhoff (1974, 1979) believed her works were not fully anthropological (Callaway 1992:32–33). During this resolutely modernist period, the subjective voice of the researcher was generally confined to nontraditional literary forms (e.g., poetry) or to journalism (e.g., Herskovitz and Victor Turner) (Poewe 1996:195; Asad 1973), or remained part of the writer's memoirs or private writing, as earlier with Malinowski.

The same period, however, wrought an abundance of "self-reflexive" (Clifford 1986:14), confessional field accounts, produced as separate entities from the finished scientific ethnography (Marcus and Fischer 1986:33–34). Many of these personal accounts were written by women (often themselves professionally trained) like Edith Turner or Marjorie Shostak, whose anthropologist husbands wrote the traditional ethnography (Callaway 1992:31; Bruner 1993:5). The recognition of a gendered differentiation of labor in the field, however, may have led some women to reflect on what it means to be a woman in the field (e.g., Golde 1986 [1970]).

Ethnography's reflexive turn

This reflection about field experiences was further bolstered by a growing crisis in anthropology. During the late 1960s and early 1970s, critics of postcolonial anthropology began to question anthropology's involvement as a neutral bystander in colonialism. Disenchanted with the discipline's continued reliance on objectivist approaches to studying politically disadvantaged "others" (Asad 1973), they turned anthropology's gaze onto itself. These critics challenged anthropology's claims as an objective value-free social science and critically examined the political and personal consequences (e.g., Hymes 1974[1972]; Diamond 1974[1972]) of such a stance. By calling for a corrective "reflexive and critical anthropology," one critic, Bob Scholte (1974[1972]), turned attention to the subjectivities of both the ethnographer and the "native" as inseparable from the processes of knowledge production.

Scholte urged that ethnographic descriptions could no longer be accepted as givens, captured by "objective" trained observers but, drawing on hermeneutics, argued that they must be seen as the products of "interpretive" activities that rest in "communicative interaction" (pp. 440–441) and "empathetic appreciation" (p. 449). This required a kind of self-understanding (see also Diamond 1974 [1972]:409–413) that could only be produced in relation to others. But for this group of critics, reflexivity was a "necessary, though not sufficient" part of a larger political and, given the period, "emancipatory" (pp. 446–449) anthropological praxis.

A few years later, reflexive ethnographies (e.g., Rabinow 1977; Dumont 1978; Crapanzano 1980) ushered in an "experimental" moment (cf. Marcus and Fischer 1986) with postmodern texts that accommodated the ethnographer's personal reflections as well as his or her dialogue with interlocutors as the source of knowledge. For Crapanzano, *Tuhami* (1980) was an "experiment" that represented a significant departure from traditional ethnographies marked unreflectively by the anthropologist's authority, invisibility, and supposed neutrality – something that had concerned him since his student days when taking a methods course with Margaret Mead (p. ix). *Tuhami* shared with the reader its author's own heavily edited field notes, inviting the reader to his or her own interpretation. Some critics have argued that "experiential" ethnographies occurred quite apart from this "experimental moment," despite being placed there (Poewe 1996). *Tuhami*, however, was also "experiential" because it used the field experiences of the ethnographer as the basis for serious epistemological questioning. It also conveyed the complexity of *Tuhami*'s experience (Marcus and Fischer 1986:42–43) and the necessarily hypothetical basis of its author's interpretations of it (Crapanzano 1980:148).

Writing during this same period, Gelya Frank (1979) added to the reflexivity discourse with her phenomenological critique of the life history method that also drew attention to the conscious, dialogic, and experiential bases of knowledge production. Contra to conventional views, she argued, life history, unlike autobiography, is a "collaboration involving the consciousness of the investigator as well as the subject" (p. 70). In fact, "in this sense it may represent a portrait of the investigator as well . . . a shadow biography" (p. 85). Despite "self-evident" presumptions that the life history is an objective document that "speaks for itself," Frank argued that it is not just a sample of the "whole person" (p. 75) or "raw data" to be used to draw social scientific formulations (p. 77). Rather, it is a form that emerges dialogically, blending together "the consciousness of the investigator and the subject" (p. 85).

During the 1980s anthropologists were also directed to more pragmatic concerns necessitated by the increasing need to work at "home" (Messerschmidt 1981; Jackson 1987). In Great Britain, this pressed researchers to be reflexive as they came to terms with their personal engagement with the familiar (Okeley 1992:11; Young and Meneley 2005:7). Marilyn Strathern (1987) both problematized the scope of "home" at the same time that she prophetically put to rest the notion that conducting anthropology "at home" would automatically guarantee ethnographic knowledge (Buzard 2003:3)[6] – an argument supported in a recent set of ethnographic studies (Hume and Mulcock 2004).[7] Still, the move to looking close to home, as Strathern observed (1987), can shrink to the borders of the individual and the autobiographical imagination, as it has increasingly been accused of doing in some autoethnographies in recent years (see below).

By the mid-1980s, two influential texts drew attention to the problems of realist ethnographic representations of the "other." Prompted in part by Edward Said's critique (1979) of Western representation of non-Western cultures, Marcus and Fischer's *Anthropology as Cultural Critique* (1986) resounded the need for ongoing critical reflection of ethnographers' moral and social engagements in the field as well as of their representations of them. They examined experimental forms of ethnographic writing as potentially more sensitive representations of other cultures as well as reflexive self-critiques. Clifford and Marcus's edited volume, *Writing Culture* (1986), examined similar issues, drawing particular attention to anthropology's literary turn to textual forms and also attuning anthropologists to the politics of representation. Clifford hoped to shift ethnography away from a visual paradigm, which would perpetuate the structure of relations that depended on traditional participant-"observation" to a more democratic discursive cultural "poetics" (p. 12), or literary text, broadly construed (Clifford 1986:3–6). However, he evoked sharp criticism from feminists (e.g., Abu-Lughod 1991) who felt he had ignored their contributions.

Fifteen years later, Scholte (1987) voiced regret that reflexivity had become restricted to the textual positioning of the self. Fischer too felt that a preponderance of ethnographies in the 1990s had touted an individualized reflexivity which his and Marcus's *Anthropology as Cultural Critique* (1986) had never advocated (Fischer 2003:12). Yet as more people began to reflexively examine their personal engagements in the field, they often justified their "solipsistic exercises" (Young and Meneley 2005:7) by citing texts that had actually objected to such restrictive practices (Fischer 2003:12). Like Fischer, Fabian argued for a return to an active processual, dialectical, and intersubjective reflexivity (2001:50) in order to produce individually and historically contextualized knowledge. Other scholars argued, however, that even a self-centered reflexivity can lead to a more radical self-awareness that can affect the politics of conducting fieldwork (Callaway 1992:33) – a view of reflexivity in radical opposition to the critical epistemic social reflexivity to which Bourdieu tirelessly subjected intellectual works (Wacquant 1992:36–46).

Empathy in fieldwork

Reflexivity legitimized examining subjective experiences as part of the research process and analysis (Clifford 1986:13). Those experiences could include feelings, intuitions, and "sympathetic identity" (Scholte 1974[1972]:443), or empathy, with ethnographic "others." Even before the reflexive turn, however, Boas had adopted an empathic approach toward marginalized persons. In fact, he and his students had used empathy, or "seeing from within," as a tool in fieldwork (Frank 2000:96). As a way of extending understanding of the "aboriginal mentality," he trained native ethnographers, locals, and women anthropologists (who could gain greater access to differently gendered experiences), and was engaged in debates about the quality of data collected by those who were heavily invested in their research (Buzard 2003:66). He also supported the work of his "negro" student, Zora Neal Hurston, to conduct anthropology "at home" in her native south (Buzard 2003:66), because he assumed a native ethnographer would achieve a fuller understanding by being a member of the group (Young and Meneley 2005:5). True to his scientific training, he felt this "inwardness" could be best achieved by "objective documentation" by natives rather than by the "uncontrollable intuitions of romantic outsiders" (Lowie 1960:133, cited in Frank 2000:96). His realist perspective, however, sometimes clashed with the views of native ethnographers (which anticipated what some call the "postmodern view") that "ethnographic truth was partial, perspectival, and embedded in social and material relations of power and obligation" (Finn 1995:140, cited in Frank 2000:96).

Ruth Benedict and Margaret Mead also appreciated the value of empathy. But whereas Benedict was concerned with how members of other cultures gain self-understanding, Mead recognized that the ethnographer must also explore her own biases and shadows before she can begin to understand others (Frank 2000:97). While empathy has been fundamental to many interpretive accounts, Bourdieu viewed it as an impediment to clarity (Reed-Danahay 2005:126) and Geertz rejected it as unnecessary (Marcus and Fischer 1986:30–31) or incompatible with understanding (*Verstehen*) (Frank 2000:97–98). What happens to understanding, Geertz wondered, when empathy (*Einfühlung*) is lacking?

Geertz's rejection, Frank argues, rested on too limited a view of empathy as simply intuition or feeling of another's state. Through empirical hermeneutic analysis, Frank moves empathy beyond intuition, with distinct ethical and moral dimensions. Like Poewe (1996:197–198) though, she found that empathy need not always be positive, and that even negative empathy can be a source of insight (Frank 2000:98–99). In fact, for Poewe, it was this very awareness of difference at times of intimacy which rendered negative empathy such a powerful tool for appreciating others (pp. 198–199). Thus, far from being "narcissistic," as has sometimes been asserted (cf. Okeley 1992:2), reflexivity can promote a political praxis consistent with Scholte's (1974 [1972]) original vision. But this can occur only by taking the intersubjective encounter to new levels.

The "auto" in ethnography: toward an economy of self-disclosure

Okeley rightly asserts that the experience of fieldwork is "totalizing," drawing upon the "whole being," and not reducible to the mere "collection of data by a dehumanized machine" (1992:3). Compellingly, she adds: "Autobiography dismantles the positivist machine." Much autoethnography in fact was written in reaction to positivist ethnographies from which the ethnographic self had been excluded. Carolyn Ellis (1991, 2003), for example, advocated an "emotional sociology" that defiantly challenged previous traditions. Anthropologists (e.g., Ruth Behar 1993, 1996) have also encouraged, though more gently, clearly articulating the relevance of emotions in ethnographic works.

By the late 1980s and 1990s, autoethnography provided a new autobiographical outlet for the ethnographic self and a particular vehicle of expression for suppressed feminist and postcolonial voices. However, there have been such a range of autoethnographic expressions that the term has lost any singular meaning (Buzard 2003).[8] This may be why Clifford could criticize them as overly self-absorbing in one writing (Clifford 1986:15) while lauding them as a "particularly promising" analytic tool in another (Buzard 2003:64).

At its most general, autoethnography is a "form of self-narrative that places the self within a social context" (Reed-Danahay 1997:9). Thus, ethnographic writing that involves reflections on one's self and one's field experiences can be considered, in the broadest sense, autoethnographic. Reed-Danahay (2005:126) describes a broad continuum from those writers whose reflexivity has been construed as individualized, self-celebratory, and "navel-gazing" to those seen as confessional, to the other extreme of those who have demanded a historical and consciously social reflexivity. Despite his distaste for explicitly revealing emotions and intents, Bourdieu's concept of *habitus* permits a different kind of noninteriorized autoethnography that allows for what Spry (2001) calls "an embodied methodological praxis" (Reed-Danahay 2005:126). Thus others argue that all ethnography is inevitably connected to the autobiographical, not only at its most passionate (Fabian 2001:12, 32), but even at its seemingly most removed.

The negative associations of autoethnography as narcissistic and confessional came to a head after Ruth Behar's publication of *Translated Woman* (1993), the life story of Esperanza Hernandez, a Mexican street peddler. In the closing chapter of her book, Behar draws upon her own life story (her "Biography in the Shadow"), making subtle connections between the violences to which both she and Esperanza had been subjected. The comparisons made by this privileged academic, in describing her innermost sense of oppression, ambition, and rage, did not convince her readers, however, and drew the ire of many.

Gelya Frank (1995) argued, however, that the problem was not in revealing too much to the reader. As Frank noted elsewhere (2000:84–85), every confession is necessarily selective, hiding as much as revealing. If anything,

Behar "underanalyzed" (Frank 1995:358) what she did reveal and failed to make explicit links between her self-disclosure and the production of knowledge. In this process, Frank asserts, no type or amount of information or autobiographical experiences should be off limits from disclosure as they can lead to new understandings. However, she cautiously adds, "reporting self-reflexive or autobiographical material is relevant *only to the point that the author shows its relevance* to the production of knowledge" (letter to Athena McLean, December 27, 2005).

We firmly adopt the position that the ethnographer's personal data are relevant only as they relate to, and help illuminate, the ethnographic process. Thus we urge caution against confessional excesses. We call further for a measured *economy of disclosure*, aspiring to "discretion," rather than "confession" (Lovell 2003) as a mode of disclosure. This means exercising discretion in sharing *only what we must* about our personal lives (while at the same time not holding back what needs to be examined) for the purposes of advancing knowledge for ourselves, our interlocutors, and our readers.

Approaching Issues in the Shadow

How does approaching the shadow compare with – and depart from – this history of personal engagement in fieldwork? The authors in this volume approach the shadow through subjective means similar to those described above. However, they tend toward critical reflexivity and dia-ethnographic approaches in examining perplexing social phenomena that produce more challenging analyses than typically found in ethnographic work. A few turn their gaze onto intimate or forbidden terrain (to a close family member, for example), confounding the borders between ethnography and private life, but do so in order to explore questions far beyond individual concerns. Several discuss situations that occurred while doing fieldwork that brought them to the edges of reality, uncomfortably pushing them beyond the realm of ordinary, taken for granted, experience.

The writers, however, do not stop here; their focus is with phenomena and relations that somehow seem amiss or extraordinary, and rarely examined in research. People become aware of something troubling because they feel it is out of place – the Jungian "saurian tail" that nags at them. In this volume, this nagging sense occurs not only in the ethnographic works that examine the personal dimension of fieldwork, but also in the only article where this relation is extra-textual, that of Jason Szabo, a historian of medicine. (Szabo could make certain observations only because of his previous education and experience as a medical doctor.[9])

Thus the articles in this volume describe processes of getting closer to the shadow and bringing into awareness at least some of what had previously been hidden. In this sense, these are hopeful accounts, even though they sometimes face disturbing sides of reality. The authors show courage in facing the darker issues of fieldwork (and life). But darkness needs not be negative; indeed in the natural sciences, shadows have proven to be a "magnificent tool" for knowledge (Casati 2003:6).

The following overview describes various ways in which the authors have conceptualized and approached the shadow in their research. While acknowledging the considerable thematic overlap among the selections, we organized them into the following topical clusters.

Secrecy and silence in the ethnographic encounter

The first two chapters deal with what is sometimes called *umbra* in optics – a region of complete shadow. More specifically, they deal with silences and secrets, something that cannot be known if they are not revealed by someone. If the revelation does not happen, both silences and secrets are, to some extent, unapproachable. Nevertheless, signs or rumors may index that "there is something."

The authors in this section approach secrecy and silence with a "critical intimacy," through which they rethink the context in which information is being revealed to them. Before writing their chapter, "Out of the Shadows of History and Memory: Personal Family Narratives as Intimate Ethnography," both authors, Alisse Waterston and Barbara Rylko-Bauer, knew that their respective parents went through major upheavals in their lives. They also were aware of silences that were necessary for their parents in order to deal with the past. Uncovering these silences – silences made up in the case of Rylko-Bauer's mother by avoiding the topic, and in the case of Waterston's father by talking incessantly about his traumata, but in a ritualized way (another form of silence) – only became a serious issue when each anthropologist decided to do research on her own parent's history. Those silenced narratives had to be treated as both "slices of larger history" and part of the authors' personal histories. Intimacy between daughter and parent had to be reworked to overcome rigid forms of relating. Furthermore, as Waterston and Rylko-Bauer sensitively show, historical categories like "survivor" or "Holocaust" needed to be rethought; they simply do not accommodate the experiences of everybody who went through World War II, even those whose personal histories concerned surviving the Holocaust.

Anne Lovell, in "When Things Get Personal: Secrecy, Intimacy, and the Production of Experience in Fieldwork," chose to write about secrets, which she conceptualizes as movement, dialogue, and micropolitics and approachable as such. Like Waterston and Rylko-Bauer, Lovell develops her arguments on intimacy and on relationships that can be built on "elective secrets." What is at stake between researchers and those researched is an interaction in which secrets tie them together. The examples given by Lovell from her own fieldwork show how certain interactions and dialogues between researcher and informant become decisive in determining whether a secret is shared or not. This results in an especially delicate relationship whenever secrets are linked to the vulnerability of anybody involved in the research.

Both chapters address the ethics of conducting research in the shadows. To conduct their research, Waterson and Rylko-Bauer were forced to repeatedly evoke painful memories in their elderly parents. This placed immense ethical responsibility on them to tread gently, to minimize pain as any researcher would. As daughters, this task was further inflected by the shadows of their ongoing relationship with their parents. Lovell's chapter, however, describes an ethical practice in which the ethnographer must carefully gauge the need to divulge something about herself – yet not too much – in order to gain access to others' secrets. She also shows how not doing so can create an imbalance in the act of sharing that risks both the ethnographic relationship and knowledge.

Transmutations of experience: approaching the reality of shadows

Can we go beyond that which we generally call reality? What is the relationship between what we do not perceive and reality? And how can we describe the relationship of something that *is* visible, but is not perceived as reality by the researcher, like illness due to witchcraft (e.g., Elenore Smith Bowen [Laura Bohannan 1954])? Vincent Crapanzano's chapter, "The Scene: Shadowing the Real," explores the point to which the notion of reality can be stretched to include the mysterious or ephemeral that is often put aside in "serious" ethnographies. Crapanzano discusses the way in which the romantic heritage in science (and its opposition) influences today's exclusion of issues such as religion from rational scientific discourse. These excluded spaces in anthropology can be evoked when the intersubjective world ("the feeling of being one" or the perceived atmospheric changes in a room due to emotions) enables a mutual understanding; however, according to Crapanzano, these moments are rare and sometimes pathologized (e.g., "folie à deux"). He advocates an "intersubjective construction of self-consciousness," but with caution.

The reality encountered in fieldwork may also radically differ from the researcher's previous experiences. Thomas Csordas' chapter, "Transmutation of Sensibilities: Empathy, Intuition, Revelation," also deals with a momentarily shared reality with the persons a researcher meets in conducting fieldwork, even when the shared reality normally lies in the shadow of the researcher's everyday experience. Drawing examples from his fieldwork, Csordas describes how he received revelations from another world within a specific religious setting, even though he did not share the specific belief system. These moments, when "transmutations of sensibilities" happen, and the reality of the other invades the ethnographer's world, can be retrospectively linked to empathy and intuition. Similarly to Crapanzano, Csordas considers these to be phenomena of intersubjectivity – "of being enfolded . . . in the flesh of the world."

Epistemic shadows

The reality of scientific arguments is the topic of Jason Szabo's chapter, "Shining a Light into the Shadow of Death: Terminal Care Discourse and Practice in the Late 20th Century." Taking as an example the hospice movement in palliative care, Szabo shows how certain assumptions of a "good death," such as being close to the patient, physically and ideologically, may result in too much certainty and make "people see what they are inclined to see."[10] Szabo claims that professionals' personal convictions about the value of palliative care also represents its Achilles' heel. Szabo disturbs the reality (and certainty) of the hospice movement, without denying its important achievements. He accomplishes this using a diachronic approach tracing the becoming of today's values (and certainties) in thanatology. This kind of critical historical analysis creates a temporal distance to the object of study that can enable the researcher to understand the (normally hidden) assumptions on which a certain phenomenon is based.

Like Szabo, Annette Leibing, in her chapter, "The Hidden Side of the Moon or, 'Lifting Out' in Ethnographies," suggests that the tensions created by Foucault's "cracks and gaps" may be important for approaching the shadow side of fieldwork. In fact, both authors seem to conceptualize the shadow in terms close to what Michel Foucault calls *episteme* (Foucault 1966). In this sense, Leibing argues that to transcend particular shadows it may be necessary to create distance, temporal or otherwise. She parts from her own experience as an ethnographer in a country where she was both a stranger and living and constructing a home, in order to describe a process she calls "lifting out." "Lifting out" is a critical confrontation of interruptions and contradictions in time and space. Elements sensed as problematic (e.g., contradictory), when past perceptions become incongruent with more recent perceptions, are recontextualized through a reconsideration of the past as related to the present. This requires repositioning and taking a critical stance toward changing categorizations.

Political shadows in the ethnographic encounter

It was just such repositioning that propelled the writers in the next section to rethink their positions of the anthropological enterprise in its moral, political, and ethical dimensions. Each writer, through her ethnographic encounters, considers issues of terror and violence, processes of "othering" and excluding, and the consequences for the victims.

Nancy Scheper-Hughes, in "The Gray Zone," sets out to expose the thoroughly cultural nature of violence, including the everyday violences that evade us. Looking back to her research in areas penetrated by political violence during her studies (Ireland, Brazil, and South Africa), Scheper-Hughes is amazed by her massive sense of denial in attending only to "*interior* spaces." She decries the "relativizing moral blinders" of modernist anthropology even during periods of genocide and mass violence. Following Levinas, she argues that morality is not confined within culture; it "enables one to judge it." Scheper-Hughes exhorts us to be hyper-vigilant to all backgrounded (*per* Douglas 1999) acts of violence, directed against vulnerable persons. But we need not look far; we are all complicit.

In "Others within Us: Collective Identity, Positioning and Displacement," Meira Weiss examines the dynamics of collective identity formation in Israel in which she is a participant and observer. Weiss writes from her perspective as an Israeli professor and former military officer, whose life course embodied all the right choices – choices she came to question. Weiss confronts violence, terror, and political deception in her country from a biographical repositioning and reinterpretation of her previous ethnographic works and memories. Her research into the forensic administration of the "chosen body" – masculine, Jewish, Ashkenazi, perfect, and wholesome – led her to see the construction of the "us/them" dichotomy on a social and political level.

Her research is controversial, and, under conditions that threaten natural security, Weiss is "torn between being an enlisted citizen and a critical anthropologist." As an Israeli anthropologist, she realizes that "the quest for collective identity" begins with the hidden "others within us," but urges anthropologists everywhere to examine the nationalistic shadows in their own work.

In "Falling into Fieldwork: Lessons from a Desperate Search for Survival," Rose-Marie Chierici directly confronts the agony of structural violence and racial exclusion when she is suddenly drawn into the life of a dying young Haitian man. Chierici's encounters with Mathias during his last tragic weeks were transformative for her, forcing her to reexamine the anthropological enterprise and her ethical role within it. By sharing in his pain, she came to conclude that anthropologists must advocate on behalf of victims. Chierici sets Mathias' tragedy in the larger "global ethnoscape" of exclusion and devastating effects of marginality and anonymity. She uses his story to return "voice" to those who have been backgrounded and silenced.

Through their various encounters with the tragic effects of political exclusion, all three writers assume the ethical stance of social critic. Scheper-Hughes and Chierici observe how invisible tyrannies are sustained by averting one's gaze from uncomfortable realities; Weiss though pays the price for confronting them. The three writers expose the tragic costs of backgrounding and silencing vulnerable persons and groups. All agree that political critique begins with self-critique – of everyday complacencies that maintain the cover of political shadows and invisible tyrannies.

Blurred borders in the ethnographic encounter of self and other

The final set of chapters examines blurred borders in the ethnographic encounter and the symbolic boundaries that limit understanding. Three anthropologists, at different stages in their careers, reflect upon their field experiences and factors that have shaped them. The first selection, "Field Research on the Run: One More (~~from~~) for the Road," is by Dimitris Papageorgiou, a young scholar writing from the periphery of Europe. As a graduate student, Papageorgiou began to resist the boundaries his mentors drew around prescriptive methodologies and between objective data *about* cultural systems and the subjective experiences *of* them. After plunging into fieldwork, he concluded that there is no substitute for intense emotional engagement (what Fabian calls "the ecstatic" side of field-work conducted *"while we are 'out of our minds'"*) (2001:31) as a source of knowledge. In fact, it was during times when he forgot himself as *researcher* and was fully absorbed into the group of *researched* that he learned the most. In contrast to theories that constrain understandings by ignoring experiences and ambiguities, he aims to address both through a critical understanding of social phenomena using a process for extracting *"noema"* from "raw" field data. This involves dialectically moving along a "continuum of 'interpretation,'" balancing between the poles of (objective) knowledge about the observed and (subjective) experience by the observer involved with the observed. This is admittedly "very hard" and he regrets periods when his research relations suffered because he favored the former over the latter.

In "Personal Travels through Otherness," Ellen Corin, an anthropologist and psychoanalyst, cuts to the core of what is at stake in pressing to reveal the shadow side of fieldwork. While affirming the importance of subjective experience for shaping ethnographic knowledge, she writes of the illusory nature of any objective reality: our very descriptions about the Other are "haunted" by other voices and visions which lie in our personal histories, often unbeknownst to us. Corin examines the forces that shape these descriptions, lending a contrived "coherence" to our narratives, and artificial understandings about others' worlds. Looking back on her ethnographic research journey, she sees her involvement in a trajectory of "interlaced motives" – some internal to her personal history; others located in external circumstances (interests, study sites, and insights from her psychoanalytic practice) – that inflected her research questions and directions. There is no simple causality here, only bidirectional resonance of influences. Her research presses the margins of her disciplines and experiences, while margins, limit-zones, and Otherness figure as major analytic devices throughout her research trajectory.

In the final chapter, "When the Borders of Research and Personal Life Become Blurred: Thorny Issues in Conducting Dementia Research," Athena McLean explores a challenging period in her life, studying dementia care at one nursing home while helping provide it for her mother at another. These circumstances enabled her to deeply penetrate the world of the institutionalized Other and learn the sentient reality of what was at stake. They also exposed artificial theoretical boundaries defining "the field," ethnographers' positions in it, and the differentiation of self from Other. Through her mother, McLean gained a indirect experience of institutional violence – and the urge to oppose it. After immersing herself in life at both homes and witnessing injustices at each, the homes merged into a single "moral terrain" for her, evoking common concerns. Once her mother occupied the position of the "others" she was studying, the distinction between them also blurred. And when a nurse discounted a resident as "very demented," McLean felt personally embarrassed: "my very personhood felt violated." By stimulating imaginings of shared vulnerabilities, she believes anthropologists can begin to dissolve the borders separating "others" from both the ethnographer and her readers and to work against injustice.

All three authors address shadows (blurrings) in their encounters with others that impacted their perceptions. For Corin, these occurred in the seepage between her private life and research career. For Papageorgiou, it was at an experiential level where researched and researcher shared a common emotional field. And for McLean these involved mergings within space (her mother's home and the field site), professional identity (daughter and researcher), and empathetic identity (her sense of shared vulnerability with the elders). The three chapters thus reveal the power of personal and intersubjective encounters in shaping ethnographic knowledge. By acknowledging this, however, they do not give up on achieving reliable knowledge, but offer hope for improving it.

As this overview shows, the shadow assumes many forms and each presents unique challenges to researchers. Ultimately, it is the responsibility of each researcher to acknowledge the shadow and decide whether or not to confront it. That decision will undoubtedly affect possibilities for knowledge, future theories, and research praxis.

This volume reflects early efforts in exploring the shadow side of research and the authors provide no recipe or final directives, only hints of possible paths of inquiry. The light we try to hold over life's blind spots might only be a candle, but it is a beginning.

Conclusion

> *The task is not so much to see what no one yet has seen, but to think what no body yet has thought about that which everyone sees . . . [Arthur Schopenhauer,* The World as Will and Representation, *1818]*

The writers of this volume have dedicated themselves to imagining various ways in which their production of ethnographic knowledge has been mediated in their work. They provide ethnographies that dare to disturb and question elements of the ethnographic encounter that usually remain in the shadows of anthropological research.

We have called the works in this collection "dia-ethnographies" to reflect the dynamic and ongoing movement that occurs between the various shadows and the ethnographer, and to note the lack of finality of their works: eventually a new text must be written, once the shadow side of fieldwork becomes an issue (see Leibing, this volume).

Reflections on the shadow side of research necessarily involve auto-biographical aspects, even though that is not their overall intent. The essays in this volume portray a special awareness on the part of their writers about the complexity of the sources of their knowledge and the interpenetration of their personal lives and experiences in the processes of producing their knowledge. For these writers, the person of the ethnographer, though central to processes of knowledge production, is rather beside the point; their focus is instead on the processes of producing the knowledge and on the various shadows that must be confronted along the way.

The engagement of the contributors to this volume with complex layers of research can be perceived as a "critical intimacy" that may involve a relational, intersubjective aspect of knowledge production or simply a heightened attentiveness to Foucault's gaps and cracks. Such an intimacy is integral to developing a critical ethnographic praxis that can further understanding (cf. Stoller 2004) and advance an ethical appreciation for the social and political issues this may entail (cf. Biehl 2005). In fact, we would argue that reflexive ethnography that excludes political dimensions is inadequately theorized and inadequately reflexive (cf. Okeley 1992:4).

But why should anthropologists venture into the shadow side of research, into these less traveled zones? Why should they risk losing the assurances of established, "safer" routes to knowledge?

Not all "shadows" in this volume are equally risky or specifically challenging. But generally we would argue that taking risks is necessary if we wish to advance the epistemological possibilities of our discipline. We do not claim that confronting the shadow side of fieldwork is the only way of engaging with "the field." However, if anthropology is to further refine its approach to studying the world we live in, anthropologists should not hesitate to imaginatively confront data that have been inadequately explored in the past. Researchers can no longer afford to marginalize these elements as irrelevant because – as many of the contributions show – they impact our research and our findings. Thus turning our attention to the shadow side of research and thoroughly pursuing what we find there should impart a distinctive nonpositivist rigor to our ethnographic exploits and *add, not shake, confidence* in the knowledge we produce.

What distinguishes the contributions in this volume is their reliance on the unique judgment of each ethnographer to confront his or her unique shadows in the pursuit of knowledge. In that pursuit, the self of the ethnographer is fundamental to that task, but cannot become its focus, except perhaps for brief interludes, on its larger mission; this is why we have called for a measured economy of self-disclosure. Schlemihl has taught us the misfortune that can result from ignoring crucial aspects of our lives – the taken-for-granted shadows. Only by engaging with the more difficult and elusive aspects of research and life can we extend our visions and advance our knowledge as ever more responsible social scientists.

Notes

1   We are grateful to Sybille Benninghoff-Lühl who introduced us to this "Wonderful History of Peter Schlemihl" at the American Anthropological Association meeting in Chicago in 2003.

2   We do not restrict "fieldwork" to a specific activity or environment, but rather to a serious *in situ* engagement with the multiple layers of a research topic. This can be undertaken in spaces as varied as a foreign country, familiar terrain, archives, the Internet, one's home, or a museum.

3   For example, in some forms of autoethnography, the unselfconscious exposure of self may appear as spectacle (Clough 2000).

4   This kind of psychologization continues to exist. A task force set up in the late 1980s on self-esteem assumed that raising it in young people would reduce delinquency, school underachievement, and pollution. Their literature review stated that "many, if not most, of the major problems plaguing society have roots in the low self-esteem of many of the people who make up society" (quoted in Baumeister et al. 2006:50f.).

5   Boas's scientific tolerance nonetheless had his limits, such as the poetry that Sapir and Benedict felt they had to hide from him (Clifford 1986:4).

6   See also Clough's challenge against assurances of autoethnographic genres as providing "fuller or more accurate" accounts "than writing what one knows about others" (2000:17). Similarly Simpson (2002) critiques the illusory assurances that come with simply defining one's position. Native anthropological voices, presented as guarantors of authentic native knowledge, have also come into question. See for example Narayan (1993, *cited in* Buzard 2003), and a recent article by the Comaroffs (2003:156).

7   Studies in the collection showed that conducting ethnographic research in familiar settings could increase anxieties of researchers. Other difficulties were "getting caught" between the field and home or "degrees" of home penetrating work (and vice versa).

8   Buzard provides a more comprehensive treatment of autoethnography's history. He asks why, despite enduring interest in it, autoethnography has met so much resistance.

9   We owe this insight to Szabo's colleague and mentor, George Weisz, who referred him to us.

10   This kind of intimacy could be called *epistemological intimacy*.

References

Abu-Lughod, Lila
   1991   Writing Against Culture. *In* Recapturing Anthropology. Richard Fox, ed. Pp. 137–162. Santa Fe, NM: School of American Research Press.
Achino-Loeb, Maria-Luisa
   2006   Introduction. *In* Silence as the Currency of Power. Maria-Luisa Achino-Loeb, ed. Pp. 1–22. New York: Berghahn Books.
Asad, Talal, ed.
   1973   Anthropology and the Colonial Encounter. London: Athlone Press.
Baumeister, Roy F., Jennifer Campbell, Joachim I. Krueger, and Kathleen D. Vohs
   2006   Exploding the Self-Esteem Myth. Scientific American Mind, February 6:50–57.

Behar, Ruth
1993 Translated Woman: Crossing the Border with Esperanza's Story. Boston: Beacon Press.

Behar, Ruth
1996 The Vulnerable Observer: Ethnography That Breaks your Heart. Boston: Beacon Press.

Benninghoff-Lühl, Sibylle
n.d. The Traveller's Shadow: Peter Schlemihl, Franz Boas and Other Unspeakable Stories. Institute of German Literature, Humboldt-University of Berlin, unpublished MS.

Biehl, João
2005 Vita: Life in a Zone of Social Abandonment. Berkeley: University of California Press.

Bluebond-Langner, Myra
2000 In the Shadow of Illness: Parents and Siblings of the Chronically Ill Child. Princeton: Princeton University Press.

Bowen, Elenore Smith
1954 Return to Laughter. London: Victor Gollancz.

Bowen, Elenore Smith
1984 Rückkehr zum Lachen, Ein Ethnologischer Roman [Return to Laughter]. Erika Stagl, trans. Berlin: Dietrich Reimer Verlag.

Bruner, Edward
1993 Introduction: The Ethnographic Self and the Personal Self. *In* Anthropology and Literature. Paul Benson, ed. Pp. 1–26. Urbana, IL: University of Illinois Press.

Buzard, James
2003 On Autoethnographic Authority. The Yale Journal of Criticism 16(1): 61–91.

Callaway, Helen
1992 Ethnography and Experience. *In* Anthropology and Autobiography. Judith Okeley and Helen Callaway, eds. Pp. 27–49. London: Routledge.

Casati, Roberto
2003 The Shadow Club: The Greatest Mystery in the Universe – Shadows – and the Thinkers who Unlocked their Secrets. New York: Alfred Knopf.

von Chamisso, Adelbert
1923 [1814] The Wonderful History of Peter Schlemihl. New York: B.W. Huebsch.

Clifford, James
1986 Introduction: Partial Truths. *In* Writing Culture: The Poetics and Politics of Ethnography. James Clifford and George Marcus, eds. Pp. 1–26. Berkeley: University of California Press.

Clifford, James, and George Marcus, eds.
1986 Writing Culture: The Poetics and Politics of Ethnography. Berkeley: University of California Press.

Clough, Patricia
  2000   Autoaffection: Unconscious Thought in the Age of Teletechnology. Minneapolis: University of Minnesota Press.
Comaroff, Jean, and John Comaroff
  2003   Ethnography on an Awkward Scale: Postcolonial Anthropology and the Violence of Abstraction. Ethnography 42:147–179.
Crapanzano, Vincent
  1980   Tuhami: Portrait of a Moroccan. Chicago: University of Chicago Press.
Crapanzano, Vincent
  1992   Hermes' Dilemma and Hamlet's Desire. On the Epistemology of Interpretation. Cambridge, MA: Harvard University Press.
Das, Veena and Poole, Deborah, eds.
  2004   Anthropology in the Margins of the State. Santa Fe, NM: School of American Research Press.
Davies, B., J. Browne, S. Gannon, E. Honan, C. Laws, B. Mueller-Rockstroh, and E. Bendix Petersen
  2004   The Ambivalent Practices of Reflexivity. Qualitative Inquiry 10(3):360–389.
Diamond, Stanley
  1974 [1972]   Anthropology in Question. *In* Reinventing Anthropology. Dell Hymes, ed. Pp. 401–429. New York: Vintage Books.
Douglas, Mary
  1995   The Cloud God and the Shadow Self. Social Anthropology 3(2):83–94.
Douglas, Mary
  1999   Implicit Meanings: Selected Essays in Anthropology. London: Routledge.
Dumont, Jean-Paul
  1978   The Headman and I. Austin: The University of Texas Press.
Ellis, Carolyn
  1991   Emotional Sociology. Studies in Symbolic Interaction 12:123–145.
Ellis, Carolyn
  2003   The Ethnographic I: A Methodological Novel About Autoethnography. Walnut Creek, CA: AltaMira Press.
Fabian, Johannes
  2001   Anthropology with an Attitude. Stanford: Stanford University Press.
Finn, Janet
  1995   Ella Cara Deloria and Mourning Dove: Writing for Cultures, Writing Against the Grain. *In* Women Writing Culture. Ruth Behar and D. Gordon, eds. Pp. 131–147. Berkeley: University of California Press.
Fischer, Michael
  2003   Emergent Forms of Life and the Anthropological Voice. Durham: Duke University Press.
Foucault, Michel
  1966   Les mots et les choses. Paris: Gallimard.
Foucault, Michel
  2000   So is it Important to Think? *In* Michel Foucault: Power. J. D. Faubion, ed. Pp. 454–458. New York: New Press.

Frank, Gelya
  1979   Finding the Common Denominator: A Phenomenological Critique Of Life History Method. Ethos 7(1):68–94.
Frank, Gelya
  1995   Ruth Behar's Biography in the Shadow: A Review of Reviews. American Anthropologist 97(2):357–359.
Frank, Gelya
  2000   Venus on Wheels. Berkeley: University of California Press.
Frankenberg, Ronnie
  2005   Restricted Reciprocity, Self-Censorship, Taboo Topics and Unshared Secrets; Burnt Bridges, and Trashed Papers in pre Audio-Technological Fieldwork. An Unduly Auto-ethnography? Department of Sociology and Social Anthropology, University of Keele, working MS.
Golde, Peggy
  1986 [1970]   Women in the Field. Berkeley: University of California Press.
Hume, Lynne and Jane Mulcock, eds.
  2004   Anthropologists in the Field: Cases in Participant Observation. New York: Columbia University Press.
Hymes, Dell, ed.
  1974 [1972]   Reinventing Anthropology. New York: Vintage Books Edition.
Jackson, Anthony, ed.
  1987   Anthropology at Home. London: Tavistock.
Jenkins, Francis A., and Harvey E. White
  2001   Fundamentals of Optics. New York: McGraw-Hill.
Jung, Carl Gustav
  1973 [1939]   C. G. Jung Psychological Reflections: An Anthology of His Writings, 1905–1961. J. Jacobi and R. F. C. Hull, eds. Princeton: Princeton University Press.
Jung, Carl Gustav
  1938   Psychology and Religion, The Terry Lectures. New Haven, CT: Yale University Press.
Kast, Verena
  2001   Die Dynamik der Symbole. Grundlagen der Jungschen Psychotherapie. Meilen: Walter Verlag.
Labaree, Robert V.
  2002   The Risk of "Going Observationalist": Negotiating the Hidden Dilemmas of Being an Insider Participant Observer. Qualitative Research 2(1):97–122.
Lambek, Michael
  1997   Pinching the Crocodile's Tongue: Affinity and the Anxieties of Influence in Fieldwork. Anthropology and Humanism 22(1):31–53.
Latour, Bruno
  2005   That Obscure Object of Politics. Domus, March, Electronic document. (http://www.ensmp.fr/~latour/presse/presse_art/GB-DOMUS%2003-05.html).
Liu, Xin
  2000   In One's Own Shadow: An Ethnographic Account of the Condition of Post-Reform Rural China. Berkeley: University of California Press.

Lovell, Anne
2003   When Things Get Personal: Secrecy, Intimacy and The Production of Experience in Fieldwork. Paper presented at the Annual Meeting of the American Anthropological Association, Chicago, November 22.

Lowie, Robert
1960   Empathy, or "Seeing from Within." *In* Culture in History: Essays in Honor of Paul Radin. Stanley Diamond, ed. Pp. 145–159. New York: Columbia University Press.

Marcus, George, and Michael Fischer
1986   Anthropology as Cultural Critique: An Experimental Moment in the Human Sciences. Chicago: University of Chicago Press.

Messerschmidt, Donald
1981   Anthropologists at Home in North America: Methods and Issues in the Study of One's Own Society. Cambridge: Cambridge University Press.

Miceli, Sergio
2004   Introdução: A emoção raciocinada. *In* Bourdieu, Pierre – Esboço de auto-análise [Esquisse pour une auto-analyse]. Sergio Micali, trans. Pp. 7–20. São Paulo: Ed. Schwarcz.

Myerhoff, Barbara
1974   Peyote Hunt: The Sacred Journey of the Huichol Indians. New York: Cornell University Press.

Myerhoff, Barbara
1979   Number Our Days. New York: Dutton Press.

Narayan, Kirin
1993   How Native is a "Native" Anthropologist? American Anthropologist 95:671–686.

Okeley, Judith
1992   Participatory Experience and Embodied Knowledge. *In* Anthropology and Autobiography. Judith Okeley and Helen Callaway, eds. Pp. 1–25. London: Routledge.

Poewe, Karla
1996   Writing Culture and Writing Fieldwork: The Proliferation of Experimental and Experiential Ethnographies. Ethnos 61(3–4):177–206.

Powdermaker, Hortense
1966   Stranger and Friend. New York: W. W. Norton.

Rabinow, Paul
1977   Reflections on Fieldwork in Morocco. Berkeley: University of California Press.

Rabinow, Paul
1996   Essays on the Anthropology of Reason. Princeton: Princeton University Press.

Rabinow, Paul
2003   Anthropos Today – Reflections on Modern Equipment. Princeton: Princeton University Press.

Reed-Danahay, Deborah
   1997   Introduction. *In* Auto/Ethnography: Rewriting the Self and the Social. Deborah Reed-Danahay, ed. Pp. 1–20. Oxford and New York: Berg.
Reed-Danahay, Deborah
   2005   Locating Bourdieu. Bloomington and Indianapolis: Indiana University Press.
Said, Edward
   1979   Orientalism. New York: Random House.
Scholte, Bob
   1974 [1972]   Toward a Reflexive and Critical Anthropology. *In* Reinventing Anthropology. Dell Hymes, ed. Pp. 430–458. New York: Vintage Books.
Scholte, Bob
   1987   The Literary Turn in Contemporary Anthropology. Critique of Anthropology 7(10):33–47.
Schopenhauer, Arthur
   1966 [1818]   The World as Will and Representation. E. F. J. Payne, trans. London: Dover Publ.
Simpson, David
   2002   Situatedness, or, Why We Keep Saying Where We're Coming From. Durham: Duke University Press.
Spry, Tami
   2001   Performing Auto-Ethography: An Embodied Methodological Praxis. Qualitative Inquiry 7(6):706–732.
Star, Susan Leigh, and Anselm Strauss
   1999   Layers of Silence, Arenas of Voice: The Ecology of Visible and Invisible Work. Computer-Supported Cooperative Work. The Journal of Collaborative Computing 8:9–30.
Stocking, George W., Jr.
   1974   Introduction: The Basic Assumptions of Boasian Anthropology. *In* A Franz Boas Reader: The Shapings of American Anthropology, 1883–1911. George W. Stocking, Jr., ed. Pp. 1–23. Chicago: University of Chicago Press.
Stoller, Paul
   2004   Stranger in the Village of the Sick: A Memoir of Cancer, Sorcery, and Healing. Boston: Beacon Press.
Stoller, Paul, and Cheryl Olkes
   1987   In Sorcery's Shadow: A Memoir of Apprenticeship Among the Songhay of Niger. Chicago: University of Chicago Press.
Strathern, Marilyn
   1987   The Limits of Auto-Anthropology. *In* Anthropology at Home. Anthony Jackson, ed. P. 16. London: Tavistock.
Strathern, Marilyn
   2000   The Tyranny of Transparency. British Educational Research Journal 26(3):309–322.
Strathern, Marilyn
   2004   The Whole Person and its Artifacts. Annual Review of Anthropology 33:1–19.

Wacquant, Loïc J. D.
   1992   Toward a Social Praxeology: The Structure and Logic of Bourdieu's Sociology. *In* An Invitation to Reflexive Sociology. Pierre Bourdieu and Loïc Wacquant, eds. Pp. 1–61. Chicago: University of Chicago Press.
Young, Donna, and Anne Meneley
   2005   Introduction. *In* Auto-Ethnographies: The Anthropology of Academic Practices. Anne Meneley and Donna Young, eds. Pp. 1–22. Peterborough, ON: Broadview Press.

Part I

Secrecy and Silence in the Ethnographic Encounter

Chapter 1

Out of the Shadows of History and Memory: Personal Family Narratives as Intimate Ethnography

Alisse Waterston and Barbara Rylko-Bauer

It is necessary to separate the past from the present and to judge the present in its own light. . . . But if we do not want to betray the past – if we want to remain ethical beings and honor our covenant with those who suffered – then moral passion needs to be supplanted by moral thought, by an incorporation of memory into our consciousness of the world. [Eva Hoffman]

Over the past few years, each of us, independently, has been talking to and interviewing a respective parent, with the goal of writing a life history that is embedded in broader frames of political economy and a sociohistorical context. Both parents, in their nineties, have witnessed some of the 20th century's major upheavals and social processes – war, fascism, the Holocaust, revolution, dispossession, migration, and exile. Our effort is to probe at a very deep level of intimacy to explore implications of their experiences for understanding the aftermaths of history as well as the world we live in today. Our parents' respective life stories form slices of larger history and offer lessons about survival, dehumanization, adaptation, memory, and identity – lessons that have great relevance for our times.[1]

Although both of us approach these life history projects as daughters, the anthropologist is ever present, posing broader questions and looking beyond the story. From the outset of the research, there has been an interplay of roles: as the daughter chronicles a family narrative, the anthropologist contextualizes the story, situating it in larger history and political economy. We have chosen to call our methodological approach "intimate ethnography" as we are focusing our ethnographic gaze upon those who are close to us.

This chapter is based on an ongoing dialogue that the two of us have had about our respective projects and on our collaborative efforts in creating our respective parent narratives. This collaboration has challenged us to more openly explore the historical context of our parents' lives, including the history of Polish Christian–Jewish relations and the experiences of World War II and its aftermath.

We undoubtedly stretch methodological boundaries in taking the deeply personal and emotional as our anthropological subject, yet in the process of comparing our respective intimate ethnographies, we bring into sharper focus epistemological, methodological, emotional, and ethical issues that all too often remain in what Athena McLean and Annette Leibing (2003) term "the shadow side of fieldwork." In this chapter, we reflect on the construction of memory, the process of collecting difficult stories, the nature of "truth" in relation to empirical accuracy, the shaping of narrative, and the role of emotion in ethnographic work. We also confront dilemmas surrounding our own positionality, examining both advantages and blind spots generated by intimacy and by our own respective emotional, cognitive, and cultural links to the larger history.

We began with a quotation from the conclusion to Eva Hoffman's book, *After Such Knowledge: Memory, History, and the Legacy of the Holocaust* (2004:278–279). We make frequent reference to this work, using Hoffman, a daughter of Holocaust survivors, as another interlocutor. Many of Hoffman's ideas, sensibilities, and words reflect our own thinking concerning the role of momentous events of the 20th century – including the Holocaust – in history, memory, and family narratives. Equally relevant is Hoffman's call to bring the past into the present, reflected in the epigraph above and elaborated more fully in our conclusion.

On another note, we faced a stylistic challenge in writing this chapter because we were working with two independent stories and projects as well as with the fruits of our anthropological collaboration. Our solution was to use the third-person narrative in discussing the daughter–parent interactions or individual aspects of each parent's life and to use the first person as our collaborative voice.

We begin with a thumbnail sketch of these two lives – that of Jadzia (Rylko-Bauer's mother) and Mendel-Miguel (Waterston's father) – touching primarily on events that shaped their trajectories. We then discuss a series of issues that emerge in doing intimate ethnography and that have implications for conducting any kind of ethnographic research.

A Sketch of Two Lives

Jadwiga (Jadzia) Lenartowicz, a Roman Catholic Pole, was a young physician at the outbreak of World War II. She was in the midst of completing her residency training at the pediatric hospital in Łódź when she was dismissed in the spring of 1940 from the hospital (along with most of the other Polish staff) and reassigned by the Nazis to a neighborhood clinic providing general medical care. On January 14, 1944, Jadzia was arrested by the Gestapo for alleged involvement in resistance activities and listening to radio broadcasts, something strictly forbidden to the general Polish population.

Over the next 15 months, Jadzia was registered consecutively in three concentration camps: Ravensbrück, Gross Rosen, and Flossenbürg. She spent much of her time in a subcamp in the town of Neusalz that was part of the extensive Gross Rosen concentration-camp system, where she worked as a physician alongside a Jewish dentist and a young Jewish nurse. Jadzia had become a slave doctor for slave laborers – about 1,000 Jewish women prisoners forced to work without pay for the German textile firm Gruschwitz.[2]

In late January 1945, as the Soviet army approached, the SS began evacuating the Gross Rosen subcamps. For the women of Neusalz, this was the beginning of a brutal 42-day death march through southeastern Germany and the western Sudentenland, an estimated 280-mile journey. Jadzia was among the fortunate minority to survive this and other travails.

Like many survivors of World War II, Jadzia ended up in a refugee camp in Germany, where she was able again to practice as a physician. She eventually married and emigrated to the United States, with her husband and ten-month-old daughter, Barbara. Although she had planned to work as a physician in her new homeland, Jadzia could not overcome barriers – financial, legal, linguistic, and personal – that prevented her from practicing her profession. Instead, she ended up working for 20 years as a nurse's assistant in a hospital in Detroit. Despite these hardships, she retains a sense of optimism and humor. At the age of 95, she still takes daily walks of a mile or more and quips, "I learned how to walk on that trek across the Reich."

★★★★★

An old Jewish man is alive today whose travels through the 20th century have been colored by tragedy, sorrow, humor, pathos, and transformation.

Barry University Library
11300 NE Second Avenue
Miami Shores, FL 33161

In 1913, he was born Menachim Mendel (Mendelee in the Yiddish diminut-ive), the youngest of Riva and Itsak Isak Waserstein's seven children. Jedwabne was their home, a village in northeastern Poland where Jews lived and provided services to the surrounding gentile farmers. World War I left the Wasersteins "helpless, the poorest of the poor," according to the old man. After the war, Riva wanted her children out of Poland, yet the United States had closed its borders to people like her. In 1924, Riva began sending her children, one by one, to Havana, Cuba.

In the summer of 1941, Jedwabne became the site of a horrific, now infamous massacre of Jews. According to historian Jan T. Gross, "half of the population of a small East European town murdered the other half – some 1,600 men, women and children" (2001:7), most of whom were forced into a barn that was set on fire by their neighbors. Mendel and his immediate family escaped the burning, having all arrived in Cuba by 1939. Among the Wasersteins who remained in Jedwabne was Szmul (Shmulke) Wasersztajn, Mendel's cousin. He was saved by a Christian neighbor, who hid him in a barn, although his mother, Chajcia, was killed in the massacre.

Shmulke provided formal testimony right after the war and this became a central source for Gross's book *Neighbors: The Destruction of the Jewish Community in Jedwabne, Poland* (2001), a slender volume that ignited intense discussion about Polish Christian–Jewish relations and the Holocaust (Brand 2001; Polonsky and Michlic 2003). Eventually, Shmulke joined the Waserstein clan in Havana, where his testimony would become fam-ily legend, passed from one generation to the next.

In the meantime Mendelee became Miguel in Cuba. Miguel and his brothers ran a general store in Manguito, a small town in the province of Matanzas. Later, they sought their fortunes in Havana, opening cloth-ing and textile shops. Miguel would open two stores of his own, which he ambitiously named El Imperio (The Empire). He learned to speak English in his late twenties when he joined the U.S. Army, discovered New York, became an American citizen, and renamed himself Michael Waterston.

By 1961, the Cuban Revolution had put this petty merchant in the same category as United Fruit and General Motors, leaving Miguel (in Havana) and Michael (in New York) the penniless head of a growing household. Another move brought him to San Juan, Puerto Rico, where he rebuilt El Imperio, and became the merchant don Miguel.

Miguel lost his wife to divorce after a 51-year marriage and saw his "empire" crumble, his properties confiscated, and the business lost to bankruptcy. Now 92 years old, he manages on Social Security and under the watchful eye of his firstborn. His short-term memory is as faded as the sun-bleached family photos that sit on weary display in his apartment, though his memories of Havana, Manguito, and Jedwabne are deep and still clear.

Points of Comparison

Both Jadzia's and Miguel's life experiences have been profoundly shaped by events that took place in their country of birth, Poland, prior to, during, and after World War II. In addition, they share the complexities of the immigration experience, even though their lives took very different paths, with Jadzia moving from Poland to Germany, and eventually the United States, and Mendel-Miguel going from Poland to Cuba and then moving between the United States and Puerto Rico.

There are, of course, important differences between this mother and this father. Jadzia is a Roman Catholic, and Miguel, a Jew. Jadzia came from the industrial city of Łódź, whereas Miguel spent his childhood in the shtetl Jedwabne. Both the large city and the small town had sizeable populations of Jews living alongside non-Jews, and both locales were profoundly altered by the events of World War II.

Writing in the town's history and memorial book, Rabbis Julius Baker and Moshe Tzinovitz describe Jedwabne as "located twenty-one kilometers northeast of the city of Lomza, amidst the forests, fields of green herbage, and pasturage; [its] Jewish families moved there . . . as early as 1664. They probably settled there because of the weekly market day, which was by then well established" (1980:231). Later, Jedwabne was the site of genocide, when the town's Jews were slaughtered by their Polish neighbors during the Nazi occupation (Gross 2001; Waserstein Kahn and Monestel Arce 2001).

Łódź also had a large, well-established Jewish community, forming about 35 percent of the city's total prewar population. During the Nazi occupation, Łódź became the site of the second largest Jewish ghetto in Poland, established in 1940 and, by 1941, "home" to over 160,000 Jews; those who did not die there from malnutrition, disease, and executions were deported to and perished in the death camps (Krakowski 1990).

The non-Jewish population also felt the heavy hand of Nazi occupation. Schools were closed, cultural activities banned, and the Polish language suppressed (Steinlauf 1997). Łódź was subjected to intense germanization, its name changed to Litzmannstadt, all streets and squares given German names, and its residents subjected to rule by terror, surveillance, deprivation, and deportations (Dobroszycki 1984:xxiv).

The lives of Jadzia and Miguel were torn apart by the upheavals of the 20th century, and both were directly, yet differently, affected by World War II and the Holocaust. How they responded in the aftermath of these upheavals reveals differences not only of personality and culture but also gender and identity.

Epistemological Challenges

The Jew and the gentile

We begin this section with an exposé – a bringing out of the shadows – of our own position vis-à-vis each other – as friends, colleagues, daughters, and collaborators. We recognize the need to confront what we, our respective parents, and our ancestral homeland may represent to the other and how that might affect the construction of this narrative and our own ethnographic projects. At the center of this existential position is that Rylko-Bauer is a Polish Catholic and Waterston, a Jew.

To paraphrase Eva Hoffman, a "shadow falls on our psyches too darkly still and it would be [a] kind of falseness to pretend it isn't there" (Hoffman 2004:128). Poland itself casts this shadow: the place, its people, and its history – in Hoffman's words, "the central site of the grotesque in the twentieth century" (2004:19).[3] She views Poland as "the site of two catastrophes. One was the Nazi war of conquest against the Polish nation and the policy of widespread murder and eventual enslavement of the Poles. The other was the campaign of extermination directed against all Jews of Europe, but executed mostly on Polish territory" (2004:16–17).

Michael Steinlauf explains that "the Jewish connection to Poland is as old as Polish history" (1997:1), with the earliest Jewish settlements dating back to the late 12th century. This is a complex history, marked by coexistence and the coshaping of Polish culture. It is also history marred by anti-Semitism and ethnic discord, and historians continue to examine and debate the nature, extent, and pervasiveness of anti-Semitism in postwar and modern Poland (Blobaum 2005; Steinlauf 1997).

This problematic history does not translate into emotional distance or distrust in our personal relationship, and we do not view each other as embodiment of a historically constituted Other. Each of us feels compassion for the other's parent, appreciating the sufferings and struggles he or she endured. Our parents' stories humanize what might otherwise be more abstract histories, thereby expanding our understanding of these seemingly different segments of Polish history and Polish life.

The meanings of Poland

For Rylko-Bauer, Poland has played a key role in shaping her core identity and it is where most of her family still lives. She is bilingual and her father was a very strong force in fostering this identification with Polish history and culture – the beautiful, heroic aspects, not the dark sides. On a trip to Poland in 2001, which she took with her mother, Rylko-Bauer felt as if she had "come home," and she felt an even greater connectedness during a subsequent visit to Łódź and sites from her mother's life.

Poland, for Jadzia, has been a source of sorrow, for the anticipated future lost to the war and its aftermath. But there is no bitterness in this sorrow, and it is tempered by many fond memories that she has of her first 33 years spent there. The fact that Poland is also a source of strength and comfort for Jadzia clearly shapes Rylko-Bauer's sense of place and history.

For Waterston, Poland had been "fixed in her Jewish imagination as the land of unreconstructed anti-Semitism" (Hoffman 2004:137), and she felt uneasy among its inhabitants while on a pilgrimage there, also in 2001. Waterston grew up on stories of Polish anti-Semitism, of its being grounded in church propaganda, and of the Jedwabne massacre. Her trip to Poland was colored by this information. How could she walk on that soiled land in comfort and with confidence knowing its role in her father's deep wounds?

"The Polish were very anti-Semitic and they had to relieve themselves to get rid of the Jews," her father says, not just as recollection but as warning to a Jewish daughter about to visit Poland. He prepared her with vivid and compelling images, with names of streets and the exact location of the family home, hovel that it was. From memory, he drew for her a map of Jedwabne, a place he had last seen 73 years earlier.

When she finally arrived in Jedwabne, Waterston remembers recoiling from the townsfolk, reaching out to no one. This was not like her, the person or the anthropologist, and she was acutely aware of the unfamiliar sensation. She looked suspiciously at the huddle of old women chatting on a stoop. Old men on the street corner peered back at her with equal suspicion.

These are the kinds of emotions both of us must confront. If not, their residues will affect the veracity of our work, because these emotions signal conflicting issues of loyalty and betrayal to one's own parent and, perhaps, to our sense of collective identity. However, as Hoffman notes, "The leap from suspicion to trust carries the danger of betraying the stern gods of tribal solidarity and fidelity to suffering" (2004:142). As both daughters and anthropologists, and for the sakes of our respective projects, each of us must discover a way to confront and resolve this central conflict.

Rylko-Bauer confronts this conflict by embracing the complexity of Poland's history and unpacking the concept of "survivor" within the context of her mother's experience in the Holocaust. Waterston does so by exploring how a broader, but still very Jewish concept of "survivor" is implicated in her father's personality, his reflexive attachment to the experience of Jewish suffering even as he reinvents himself in new circumstances.

Survivors

It strikes us as ironic that Jadzia became a concentration-camp prisoner, a slave in her native land, whereas Mendel escaped the "Main Event." The Polish Catholic, immediately caught up in the events of World War II, is a Holocaust survivor; the Polish Jew is not. This statement is "true" in that it accords with the U.S. Holocaust Memorial Museum's inclusive definition of the term survivor.[4]

If we accept the statement as true, what does that signify for us, as daughters, and for our respective parents? In what ways does our acceptance or rejection of that category affect how our subjects are placed in history by us and by others, and how does it affect our positionality as members of the "post-generation"? Who "counts" as a survivor matters for how history gets interpreted and for locating the points of commonality and difference among groups who have suffered the results of genocidal hatred.

Jadzia, in a very basic sense, is a survivor of what transpired during the Holocaust – she is part of that event in history. She often describes situations in which some person or policy made the difference between a good and a bad outcome, perhaps even the difference between life and death. "When I look back in time," Jadzia will say, "I wonder how was I able to do all this, to endure all this, and to *survive*?"

Yet, in all the recounting of her concentration-camp experiences, Jadzia never identifies herself as a "Holocaust survivor." Instead, she sees herself as a Catholic Pole, a survivor of Nazi brutality, of Hitler's madness, caught up in the events and aftermath of World War II, of which the persecution of the Jews was a critical part. Jadzia's story blurs the boundaries of labeled experiences, such as the Holocaust, survival, and suffering. Such points of blurring accord us, as scholars, the chance to expand our understandings of social phenomena.

In Jadzia's case, we have a Polish Catholic who was swept up in the maelstrom of the Holocaust, working as a prisoner-doctor for, and alongside, Jewish slave laborers. "I didn't feel any different from the rest of them," Jadzia says of her Jewish co-inmates in the camp. This, of course, belies her more privileged position (if such a term can be used in the context of slave-labor-camp imprisonment) relative to the average young women who lived in that camp. But from Jadzia's perspective, such differences were less important than the overarching point of convergence: She and the others were fellow prisoners, ultimately at the mercy of their Nazi masters. This shared status was starkly illustrated on that 42-day death march, when, in the eyes of the outside world, Jadzia merged with the other, Jewish women. To the bystanders who watched and at times mocked the women as they stumbled by, or to the German farmers in whose barns and stables they slept, one dirty, thin, lice-bitten woman looked like any other.

Even as she explores the points of commonality shared by Jadzia and other survivors, Rylko-Bauer also recognizes the significant role of one other factor in Jadzia's survival: She was not a Jew. Thus, while locating her mother within the Holocaust, Rylko-Bauer also situates Jadzia apart from the Holocaust's deep and complex meanings.

One point of departure lies in the aftermath of this violence. Hoffman notes that the traumatic memories of suffering experienced by Holocaust survivors can express themselves in personality and behavior. Survivors, not surprisingly, "are often difficult people, and are found to be so by others" (2004:54). Many – although not all – continued living with a sense of guilt, stigma, or shame, which often was passed on to the next generation. "Over and over, the children speak of being permeated by sensations of panic and deadliness, of shame and guilt. . . . there is the need – indeed, the imperative – to perform impossible psychic tasks: to replace dead relatives, or children who have perished; to heal and repair the parents; above all, to rescue the parents" (Hoffman 2004:63).

Rylko-Bauer's parents did not dwell upon their wartime experiences, but the past was always there, in the background; it was not masked in a mantle of silence. They attached no shame or stigma to having been a prisoner-of-war (in the case of her father) or a political prisoner in the concentration camps. Most importantly, throughout Jadzia's narrative there is no evident sense of "survivor guilt," perhaps because everyone in her immediate family survived, even as they suffered during the war. Would Jadzia have felt differently if her sisters or parents had died? Poles undoubtedly suffered tremendously during the war, in terror endured, lives lost, and in the extensive damage that the Nazis wrought with special fury on the Polish landscape (Davies 2004; Rossino 2003; Steinlauf 1997). For the non-Jewish Poles, what was left from the rubble of war was a nation and a culture – deeply wounded but still intact, waiting to be rebuilt.

But for many of the Jews of Poland, nothing remained to return to or to rebuild. Entire families, shtetls, and communities were massacred. This is part of the Holocaust's painful legacy – a world, a culture, a people, and a history, by design, nearly wiped out.

The Holocaust, for Jews, has multiple, complex, and dark meanings, shaped by this profound collective reality that Rylko-Bauer and her mother can never internalize. In this sense, although Jadzia is a survivor of the Holocaust, she is apart from this collective legacy.

Without question, Waterston's father is not literally a "Holocaust survivor." Erika Bourguignon, a refugee from Vienna who managed to leave soon after the Nazi annexation of Austria, writes about this experience. "To be considered, and to consider myself, a 'survivor' seems nothing short of indecent. . . . what did I survive? Can early escape and the resulting avoidance of danger classify one as a survivor?" (Bourguignon 2005:72). Refugee might be a term that better fits Miguel's profile, or, perhaps, his self-description as a person who fled persecution. In considering such labels, Waterston is most concerned with avoiding distortion and invoking images that do not resonate with her father's experience. Labeling her father as "survivor" exaggerates the role of the Holocaust in his saga and shuts out other events of the century that significantly defined his experience.

At the same time, Miguel seems to share with survivors certain psychological traits often attributed to the Holocaust experience. He is a difficult person: narcissistic, prone to depressions and nightmares, exacting self-sacrifice from close family members, and privileging his own emotional needs over those of others as entitlement for suffering that, in his view, others could never know or experience (Krell, Sherman, and Wiesel 1997; Marcus and Rosenberg 1989; Spiegelman 1997). If not the Holocaust, what else accounts for these strong similarities? This question becomes even more pointed given the absence of such traits in Jadzia's case.

Waterston recognizes, as both daughter and as anthropologist, the significance of her father being a Jew in the 20th century. George Steiner (1988) notes that collective traumatic memory is shared by Jews throughout the world and is situated in the deep recesses of Jewish identity: "The Shoah, the remembrance of Auschwitz, the haunting apprehension that, somewhere, somehow, the massacres could begin anew, is today the cement of Jewish identity . . . Above all else, to be a Jew in the second half of this century is to be a survivor, and one who knows that his survival can again be put in question" (1988:159–160). Above all else, to be a Jew is to hear the "echoes of persecution" that began long ago with the destruction of the first temple in 586 B.C.E., which is remembered and marked by religious ritual like "the Sabbath before Tish 'ah be-Av when the Jews recall all the major catastrophes in their history" (Cohen 2004:160).

Jadzia's story shows how a narrow application of the term *survivor* can erase the reality of the non-Jewish experience of the Holocaust. Miguel's profile suggests that Holocaust particularism may blind scholars to the workings of collective memory and cultural legacy on identity, disposition, and even one's worldly fate. Like many Holocaust survivors, Miguel views his life "as if it were always being lived under the sign of extermination" (Mintz 2001:163). The theme of impending doom is ever present in his conversations, and his fear borders on paranoia. Victimization is a key motif of his narrative, and he often describes himself in the process of running, suffering, barely surviving, and persecuted. Miguel has never gotten over the feelings of isolation and loneliness that come from being cast out, from forced absence. In his case, the metanarrative of inevitable destruction and loss has actually played out in his life.

From Epistemology to Methodology

Ethnographers spend their lives in immediate history, gathering information and insight about on-the-ground realities captured in a moment in time. Notwithstanding problems of "romanticized timelessness" characteristic of many classic ethnographies (Kottak 2002:42), anthropological training is invaluable for uncovering the forces implicated in those ethnographic moments.

Intimate ethnography as method

A long tradition exists in anthropology of using personal experience as impetus for studying a particular subject or of actually incorporating those experiences into the process of research and analysis. The work ranges across related and overlapping genres: life history, cultural biography, memoir, autoethnography, and personal narrative (e.g., Bateson 1984; Behar 1993; Crapanzano 1980; Frank 2000; Orlove 1995; Scheper-Hughes 2000; Shostak 2000). In some cases, personal experiences and reflections are interwoven with analysis of the broader topic at hand (Brodkin 1998; Hutchinson 2005; Myerhoff 1978; Zola 1982). These approaches enrich ethnography while challenging anthropologists to represent ourselves and those from whom we are privileged to learn in ways that honor and do justice to the reality of our informants' lives and their history.

One such genre, autoethnography, specifically focuses on a person and his or her "ever-changing relationships" (Abu-Lughod 1993) and on movements between the personal and the cultural, historical, and social structural (Angrosino and Mays de Pérez 2003; Ellis 2004; Reed-Danahay 1997). "Produced by an 'insider' or 'native' observer of his or her own cultural milieu" (Reed-Danahay 2002:423), it offers a way to expose "multiple layers of consciousness, connecting the personal to the cultural"

(Ellis and Bochner 2000:739). While our projects could be considered experiments in autoethnography because of the intimate connection between ourselves and our subjects, our ultimate goal, however, is to go beyond the reflexive "I." To underscore the distinction between these related methods and our perspective, we call our approach "intimate ethnography." The challenge for our respective intimate ethnographies is to chronicle our parents' rich and complex lives while also understanding and accounting for the methodological, emotional, and ethical issues attendant to such intimate life histories and finding ways of linking the individual stories to larger social processes.

The ethnographer's stance

The actual practice of interviewing our parents, although not without its own challenges, is in some ways no more difficult than conducting research among strangers, some of whom may eventually become intimates.[5] We are comfortable in the role of ethnographer, in getting very close to another without losing ourselves in that person, and in standing apart, somewhat detached but with empathy and compassion. With our parents as ethnographic "informants," however, we started our projects with old intimates as research subjects and with dynamics (of power, duty, and status) in our relationships with them that were determined long before the projects began. We have found the power dynamic to manifest itself most clearly in what we call "narrative management" – the matter of who controls the story.

For Rylko-Bauer, the process of chronicling her mother's life began slowly, because Jadzia was an ambivalent participant, not convinced that her story was so special. She was initially reluctant to let her daughter document, with notes or tape recorder, the accounts of her experiences. Miguel, on the other hand, was always eager to talk, but he could rarely be led away from the same narrative he had been telling for 30, 40, or 50 years.

Jadzia managed the narrative by silence. For example, Rylko-Bauer recalls sitting at her kitchen table, ready to tape record an anecdote about how her mother helped rescue a close friend from Nazi deportation. But Jadzia refused and her response to the ethnographer's pleadings was an emphatic "No!" as she flashed an impish grin and stuck her tongue out at her daughter. Jadzia did not like being portrayed as a heroine and having the story formally recorded, thus transforming it into the anthropologist's project. Rather, the story was hers, to be related on her own terms.

In contrast, Miguel has repeatedly managed the narrative by remaining rigidly faithful to the same tale, retold again and again, another kind of silence.

The ethnographic dance

The negotiation for control between ethnographer and key informant is exposed in raw form as daughter transacts with parent for more information. This negotiation occurs in every ethnographic exchange. It constitutes the "art" of the method, a kind of dance mediated by social distance, rules of politeness, and the anthropologist's ethical concerns about exploitation and rudeness. Like researchers everywhere, we wonder what we can ask of whom and when, how to frame effective questions, how far we can probe. With parents as subjects, this negotiation becomes more up front, more honest. Waterston, for example, is comfortable crossing certain boundaries with her father, pushing him harder to enter new territory, whereas she might hesitate to do so with less intimate informants. As ethnographer, she knows when she has "pushed" her father to the limit of his ability; with other, more distant informants, she is never as sure.

Less clear is how this research-driven dynamic shifts the power relationship between parent and child. Parents may cooperate because they value time spent with children and the attention and interest that are being focused on their lives. Parents may also concede control that they might not otherwise give up, because they implicitly understand the nature of the research relationship. In fact, this is what often happens in the field, where "informants" seem rarely to contest the unspoken deal – the researcher asks the questions, the key informant answers them.

The ethnographic field we enter in these projects is marked by such multiple layers of tension. Each of us must unravel the specifics of our particular case to reveal what aspects are operating in this struggle for power because how it gets resolved will affect the outcome of the project.

Rylko-Bauer and Jadzia are intertwined in a powerful mother–daughter bond of mutual nurturance and deep affection that also involves tensions arising from evolving role reversals. Widowed decades ago, Jadzia is fiercely independent and lives on her own yet relies on her only child for many daily needs common to a woman in her nineties. In life-history work, the ethnographer (or biographer) can easily slip into speculating or interpreting what the informant may be feeling or thinking (Linden 1993:140–142). In a close mother–daughter dynamic, as Rylko-Bauer discovered, this is even more likely to happen.

Initially, Rylko-Bauer had planned to conduct systematic interviews with her mother, but matters of ethics and emotions caused her to shift instead to doing this project as a daughter who just happened to be an anthropologist. She worried about the impact on her mother of dredging up past history and reopening old wounds, and wondered what she herself might learn about her mother that could break the daughter's heart. So the project proceeded cautiously, giving the mother space to find her own voice and the daughter time to hear what might be revealed. This approach reflected both the daughter's commitment to her mother as well as the anthropologist's responsibility to her informant.

The process of remembering and recounting was distressing at times. "Let's not talk anymore," Jadzia said after one poignant encounter, "because then I don't sleep nights, thinking of all this." At one point, Rylko-Bauer voluntarily suspended formal "information gathering," sensing that too many memories were being stirred. Interestingly enough, during this fairly long period, Jadzia would bring up vignettes from the past, even painful ones. She seemed to have a growing need to talk but to do so on her own terms.

Jadzia's story is also characterized by silences that the daughter initially interpreted simply as "gaps" in her mother's narrative. But as Paul Farmer (2003:26) notes, sometimes one must "scratch at this surface silence, to trigger that painful eloquence" while at other times, one should simply listen to the silence, note it, learn from it, and respect it. Soon, the ethnographer began to pay attention to the silences (or the spoken equivalents "don't know" or "can't remember"), which she believes have meaning in her mother's case.[6]

Some of the silence may reflect Jadzia's efforts to normalize memories of daily life in the camps. When Rylko-Bauer presses her mother for details about everyday tasks, the food she ate, the patients she saw, routines of life in the slave-labor camp – what any ethnographer is eager to know – Jadzia becomes impatient. "I don't remember, I just did what had to be done," suggesting that survival depended on being able to live as normal a life as possible, under stressful, abnormal circumstances and with a minimum of resources. What she remembers are those events or actions that were outside the norm, like stemming a threatened outbreak of diphtheria, gestures of solidarity and kindness, or moments of humor or anguish.

Finally, silence may also reflect Jadzia's lack of awareness of what was happening around her, because of her intense focus on the simple but difficult task of survival. When talking about the death march, she notes, "I have no idea how we survived. When you're marching from morning 'til night, then get just a bit to eat and not that nutritious . . . your brain stops working. After a while, you are like an automaton, placing one foot in front of the other, not at all aware of what is going on around you." Jadzia repeatedly wonders what exactly occurred on those final days of the march and how she even made it, for she is convinced that she was close to collapse.

Rylko-Bauer has her own silence. Ethnographic intimacy creates cognitive and emotional blinkers, thus increasing the risk that painful issues may be skirted. The complex topic of Polish Catholic–Jewish relations was one such area for Rylko-Bauer. Like most Poles who grew up during the first half of the 20th century, Jadzia was raised in a milieu of endemic anti-Semitism, and the daughter hesitated to explore this topic, fearing her mother also carried some of that baggage. It was, in fact, the joint effort of writing this chapter that opened up the cognitive space that allowed Rylko-Bauer to explore these important issues, as both daughter and anthropologist.

The negotiation between Waterston and her father entailed different issues, arising partly from Miguel's temperament and history. Waterston's father was domineering, exacting obedience, service, and "respect" from his wife and children in true patriarchal fashion. The wife he had chosen, however, came from New York, Jewish-liberal stock, and she rebelled against the principles central to her husband's worldview. Waterston followed her mother, ideologically speaking, although her father would hear nothing of it. With his daughter, as with all his children, Miguel's stories were also lectures, and a lesson was always involved. The more the wife rebelled, the louder the lectures became. The child must hold onto fear (of death, illness, and accident) and conformity (obedience, self-sacrifice, and silence regarding one's own psychic needs). These were key motifs.

Waterston is conscious of the limitations in "interviewing" her father, knowing full well that his compulsion to impart advice may motivate what he tells her and what he leaves out. In light of this information, how can we trust Waterston's ethnography, marked as it must be by such blemishes? But all ethnographies have blemishes, and they need to be brought to the surface. Part of this process involved forcing a change in the terms of her relationship with her father, which ultimately had an unintended, but positive, effect on the anthropological project.

For a four-year period when Miguel was in his eighties, Waterston severed ties with him, not calling or seeing him. She could no longer swallow what she perceived to be assaults on her dignity or suppress her adult self in the service of his requirements or needs. His assaults were always verbal and the demands trivial but constant and overbearing.

Waterston always knew she would write about her father, although she did not know when or how it would happen. When she returned to him (a phone call, without drama), their relationship had undergone a shift. Even if the transformation was not complete, her father seemed better able to hear her, acknowledge her autonomy, and even respect it. Miguel tended now to glorify this daughter, showering her with exaggerated praise at the expense of his other (more dutiful) children. Still, the shift was very important because the daughter was no longer so enveloped in the father.

This opened up space for the project to occur, for the anthropologist now felt emotionally brave enough and competent enough to proceed.

The most difficult aspect of this project for Waterston was grasping and understanding the sources and consequences of her father's becoming a deeply wounded person. The presence of loss penetrates all his stories. This has captivated Waterston and shaped her own sensibility, allowing her to recognize that his sorrows have become her sorrows, his losses her motivation to understand them (Boyarin 1996:31). Her objective is to uncover the legacies of cultural and political history that are reflected in the psychology of this complex man.

The project gave them common ground, something they could talk about that was of genuine interest to the daughter and flattering to the father. With his newfound respect for Waterston as an adult and a professional, the father could dialogue with her about people, places, and his feelings and thoughts over the past 90 years. In this dialogue, they return to the various settings of his life. Waterston has also literally returned to the main sites. The first was a trip to Cuba with her father in 2000, then, one year later, to Poland. Although he did not accompany her on this second trip, he provided a guided tour from afar, drawing the map of Jedwabne from long-ago memory.

Waterston's relationship with her father looks a lot like that of an anthropologist with her informant. When they see each other, they sit down together with the purpose of his telling her stories, of her asking him questions, most of it captured on audiotape and some of it on videotape. He is an eager participant. But she also approaches him as a daughter, responding to him in the language of family, with sadness and joy, disgust and sympathy, anger and patience, as these acute emotions surface. Nevertheless, that she is an anthropologist is not accidental, and it also shapes what she intends to do with the narrative he recounts.

From memory to narrative

"Narratives are versions of reality," and "lives are the pasts we tell ourselves," write Elinor Ochs and Lisa Capps (1996:21). This idea raises questions about the relevance of "truthfulness" as related to accuracy and veracity, when one is using personal experiences or knowledge in doing research. Each of our parents' reconstruction of her or his history and their understanding of its context are "right" in the sense of "story," even if not always "historically factual." Poet and Auschwitz survivor Charlotte Delbo makes a similar observation: "Today, I am not sure that what I wrote is true. I am certain it is truthful" (1995:1).

In discussing Delbo's prose and poetry, Holocaust scholar Lawrence Langer (1991) notes that survivors who speak, and especially those who write, about their experiences must find some way of communicating about daily life in what was a grotesquely alien world. They need to convey not only what happened but how it happened, what it felt like, how it looked, sounded, smelled – the context of the moment. Jadzia echoes the sentiments of many survivors when she says, "Unless you go through this yourself, you can listen, someone can tell you all about it, but you have no idea what it is like, you can't even imagine." In a sense, this is always the ethnographer's dilemma, how to get across to listeners and readers the "truthfulness" of an event, a culture, a group, or an individual that is completely foreign to them.

Perhaps the challenge lies in knowing when "accuracy" of details about experiences and events truly matters. In the specific instance of the Holocaust, two refrains permeate much of what is written: "lest we forget" and "never again." Irrespective of the "accuracy" of specific details, what comes through in all accounts – historical works, memoirs, documentaries, and photographs as well as eyewitness testimonies – are the themes of injustice, capricious cruelty, dehumanization, racism, suffering, and death and how these become embodied in specific experiences of individuals.

Our job as ethnographers in these life-history projects is to work towards capturing truthfulness, the embodiment of experience and how it is understood – so that it resonates as true, even if some facts are not empirically correct. Here is where ethnographic writing borders on art. This is also where ethnography borders on political project, because this kind of "truth" is critical to the task of "never forgetting" and of resisting the erasure of history.

Our challenge is to discover what that "truthfulness" is for each of our parents and why it is "true" for them. What ideas about their lives and place in the world get expressed symbolically through their words and actions? Can we unravel the psychological, cultural, and political roots of those ideas?

We might take, for example, Jadzia's reticence or Miguel's eagerness to tell their story as clues (some might call this "data") and theorize the meanings in terms of where each is placed in history. Why would he be so desirous and she so reluctant to speak? After all, Jadzia has a special story to tell, having lived through three concentration camps and a death march. She is a survivor, though her self-identity seems not to be linked to this symbolically and politically imbued category as it is for many Jewish survivors of the Holocaust. Her reticence may stem, in part, from her belief that these wartime experiences were not the only defining moments of her life. From Jadzia's perspective, the inability to practice her profession, to be a physician in the United States, had an equally devastating impact on her psyche and her life.

Miguel, by contrast, wants to talk, although his narrative is only partially an accounting of events – the "happenings." His rendition of the massacre in Jedwabne is a good example of the tension between myth and fact so evident in his stories. In his telling, the story becomes a Jewish legend, even as it "speaks truth" to the violence and horror. In Miguel's hands, Jedwabne is a parable of Jewish martyrdom, with young boy-heroes shouting the main statement of their belief (the Shema) at the moment of their deaths. Waterston suspects that Miguel embodies the diasporic Jew whose habitus drives his belief in telling the story, keeps him faithful to the suffering he really does endure.

Jadzia's reticence and Miguel's craving may be related to their respective selves located in sociocultural and political-historical contexts: She is the non-Jew in the war that held the Holocaust, and he is ever the Jew, relentlessly pursued by annihilationists. And still, our parents are "subjects who remember" (Hoffman 2004:166). Even if we discover in them traces of collective memory, they will always be flesh and blood to us. Our depictions will show them as we know them – with their strengths and their vulnerabilities, their flaws and their virtues, their insights and their ignorance, neither all good nor all bad, just real. Our depictions will show their individuality and their humanity even as we theorize their place in history. It is the very aspect of balancing the two dimensions that represents the strength of our approach.

From Narrative to the Worldly Shape of Events: Linking Story to History

> But the Holocaust past, aside from being a profound personal legacy, is also a task. It demands something from us, an understanding that is larger than just ourselves, that moves beyond the private vicissitudes of the inner life. The second generation after every calamity is the hinge generation, in which the meanings of awful events can remain arrested and fixed at the point of trauma; or in which they can be transformed into new sets of relations with the world, and new understanding. How we interpret the implications of our primary narrative, how we translate psychic information into information about the world, matters for more than ourselves. [Eva Hoffman[7]]

Hoffman writes specifically about the Holocaust and explicitly from her vantage point as a "second generation" daughter of survivors. Her summons to translate psychic information into information about the world, however, reflects the overall mission we have set for ourselves, informed by our understanding of political economy, a perspective that necessitates commitment to making the world a better place, not just explaining it (Farmer 2003; Singer 1993, 1994).

Rylko-Bauer approaches the project of chronicling her mother's story by asking, "What are the structures, at all levels, that allow suffering, oppression and genocide, great privation and profound inequities to continue, seemingly unabated? Anthropology may be about studying what it is and what it means to be human. But surely it is also about what it means to barely live as a human being. Or to be treated as less than human" (2003:2).

Similarly, Waterston explains the fundamental purpose of her task: "Telling my father's story and exploring what it might mean for 'bringing the past into the present' . . . Memory with its root in the Latin memoria – mindful, is key to my purpose. After all, to be mindful is to be aware, an essential step in preventing 'genocides, ethnocides and die-outs' (Scheper-Hughes 2002:351) . . . It is my hope that in the strands of this tale, we might learn more about what Paul Farmer (2003) calls the mechanisms of structural violence and the machinery of political economy that continue to wreak killing force on millions of people today" (2005:46).

Anthropology leads us to examine the multiple connections between individuals and larger histories, and we use the discipline as our guide to understanding how social forces become embodied as individual experience. Our positionality as anthropologists allows us to explore intimate domains without obscuring the role of cultural, historical, and social structural factors in causality, thereby rescuing our projects from solipsism, psychological reductionism, and the distortions of disembodied abstraction.

Like others, our parents have faced the cruelties of modernity, the consequences of empire and nation-state building, the violent oppression of difference. As we move away from our parents into the "worldly shape of events" (Hoffman 2004:16), we search for connections between their biographies and the suffering of others who – although the specifics of the histories differ – share some aspect of our parents' experiences and the consequences of their being dehumanized and displaced. Nancy Scheper-Hughes's (2000, 2002) concept of the "genocidal continuum" provides an analytic tool for linking the everyday violence and dehumanization characterizing the lives of the poor and dispossessed to the more spectacular violence of massacres and genocides. The current condition of our world, marked as it is by the shadows of war and genocide, as well as the less visible "small wars" (Scheper-Hughes 1996) and largely invisible structural violence of poverty and racism, adds urgency to our task. These events and the social processes that give rise to them are not unique in history and yet they are avoidable.

Our objective, ultimately, is to contribute to understanding violence in its many guises – and its cruel and unjust consequences – by means of ethnographic characterizations of our parents, by our written narratives of their stories, and by our anthropologically informed reckoning with the past for lessons about the present. In this way, we also hope to honor the memory of our parents' ordeals.

Acknowledgments

Alisse Waterston offers special thanks to Howard Horowitz and Adriana Waterston, and dedicates this chapter to her mother, Louise M. Waterston. Barbara Rylko-Bauer acknowledges a great debt to her mother, Jadwiga Lenartowicz Rylko, and dedicates this chapter to the women of the Neusalz slave-labor camp. We also thank Athena McLean, Annette Leibing, Virginia Dominguez, and several anonymous reviewers for their helpful comments.

Notes

1   See Rylko-Bauer 2005 and Waterston 2005 for more detailed presentations of these stories, their historical and political-economic context, and the lessons they offer. The current chapter is an adaptation of a previously published article. Waterston, Alisse, and Barbara Rylko-Bauer, "Out of the Shadows of History and Memory: Personal Family Narratives in Ethnographies of Rediscovery," American Ethnologist, 33(3):397–412. © 2006, American Anthropological Association. Used by permission. All rights reserved.

2   All the main concentration camps administered large networks of subcamps, totaling an estimated 1,634 in number, and employing several million persons in forced labor, much of it for the German war effort and for German industry profits (Allen 2002; Ferencz 2002:187, 240; Simpson 1995:86–87). See Waterston and Rylko-Bauer 2006 for more details about the structure of Nazi forced labor.

3   Hoffman here cites literary critic Jan Kott. She notes that "most of the concentration camps were situated on Polish soil, and it has often been assumed that the Germans had placed them there because they counted on the collusion of the Poles in their annihilationist project. This has been repeatedly shown to be untrue" (Hoffman 2004:17). The actual history from that time is more complex, characterized by both heroism and betrayal and shaped by the pervasive anti-Semitism that has been a waxing and waning feature of Polish Christian–Jewish relations throughout the centuries.

4   "The Museum honors as survivors any persons, Jewish or non-Jewish, who were displaced, persecuted, or discriminated against due to the racial, religious, ethnic, social, and political policies of the Nazis and their collaborators

between 1933 and 1945. In addition to former inmates of concentration camps, ghettos, and prisons, this definition includes, among others, people who were refugees or were in hiding" (U.S. Holocaust Memorial Museum n.d.). Scholars continue to debate what constitutes the Holocaust and who it encompasses (Berenbaum 1990), with some calling for a more inclusive notion (e.g., Friedlander 1995) and others arguing for a more restrictive one (e.g., Bauer 2001). See also Waterston and Rylko-Bauer 2006 for a discussion as to why such debates, when focused on definitions and boundaries, may be counterproductive to the larger goal of preventing genocides.

5 All interactions between Rylko-Bauer and her mother were in Polish, and Rylko-Bauer translated them into English. Waterston's interactions and interviews with her father were in English.

6 In some cases, of course, the silence is attributable to faded memory. Although Jadzia has amazing recall for all sorts of details, she often reminds her impatient daughter that "it's been over 60 years, so how can you expect me to remember everything!" Likewise, Miguel at times can be transported as far back as his childhood in Jedwabne, even recalling minute details of a day in his life there. At other times, he needs the daughter to prompt him with names, dates, or circumstances to trigger his fading memory.

7 Hoffman 2004:103.

References

Abu-Lughod, Lila
  1993 Writing Women's Worlds: Bedouin Stories. Berkeley: University of California Press.
Allen, Michael Thad
  2002 The Business of Genocide: The SS, Slave Labor, and the Concentration Camps. Chapel Hill: University of North Carolina Press.
Angrosino, Michael V., and Kimberly A. Mays de Pérez
  2003 Rethinking Observation: From Method to Context. *In* Collecting and Interpreting Qualitative Materials. Norman K. Denzin and Yvonna S. Lincoln, eds. Pp. 673–702. Thousand Oaks, CA: Sage Publications.
Baker, Julius L., and Moshe Tzinovitz
  1980 My Hometown Yedwabne, Province of Lomza, Poland. *In* Yedwabne: History and Memorial Book. Jerusalem and New York: The Yedwabne Societies in Israel and the United States of America. Electronic document, http://www.jewishgen.org/yizkor/jedwabne/Yedwabne.html, accessed July 7, 2005.
Bateson, Mary Catherine
  1984 With A Daughter's Eye: A Memoir of Margaret Mead and Gregory Bateson. New York: William Morrow.
Bauer, Yehuda
  2001 Rethinking the Holocaust. New Haven, CT: Yale University Press.

Behar, Ruth
  1993   Translated Woman: Crossing the Border with Esperanza's Story. Boston: Beacon Press.
Berenbaum, Michael
  1990   The Uniqueness and Universality of the Holocaust. *In* A Mosaic of Victims: Non-Jews Persecuted and Murdered by the Nazis. Michael Berenbaum, ed. Pp. 20–36. New York: New York University Press.
Blobaum, Robert, ed.
  2005   Antisemitism and Its Opponents in Modern Poland. Ithaca, NY: Cornell University Press.
Bourguignon, Erika
  2005   Memory in an Amnesic World: Holocaust, Exile and the Return of the Suppressed. Anthropological Quarterly 78(1):63–88.
Boyarin, Jonathan
  1996   Thinking in Jewish. Chicago: University of Chicago Press.
Brand, William, ed.
  2001   Thou Shalt Not Kill: Poles on Jedwabne. Warsaw: Towarzystwo "Więz."
Brodkin, Karen
  1998   How Jews Became White Folks and What That Says About Race in America. New Brunswick, NJ: Rutgers University Press.
Cohen, Jeremy
  2004   Sanctifying the Name of God. Jewish Martyrs and Jewish Memories of the First Crusade. Philadelphia: University of Pennsylvania Press.
Crapanzano, Vincent
  1980   Tuhami: Portrait of a Moroccan. Chicago: University of Chicago Press.
Davies, Norman
  2004   Rising '44: The Battle for Warsaw. New York: Viking.
Delbo, Charlotte
  1995   Auschwitz and After. Rosette C. Lamont, trans. New Haven, CT: Yale University Press.
Dobroszycki, Lucjan, ed.
  1984   The Chronicle of the Łódź Ghetto 1941–1944. New Haven, CT: Yale University Press.
Ellis, Carolyn
  2004   The Ethnographic I: A Methodological Novel about Autoethnography. Walnut Creek, CA: AltaMira Press.
Ellis, Carolyn, and Arthur P. Bochner
  2000   Autoethnography, Personal Narrative, Reflexivity: Researcher as Subject. *In* Handbook of Qualitative Research, 2nd edition. Norman K. Denzin and Yvonna S. Lincoln, eds. Pp. 733–768. Thousand Oaks, CA: Sage.
Farmer, Paul
  2003   Pathologies of Power: Health, Human Rights, and the New War on the Poor. Berkeley: University of California Press.

Ferencz, Benjamin B.
  2002 [1979]   Less Than Slaves: Jewish Forced Labor and the Quest for Compensation. Bloomington: Indiana University Press.
Frank, Gelya
  2000   Venus on Wheels. Berkeley: University of California Press.
Friedlander, Henry
  1995   The Origins of Nazi Genocide. Chapel Hill: University of North Carolina Press.
Gross, Jan T.
  2001   Neighbors: The Destruction of the Jewish Community of Jedwabne, Poland. Princeton: Princeton University Press.
Hoffman, Eva
  2004   After Such Knowledge. Memory, History, and the Legacy of the Holocaust. New York: Public Affairs.
Hutchinson, Janis Faye
  2005   Power, Race, and Culture: The Evolution of a Black Anthropologist. Blue Ridge Summit, PA: Hamilton Books.
Kottak, Conrad
  2002   Cultural Anthropology, 9th edition. New York: McGraw Hill.
Krakowski, Shmuel
  1990   "Lodz." *In* Encyclopedia of the Holocaust. Israel Gutman, ed. Pp. 900–909. New York: Macmillan.
Krell, Robert, Marc I. Sherman, and Elie Wiesel
  1997   Medical and Psychological Effects of Concentration Camps on Holocaust Survivors. Genocide – A Critical Bibliographic Review, Vol. 4. New Brunswick, NJ: Transaction Publishers.
Langer, Lawrence L.
  1991   Holocaust Testimonies: The Ruins of Memory. New Haven, CT: Yale University Press.
Linden, R. Ruth
  1993   Making Stories, Making Selves. Columbus: Ohio State University.
Marcus, Paul and Alan Rosenberg, eds.,
  1989   Healing Their Wounds: Psychotherapy with Holocaust Survivors and Their Families. New York: Praeger.
McLean, Athena, and Annette Leibing
  2003   Abstract for panel, "The Shadow Side of Field Work: Theorizing the Blurred Borders Between Ethnography and Life." Annual Meetings of the American Anthropological Association, Chicago, November 22.
Mintz, Alan
  2001   Popular Culture and the Shaping of Holocaust Memory in America. Seattle: University of Washington Press.
Myerhoff, Barbara
  1978   Number Our Days. New York: Simon and Schuster.
Ochs, Elinor, and Lisa Capps
  1996   Narrating the Self. Annual Review of Anthropology 25:19–43.

Orlove, Ben
  1995 In My Father's Study. Iowa City: University of Iowa Press.
Polonsky, Antony, and Joanna B. Michlic, eds.
  2003 The Neighbors Respond: The Controversy over the Jedwabne Massacre in Poland. Princeton: Princeton University Press.
Reed-Danahay, Deborah
  1997 Auto/ethnography: Rewriting the Self and the Social. Oxford: Berg.
Reed-Danahay, Deborah
  2002 Turning Points and Textual Strategies in Ethnographic Writing. Qualitative Studies in Education 15:421–425.
Rossino, Alexander B.
  2003 Hitler Strikes Poland: Blitzkrieg, Ideology, and Atrocity. Lawrence: University Press of Kansas.
Rylko-Bauer, Barbara
  2003 In the Shadows of History and Memory. Using Personal Family Narrative in an Ethnography of Rediscovery. Paper presented at the 102nd Annual Meeting of the American Anthropological Association, Chicago, November 22.
Rylko-Bauer, Barbara
  2005 Lessons About Humanity and Survival from My Mother and from the Holocaust. Anthropological Quarterly 78(1):11–41.
Scheper-Hughes, Nancy
  1996 Small Wars and Invisible Genocides. Social Science and Medicine 43:889–900.
Scheper-Hughes, Nancy
  2000 The Genocidal Continuum: Peace-Time Crimes. *In* Power and the Self. Jeannette Marie Mageo, ed. Pp. 29–47. Cambridge: Cambridge University Press.
Scheper-Hughes, Nancy
  2002 Coming to our Senses: Anthropology and Genocide. *In* Annihilating Difference. The Anthropology of Genocide. Alexander Laban Hinton, ed. Pp. 348–381. Berkeley: University of California Press.
Shostak, Marjorie
  2000 Return to Nisa. Cambridge, MA: Harvard University Press.
Simpson, Christopher
  1995 The Splendid Blond Beast: Money, Law and Genocide in the Twentieth Century. Monroe, ME: Common Courage Press.
Singer, Merrill
  1993 Knowledge for Use: Anthropology and Community-Centered Substance Abuse Research. Social Science & Medicine 37(1):15–25.
Singer, Merrill
  1994 Community-Centered Praxis: Toward an Alternative Non-Dominative Applied Anthropology. Human Organization 53(4):336–344.
Spiegelman, Art
  1997 The Complete Maus. A Survivor's Tale. New York: Pantheon Books.

Steiner, George
  1988   The Long Life of Metaphor. *In* Writing and the Holocaust. Berel Lang, ed. Pp. 154–171. New York: Holmes & Meier.
Steinlauf, Michael C.
  1997   Bondage to the Dead: Poland and the Memory of the Holocaust. Syracuse, NY: Syracuse University Press.
U.S. Holocaust Memorial Museum
  n.d.   Benjamin and Vladka Meed Registry of Jewish Holocaust Survivors. Electronic document, http://www.ushmm.org/remembrance/registry/index.php?content=intro/, accessed March 8, 2006.
Waserstein Kahn, Samuel and Yehudi Monestel Arce
  2001   La Denuncia. 10 de Julio de 1941. San José, Costa Rica: Editorial Guayacán Centroamericana, S.A.
Waterston, Alisse
  2005   The Story of My Story: An Anthropology of Violence, Dispossession and Diaspora. Anthropological Quarterly 78(1):43–61.
Waterston, Alisse, and Barbara Rylko-Bauer
  2006   Out of the Shadows of History and Memory: Personal Family Narratives in Ethnographies of Rediscovery. American Ethnologist 33(3):397–412.
Zola, Irving Kenneth
  1982   Missing Pieces: A Chronicle of Living with a Disability. Philadelphia: Temple University Press.

Chapter 2

When Things Get Personal: Secrecy, Intimacy, and the Production of Experience in Fieldwork

Anne M. Lovell

In much ethnographical writing, the treatment of secrets constitutes a criterion for how the text and the ethnographic work behind it will be evaluated. The ethnographer's ability to penetrate the secrets of his or her subjects becomes a major stake in the ethnographic quest. The conventions of the text orient the reader's understanding of the secret and its piercing, at once the successful culmination of the harrowing work of the ethnographer and the climax of the narrative. Supposedly at stake in the secret are truths to which the ethnographer may or may not accede: truths unquestionably personal, or collective and dangerously political, or both.

Maurice Godelier's treatment of the secret of sacred objects of the Baruya illustrates this very well. Godelier sought the secret of a sacred object, the *kwaimatnie* (a wrapped bark package, opened for ritual purposes) kept by Baruya masters of male initiation rituals. Godelier recounts what he finally sees when, many years into the field, an initiation master reveals what lies inside the *kwaimatnie*. The textual presentation borrows from the genre of the detective story such conventions as suspenseful build-up, anonymity, a general atmosphere of anxiety, and intimations of danger:

> Even before he [an initiation master] arrived, I had felt something unusual was afoot. A heavy silence hung in the air. The village was suddenly deserted. Everyone had left, having caught wind of something serious in the offing. Then the man arrived. His son . . . was with him. I was not expecting this. The two men came into the house and sat down, one at either end of the table. I put my head out to make sure no one could listen in, and saw two or three men from the Bakia clan, armed with bows and arrows,

discreetly posted around the house so that no one could approach. The man opened his net bag and took out a long object wrapped in a strip of red bark. Without a word, he laid it on the table, untied the strip and began undoing the packet. This took some time. Carefully and delicately, his fingers spread the bark. Finally he opened it completely. [Godelier 1999:125]

The uncovering of the "most secret of all the Baruya's secrets" enables Godelier to grasp the principle of Baruya men's domination over women, through the mythical but lived appropriation of the sources of women's powers. It also enables him – taking off from Annette Weiner's work on inalienable possessions – to understand the primacy of the imaginary realm (to which the inalienable possession refers) and how the imaginary is in turn invested symbolically, made "real" so to speak (e.g., initiation rites), and thus invests and reproduces social relations of gender. The uncovering of this most secret of secrets leads to one of Godelier's major contributions to contemporary anthropology.

A more ambiguous treatment of the secret emerges in the biography of the Nobel Peace Prize Mayan activist, Rigoberta Menchù (Burgos-Debray 1984). In what appears textually as a major "dialogic moment" with her biographer, Menchù states her position vis-à-vis the ethnographer: "I am still keeping my Indian identity secret. I am still keeping secret what I think no one should know. Not even anthropologists or intellectuals, no matter how many books they have, can find out all our secrets."

Here the status of the secret opens itself to multiple interpretations. The biography, a best-selling academic book, is alternately critiqued as "monological in voice and dialogical in writing process" (Ryang 2000), material for exploitation and "facile consumption of Otherness,"[1] factual, counter-factual, and the authentic voice of a subaltern woman and revolutionary.[2]

In both ethnographies, the treatment of secrets both analytically and textually (through tropes, narrative construction, etc.) brings to light the power relations between anthropologist and interlocutors in the field. The secrecy of ethnographic subjects may be read as forms of resistance – to the anthropologist or to others who exercise power – as Rigoberta Menchù implies. Secrecy, on the other hand, may constitute at once the expression of a form of resistance *and* the recognition of the power of the other (Fainzang 2002). Or secrecy refers to something static, information accorded the same status as the other pieces of data alongside which it is placed.

What I have presented is very similar to the commonsense, everyday notion of the secret, its holder and beholder. It involves at least two parties. Discretion, dissimulation, and secrecy include (those who share the secret) and exclude (the non-initiated). The excluded is very often the anthropologist, but also the presumed audience to which the anthropological text will be addressed. What though of secrecy and self-revelation not only of the anthropologists' interlocutors in the field, but of the anthropologist her or himself? How, through the play of secrets, is anthropological knowledge constituted from *both* sides of the anthropological encounter? How does working with secrecy multilaterally contribute to anthropological understanding? Shifting the problematic from the text's treatment of the secret to the dynamics of secrecy itself and to its effect on anthropological knowledge compels the anthropologist and his or her readers to reposition themselves. Rather than "seeing" secrets as a bounded though unfathomable (to the other) "thing," which can be possessed or "cracked open" or verified, it is now necessary to apprehend secrecy as movement. Questioning the truth-value or the social and cultural uses of secrets, as is common in this first genre of anthropological production, may bring to light the power at stake in secrecy. But analyzing the dialectic of secrecy and self-revelation between ethnographer and interlocutor in the field engages relations of power at another level as well, that of dialogue and micropolitics. And it undermines the notion of absolute truth because it depends on the vantage point, the position from whence one party "knows" the other, as well as what the "other" reveals.

This paper offers a modest contribution to our understanding of how the lived, but often unspeakable – because deeply personal – experience of the ethnographer interfaces with similarly intimate and emotionally charged experiences of her or his subjects. However, it focuses specifically on the secret to emphasize the degree to which self-revelation and withholding, far from being a mere "choice" or "emotional style," are intertwined with the dynamics of the ethnographic situation: the necessarily asymmetrical relationship between (participant) observer and subject; and the respective shadow dialogues of the two – what they silently articulate, or the ruminations and reflections that take place alongside their shared primary, self-constituting discourse (Crapanzano 1992). In doing so, I show that the ethnographic situation itself – and not solely what the ethnographer brings to the field from some preexisting personal experience, or expresses later in writing ethnography – produces the contours of what is "personal."

After presenting the conceptual issues around such linked notions as secrecy, discretion, and self-revelation, I will illustrate these dynamics through two sets of examples from situations in which revelation and withholding imply stakes around social survival itself. The first draw on my research in New York City with persons who experience psychosis and other anomalous states but who, at the same time, developed, individually and through collectives such as self-help groups, networks, or patient-run alternatives to hospitalization, non-institutional ways of working with their illness. The second is based on the life story of a young man in Marseilles (France), who secretly turned to injecting illicit drugs after being released from a prison where he had spent all his adult life until then. In the first examples, the dialectics of secrecy and self-revelation emerge through that most traditional of anthropological tools, namely the everyday conversations of participant observation. The second concerns the more formal interview method of the life history, which, I suggest, creates a different kind of space of encounter between ethnographer and subject, with different connotations for secrecy. For both, ethnographic and sociolinguistic analyses are used to understand how ethnographer and subject, moving between discretion and intimation of secrets, actually *produce* that experience we call "personal" rather than the personal being a dimension that lies outside the dynamics of the field encounter – pre- or post-hoc. Each set of examples thus reveals from a different angle the work of constituting anthropological knowledge.

The Coordinates of the Personal: Secrecy, Discretion, Intimacy

In cases as distinct from one another as the classical anthropological quest to reveal the contents of a Baruya cult object (Godelier 1999), concerns with the hidden agenda of political groups in the anthropology of democracy (Eliafson 2003), or more recent ethnography of the practices of "heterosexual" men in "gay" cruising sites (Gaissad 2000), the secret implies something bounded and static. The secret is potentially given or taken, grasped, apprehended. A secret "secretes," which implies a metaphorical membrane through which it oozes, before attaching itself to a word, a gesture, or leaving a trace that suggests that "thing" of which it is only a small part, a hint. Discretion – the veils covering the secret – imply separateness, distinctness of the secret and what lies around it, of those privy to the secret and those desirous of knowing it. Secrets are, in this sense, discrete entities (see also Deleuze and Guattari 1987).

In modern Western history, secrecy also implies intimacy, or that which is most private and personal. The term "intimacy," derived from the Latin *innus*, refers to "the superlative of the inner," the innermost." The German historian Kosselek shows how from the 19th century on, the state cedes legitimate secrets to its citizens and allows a private sphere, a sense of the intimate, a separation which, coupled with citizens' confidence in the state, is necessary to political mobilization and involvement in the public sphere (Laé and Proth 2002). "Inner" comes to qualify, with modernity, a "self," a "mind," a "consciousness."[3] Hence, the very notion of intimacy is necessarily caught up in the webs of meaning particular to a time and place – such as the Western notion of an authentic, autonomous, inner self. In contemporary European and North American societies, intimacy has come to be what the historian Arlette Farge and sociologist Jean-François Laé define as a "space of attitudes, manners, roles, words, actions that, through secrecy, keep social sanctions at a distance. It is an authorized silence which authorizes a sort of self-possession and deviations which would otherwise be judged or sanctioned" (Farge and Laé 2000).

But in contemporary Western societies, intimacy is also, paradoxically, overexposed. From blogs to reality TV to a certain ethos of "authenticity" and openness to the various techniques of self-help among strangers, the uncovering of what is supposedly most personal, most secret, is now intrinsic to the heightened cultures of mutual self-exposure, biography, and continual self-representation in late modernity. What is left to secrete? As Kosselek's perspective indicates (but also Norbert Elias' history of manners, among other historical sociology), intimations and self-narrations of individuals are in fact historically and socially embedded, reproducing the socio-historical contours of larger institutional or cultural frames and values. This does not, however, reveal the current meanings attributed to an increasingly visible intimacy.

Yet the conditions under which intimacy is exposed, and the mastery of the very acts of revealing or withholding, are not equally distributed.

Thus, intimacy may be knowingly shared for some, forcibly revealed (or revealed by default[4]) for others. Particularly exposed are people who inhabit those social spaces and physical places sometimes called "zones of vulnerability" (Laé and Proth 2002). These zones refer to marginal statuses, disciplinary institutions, and interstitial public spaces. There the act of self-revelation and of maintaining secrecy is far more heteronymous – controlled by the surveillance and rules of others – than on reality shows, blogs, or other stages for manifesting the intimate.[5] Secrecy as an issue, a stake, an omnipresence, infuses these zones of vulnerability. The social precariousness, stigma, madness, institutionalization, and more generally lack of social margin prevalent in such spaces expose the intimacy of the person to the mere gaze of the Other (cf. Lovell 2001a; Lovell in press). In most cases, the relative position of the anthropologist is that of the temporarily sane, the momentarily well, the stably domiciled who interacts with the not sane, the ill, or the displaced.

For persons who suffer from psychosis and/or have experienced psychiatric treatment, the sense of invasion of their most private sphere and innermost self may grow on them, as if their zone of vulnerability were an invisible sphere that had attached itself to them, always to be carried

with them, always vulnerable to the interplay of stigma.[6] What is at stake
in revealing intimacy may be a sense of shame, a loss of self-protection,
or fragile sense of control over themselves. In prison, or among those
involved in at once stigmatizing and illicit activities, secrecy is also a form
of legal protection. But the intimate is highly visible. Anthropological
descriptions often unconsciously reproduce this very control of intimacy,
particularly through the gaze of the anthropologist-Other, that is characteristic of these zones (I have been prone to the same tendency myself,
even in the later parts of this paper).[7]

In the dynamics of secrecy and self-revelation, a power relation is
incarnated through the primary, but unequal mediation, of (at least) two
bodies. While my body projects the outer signs of my social place, the
bodies I encounter in the zones of vulnerability carry the signs of their
potential stigmas: the acrid, benzene-like odor of cheap, industrial disin-
fectant from shelters and other institutional settings; the Parkinsonlike
gestures and incessant monologue spoken aloud; the unkempt hair, urine
stains, worn bags, and tattered clothes. In many of these situations, people
do not have access to the codes necessary to maintaining the most fundamental civility assumed in public or institutional space. Cognitive confusion and other psychic conditions impede picking up on hints or sensing
the doxa (Bourdieu 1977 [1972]), the "goes without saying" of such codes
as the amount of space to maintain between oneself and others, or how
and when different parts of one's body can show, or the sound, odor, sight,
touch one can emit. Similarly, people in highly marginal social situations
may lack the symbolic and material "props" through which they represent
themselves in a certain way. In public space, these may be so basic as a clean,
still smooth shopping bag full of groceries or a tool sack or computer case
that leaves no ambiguity as to where one has been or is going.[8]

Yet these forced revelations of intimacy do not necessarily indicate a
total absence of agency. First, what really constitutes the "innermost" or
most private domain of existence is not so clear: the frames of interpretation anthropologists apply to their understanding of zones of vulnerability
draw on normative codes and conventions to establish what is shameful
or threatens the integrity of others. One need not fall into relativism to
grasp that hierarchies of dignity may vary (Lovell 1996), as do the sense
of violation, the notion of privacy and "inner" and even "self." Second,
even in the most extreme situations (concentration camps, imprisonment)
in which all intimacy seems to be exposed, intimacy itself becomes the
only stake in a struggle for preservation. Allen Feldman illustrates this clearly
and painfully through his analysis of scatology in the breaking of the PIRA,
the armed Irish nationalist units, through the complete domination and
inscription of the body in the prison system (Feldman 1991). But even in

his account there is a slim margin of resistance, dehumanized as it may be, hideaways of intimacy, just as Goffman shows more generally for other total institutions like the asylum (Goffman 1961). Third, in urban public space, bizarre or odd behavior may serve to turn if not scare away an onlooker. Strong odors emanating from one's body may have "sociofugal" effects, physically (and hence socially) distancing others (Raybaud 2002). Amplifying a conversation with "no one" or repeatedly beating a stick in the personal space surrounding oneself, or urinating or defecating within the sight of others, also delineates invisible spaces of protection (Lovell 1997). The observed body, it has been suggested, constitutes the last vestige of intimacy in zones of vulnerability (Lanzarini 1998). Through physical repugnance, the body paradoxically reveals and preserves intimacy, by repelling those who might look too closely or be too eager to offer their services. At issue, though, is the extent to which conscious agency and intentionality are actually involved. Here, too, I suggest, the anthropologist must engage herself in a dialectic of secrecy and self-revelation to understand what is at hand.

The Dialectic of Self-Revelation

Ethnography of a patient-run alternative to the regimens of psychiatric hospitalization and traditional rehabilitation (such as sheltered workshops) provides me a first series of examples with which to work through the dialectics of secrecy and self-revelation. For several months, I became a participant observer of women and men who had been and are constantly threatened by the constraints of zones of vulnerability (Lovell 1991). The French expression "s'incruster" ("take root") expresses metaphorically how I put my methodology to work: by maintaining an as unobtrusive as possible presence in the three-room, makeshift office space above a bicycle repair shop and next to a noisy elevated subway in the Bronx, rented by the group. From this space they ran a food bank, collecting from supermarkets food whose date of expiration had passed, making sandwiches and filling brown bags, which they then distributed, on foot, to homeless people in Manhattan. The office also provided a place where they slept, talked, played scratchy old tapes, smoked lots of cigarettes, and opened the door to drifters, the occasional evicted mother and baby, or down-and-out adolescent trying to kick a drug habit, or hungry and curious neighbor. I also accompanied some of them to meetings and events in which they met other self-designated "consumers" (of mental health services) and "survivors" (of psychiatric internment and treatment) from around the United States.

Taking root in this setting means fitting into a different sense of time, where days seem long and slow, often eventless and mostly unplanned. But this sort of time is conducive to conversation, and conversation often turns to experience of the present. Through these conversations, and my understanding of events that did interrupt them, began to emerge a sense of what intimacy and secrecy might mean to the members of this group.

The eventlessness in fact belonged to a space that they had appropriated as their own, as autonomous and, in the sense of being untouchable (by outsiders, such as the Department of Mental Health, which was very interested in it as a model to replicate), their own private sphere. For example, while some applied long unused skills to the logistics of the food bank and others enjoyed the sense of achievement and human contact from distributing the food to homeless people in the subways and train station (several had been homeless before being hospitalized), others were content to spend the day in the office space. Some consciously mimicked the trappings of the corporate world – watching computers all day "like the corporate guys" rather than learning how to use them. Some started using hard drugs again, or became so delusional as to be rehospitalized. Members of the food bank interpreted their own or others' relapses into drug use or rehospitalizations as normal ("we're just like a corporation, we're human too" – this is at the height of Wall Street scandals around cocaine use). They showed tolerance for "word salad" and other manifestations of "crazy talk" among themselves (though not all expressed these symptoms) or simply didn't notice it. Basically, they rejected what the hospital staff supporting their project defined as a work ethic, let alone a managerial ethic, such as a clearer organizational structure and the transformation of their way of working into quantifiable "deliverables."

Intimacy, however, was a crucial stake in their feeling of autonomy or control over their own lives. One event, four years into the project, illustrated the group's struggle between autonomy and heteronomy, their desire for self-reliance and self-defined sociability versus the goals the officials, mental health and hospital administrators sought to impose. And central to this struggle was the notion of intimacy. Hospital administrators were completing a grant proposal to expand the food bank into "consumer-operated housing," that is, a residence in the Bronx where they would live together, with other patients and former patients, and more or less run the building themselves. But the food bank members showed little enthusiasm for this project. I came to understand that for them, the consumer-operated housing represented a fall back into group living, which they imagined as too similar to the hospital. Both the former and current hospital patients described life in the hospital in negative terms. There they acted "like little children," were always on bad behavior, screaming, crying, talking to themselves, vomiting in the unwanted presence of others packed together in close quarters. In the hospital, intimacy was dissolved before enforced promiscuity: the indiscriminate mingling of bodies and odors and sounds, the intrusion of staff and other patients alike into what are normally the private niches of daily life. It was like the underside of family life. In the rooms above the bicycle shop, on the contrary, the members controlled the boundaries around their intimacy. The administration eventually closed down the project but not before key members of the group had already left. Ironically, members had rejected the community the hospital had enforced on them, the externally imposed promiscuity that moving into shared housing threatened to reconstitute.

Thus far, I have presented the stakes around intimacy and, consequently, secrecy in a particular zone of vulnerability. But what happens when the anthropologist's intimacy and secrecy are also at play? I shift here from general observations of life above the bicycle shop to one-on-one conversations during meetings with other consumers or consumer groups. In the following two examples, the explicit role of the anthropologist produced another type of dynamic.

During a discussion among several of us, Carola, a striking woman who towered over me, whom I knew to be a graduate student in psychology when she wasn't experiencing acute bouts of psychosis, turned to me, and, lowering her voice, asked what I thought of the "soft consumer talk" going on. "When I get psychotic," she told me, "I'm not like *them*. I'm homicidal. They hospitalized me because I tried to kill my boyfriend." Did I, too – she wanted to know – feel uncomfortable with the "easy stuff" – the depression, the mild hallucinations that others were describing? In retrospect, she may have been seeking an alliance with someone who, like her, benefited from middle-class origins. She was the daughter of an African-American businessman and a Swedish professor. Like me, she benefited from the cultural capital that most of the others – young African-American, Afro-Caribbean, and Puerto Rican men and women from poor neighborhoods not far from the hospital, former homeless kids, informal market workers and low-paid clerks – lacked. But it was somewhat disconcerting for me when I realized that she assumed that, like her, I, too, suffered from schizophrenia. I felt in an ambivalent, if not dishonest position. I explained to her that although I had experienced some of what the others were describing, I was not a "consumer." No one had ever diagnosed me with schizophrenia. And I had never been the object of surveillance or forced treatment.

In a second example, a man about my age, Gerald, struggled to explain his terror of psychosis. This was a moment of exposed intimacy. I couldn't totally understand his experience, I told him. But I related my own odyssey. I imparted my experience of near-death, while giving birth to my daughter; my subsequent, terrifying, medically-induced psychosis and depersonalization, my (non-medically induced) paranoia when, fearful of malpractice repercussions, the doctors denied what I was experiencing; my isolation on the "high risk" maternity floor where it took those closest to me over 24 hours to get through to me; and finally, once on a regular maternity floor, the alienation from even those closest to me as I struggled to hide what I was experiencing for fear of it being misunderstood or, worse, unacknowledged.

All three examples involve some play with discretion and self-revelation. To understand what intimacy and privacy meant for the food bank members, and how that related to a larger conflict over autonomy with the mental health administration, I had first to become "discrete" myself. In fact, so discrete that I experienced what happened on at least four other occasions in fieldwork in psychiatric settings or with patients and former patients – and with Carola. I was taken (at least by some) for a patient myself. Some didn't even question my presence. (Of course to others I was clearly doing research.)

But with Carola and Gerald my own vulnerability to exposing an intimate side of myself created or impeded a "personal experience" within the fieldwork itself, which in turn produced further understanding as part of anthropological knowledge. Carola's response had been to cut me off, to stop the dialogue and shorten the presentation of part of her self. Perhaps she felt betrayed. Perhaps she expected discretion on my part, like an annulment, an immediate forgetting that I had heard that part of her that she had divulged. Gerald, on the other hand, remarked that he had never met anyone before who did not "have" schizophrenia but understood the terror of the experience. A moment of authenticity in our dialogue opened the possibility for further (but not necessarily authentic) dialogue.

With Carola, self-revelation prevented the possibility of further dialogue and heightened the incommensurability (I believe she sensed) between us. For this reason, it may have halted the process of ethnographic understanding. But it did provide, I believe, ethnographic insight into the nature of intimacy and secrecy in zones of vulnerability.

With Gerald, the moment of mutual self-revelation was also the *acknowledgment* of the incommensurability of our parallel experiences – of the two "dialogues" that were the theme of the dialogue at hand. What linked us is not that illusion of authenticity that Crapanzano calls a "kind of phatic affirmation of a shared view" or social support (Crapanzano 1992:90). Rather, we were recognizing in each other the singularity of an experience we perpetuated through our respective shadow dialogues.

Gerald and I presented to each other nonconsensual experiences, the sense of having fallen through the barrier of "normative cognition" and consensually validated ways of interpreting and contending with the external world – hence nonconsensual in an existential sense. But we also relate the experience of our respective shadow interlocutors, those who are absent from our conversation but reappear to each of us, as if invisibly attached to our narrative. In my case, that side dialogue involves those doctors who could not listen as they made their rounds with a herd of interns on a busy night in a giant metropolitan hospital (and wary of a malpractice suit because that very organizational chaos caused them to neglect routine tests that would have alerted them to my pre-eclampsia, if not prevented it). For Gerald, the interlocutors were probably among those for whom his experience remained unheard – such as the medication-oriented psychiatrist caught in the temporality of a logic of cost- and hence time-effectiveness that excluded the patient's narrative.[9] These parallel experiences reinforced a shared sense of incommensurability and opened the way to further discursive possibilities, which, at the next level of dialogue (the working through, the textualizing of my materials), promises ethnographic understanding.

The shadow dialogues as I have borrowed and worked the concept are not the same as what Gelya Frank (1979) refers to as a "biography in the shadows." Ruth Behar (1993) adopts Frank's coinage and attempts to reconstruct her own history in such a way as to create the links between her personal, emotional, and historical experiences and the choices, attitudes, and empathy she exercises during the four years of taping of Esperanza's life story. Behar compares the rebelliousness and redemption of a dominated, translated woman to her own border-crossing, constraints, and fighting back. The degree to which Behar succeeds in connecting the biography in the shadow to her ethnographic work is subject to controversy, although no one questions the originality of the remarkable life history she has produced with Esperanza. Ruth Behar recognizes, post-hoc, what unconscious signs of her personal history connect to her anthropology – for example, that her Cuban-Jewish grandfather peddled cloth and that she has written the life history of Esperanza, a street peddler in Mexquitic.

In reflections on my *own* biography and research, I have moved the shadow to the moment of encounter in the field. It emerges *with* dialogue rather than being something that I bring with me into the field. I intend "shadow" in two senses, once again in reference to Crapanzano's usage. In the psychoanalytic sense, the shadows are the absent interlocutors who operate through transference and counter-transference. In the anthropological/literary sense, the shadow refers to theoretical perspectives or indigenous beliefs. Hence, we were the two partners to the dialogue at hand, about psychotic experiences, yet each of us was ". . . simultaneously participating in shadow dialogues with absent (though significant) interlocutors who change as the primary dialogue changes."[10] There can be an *unintentional* process of transference and counter-transference in the anthropological field situation, and not simply the analogy of one. This was less evident to me in my dialogues with Gerald and Carola, although it probably underlies my discomfort in being "taken" for a psychiatric patient.

Distance, Discretion and the Construction of the Personal

The second set of examples draws on more recent field experience in Marseilles, France, where I am studying the circulation and social uses of psychotropics among young, mobile (Magrebin, Russian, Ukranian, gypsy, Caribbean . . .) men and women, in a transnational setting. Much of my methodology involves recording life histories, although far less extensive than classic examples such as Behar's and with much emphasis on the present. In some ways, I sense a parallel between the experiences of those whom I have encountered and aspects of my own life – once-removed. By once-removed, I mean that my personal trajectories have exposed me, by *proxy*, to episodes and feelings similar to the institutional and psychological experience constitutive of the lifeworlds of those I study. These parallels, as I will show, must be understood in a particular, restricted sense, without any assumption that there is any commensurability between the historical moments or the societies they have lived and those of my family and hence myself.

In Marseilles, I have rarely engaged in the level of self-revelation that I describe in the first part of the paper. The damaged-by-proxy facets of my personality remain secret, rarely exposed to my interlocutor(s) in the field. Perhaps the social distance of gender (without a slot to fit into, in a youth culture where women are to a great extent, in a secular manner, relegated to the status of either pure or impure, although collective resistance has been building),[11] of social class, and of the lack of a common language[12] (but see below) impede self-revelation. Yet I think my emotional legacy and discretion enable me to avoid the morbid fascination that the people I work with complain about in many researchers they encounter. (Unlike those researchers, I don't see them as "exotic,"[13] as one person put it.) Hence, in Marseilles I am also practicing a shadow ethnography, but in a different, less ethnographically explicit way.

For paradoxically, it is this *non-engagement* in mutual self-revelation that allows a dialogue between myself and my "subject," a dialogue that, again, reflects the asymmetry of our power relations but nevertheless permits ethnographic insight. I draw my examples from exchanges with a 30-year-old man, José, who had spent most of his adult life in prison. Since his release a few months before we met, he had become initiated into injection drug use by the woman who constituted his only close relationship.

Our social distance was marked immediately because neither I nor his friend, Driss (my field assistant), were welcome in the *baraques* (huts), the makeshift, prefabricated housing where his family and community, gypsies who immigrated to Marseilles from Algiers in the 1950s, have lived since their original housing was torn down to make way for a mall. We first met in Driss's car, outside the neighborhood, then in a café.

Our bodies also signified almost instantly the distance between José and me, a distance of social class and domination. If who I am was not immediately visible to him (other than an older, middle-class, foreign woman), references to who he was were inscribed on his body: through spaces from missing teeth, emaciation, swollen hands dotted with track marks, the roughly-made tattoo between thumb and index that symbolizes a brotherhood-behind-bars and indelibly marks him as a former prisoner, and the lips stained purple from the tablets of "rups," a powerful hypnotic he swallowed in large quantities when no opiates were to be had.[14]

The distance between us intensified through our use of French, which is neither his maternal language nor mine. He normally speaks a Spanish-derived *gitan* (literally, gypsy language). Thus each of us used the mediation of a third, common language. French is at once an imposed language (deployed in situations in which we assimilate, even temporarily) and a neutral ground, a public social space or passage way between our respective private lives.

Paradoxically, it is this neutral ground that allowed an encounter between José and myself, that made it possible for him to disclose a stigmatizing experience and for me to begin to grasp the institutionalized violence and sense of alienation and exclusion from his own community that his drug use symbolically condensed. Over time, he revealed the facet of his biography whose secrecy he had made a condition of our encounter: the reason for his incarceration. Behind this secret lay another, more difficult to verbalize: that his past inverted his place in the family hierarchy, through a reversal, when applied to him, of the cultural codes of his community. And this secret – that not even the nephews and nieces born while he was in prison respected him, even though he is the oldest – was revealed first. During the interview, he explained how he left prison for his mother's overcrowded house. There the brothers and grandchildren doubled up in the living room and slept several to a bed, while he was relegated to a room by himself – not as a privilege, but as a pariah within his own family.

The "bargaining chip" of our encounter – discretion about why he went to prison – metamorphosed into a different stake much later. José, it turns out, was in fact imprisoned for a crime of passion, a murder-vendetta, committed when he was still a teenager. But behind these layers of exposed intimacy lay the reality that the vendetta-murder is excusable. José was rejected by his family not because he committed a murder, but because he was caught. By exposing the community's acceptance of vendetta in dialogue with me, Jose acquitted himself of guilt while indicting his community. In fact it is the third party to our encounter, Driss, in the role of interpreter/messenger/trickster,[15] who brought this meaning to the surface. When José disclosed the murder, Driss interjected that vendettas are acceptable to *gitans*, "comme pour les Corses." José acknowledged what Driss said: "c'est comme ça."

But there is a third instance of self-revelation, in the following conversation. In it, José repeats the term "*caler*," which in slang means to shoot up (heroin or another drug) and in standard French means "to fill up or become satiated," as after a big meal.

"*Pourquoi tu te cales?*", I asked him: "Why do you shoot up?" I was referring to buprenorphine, an opiate substitute that leaked into the illicit drug market, and is now the most commonly injected drug in the streets of Marseilles, where cocaine is too expensive and heroin scarce (Lovell 2001b, 2006). José had told me previously that in prison, the doctor prescribed oral buprenorphine for him, "to calm him down" (although it is an opiate agonist-antagonist, not intended as a tranquillizer).

I asked him this question after he told me that, shortly after being released from the Baumettes, the notorious Marseilles prison, he became sexually and emotionally involved with the widow of a fellow prisoner who had committed suicide. Caty was dependent on opiates, but her veins were too damaged to inject easily. José was injecting her regularly in her neck and other hard-to-reach areas. But after a while, he began injecting himself, with a concoction[16] made from the tablets of buprenorphine he still received through prescription. At the time I met him, he was sharing his daytime life with Caty, his drug use unbeknownst to his family (though surely, I thought, they could see the track marks inscribed on his body; was there mutual denial?).

"*Pourquoi tu te cales?*"

"It's faster [the effect] when you shoot up ['*quand tu te cales*']. It relieves me; it has to do with feelings, with nerves . . . When you shoot up, Madame, it's to fill up" [*here he uses "caler" in the non-colloquial sense: "to satiate hunger," as when one feels full after a big meal*].

"As I haven't eaten in a month, it's to replace all those things I need. My problems come from everything, from hunger, from lack of calcium. It's to console myself, to reassure myself that I shoot up/fill myself up" [*Here I interpret his use of the word "caler" as connoting both meanings*].

He continues, going back further in time: "I was so deprived from not being able to eat enough [*literally, 'being able to fill up the hunger'*], during all those years in prison. At home, I can't fill my stomach and deprive the others from eating. I prefer to take something to fill me up, to calm me down. I am always looking to comfort myself, to feel satisfied, reassured."[17]

Although, when I asked the question, I used the vocative "tu" ["*pourquoi tu te cales*"], the familiar form, as I did with Driss and as was expected in many of my interviews (I think as a sign that I'm willing to put myself, in the field situation, on equal footing with my interlocutors), José responded to me differently. At first, when he described why he shoots up, he used the familiar "tu" form, which communicates the immediateness of the experience (as if I were the one shooting up). But then, he retracted it, addressing me directly with the honorific "Madame" (and continued for the rest of our conversation to use the "vous" form).

In this way, we created a public space in a dual sense. By recording José's life history, I in some sense simulated the process of rendering what for him is private, public, by publicizing it, allowing it to «become public» (in French, *publicisation*). In agreeing to be interviewed by me (which did not happen immediately, for he had many misgivings and finally agreed to be interviewed only by putting his bargaining chip on the table: that we would not discuss why he went to prison), he knew that what he communicated would eventually be transcribed and find its way into my writing, though of course without identifying him and in accordance with the restrictions he demanded. (These restrictions evolved over time.) In other words, what he said would eventually find its way into other interpretative frames, of readers unknown to him.[18]

The use of what is for both of us a third language, French, in the sense of a third presence,[19] also creates a public space. Public spaces are necessarily interstitial, that is, they create social spaces in between more stable domains, or networks, of social action. As Mische and White have theorized them (1999), public spaces are liminal, characterized by the short-term co-presence of, often, strangers. They serve temporally as moments of transition between the spaces of social action linked to longer-term ties, identities, and social worlds. French created such a temporary space, neither here nor there, neither his community nor mine, of transition.

The publicness was doubled by the vocative used to address both a stranger and a superior. For to him, I am both. By distancing me through language, José at the same time created a space in which an anonymous intimacy could be revealed.[20] He enabled me to grasp how the drug and the act of injecting become the relationships he doesn't have, the substitute for needs he can't meet. And in this revelation he allowed me to understand how the drug works far more than in a physiological sense; it is symbolically "efficacious." It condenses all of which he is deprived, it counteracts the institutional violence inflicted on him. It buffers, it fills in the void in his relationship to his family and community, where his place as a man in a very virile, male-dominated culture has been taken away, depriving him of a compensatory mechanism in a community that itself has experienced constant displacement and exclusion.[21]

What still remains unexplained in my analysis is why José opened up to me without the tacit understanding – as had happened in my New York examples – that I would reciprocate in the same way. I can only suppose that the attitude or stance others in my fieldwork saw in me perhaps also affected my relationship with José. I extrapolate in suggesting that it is my lack of awe and curiosity for the "exotic," an attitude that stems from my own biography, that affected José's attitude towards me. Without in any way suggesting that our experiences are at all comparable, let me deviate slightly to explain what I mean.

By the time I was born, my parents had achieved middle-class status. And although I was raised in relative comfort, on four continents and in three languages, I am only one generation removed from a large, dirt poor, Southern Baptist family of sharecroppers (on one side) and marginal laborers (on the other). This legacy separates the remnants of my extended family between "haves" and "have nots," between those who "got themselves an education" (as my paternal grandmother used to say) and those who hold unskilled jobs in the mobile home industry or at the local refinery, hunt for their meat, and have lived in trailers or patched-together houses. While I grew up economically secure, for some of them, the indoor toilet was the first sign of upward mobility. Yet although my habitus is shaped by a privileged, cosmopolitan experience, I have incorporated from my parents' culture traces of the habitus of poverty, that habitus which is carried by the upwardly mobile into their new world, and partly transmitted through socialization to the next generation – in this case, me.[22] Most of us are born swathed in an old man or an old woman's clothes, a metaphor that lives in and shapes us. Comparisons with living and deceased kin, second-hand nicknames and patronyms, family stories overheard surreptitiously and snippets of biography recounted with a moral purpose or just for the hell of it – this is my heritage, as such birthrights are anyone's, so to speak.[23] And so shame, remorse, stigma, invisibility, marginalization, and inferiority are all feelings I have experienced either directly, or by proxy, as if the stories with which I grew up were my own. And so the situations I encounter in my fieldwork – alcoholism, drug use, imprisonment, psychiatric hospitalization, sexual and economic exploitation, displacement, social precariousness – are all situations I have encountered before, in my immediate or extended family, as direct experience or as emotional legacy.

Thus while I do not expose my own intimacy, my own secrets (of various degrees) create, I believe, an empathy which may be sensed by the other. For this I have no direct evidence, only my reflection on our intersubjectivity.

The Social Sources of Secrecy

The above examples illustrate how our understanding of others follows from our own experience, a point often made in contemporary anthropology, whether from a phenomenological (e.g., Jackson 1986), feminist (Behar 1993), or other perspective. But they also emphasize the necessity of a common ground, in this case constituted by the confrontation and sometimes sharing of secrecy, or at least the tension that surrounds it. And in this sense, these examples presume secrecy as already a social act.

Georg Simmel's theory of secrecy shows all of its pertinence here. For him, secrecy is as constitutive of the social as language, and this in several ways (Simmel 1996 [1908]). If society is conditioned by the fact of speaking, of communicating, it is also modeled by the ability to be silent. Simmel's reasoning lies in both cognitive and social arguments. On the one hand, social interaction becomes possible only because the parties to the situation are able, consciously or unconsciously, to sift through and discriminate among their subjective feelings, instincts, or secrets. They are able to withhold, to leave beneath the surface, much of their experience. The incapacity to do so, cognitive disorganization, is the essence of "insane dialogue," which risks being reduced to monologue, given its non-consensual foundation.

On the other hand, secrecy is bound up in that basic building block, the social form, at the basis of all society: sociability. Secrecy is social in the tension that it creates: social interaction in this sense is possible only because humans know something about one another (Simmel 1908/1996:7). Mutual recognition is the a priori of every social relation. And of course revelation and dissimulation come into play, as tactics in the games of power through which this universal principle interacts with the particularity of individuals and situations.

In a second way, secrecy is a social act. In the revealing of a secret, the receiver is placed in a situation of reciprocity (asymmetrical or not): she must reveal her own (secret works as a currency, to use Simmel's metaphor for social relations in modernity), or she must at least exercise discretion, a pact that the secret will not go further.

I would, however, argue against Simmel, for whom the secret exists independent of its potential revelation, that the secret is constituted as such when its content is revealed or its existence (but not content) is communicated. This confusion between secret as a social form and secret as inner life – Simmel uses both definitions – could be cleared up by using, as I suggest, the notion of secret to refer to the social form and the notion of intimacy to refer to the "*for intérieur*," the innermost recesses of the self. Again, the notion of intimacy need not imply an essential, continuous inner self.

Any secret will only concern one (or selected) facets of the Other. Hence self-revelation does not imply a stable inner self. This is not always intuitive to grasp. In the modern, market societies such as that from which I have drawn my examples, the biographical model (many argue) has replaced institutional models as the frame of interpretation (e.g., Murard 2002). In other words, reflexivity, narrative, and the ability to decipher oneself and one's environment become the only guide for action.

Conclusion

Self-revelation is not independent of the ethnographic situation. It is the ethnographic situation itself and the interaction between ethnographer and subject that "produce" what "gets personal."

The various examples have illustrated this potential variability. First, with Carola, I did not reciprocate with the same currency, with self-exposure. I declined her invitation to "get more personal," hence to understand. With Gerald, on the contrary, there was both exchange and recognition; incommensurability was momentarily suspended. We might call these "elective secrets," as not only do they tie individuals to one another (in French, *lier*) but individuals *choose* (in French, *élire*) to share them or not.[24] I think Carola recognized this and Gerald did not.

With José, my personal experience was never solicited as such. Yet there is the recognition that a secret, a personal experience, is something that can be given or handed over to another – again, creating ties while expressing a willingness towards exposure or not. José did not ask me explicitly to reveal, he "lent" me the experience when he evoked his relationship to injecting by the use of "tu." The "tu" is performative, in that he places me on the scene, the representation of an experience that is his, by presupposing that it is shared. But he immediately retracted it, by addressing me as "Madame," hence reestablishing another space, our institutional distance. That is, he spared me of having to tell my own personal story and spare me of having to retract with the entailing sense of a betrayed pact; he performed in my place the perilous task I faced with Carola.

The three sets of experiences have much to teach about the stakes in zones of vulnerability, where secrets can intensify the power imbalance. Secrets act as extensions of one's self. Yet they can also operate as still another "currency of the deprived" in the same way words, jokes, tales, gossip operate as a "currency of the poor," in the absence of other resources that are displayed in the constitution of a social self (Laé and Murard 1985). "Getting personal" does not depend solely on the unconscious experience of the ethnographer, but rather on the specificities of the field encounter and the stakes at hand. The shadows are in the dialogues at hand, rather than the personal in the shadows.

Acknowledgments

My thanks to Sue Makiesky Barrow, Samuel Bordreuil, and Robert Desjarlais for their thoughtful readings of this paper and valuable suggestions.

Notes

1 Salazar, quoted in Ryang, 2000.
2 See Ryang's (2000) review of reviews. A popular trade book translated into many languages, Burgos-Debray's life history of Menchù functioned as a testimony of poverty and the massacre of Mayan people that politicized its readers to the situation of First Nations peoples in general, and Guatemalan army repression in particular. The truth-value of the text was challenged by an anthropologist who retraced Menchu's trajectory with her own villagers and others from her life (Stoll 1999), only to be severely criticized himself for conservative political motives and partiality. At stake are the conventions of anthropological writing, postmodern or not, and thus the very question of how knowledge is constructed.
3 In French, the "innermost" is conscience, the "heart of hearts" or the mind, as in the term "*for intérieur.*"
4 In modern societies, excluded persons and the mad may reach such levels of a-sociality (as opposed to anti-sociality) that they are no longer aware of how they present themselves to others. Compare for example the meaning of agency and intentionality in a chronically homeless man, delirious perhaps from lack of sleep and malnutrition, and lying half naked in his own excreta,

in the middle of a busy metropolitan railway station, supposedly oblivious to others; and in the wild-haired, similarly naked Indian *sadhu*, begging for food in an Indian city.

5   Of course, the same media techniques and network structures that permit overexposure of intimacy also facilitate the expropriation and circulation of secrets, against the wishes, and often to the detriment, of those who would prefer to remain discreet: political rivals, entertainment personalities, wealth celebrities ("the rich and famous"), and moral entrepreneurs, such as clergy, teachers, doctors, and so forth.

6   I see stigma as a process, an interplay between real and virtual selves, between what the potentially stigmatized person can and/or will reveal or dissimulate, on the one hand, and the interpretation of the other, in any situation.

7   For example, the following description, which places the reader in the position of the anthropologist observing, like any other passer-by, a homeless woman as she tries to dissimulate the degrading behavior of rummaging through garbage. (This takes place in a middle-class town in France):

> *"A woman stops near the garbage; she's walking slowly, as if on a stroll. She stops, hesitates with her gestures near an overflowing garbage can. She grabs a plastic bag with the ends of her fingers, tries to look through it at what's inside. Her body is turned away from the garbage, as if she is about to start to walk again after this parenthesis of a chance stop. Only one arm and her head, facing the garbage, seem engaged in the action. The woman starts to walk again, takes two or three steps, then stops again near another bag in a garbage can and takes up the same stance . . ."* [Raybaud 2002:20]

But never is it a question, for the ethnographer, of understanding through interaction.

8   Following Ann Mische and Harrison White (1999), I have argued that public space constitutes "holes" in the networks in which people are inscribed, neutral zones between the social worlds through which they move. Social interaction, including the silent conventions or "asocial sociability" and polite avoidance that allow co-presence and civility in (North American or European) urban public space, nevertheless depends on a minimum ability to sense who the other is. Identities are emergent in public space, as strangers cross paths, but they also depend on minimal signs, or what Goffman calls "props." The most marginalized lack such props and must often project and/or protect identity with what is at hand (Lovell 2001a). Intimate aspects of the body itself become props.

9   I would argue that this logic precedes managed care.

10 Like figures of transference and counter transference in psychoanalysis, absent interlocutors are subject to the complex play of desire and power (Crapanzano 1992:6).

11 I refer to a youth culture in which some of these men have grown up, and not to their individual opinions or attitudes. At the same time, all the women

I have interviewed in my study who share this culture have experienced extreme gender-related violence, including the initiatory ritual (for boys) of gang rapes ("tournantes"), while growing up.

12   Interviews with Russians and Ukrainians who spoke no French were carried out with a Russian-French interpreter.

13   During my fieldwork, several drug users and outreach workers complained to the Marseilles health department about the researchers being deployed to study them. They accused them of exploitation and of allowing their data to be used for political purposes (the implementation of the so-called Sarkozy laws against "public insecurity," such as arrests) and of not being able to adequately understand the conditions of their drug use and lives. They likened researchers to *voyeurs*. At the same time, they presented me to the city officials as a researcher ("l'anthropologue") they would work with. Of course, I am the one who is attributing their action, post-hoc, to my stance, which I assume comes from my own exposure, in my life, to much of what they experience and that humiliates them.

14   In a contradictory attempt to stop pharmaceutical leakage without taking the molecule off the market, the pharmaceutical makers of Rohypnol® ("rups") inserted a dye that turns the lips and tongue purple. Opiate users might consume 30 or 40 "rups" at once, which notably mark the mouth and tongue. This is more a technique of abeyance than surveillance, in the sense that a harmful practice (the hypnotic effect, aggressiveness, and subsequent amnesia that the drug brings on – hence the designation as a "rape" drug) is perpetuated but contained.

15   In a twist on the typical situation analyzed by Crapanzano (1992), Hermes is played by the field assistant, rather than the anthropologist.

16   In Marseilles, drug injectors call this their "cuisine." José is unfamiliar with this language and with many other colloquialisms that others I have interviewed use. His trajectory and how he came to inject drugs is singular.

17   "C'est plus vite quand tu te le cales . . . ça soulage, c'est sentimental, nerveux . . . Quand tu te cales, Madame . . . c'est pour caler. Comme je n'ai pas mangé pendant un mois, c'est pour remplacer tout ce qui me faut. Les problèmes viennent de tout, de la faim, du manque de calcium. C'est pour consoler, rassurer moi-même, que je me cale. Pour être bien normalement. J'étais tellement privé de manger à ma faim [pendant toutes ces années d'incarcération]. [A la maison] je ne peux pas remplir mon ventre et laissez les autres sans manger. Je préfère prendre quelque chose et me caler pour me calmer. Je cherche toujours à me soulager, à être satisfait, rassuré."

18   Michel Callon and Vololona Rahebarisoa (1999) analyze, in a case study, how they simulate a public arena with a man, Gino, who carries the gene for muscular dystrophy. The interview is part of a study of the Muscular Dystrophy Association of Reunion Island, in the Indian Ocean. Gino has refused medical knowledge, medical treatment, and participation in the local consumer group, despite the consequences for his own suffering or for

his offspring. His barely audible speech and silences during the interview are at first interpreted by the sociologists in terms of this refusal. But through the interview process, the sociologists have placed Gino in a situation of having to justify his actions – because he is in a public situation (that of the interview itself, which included family members within earshot; and that of those who will hear or read the interview). It is by rendering visible what is barely so that the sociologists "publicize" the deeply private feelings of Gino. In the end, Gino seems to be embracing a morality of immediate experience, emotional and (in his own way) interactive, rather than an essentialist or relativist sense of moral agency.

19   In fact, French is the second language each of us speaks. But it represents a third presence because of the additional mediation it forces upon us: that of a foreign language in which neither of us is at home, regardless of our fluency. For each of us, our very slight accents "betray" our origins, although for José that accent probably invites discrimination that I do not suffer in France.

20   Perhaps similarly to the neutral screen at work in the Lacanian theory of transference.

21   That historical process does not "explain" the virility of the culture, and I am not presenting it as unproblematic. But the dominant status and importance of virility within the community may be operating as a balance to the domination and humiliation men experience outside. Alain Tarrius (1999) has shown how in another gypsy community, on the border between Spain and France, heroin trade and then consumption by the men, often in father–son dyads, reversed the traditional hierarchies, empowering the women and opening the community to heterogamy.

22   Although Bourdieu's schema of habitus is too rigid, his agents overdetermined by their place in the structure, with restricted possibility to maneuvering – their tactics may bend rules, but they maintain structure and false consciousness.

23   Among the social scientists who have studied primarily negative and destructive aspects of working-class culture, see de Gaulejac, Vincent de. 1992. *La névrose de classe*. Paris: Hommes et Groupes. For a corrective to the contemporary social use of "poor white trash" as a condescending icon of popular culture in the hyperconsumerism and logo consciousness of contemporary America, see Howell, Joseph T. 1973. *Hard Living on Clay Street. Portraits of Blue Collar Families*. Garden City, NY: Anchor Books. These and an important body of contemporary literature, from Barbara Kingsolver to Dorothy Allison, provide a counterpart to the triumphalist – though certainly valid – literature of working-class solidarity and culture. Pierre Bourdieu, to prove that we *are* indeed cultural dopes (pace Garfinkel), represents the working class and the poor in disdainful, almost mocking descriptions, at least until his late work (compare *La Distinction* (1979) with *La misère du monde* (1998)).

24   I thank Samuel Bordreuil for bringing this to my attention.

References

Behar, Ruth
  1993 [1983] Translated Woman: Crossing the Border with Esperanza's Story. Boston: Beacon Press.
Bourdieu, Pierre
  1977 [1972] Outline of a Theory of Practice. Cambridge, UK: Cambridge University Press.
Bourdieu, Pierre
  1979 La Distinction: Critique Sociale du Jugement. Paris: Les Editions de Minuit.
Bourdieu, Pierre
  1998 La Misère du Monde. Paris: Points.
Burgos-Debray, Elisabeth, ed.
  1984 I, Rigoberta Menchù. London: Verso.
Callon, Michel, and Rabeharisoa, Vololona
  1999 Gino ou la leçon de l'humanité. Réseaux 17:197–235.
Crapanzano, Vincent
  1992 Hermes' Dilemma and Hamlet's Desire: on the Epistemology of Interpretation. Cambridge, MA: Harvard University Press.
Deleuze, Gilles, and Felix Guattari
  1987 A Thousand Plateaux. Minneapolis: University of Minnesota Press.
Eliafson, Nina
  2003 Publics fragiles. Une ethnographie de la citoyenneté dans la vie associative. *In* Les sens du public: publics politiques, publics médiatiques. D. Cefai and D. Pasquier, eds. Pp. 225–268. Paris: PUF.
Fainzang, Sylvie
  2002 Lying, secrecy and power within the doctor–patient relationship. Anthropology and Medicine 9:117–133.
Farge, Arlette, and Jean-François Laé
  2000 Fracture Sociale. Paris: Desclée de Brouwer.
Feldman, Allan
  1991 Formations of Violence. The Narrative of the Body and Political Terror in Northern Ireland. Chicago: University of Chicago Press.
Frank, Gelya
  1979 Finding the common denominator: a phenomenological critique of life history method. Ethos 7:68–94.
Gaissad, Laurent
  2000 L'air de la nuit rend libre? Lieux et rencontres dans quelques villes du sud de la France. Les Annales de la Recherche Urbaine 87:36–42.
Gaulejac, Vincent de
  1992 La névrose de classe. Paris: Hommes et Groupes.
Godelier, Maurice
  1999 The Enigma of the Gift. Chicago, University of Chicago Press.

Goffman, Erving
    1961   Asylums. Essays on the Social Situation of Mental Patients and Other
    Inmates. New York: Anchor Books.
Howell, Joseph T.
    1973   Hard Living on Clay Street. Portraits of Blue Collar Families. Garden
    City, NY: Anchor Books.
Jackson, Michael
    1996   Things as They Are. New Directions in Phenomenological Anthro-
    pology. Bloomington, IN: Indiana University Press.
Laé, Jean-François, and Numa Murard
    1985   L'argent des Pauvres. Paris: Seuil.
Laé, Jean-François, and Bruno Proth
    2002   Les territoires de l'intimité, protection et sanction. Ethnologie Française
    23:5–10.
Lanzarini, Corinne
    1998   Un autre monde. Situations extrêmes et tactiques de survie des sous-
    prolétaires de la rue. Ph.D. dissertation, University of Paris 8.
Lovell, Anne M.
    1991   Meaning, De-Meaning and Empowerment. Paper presented at the in
    90th Annual meeting of the American Anthropological Association. Chicago,
    November.
Lovell, Anne M.
    1996   Mobilité des cadres et psychiatrie hors les murs [Mobile frames and psy-
    chiatry outside the walls]. Raisons Pratiques 7:59–85.
Lovell, Anne M.
    1997   "The city is my mother": narratives of homelessness and schizophre-
    nia. American Anthropologist 99:355–368.
Lovell, Anne M.
    2001a   Les fictions de soi-même ou les délires identificatoires dans la rue.
    [Romancing the self: Delusional identities on the street]. *In* La maladie
    mentale en mutation. Psychiatrie et société [Mental illness in transformation.
    Psychiatry and Society]. Alain Ehrenberg and Anne M. Lovell, eds. Pp. 127–
    161. Paris: Odile Jacob.
Lovell, Anne M.
    2001b   Ordonner les risques: l'individu et le pharmaco-sociatif face à la
    réduction des dommages dans l'injection de drogues. *In* Critique de la santé
    publique. J. P. Dozon and D. Fassin, eds. Paris: Balland.
Lovell, Anne M.
    2006   Addiction Markets: The Example of Opiate Substitutes in France. *In*
    Global Pharmaceuticals. Ethics, Markets, Practices. A. Petryna, A. Lakoff, and
    A. Kleinman, eds. Pp. 136–170. Chapel Hill, NC: Duke University Press.
Lovell, Anne M.
    In press   Hoarders and Scrappers: Madness and the Social Person in the
    Interstices of the City. *In* Ethnography and Subjectivity. Joao Biehl, Byron
    Good, and Arthur Kleinman, eds. Berkeley: University of California Press.

Mische, Ann, and Harrison T. White
   1999   Between Conversation and Situation: Public Switching Dynamics Across Network Domains. Social Research 65(3):695–724.
Murard, Numa
   2002   Biographie: à la recherche de l'intimité. Ethnologie Française 22:123–132.
Raybaud, Vincent
   2002   Les signes faibles du discrédit. Ethnologie Française 22:115–122.
Ryang, Sonia
   2000   Ethnography Or Self-Cultural Anthropology? Reflections On Writing About Ourselves. Dialectical Anthropology 25:297–320.
Simmel, Georg
   1996 [1908]   Secret et sociétés secrètes. Courtry: Circé Poche.
Stoll, David
   1999   Riboberta Menchù and the Story of All Poor Guatemalans. Boulder: Westview Press.
Tarrius, Alain
   1999   Fin de siècle incertaine à Perpignan: Drogues, pauvreté, communautés d'étrangers, jeunes sans emplois, et renouveau des civilités dans une ville moyenne française. Barcelona: Libres Del Trabucaire.

Part II

Transmutations of Experience: Approaching the Reality of Shadows

Chapter 3[1]

The Scene:
Shadowing the Real

Vincent Crapanzano

Ce que je vois existe. Seulement, on ne croit en ce que l'on voit que parce qu'on voit ce en quoi on croit. [J.-B. Pontalis, Perdre de vue*]*

Over my desk is a large etching called *Crépuscule*, Twilight, by the contemporary French artist Gérard Trignac. It is a shadowy depiction of a large castle surrounded by an enormous moat over which stretches a massive bridge. The view is from under the bridge, and the viewer feels the bridge's enormous weight. Behind one of the pylons that support the bridge one sees the top of a white sail which is lit by a beam of light. On first viewing, the engraving is reminiscent of Piranesi but it is less dramatic than Piranesi's works, far warmer, and though suggestive of dark castle keeps, lurking danger, and the river of death, death itself, there is something calming about the mystery, the aura, the work projects. At least I have found it so, these many years that I have worked under its silent surveillance.

As I look up at Trignac's etching I think of shadows and shades – the shadowy dimensions of social and cultural existence that we anthropologists have so often encountered in one guise or another and which we have tended to keep at a distance from our "serious" work as if embarrassed by mystery, danger, and the imminence, the immediacy, of what we presume to be the irrational or at least the ephemeral, the epiphenomenal. Of course, other ages took pleasure in what Shelley refers to as the "unfathomable world." In his first major poem, *Alastor or The Spirit of Solitude*, he addresses the "mother of this world, of Nature and Necessity."

> I have watched
> Thy shadow and the darkness of thy steps,
> And my heart ever gazes on the depth

> Of thy deep mysteries. I have made my bed
> In charnels and on coffins, where black death
> Keeps record of the trophies won from thee,
> Hoping to still these obstinate questionings
> Of thee and thine, by forcing some lone ghost,
>   The messenger, to render up the tale
>   Of what we are. (ll.2–28)

I want to resurrect the romantic dimension of anthropology not because I want to propose a romantic anthropology, not at all, but because I want us to come to terms with our romantic heritage and the effect that heritage has had on us, if only through its insistent ideological rejection. The rejected – the categories, themes, and sensibilities of romanticism in case in point – is not without influence if only through its forced absence. With this rejection, as with the rejection of the religious – the Judeo-Christian – roots of our discipline which have played so fundamental a role in our understanding and interpreting of the phenomena we study, there often slips away a dimension of the reality that is most dear to those we study (and to us too in our other lives). Or if it doesn't slip away, if it is not ignored, suppressed, or repressed, it is so reduced to one deadening paradigm or another that those shadowy worlds – or experiences – lose whatever empirical reality they may have and whatever influence they may have on the conduct and thoughts of those we study.

I have recently been thinking of the way in which we have tended to ignore (for lack of a better term and therefore provisionally) the "subjectification" of the putatively objective contexts to which we look for explanation of the phenomena we observe. In a preliminary way, one which requires considerably more epistemological rigor than I can yet give it (if I ever can), I have attempted to differentiate between "objective" reality – and what I call the scene.[2] By "objective reality" I mean something like what Alfred Schutz (1970:253) calls "paramount reality," or the commonsense reality of everyday life we take for granted. It includes, in Schutz's phenomenological terms, "not only physical objects, facts, and events within our actual and potential reach perceived as such in the mere apperceptual scheme, but also appresentational references of a lower order by which the physical objects of nature are transformed into socio-cultural objects." It is the "finite province of meaning upon which we bestow the accent of reality" and, as such, differs dramatically from other such provinces as "the world of imaginings and fantasms" or the "world of scientific contemplation."[3] Whether we understand paramount reality in terms of coerciveness, as William James might, or resistance, as the phenomenologists would, or in terms of (socially constructed and accepted or acceptable) conventions, we assume, I believe, a certain constancy that is shared or at least negotiable from different perspectives (Husserl 1931: 129ff.). It is, in short, the reality of primary reference. Within our ordinary empirical, or, if you prefer, pragmatic assumption, paramount reality is shorn of the fanciful, the temporally, indeed the spatially, capricious – those shiftings of attention that we relate to feelings, emotions, and moods, all of which we identify with the subjective. They are mere decoration, epiphenomena, or, as some would have it, epiphenomena of epiphenomena. It is to precisely this decoration, these epiphenomena, that I want to draw attention, for they are, in their own special way, a significant and effective dimension of the world in which we live, think, and act.

I do not want to reduce the scene to the subjective, however, for I think that would lead us away from what I take to be its intersubjective foundation. In this respect, I differ from the usual singular consciousness- or intention-centered approach of phenomenology and, indeed, commonsense. I should add, but cannot pursue my argument here, that subjectivity, however particularly mine it may appear to be, is essentially intersubjective, both in a mediated way, through language, for example, and immediately, through real and imagined encounters with real and imagined, at times, shadowy figures of import. For me, at least, the scene is that take on – or refraction of – the "objective" situation in which we find ourselves which colors and tones that situation and, thereby, renders it other than we know it to be, if we bother to think about it objectively, and yet, however deeply colored, however intensely toned, rests on that objectivity. Indeed, however disturbing we may find that objective reality, in its objectness, its firmness, its constancy, it gives us epistemic if not ontological security. We may perhaps speak of the scene, by analogy with double-voicing, as double-sighted. We recognize at once what we take to be the objective reality of the situation in which we find ourselves, however that objectivity is taken (as empirical reality in a crudely Lockean sense, for example, or the product of a set of social and cultural conventions) and our direct experience of that reality in all its eccentricity. I will return to the way in which the intersubjective nature of our experience of the scene facilitates this double-sightedness.

In giving objective reality refractory priority over the scene, I do not want to imply that reality is immune to the effects of the scene. The two are mutually engaged, but the "weight" of their influence varies, no doubt, with pertinent epistemological regimes. The point I am making is that the (immediate) experience of "objective reality" cannot admit the effect of the scene on it if it is to remain objective, a primary reference, firm and constant.

Here I want to stress the fact that it is the acknowledgment of the objective that facilitates the precipitation of the scene and our experience of it, much as it is the objective reality of the psychoanalyst as psychoanalyst and the patient as patient that facilitates the projections of transference and counter-transference. As the projective identity of the psychoanalyst or patient may become so intense in transference and counter-transference that either or both of the parties to the encounter may lose track of their object-ive identities, so there are moments when the scene may supersede the objective reality upon which it rests or is at least facilitated. The converse is equally true. For, there are also moments, far more frequent, when object-ive reality so supersedes scenic reality that it obliterates it. It is as though we take refuge in the objective for fear of the scenic, its elaboration, its implication. Think of those terrifying images that sometimes flash through your mind without connection or explanation. Or, the clutching at reality – the walls, the pillow, a dressing table – that follows instantaneously upon waking from a nightmare.[4]

★★★★★

Yesterday one of my students who was in the last stages of her field research came to my office. Uncertain about whether or not she had finished up – "I haven't had enough interviews" – confronted by the mass of dis-ordered and as yet unassimilated material she had collected, she was drained and distraught. Her eyes, which are usually bright and lively, were dull and furtive. I remembered how shocked I was the first time I had seen her like this. It was just before her oral examinations. As then, yes-terday, she carried into my office a darkness – "gloom" would be too strong a word – that was so intense that I actually looked up to see whether the lights had dimmed. They had not. And then, a few minutes later, after talking about her doubts, her eyes suddenly lit up as she pulled out a sheet of paper on which she had scribbled a hodgepodge of ideas. Her move-ment was so abrupt, so spontaneous, so filled with relief, as though she had suddenly remembered what she had long forgotten, that my office brightened. I felt that the bluish florescent lighting had turned yellow, like the light from an incandescent bulb. We were able to talk easily about her research, and as we talked, my office, its lighting, indeed, her face, her eyes, fell away. . . . At the end of our discussion I told her about my notion of the scene and my response to her anxiety and relief. She acknowledged that she herself had felt a change in the "mood in the room." I should add that she is an independent spirit who does not hide her skep-ticism about my approach to anthropology.[5]

There is, in fact, nothing particularly unusual about my – our – experi-ence. We have all experienced such changes, which we associated personally with changes in mood or collectively with changes in atmosphere.[6] They are described again and again in literature. Kate Leslie, the heroine of D. H. Lawrence's *The Plumed Serpent*, reads one of Don Ramón's lengthy hymns. (Don Ramón is the leader, indeed the prophet, of Lawrence's fantasized Mexican nativistic movement that proclaims the return of the Aztec sun-god Quetzalcoatl.)

> Kate read this long leaflet again and again, and a swift darkness like a whirlwind seemed to envelop the morning. She drank her coffee on the veranda, and the heavy *papayas* in their grouping seemed to be oozing like great drops from the invisible sprouting of the fountain of non-human life. She seemed to see the great sprouting and urging of the cosmos, moving into weird life. And men only like green-fly clustering on the tender tips, an aberration there. So monstrous the rolling and unfolding of the life of the cosmos, as if even iron could grow like lichen deep in the earth, and cease growing, and prepare to perish. Iron and stone render up their life, when the hour comes . . . (Lawrence 1950:256)

A shift in mood darkens the atmosphere in which Kate finds herself. Her immediate perception of the scene leads, as it often does, to a vision that has perhaps as much reality as the darkened veranda, the veranda in the full light of the morning sun. Such shifts from objective reality to the scene to visionary experiences may play an important role in our creative lives by opening up imaginative horizons – possibilities that hover at the edge of ordinary perception (Crapanzano 2004). But, I should add, they may also constrain, if only by negation, by terror, paramount reality. They may call attention to the artifice, as I see it, of that reality. They may cast a shadow on its givenness, its facticity.

> While daylight held
> The sky, the poet – [Alastor] – kept mute conference
> With his still soul. At night the passion came
> Like the fierce fiend of a distempered dream,
> And shook him from his rest, and led him forth
> Into the darkness. (*Alastor or The Spirit of Solitude* ll. 221–226)

In harrowing darkness of the death-haunted dream, despite his effort, the poet can give no life in "vacant" Nature. He cannot conjoin the two worlds, the wakened and the dreamt, the real and the ideal.

Shelley aside – I may be misreading him – we must note that the overlay of "objective reality" by the scene is itself subject not only to cultural and epochal differences but to genre and convention within any one culture or period. No doubt, there are societies that are willing to surrender objective reality to the scene, but to speak in such *mentalité* generalizing terms not only risks stereotypy but misses the subtle economy of the relation-ship between the two and the dynamics of their encounter. The romantic poet – Shelley, Novalis more so – may indulge in the scene hovering over reality like a dream, a shade, or a vision in their poetry – in their inspira-tion, but they must certainly have experienced a hard reality that resisted that indulgence or led them, as it did de Quincy and Coleridge, among others, to find escape in opiate reverie or some mysticism. My point is that the way we respond to – indulge, dismiss, or ignore – the scene is subject to the way in which the situation in which we find ourselves is framed – and not, at least less so, by character or disposition. With auth-orial control, Lawrence set up Kate's response to Don Ramón's hymn. In less personal, though equally, if not more, effective ways, such control – the choreography of scenic reality and the pressure of its assumption – operates in ritual and theater.

★★★★★

I look up at Trignac's *Crépuscule* and suddenly recall a scene from my ear-liest childhood. I am just under 4 years old and am in a church for the first time. My mother had, I learned later, become convinced that the Nazis would win the war. Though she and my father were stubbornly secular, she decided that my sister and I should be baptized – "to set the record," as she told me years later with considerable embarrassment. I had never been in a church before and was terrified by its darkness, the stale odor of incense, and above all the priest whom I was told to call father though I had never even seen him before and immediately disliked him after he called me "my son." I was not his son, and he was not my father. I wanted to cry, but I contained myself, particularly after my sister, who was less than a year old, burst into tears. I was the first to be baptized and remember nothing of it but the priest's bad breath, the taste of salt, wet hair, and mumblings in a language I did not understand. Above all I remember a beam of light that got in my eyes which came through a panel or two of transparent glass in a stained glass window from which a man in a long white and gold robe and a conical hat like the dunce caps I saw in the comics looked down at me menacingly. My eyes were so blinded by the light that they filled with tears, and the man's expression, whoever he was, kept changing in one grotesque way or another. For some reason the beam of light that illuminates the sail of the boat in the moat in Trignac's etching reminds me of that beam. I wondered whether my sister would also be blinded by it. She was tiny and was held up, not in my mother's arms but in those of one of my father's friends – my mother didn't like her – who gave me a little gold cross on a necklace that I was supposed to wear, like a girl, but which my mother told me later I never had to. My sister was lucky because she was protected from the light by the priest's shadow as he bent over her. Though I do not remember his placing a white veil over my face, I do remember his covering my sister's with it. I had to squint when we left the church because everything was so bright.

★★★★★

I will return to the diachronic dimension – the narrative potential – of our experiences of the scene. Now I want to describe its choreography in a communion service I witnessed in a conservative evangelical church in southern California where I was doing research on Christian Fundamentalism. The church was known for its theatrical baptisms, which were performed on a balcony high above the altar. The communion service was an experiment. Tables, set for communion, were placed in the aisles throughout the church, and the communicants were asked to administer communion to each other. At first everyone hesitated, but as the lights dimmed and the organ played softly seductive music – I did not recognize it – one couple after another were drawn to the tables. Some were embarrassed but most were caught up in the occasion. They gazed in each other's eyes, sometimes weeping, whether in pain or joy I could not always tell, as they gave each other communion. Their mutual gazes conveyed not only their love for each other, for Jesus, but also – I felt – personal stories that demanded forgiveness. For me, despite myself, as for them, the atmosphere was suffused with a moving sentimentality that transformed the church into a scene of such intimacy, such love, as they would no doubt put it, that the church itself seemed to slip away. It became a vast theater of at once intensely personal and equally transcendent communion. Both those who administered the communion and those who simply watched were caught. I wondered if I was the only one, among the several thousand members of the congregation, who was removed from the scene, less, I suspect, by my "professional" gaze than by voyeuristic embarrassment. The experiment was considered to be an enormous success, I learned later, and it was hoped that it would increase church attendance.

That ritual promotes a sense of community, or, as Victor Turner (1969:94–165) would put it, communitas, was common knowledge long before the birth of anthropology. The social effervescence that Durkheim saw at its core, at least at the core of primitive rituals, is, I suspect, rather more a projection of the desiccated Western mind than an objective fact. I do not want to deny that there are rituals whose denouements are so frenzied that there is a loss of individual consciousness and a submergence in the group, disco-fashion, I might say. I have, in fact, witnessed such denouements, among the Hamadsha, the members of a Moroccan religious brotherhood known for their wild exorcistic rites, when suddenly, late in the night, after hours of entranced dancing and chanting, the lights are suddenly extinguished and in loud hush – only an oxymoron can do justice to that moment – 'A'isha Qandisha, the she-demon they venerate, makes her appearance. Though I cannot know what the participants actually experienced at such moments, they all recall seeing 'A'isha in one manifestation or another. (Psychologists would, no doubt, say that whatever the participants' individual experiences were, they were immediately interpreted in the collective idiom as a manifestation of the she-demon.) Though I myself did not see 'A'isha, I did feel a shadowy presence, which I immediately attributed, given my (perhaps defensive) rationalism, to the intense focalization of the ritual participants on the she-demon. Later I likened it to those experiences we have all had when, believing we are alone, we suddenly feel the presence of someone in a room before we actually see him or her.

Most rituals I have witnessed, including many Hamadsha performances, or read about are, in fact, rather desultory affairs without much dramatic intensity. And where there is such intensity, it is not clear that they produce any effervescence. Describing the divinatory séances Azande witchdoctors perform, Evans-Pritchard (1937:177) noted that their dance is "the most spirited performance" he had ever witnessed and that the music the doctors make – the "conjunction" of gong and drum – is intoxicating to both performers and audience. "Music, rhythmic movements, facial grimaces, grotesque dress, all lend their aid in creating a proper atmosphere for the manifestation of exotic powers." Though the audience follows the display eagerly, moving their heads to the music and singing along when it pleases them, it would be a mistake, Evans-Pritchard assures us, to assume that the atmosphere is awe-filled. Rather people are jovial, talk to each other, and joke. And yet Evans-Pritchard reminds us

> that the audience is not observing simply a rhythmic performance, but also a ritual enactment of magic. It is something more than a dance, it is a fight, partly direct and partly symbolic, against the powers of evil. The full meaning of a séance as a parade against witchcraft can only be grasped when the dancing is understood. . . . A witch-doctor "dances the questions," [Evans-Pritchard, 1937:178]

What Evans-Pritchard fails to explore is the ritual (the dramatic, indeed the psychological) effect of the disjunction between the seriousness of the séance – the awe it might inspire – and the (sometime) jovial attitude of its audience. There does not seem, in the event, to be group effervescence or even constant focus. Might we argue that there is persistent deflection? It is perhaps abstraction, as personal in its impersonality as it is communal, which is the most characteristic ritual attitude. One of the mistakes of many ritual studies is, in my view, their derivation of dramatic form and intention from an assumed denouement. As I noted in *Imaginative Horizons*, I have been told by many ritual participants that it was in ritual that they felt their loneliness most intensely.

How often have I – and other anthropologists – been unable to distinguish between the unrealized ideal and the actual experience in the ritual participants' descriptions of their experiences. I recall attending a Hamadsha *musem*, the annual pilgrimage, which culminates in the meeting of the leaders of two rival villages, one, Beni Rachid, of higher status than the other, Beni Ouarad.[7] The leader, or *mizwar* of Beni Ouarad, trailed by thousands of his followers, arrives on a stallion at the entrance of Beni Rachid, where its *mizwar* awaits him on a white stallion, surrounded by thousands of *his* followers. The *mizwar* of Beni Ouarad dismounts and follows on foot the leader of Beni Rachid, who remains mounted, through the village to the sanctuary of the Hamadsha saint they venerate, where they pray, and then return to the village entrance. Such is the ideal, "the way it used to be" performed, but I was told that now the two leaders meet, the one dismounting, the other remaining on horseback, greet each other, and then depart. This, it was explained, is because they cannot easily make their way through the milling crowds of entranced and frenzied worshipers. In fact, the two men were jealous of each other's prerogatives and were embattled in court in land disputes. What I observed was neither the ideal nor the "realistic" version. The two leaders met at the edge of the village. They did not greet each other. They simply paused and then turned around and proceeded back to their respective homes. When I asked the spectators what had happened, they assured me that the two leaders had not only greeted each other but shook hands. Several insisted that the *mizwar* of Beni Ouarad had dismounted! When I questioned them further, they became so violently angry that I had to stop. It is perhaps the hovering between the ideal and the real, the elation and the sense of insufficiency, that characterizes much ritual experience and, as I (Crapanzano 1992:260–280) argued for Moroccan circumcision rituals, its efficacy. The one casts a shadow over the other, the other over the one. What is important in their mutual implication. The ideal cannot be fully disengaged from the actual experience, though they may be, with some success, analytically distinguished. It is, for this reason, that I would hesitate to equate the ideal with the scene. Their relations with the real have divergent grammars.

★★★★★

Many ritual studies, even those that lay emphasis on communitas, resist the sense of the miraculous, mystery, and the uncanny that the participants describe, as if, however metaphorical, however symbolic, they have no *real* referent. Though I am personally unwilling to accept a miracle interpretation, I believe that we have to ask what is being described by the "miraculous," "mystery," and the "uncanny." Before we attribute to these glosses of experience, or their indigenous approximations, a predetermined and comfortable referent – castration anxiety, say, in the case of the uncanny, the transcendent powers of the social in the case of the miraculous or the mysterious – we should attempt to understand how these and analogous terms are used and how they figure in the cultural outlook under study. The "miracle" suggests in Euro-American culture a break with the "natural" chain of events that are causally conjoined in mediate as well as immediate ways. Indeed, the "miracle" is doubly miraculous, for not only is it miraculous in its own terms but it miraculously creates a rupture in our naturalized sense of history and becomes all the more extraordinary. Freud's (1963) discussion of the uncanny might serve us as a model, for, though he relates the uncanny, one of its manifestations at least, to castration anxiety, he resists, or rather his material forces him to resist, the postulation of a single causal referent. "An uncanny experience occurs either when repressed infantile complexes have been revived by some impression, or when the primitive beliefs we have surmounted seem once more to be confirmed" (Freud 1963:55). What is important in our reading of Freud is the mechanism that produces a sense of the uncanny: the familiar unfamiliar, something terrifying that has been long known but forgotten until it, its effect, is triggered by some impression in the present. I would stress the paradoxical relationship between contingency and repetition – a repetition that enhances the contingent as it disarms it.

Freud (1963:50) remarks elsewhere in his essay that "an uncanny effect is often and easily produced by effacing the distinction between imagination and reality, such as when something that we have hitherto regarded as imaginary appears before us in reality, or when a symbol takes over the full function and significance of the thing it symbolizes, and so on." Freud relates this "over-accentuation of psychical reality in comparison with physical reality" to the infantile feelings of omnipotence and to magical practices. His search for endopsychic origins for the experience reflects, of course, the culture-specific historical assumption of his times. I would rather stress the interpersonal dimension of the experience of the uncanny in both its synchronic and diachronic dimensions; that is, in terms of the situation in which whoever experiences the uncanny finds him or herself at the time of the experience and (insofar as it is evoked anew) at the time it is described and in terms of the con-figured past that inserts itself, through witting or unwitting remembrance in the present. I use "con-figured" here to suggest both the articulation of the past event and its – shall I say, animistic? – figuration: one that affords interlocutory possibility.

★★★★★

Anxiously I look up at Trignac's etching. I note the way in which the pylons that support the bridge over the moat are reflected in obverse in the dark waters of the moat. Their reflection, like an inverted triangle, an arrow, points downward, into the mysterious depths of the water and all that lies at its bottom. It is highlighted by a sail that for no apparent reason is stretched out at the pylon's base. Illuminated by the same beam of light that shines on the sails of what I now see as the ship of death, its reflection darkens as it plunges into the moat's depths. Whatever personal associations it evokes – of drowning, of fear of being swallowed up – the pylon and the sail and their reflections suddenly become a rather menacing map of psychic reality – one version of it at least – in which the line between the pylon and the sail's reality and their reflection, the line of contiguity, which the Sufis would call *barzakh*, is reduced to a darkened strip that can be identified as neither reality nor reflection.

★★★★★

The Fang of Gabon, who are participants in a syncretistic religious movement called Bwiti, stress the role of amazement or the miraculous – *akyunge* – in their ritual performances. Though usually translated as miracle, *akyunge* means, as James Fernandez (1982:436) puts it, "anything done with such surpassing skill and subtlety as to amaze and be beyond ordinary understanding and imitation."

> Supernaturals amaze by intervening in the natural order of things and contravening the normal. Bwiti amazes its members by intervening in their lives in such a way as to enable them to surpass themselves and come to an understanding of the extraordinary, the unseen, the "death side" of things. And thus to be in communication with it.

The Fang Bwiti set their standards of ritual practice by those of the neighboring Gabon people, the Metsogo. Fernandez (1982:438) describes the "amazements" of an *obango* – an ecstatic dance performed by the Metsogo people: "torches that glided eerily across the courtyard, the apparent growth over several hours of a small tree from a banana shoot, the sudden production of a cock from an egg, and the falling of a dancer into the fire without being burned." Some of these, Fernandez tells us, were simply sleights of hand but others were the result of extraordinary skill and planning.

> Wires had to be carefully guyed to "float" the torches across the courtyard. Or take a strange sound in a nearby tree top. Is it a spirit? A dancer volunteers to climb the tree and find out. And he does so with a torch tied to his arm. But just as he reaches the top he is cast down, the torch and what appears to be his body falling with a terrific scream through the trees. In the next instance the same man jumps out of the secret chamber [presumably of the Bwiti chapel].

Such spectacles are appreciated for their artistry but, as they edge on the extraordinary, they seem easily to be taken as miracles, at least in the moment – the high – of their performance. At the end of a night-long ceremony, the Path of Birth and Death, in which the liturgical-cosmic cycle of Bwiti belief is rehearsed in song, prayer, and dance, enhanced by the use of *eboga* (ibogaine, a mild hallucinogen). The last part of the ceremony, the Path of Death, culminates in the death, transformation, and ascension of the god Eyen Zame and the liberation of imprisoned ancestors. This complex ritual includes two highly dramatic *obango* episodes, separated by less intense periods of singing and dancing (Fernandez 1982:453–454). The two episodes, which take place after midnight and just before dawn, culminate in what the Fang call oneheartedness (*nlem mvôre*) – a flowing together. The ritual participants, carrying candles, follow the cult harp through the forest in search of those lost ancestor spirits who have not yet found their way to the chapel and are then led back to the chapel where they press around the central pillar and the cult leader, becoming, as Fernandez puts it, virtually one being. "Raising their candles above their heads (ideally they should be able to make one flame out of all the candles) they intone . . . now we become one heart."

For Fernandez (1982:466–469) the amazements of the ritual performance stir the Fang religious imagination by confounding ordinary categories of experience: "We find in them [the Fang Bwiti ceremonies inspired by the Metsogo] a liminal atmosphere in which the dead are suddenly again living, animals are yet men, seedlings are suddenly mature trees, and white-men are really blackmen, or vice versa. Things are confused, lose their categories – Metsogo 'miracles' make things 'amazingly ambiguous'." As Fernandez sees it, the ritually induced semantic confusions are eventually resolved, as the Fang see it, by their ancestors, the living dead. It is they who reclassify and line up men and women in genealogical allegiance – on the path of birth and death. Though Fernandez (1982:476–487) reports some of the visions of initiates under the influence of *eboga*, he does not tell us how the participants in the Path of Birth and Death describe their experiences during the ceremony. It is left to our imagination. We might imagine that hours of dancing, singing, imbibing moderate doses of a mild hallucinogen, candle-lit midnight marches into the forest, always shadowy and filled with potential dangers, (imagined) encounters with dead ancestors all produce multiple and ever-changing scenes that are ever more removed from "paramount reality."

Whatever else we may say about the Bwiti ritual it is theatrical, and as such it so enhances the scenic, so it would seem to the outsider, that paramount reality slips away. How this affects the Bwiti outlook on life in general, their perception of everyday life, the acknowledgment of the artifice of the scene(s), indeed of ordinary reality, their realism, and the way they con-figure and figure – metaphorize – the scene on, and for, other occasions has to be determined. Such determinations would have to rest not only on experiential accounts (for these, alone, would foster, perhaps, too great a stress on the individually subjective at the expense of the intersubjective, the interpersonal, the choreographed); but also, more formally, on how the scenic experiences are framed and, in consequence, subjected to a metapragmatic regimen. How the framing of the framing of the scene – the miracles – governs the way the scene is articulated, evaluated, and con-figured. How, in other words, the "experientiality" of the experience is constituted.

★★★★★

I glance nervously at Trignac's fortress. It reminds me now of an opera setting. I think of dungeons, incarceration, the prison scenes in *Little Dorrit*, the *Count of Monte Christo*, tunneling, escape, the slowness of escape . . . entrapment in one reality or another, the illusions of freedom, the constraints of realism, imaginative release, the illusions of that release, *maya* . . . All the world's a dream. All the world's a stage. Can we escape from the dream? Can we see beyond that stage? Why would we? One of my students, an actor, remarked a couple of days ago that when you are on stage, you cannot really see your audience. They are simply shadows. But you feel their presence, that is, when you are not fully transported. And even then . . .

★★★★★

I will not touch on the use of drugs to produce a counter-reality. As my argument goes, whatever reality they produce physiologically, it is still an encultured response – the product of complex interlocutory play. In my senior year at Harvard, to earn a few dollars, friends of mine participated in psychological experiments in which they were given a drug – they didn't know what it was – and had to report what they experienced. They saw lights, stars, "illuminations like the northern lights," one of them put it. That was all. They had been given LSD. The psychologist was Timothy Leary. A couple of years later (if that long) they would have been tripping: meeting their doubles, bathing in ecstasy, voyaging to the heavens, to hellish depths, experiencing nirvana, suffering the Boschian pleasures of the Garden of Heavenly Delights, in touch with their archetypes. Some would cross over, lose their bearings, and never return. To what? I shall never forget the day one of my students at Princeton came to my office high on acid, hoping, he told me, never to come down. It was the day after the Kent State killings . . .

Am I going too far here? Am I breaking the conventions of my chosen, my prescribed, genre? I hope I have made my point. Reality, paramount reality, can be painful. Freud said it. The Buddhists, the Hindus, say it. Plato understood the exquisite pain of reality – *the* reality, that of the Ideas. We are condemned, so he thought (and his thought has insinuated itself ever since in *our* thought), to a world of shadows, refractions of a reality we can never experience directly, however great our longing, our discipline . . .

But, why do we postulate such an unattainable reality?

The question is important, less because of its idealist entailments, than in empirical implications. Why do we – some of us at least – cling so obsessively to what we call empirical reality? Why has *that* reality become the bulwark of an epistemological discipline that, despite its rejection of any ethical foundation, is carried out with such moral – yes, moral – rigor: preclusive rigor?

I recall a lecture I attended when I was a graduate student by an anthropologist whose identity I will not reveal. He spent an hour describing his empirical methodology. He lived in a village in which he simply recorded what people did in minute detail without ever paying attention to what they said. I don't think he even learned their language, for fear that it would contaminate his objectivity and compromise his methodology. Extreme, to be sure, absurd, but it is not without resonance within our empirical assumption.

Again, I feel compelled to reiterate that I am not making a plea for the irrational. I am asking rather for an opening up of our empiricism to include within its purview the irrational – the less than rational. There is, in case in point, nothing irrational, nothing even fictive, about the scene. In its experience, in its description, and in its glosses or non-glosses, it is a given.

★★★★★

I have been reluctant to reduce the scene to the merely subjective on two grounds. The first is that given the empirical regimen I am contesting, not empiricism generally, the subjective is often a category of dismissal. The second is that both the scene and, as Goethe understood, objective reality are subjectively experienced. The third is that the way we conceive of the subjective is so individualized as to preclude its interlocutory, its interpersonal foundations. Even when we try to delve into its structure we tend to look to biographical (that is, individualized) causes. Or, with the so-called linguistic turn, to the formative role of language. As I began, before my rhetorical descent into the seemingly irrational, I want to stress the way in which the scene, and indeed paramount reality, are constructed. We talk too facilely about the social construction of reality when we should perhaps be talking about the social construction of scenes and realities and – more important – the social construction of the way scenes and realities are related or not related to one another. To the way they are hierarchized, if indeed hierarchy is the appropriate figure. Other arrangements are possible. These might include equations of different scenes and realities, the dismissal of certain of them, indeed, their foreclosing, their *Verwerfung*, or their obliteration without a trace. They may be organized temporally, say, in an oscillating fashion, a hide-and-seek mode, or quantum-mechanics-like flip-flop from one interpretive or positional modality to another.

Social constructivist approaches are always a bit troubling in their generality. Here I would like to restrict my discussion to the way in which the interlocutory exchanges precipitate the scene and, if not paramount reality, its articulation and evaluation as well as the relationship between scene and reality. As I have suggested when discussing framing and the metapragmatics of framing, the constitution of scene, reality, and their relationship is the result of complex indexical play between interlocutors who have themselves wittingly or unwittingly to index themselves and their relationship over a span of time. There is nothing particularly new about this observation. What I want to stress, however, is that the self- and other-constituting interlocutors need not be individuals with whom one is immediately engaged or mediately engaged, as for example, when reading, but they may also be figures of the imagination or memory edging on the shadowy world of the phantasm. (In many cultures memory and imagination are conceptually conflated.) We may conceive of these two categories of interlocutors in synchronic and diachronic terms or, if you prefer, in terms of a horizontal and vertical axis whose intersection is the experiential moment. Depending on the situation in which one finds oneself – the way it is framed – the immediate or mediate interlocutors or the imagined or remembered ones may be dominant, but, I suggest, the latent interlocutors are never wholly absent or without influence on interlocution. How the focalization on one interlocutory type or another relates to the constitution and evaluation of scene and reality has to be determined case by case.

Indexical processes are never simple ostensive acts that point to, or call forth, a single element in a constituted reality – a context. Aside from the rather obvious point that in indexing a contextual element, they also index the context in which that element occurs, as being, say, a context in which such an element can occur. Or, they may play, ironically, comically, transgressively, on contextual "inappropriateness" or "unexpectedness." I remember how my daughter, at three, burst into laughter when, without thinking, I put a carrot I was eating in an empty wine glass in order to free my hands to pet the dog. Irony, play, and transgression call attention to the complexity of pragmatic and metapragmatic dynamics, the analysis of which are beyond the scope of this essay (see Crapanzano 2003).

The indexing of any element and in consequence its context is minimally a double indexing; for not only does it point to what it is – the contextualizing element, the context – but also what it is not. This Hegelian play with negation is so inevitable, at least from a communicational point of view, as to be meaningless under most circumstances, that is, unless the negated itself is highlighted as it frequently is in word play. But, whether through negation or positive affirmation, indexicals may, as I suggested, point simultaneously to paramount reality and one or more "coincident" scenes. In so doing, the indexicals also "define" the relationship between the scene and reality. At least in those societies that privilege realism, their realism, it seems likely that privileging masks the way the indexing of that reality also indexes the scene. When the scene is the indexical focus, however, it seems likely that the indexing of reality is more salient. Of course, these hypotheses require confirmation. What is clear – and what I have tried to demonstrate in my discussion of ritual – is that there are times when the indexing of the scene may so mask the indexing of paramount reality that that reality slips away.[8]

★★★★★

Thus far I have stressed the indexical play between reality or realities and scene or scenes from the point of view of a single discursive position, that of the speaker or thinker, but, as my stress on interlocution suggests, no discursive position is ever *sui generis*. It is always the result of complex interlocutory dynamics that are born by the discourse or conversation. They include indexical play or, perhaps more accurately, struggle (except in the most conventional situations) between differently positioned interlocutors, including both the real and the remembered and imagined ones. This play is, as I (Crapanzano 1992) have frequently argued, governed by a set of determining (or metapragmatic) conventions that I have referred to as the Third, itself a focus of interlocutory struggle (Crapanzano 1992: Introduction, Chapters 3 and 4). Put simply, any interlocution always involves a negotiation for the way interlocution will be framed, what discursive conventions will prevail, and which hermeneutic and axiological procedures are appropriate for interpretation and evaluation. It is at this metapragmatic – this framing the frame – level that power, whether understood in Foucault's pervasive sense or in a more institutionally centered one, as in Marxism, insinuates itself most effectively and blindingly into discourse and its precipitation of reality, the scene, and their relationship.[9] For any communication to be successful, there is always an accommodation – an acceptance of the frame, conventions, and relevant hermeneutics and axiology – for the occasion. This acceptance need not, of course, be believed in or heartfelt. It may be practical, politic, or simply hypocritical. It is only the naïve who accept accommodation without suspicion. There lurks behind every interlocution the opacity – the mind – of the other that casts its shadow on that interlocution.[10]

There are moments, however, when the parties to the interlocution surrender not so much to one another as to the intersubjective world they have co-created. At least since Winnicott's (1982:104–110) work on potential space and the intermediate area of experience – roughly the transitional space between inner and outer reality – object relations theorists in psychoanalysis have been concerned with the dynamics of the space-time of the psychoanalytic session. Among the most important of them is Thomas H. Ogden (1999) who explores the intersubjective space created during the psychoanalytic hour, which he refers to as an "intersubjective analytic third" or simply a "third."[11] He argues (p. 462) that contemporary psychoanalytic thinking "can no longer simply speak of the analyst and the analysand as separate subjects who take one another as objects." They are caught, at least during the analytic session, in so strong an intersubjective engagement (or dialectic) that that engagement becomes (experientially) a third subjectivity with which they have to reckon both from within and without it. "The intersubjective and the individually subjective each create, negate, and preserve the other" (p. 463).

> I believe that a major dimension of the analyst's psychological life in the consulting room with the patient takes the form of reverie concerning the everyday details of his own life . . . [T]hese reveries are not simply

reflections of inattentiveness, narcissistic self-involvement, unresolved emotional conflict, and the like; rather, this psychological activity represents symbolic and proto-symbolic (sensation-based) forms given to the unarticulated (and often not yet felt) experience of the analysand as they are taking form in the intersubjectivity of the analytic pair (i.e., in the analytic third). [p. 476]

Ogden (p. 487) stresses the unconscious dimension of the co-created intersubjective third. He emphasizes the way the analyst will suddenly focus on a common object he has ignored, as, for example, the bulk postmark on the envelope of a letter he took to be confidential. He recognizes that the co-creative relationship is doubly asymmetrical: for, (a) "the exploration of analysand's unconscious internal object world and forms of relatedness to the external world" is privileged, and (b) the two participants experience the third from their differing perspectives, personalities, modes of adjustment to their respective worlds, their world.

Ogden restricts his discussion to the analytic session, but I would argue that we are often so intersubjectively captivated that we have to reckon (no doubt with less critical self-reflection than the psychoanalyst) with one experiential figuration of intersubjectivity or another. Two examples immediately come to mind: the first is those entanglements of longstanding anger and bitterness of the sort that Strindberg depicts in "The Dance of Death"; the second are those moments of amorous enchantment when lovers feel one with each other and have yet to separate themselves. There are also all sorts of pathological conditions that can be understood in terms of intersubjective captivation, the most obvious of which is the *folie à deux*, but we would have to include "family disturbances" which so knot family members in one another that they cannot disengage themselves or do so poorly. All of these as well as those ritual moments I have discussed are differently structured than the psychoanalytic session. The intersubjective claims may be so intense that subjective differentiation may fall by the wayside. Certainly I have heard psychoanalysts speak of rare moments when they felt that they and their patients actually felt one with each other, "as though they shared a single consciousness". Such moments are rare and are not cultivated in Western societies, where they are usually considered to be delusional, but they are given greater credence in other societies, as we saw in Bwiti oneheartedness when the ritual participants were clutched together each holding up candles to form a single flame.

As part of my recent research on the Harkis, those Algerians who sided with the French during Algeria's war of independence, I visited one of the most notorious French camps in which those who managed to escape slaughter after Independence were incarcerated. (Of the roughly 250 thousand Harkis, between 70 and 150 thousand were mutilated and murdered by the Algerian population at large at the time of Independence. Despite de Gaulle's attempt to prevent the Harkis' flight to France, about twenty thousand families managed to make it and were immediately put into camps, some for as long as sixteen years.) Mohammed B. had grown up in this camp – an isolated *camp de forestage* in the mountains around Carcassone – which he visits at least once a year "to remember." Today, with the exception of a few German hippies who have camped out there, the village is abandoned, the stone huts in ruins, and the entrance square filled with derelict cars and old tires. Only the camp commandant's house, now his hunting lodge, which overlooks the village, is kept up. Mohammed was anxious to show the camp to me. On the long drive there we talked about the Harkis, mercenaries, the French economy, politics, and inevitably the war in Iraq. As we approached the camp, Mohammed grew pensive, lost, I supposed, in memory. I was shocked by how isolated the camp was. On several occasions he asked me to stop and take pictures of the village and its surroundings, and when I did, dutifully, he would tell me about a friend of his, a *pied-noir*, who was so moved by the dehumanizing conditions that he couldn't take any pictures. I felt taken. I had done what Mohammed had asked me to – I don't particularly like taking pictures – and was then shown to be callous. I was outraged and yet filled with understanding for Mohammed's ambivalence. Sometimes with tears in his eyes, he showed me the sty in which he, his mother, and sisters had been housed, the school he had been sent to, the lot where he had played, the well. . . . I was overcome by the thought of all that was passing though his mind that I couldn't know in fact but somehow knew. On the way back, we stopped for lunch. Mohammed drank a lot of wine, was sullen, and back in the car dozed. It was an obliterating sleep, I thought to myself. When he awoke, he sat silently, occasionally fidgeting with his cell phone, hoping, I suspected, for a call that would remove him from the implosion of his memory world. I too hoped it would ring. Finally, after about an hour, Mohammed turned to me and said that were it not for his mother who had always insisted that he look positively to the future, he would commit suicide. But he could not disappoint her. (She is, in fact, a remarkable woman who managed not only to survive the horror of seeing her husband's throat slit in front of her and the ensuing camp life, but succeeded in finding a job that enabled her to raise and educate her three children.) I was stunned by Mohammed's words, less because of what he had said but by the fact that I had been thinking he was having suicidal thoughts as he sat next to me. I could say nothing. There was nothing to be said. The car became a sort of prison. I wanted to flee. Fortunately, Mohammed's cell phone rang. It was one of his clients. He is a builder.

Anthropologists have all had such experiences. We have an asymmetrical relationship with our informants. It is the informant's words that are privileged. Ogden might say that I was caught in *something like* the intersubjective third, but though I experienced a captivating closeness to, perhaps even a merging with, Mohammed's thoughts at the time, I am hesitant to refer to that closeness, that possible merging, as a third. Ogden's understanding arises out of the experience itself. He himself speaks of being at once in and out of the intersubjective third. His theorizing reflects – and mystifies, inevitably – the experience. It is, if you will, a symptom of the experience. He can neither attain requisite distance to view it as if from the outside nor can he possibly reflect on the indexical play – the struggle – that is occurring as he experiences it without disturbing, indeed destroying, the experience itself. There is always a limit to our self-doubling and -trebling consciousness. Given the intersubjective construction of self-consciousness that I am advocating, I would have, in any case, to ask how a putative awareness of intersubjectivity, its captivation, relates to intersubjectively constituted subjectivity. We must not be seduced by the gloss into even spotty omniscience.

★★★★★

I look up one last time at Trignac's fortress and suddenly realize that I have never asked myself who lives there. There are windows, but they are darkened. I cannot see in any more than I can look into someone else's mind. Is anyone looking out at me? At any viewer? My study darkens. It is a late wintry afternoon – twilight, *crépuscule*.

Notes

1   A version of this paper was first published in Portuguese in the Brazilian journal *Mana* 11 (2005):357–383.
2   As will become clear, my use of "scene" should not be confused with Erving Goffman's (1959) theatrical metaphor. Goffman's particular style of empiricism precludes precisely what I mean by the scene. In oral versions of this paper, to differentiate my notion of the scene from the more standard sociological ones, I used the French *scène*, but, in the end, this seemed to be pretentious word magic. I should note that in using the English, I have lost the immediate reference to Lacan's translation of Freud's *der andere Schauplatz* as *scène*: the dream scene.
3   We should note that Schutz recognizes his debt to William James's notions of "subuniverses". Schutz's paramount reality corresponds roughly to James's

"world of sense." See James's (n.d.:1028–1030) essay, "The Psychology of Belief."

4   It could be argued that scenic reality precipitates objective reality, but I would be reluctant to accept so idealist a position. No doubt, it can intensify the experience and evaluation of objective reality, as, I believe, these last examples suggest. It can be argued, indeed in different terms it has been argued, that what might be called the exaggeration of scenic reality in some rituals confirms and intensifies the (conventional) experience of objective reality. It would be, in my view, a mistake to identify objective reality with everyday reality, since the quotidian is not without its scenes. In any case, I would still argue, as I did above, that, however influenced by the scene, the experience of objective reality cannot admit of this influence, for it would lose its objectivity.

5   I have discussed the scene with a number of psychoanalysts. Though they are, as a group, sensitive to changes in the mood and character of their patients and themselves, they were surprised when I asked them about changes in their sense of immediate reality during the psychoanalytic sessions. The context was simply their offices. But, once they reflected, they began to recall such changes. When their patients were depressed, they said the room darkened and felt smaller. Several stressed blue light. With maniacally happy patients, the room brightened, and several said it turned yellow. Some felt the room became larger; others felt claustrophobia. Anger and aggression were associated with red. Objects also changed. They were suddenly aware of the shoddiness of a couch or the dust on a lampshade which they had never before noticed. One analyst said that a small, highly abstract picture, which she faced and was often a focus of reflection as she listened to her patients, became larger at times and smaller at others. She was not able to say when or why.

6   Though mood and atmosphere no doubt play an important role in the description, if not the constitution, of the scene, I do not want to reduce the scene to them. Both are, as Charles Altieri (2003:54) observes, encompassing. Moods relate roughly to inner experience; atmosphere to outer experience. Moods are pervasive and do not attach themselves, as Altieri (p. 54) argues, to specific objects.

> In moods the affects seem continuous with some overall state of the subject. But the continuity is insistently not one for which we can provide a narrative, perhaps because moods seem total and so have no beginning and ending, only extension and duration and evanescence . . . Moods are synthetic and imperialistic, absorbing details rather than conforming to their specific appearances (p. 54).

Altieri insists that as moods are pervasive, the intentional subject is not particularly important. "We certainly feel ourselves involved as subjects, but we do not organize the scenes in terms of our specific interests or perspectives as subjects. Rather subjectivity floats, modulating between a sense of one's own participation and a sense of being taken up into states of mind that any subject might enter because states of mind seem to exist independently of practical perspectives." They absorb agency into the transpersonal. Though atmosphere can be distinguished from moods in terms of its exterior focus, the two can metaphorize each other, as when my student referred to a change of mood in the room. Both mood and atmosphere differ from what I mean by the scene. It is "objectivistic," defined in terms of specific elements and events, and has great narrative as well as theatrical potential. I do not want, however, to belabor these differences, for the distinction between mood, atmosphere, and scene is inevitably messy.

7   For a more detailed description of the Hamadsha rituals and pilgrimages, see Crapanzano 1973, especially pp. 115–118.

8   See note 3 for the converse.

9   I do not mean to suggest that there is no "hard" reality out there but rather that reality, what the phenomenologists refer to as resistance, is called forth and given articulate form and value – precipitated – through discourse.

10   See my discussion of shadow dialogues, those interior dialogues that each dialogical participant has silently with himself as the dialogical exchange with an other, with others, progresses (Crapanzano 1992:213ff.).

11   Ogden (1999:464, fn. 2) is careful to distinguish his notion of the third from Lacan's "name of the father" ("*nom de père*"), which Ogden understands as "a middle term" standing between symbol and symbolized, between oneself and one's immediate environment, which creates "a space in which the interpreting, self-reflective, symbolizing subject is generated." Nor, I would add, is Ogden's third equivalent to my usage of the term as a metapragmatically authoritative term. Though closer to Lacan's name of the father, the Third, as I use it, is at another level of abstraction, which can be symbolized by the "name of the father" as it can be by the "Law" or incarnated by a father or, for that matter, a totemic figure or god. I want to avoid the psychogenetic implication of Lacan's term.

References

Altieri, Charles
   2003   The Rapture: The Aesthetics of the Affects. Ithaca, NY: Cornell University Press.
Crapanzano, Vincent
   1973   The Hamdsha: A Study in Moroccan Ethnopsychiatry. Berkeley: University of California Press.
Crapanzano, Vincent
   1992   Hermes' Dilemma and Hamlet's Desire: On the Epistemology of Interpretation. Cambridge: Harvard University Press.
Crapanzano, Vincent
   2003   Afterward. *In* Illness and Irony: On the Ambiguity of Suffering in Culture, Michael Lambek and Paul Antze, eds. Pp. 135–148. New York: Berghahn Books.

Crapanzano, Vincent
  2004   Imaginative Horizons: An Essay in Literary-Philosophical Anthropology. Chicago: University of Chicago Press.
Evans-Pritchard, E. E.
  1937   Witchcraft, Oracles, and Magic Among the Azande. Oxford: Clarendon Press.
Fernandez, James
  1982   Bwiti: An Ethnography of the Religious Imagination in Africa. Princeton: Princeton University Press.
Freud, Sigmund
  1963 [1919]   The 'Uncanny.' *In* Studies in Parapsychology. Philip Rieff, ed. Pp. 19–66. New York: Collier Books.
Goffman, Erving
  1959   The Presentation of the Self in Everyday Life. New City, NY: Doubleday Anchor.
Husserl, Edmund
  1931   Ideas: A General Introduction to Pure Phenomenology. London: George Allen and Unwin.
Lawrence, D. H.
  1950   The Plumed Serpent. Harmondsworth: Penguin.
Ogden, Thomas H.
  1999   The Analytic Third: Working with Intersubjective Clinical Facts. *In* Relational Psychoanalysis: The Emergence of a Tradition. Stephen A. Mitchell and Lewis Aron, eds. Pp. 459–492. Hillsdale, NJ: The Analytic Press.
Schutz, Alfred
  1970   On the Phenomenology and Social Relations. Helmut Wagner, ed. Chicago: University of Chicago Press.
Turner, Victor
  1969   The Ritual Process: Structure and Anti-Structure. Chicago: Aldine.
Winnicott, D. W.
  1982   Playing and Reality. New York: Tavistock.

Chapter 4

Transmutation of Sensibilities:
Empathy, Intuition, Revelation

Thomas J. Csordas

There are moments in the course of ethnographic work that occupy a particular position on the continuum between going native and feeling the absolute stranger. These moments occur on what the editors of this volume have called the "shadow side" of ethnography, and are quite different from moments of insight, apt translation, feeling at home, attaining to fluency, relaxed comfort, or true friendship with one's informants. They are moments that can best be described as the transmutation of sensibilities, when one has an unexpected and striking experience in a modality typical of the setting in which one is working. The experience is one that could have been experienced by an indigenous person in the sense of its form and its relevance to the immediate setting, but not in terms of its psychodynamic content or the dispositions upon which it is founded. This chapter describes three such moments that I have experienced, and examines the conjunction between existential and ethnographic significance to which they point.

★★★★★

Beginning in 1973 I began fieldwork in the Catholic Charismatic Renewal, a neo-Pentecostal movement within the Roman Catholic Church. One of the features of Charismatic ritual life that I found most intriguing was a system of genres of ritual language that included prayer, teaching, witnessing, and prophecy. Among these genres, prophecy was particularly potent in that it was understood as God speaking though the mind and mouth of the one gifted to deliver the utterance. It is a charism or gift of the Holy Spirit mentioned by St. Paul as among those granted to the apostles at Pentecost. In form, prophecy as I heard it in the 1970s and 1980s was often an elegant kind of inspired oral poetry produced in couplet form. In rhetorical effect it occasionally moved people to act in certain ways or undertake certain projects that were highly consequential for their lives.

Charismatic prophecy is readily recognizable by prosodic features such as an authoritative vocal tone, and an opening formula of address such as "My children," and as a first person utterance in which the "I" is God. It articulates an identifiable vocabulary of motives and exhibits a repertoire of typical themes. The prophet is responsible for exercising "discernment" with respect to whether his or her inspiration is authentically from God as well as whether the message is intended for personal edification only or for the edification and exhortation of the larger group. In short, it is a full-fledged genre with conventions that can be assimilated by cultivated listening and that can be performed by all participants with appropriate legitimation from the community of devotees.

Soon after I began working in a Catholic Charismatic group in the city where I attended university as an undergraduate, I became aware that the movement had become widespread in the United States and had begun to expand abroad as well. I realized that if I were to claim to be studying the movement rather than a local instantiation of that movement my ethnography would necessarily be multi-sited. As I traveled among Charismatic communities I learned that various among them were allied into networks, were in regular contact with one another, and in symbolic terms tended to distinguish among themselves by adopting names that often reflected the notion that each community possessed a unique charism that it contributed to a "community of communities" just as within each community individual members were granted charisms that in their ensemble would contribute to the building of that community.

Small prayer groups sometimes aspired to grow into communities with a full complement of spiritual gifts, or at least to be able to develop a particular "ministry" in service to their own members and others who might seek their help or seek to join them, and by which they would be recognized among other groups. In the course of my travels, having spent time with a variety of groups over the course of several years, I visited the weekly prayer meeting of a small group of perhaps thirty members, coincidentally (perhaps) in the town where I had spent part of my childhood and adolescence. It became clear that the group had been prayerfully discussing whether to initiate a "healing ministry" which would become their defining activity. Such a healing ministry is one in which a team of people are chosen based on their perceived maturity and caring. They and other members pray to receive the charism of healing, and subsequently they can be approached by others for healing prayer and the laying on of hands. The prayer meeting itself was not an appropriate venue for discussion, but for "seeking the Lord's will" via prayer and openness to the divine response in prophecy.

At some point during the meeting, as I listened and observed the process of collective inspiration potentially giving birth to social form and practice, a brief sentence took form in my thoughts, or perhaps I could say that the following words came to me: "My children, be cautious." After perhaps a moment's lag time I did a mental double take, and said to myself, "O my God, I just got a prophecy." There was no mistaking the phenomenon, having studied it, listened to it, transcribed it, conducted interviews about it, read Charismatics' own manuals on how to recognize and use the gift. The words had emerged in thought spontaneously, fully formed and in effect with quotation marks already inscribed, though as I recall it the presentation was not in visual but in purely verbal form. It was more like the way a line of poetry or song lyric might come, visual only in the sense that it appealed to a disposition to commit such words to writing. This was my first encounter with the shadow side of ethnography.

What is required here is a precise phenomenological account of what happened to me in this instance, for it is perfectly inadequate to say that for a moment I was converted or that for a moment I went native. We would be getting closer by saying that my prophecy was an upwelling of empathy for their struggle, an authentic struggle to discern what they imagined as God's will for them as a group, a struggle to do the right things and provide service to their fellow Christians in a way for which they were best suited, a struggle to play their part in bringing about the kingdom of God, a struggle which I was able to recognize having observed others trying to create similar ministries, sometimes with greater resources. Associated with this empathy in a way that is critical and in need of further elaboration is a specific intuition about the circumstances under which this decision was being undertaken and the feeling of tension about something being at stake. Specifically, the intuition would be awareness of the risks involved based on ethnographic background knowledge of the stress and potential for "burnout" faced by those who placed themselves in the position of praying for the healing of others, others who could be emotionally quite needy and demanding. Risks, too, of "getting in over one's head," in situations where what was needed was a fully trained psychotherapist rather than a well-meaning layperson.

Still, empathy and intuition do not account for why my experience took the form of a prophecy. I have hinted at two possible idiosyncratic features that would incline the situation in that direction. The fact that it took place in my home town perhaps created an element of entitlement to speak authoritatively. The fact that I had some experience writing poetry and song lyrics and in addition studied the work of Alfred Lord on oral composition among folk poets perhaps created an element of subjective familiarity with the kind of genre conventions in question. However, the principal factor was that I had studied this genre of ritual speech and the system of genres in which it is embedded thoroughly enough so that, without being fully aware that this was taking place, I had both incorporated its performative conventions and inculcated within myself its performative dispositions. I am intentionally evoking language reminiscent of Bourdieu's discussion of habitus because it is only by immersion within a habitus that one can experience what I want to call the transmutation of sensibilities that occurred in my revelatory experience. That is, my upsurge of empathy and intuition was clothed in the immediacy of appropriate cultural form because I was immersed in the charismatic habitus. And by sensibilities I am not referring only to empathy and intuition, but to language and expression as they are evoked in an intersubjective setting of bodily being in proximity to others who are simultaneously open to inspiration.

It is hardly relevant from this standpoint that I was not, nor could I be, actively engaged in the collective act of "seeking the Lord's will." What I will submit in evidence for my interpretation is the fact that my empathic/intuitive insight that took the form of revelation – that is, conformed to the genre conventions of prophecy – created a dilemma. Was I somehow obligated to pass on the message to the participants? The point is that I took this question quite seriously. It was not because I thought God was perhaps using me the non-believer as a messenger, though I have heard that possibility articulated. It was rather – again thinking retrospectively – that I respected the authenticity of inspiration, whether the source was actually the human imagination or misrepresented as divine intervention in human consciousness. The point is that the transmutation of sensibilities was sufficiently thorough that it made me actively question how to comport myself. So how did I handle it? The genre convention requiring discernment on the part of the prophet made it evident that a stranger, let alone a non-believer, should not speak out publicly without the most powerful sense of conviction. The question was whether to share the revelation with the priest who was leader of the group after the meeting. I did so, at the same time identifying myself as an anthropologist studying the Charismatic Renewal. He thanked me politely, and that was the end of the episode.

★★★★★

My second encounter with the shadow side of ethnography occurred more than twenty years later while I was participating in a Navajo Night Way ceremony. The Night Way is one of the crown jewels of the Navajo ritual system, a nine–night ceremony conducted during the winter months and featuring the appearance of troops of masked dancers representing the *yei-bi-cheis*, that is, the Navajo deities or Holy People. On the fourth and ninth nights of this ceremony ritual activities continue till dawn, with prayer, song, manipulation of ritual objects, and ministry to the patient – virtually every Navajo ceremony except those marking life cycle transitions is directed toward healing and has a patient.

Late on the fourth night of this particular ceremony, perhaps at four o'clock in the morning, a bucket of water was passed along with a wooden dipper for participants to take a drink. As is often the case in such situations, the passing of the water was not merely instrumental in the sense of recognition of the need to satisfy thirst, but was a ritual act involving the symbolic importance of water. The wooden dipper was hand carved such that the rounded bottom was not smooth but rugged from the action of the tool that had created its hollow. At the moment that I lifted the dipper to my mouth, light glinted off the wet and uneven inner surface of the dipper. I had two thoughts simultaneously as the light struck my eye. The first was that it appeared to have reflected from the lantern in the Hogan off my glasses and into the dipper. The second was that, for only an instant as the angle of the dipper and the reflected light changed with my movement, the reflection took the shape of a *yei-bi-chei*, specifically the hump-backed deity who is one of the participating gods in the Night Chant and who is related to the commonly depicted Kokopeli figure of the Pueblos.

We can consider this the apparition of a deity in the same sense as my Charismatic experience was an instance of prophecy. It was by no means a hallucination in the sense of an image suspended indeterminately in space, and neither was it an inward phenomenon like the prophecy (which as I noted emerged in consciousness as a line of poetry might). It appeared in concrete sensory form as a silhouette formed of light, although so instantaneously and briefly that it seems it could have passed unnoticed by me. I did notice it, however, again because of incorporated performative conventions and inculcated performative dispositions. To be more precise, I not so much recognized a form as endowed the shifting reflection with form. I in-formed it by means of a synthetic bodily act including not only the coalescence of a visual gestalt but the synchronization of lifting the water-filled dipper at a certain angle in relation to the lantern and in so doing performing a ritual act of the most minimal sort. I was rewarded with a revelation of the most minimal sort, just as my Charismatic prophecy was a minimal prophecy.

This time I felt no obligation to narrate the incident, although it can be considered important to share such information in Navajo ceremonialism since it may suggest some unanticipated ritual need to the chanter or indicate some danger to which the chanter must respond ceremonially. My motivation for telling the chanter what had happened was more to use the incident as a way to elicit a comment from him. I was interested in whether he would regard my experience as meaningful or epiphenomenal. In fact, he said "What you thought you saw is probably a sign that they're around [i.e., the yei-bi-cheis], intended to show someone who's not a believer that this is real." Note that in judging the apparition to be a sign from the deities he hedges by referring to what I "thought" I saw, and by saying that it was "probably" a sign. Yet later at end of the night's prayers he asked if I wanted to say anything, which I took as a cue to give a general thank-you speech to the healer and his team as well as the patient and his family for the privilege of participating and helping with the ceremony. In addition, however, the chanter prompted me to narrate the image for the edification of those in attendance, and pointedly stated in summary that "It wasn't just light reflected from your glasses."

Beyond this performative moment, my opening to the shadow side created a framework of intersubjectivity that was in turn grounds for an empathic bond that I had not anticipated. Later while we sat together eating at one of the tables in the large cook-tent set up to accommodate participants in the nine-night ceremony, he narrated an experience of his own in having direct contact with the Holy People. He began by noting that he built his house in 1960, and said that an event happened there in 1965. He was lying down on the couch, and though he thought he was awake at the time said he may have been asleep. He felt something on his toe, and saw one of the Holy People grabbing his toe and wiggling it, with all the holy paraphernalia spread out near the chanter's feet. He blinked and it was gone, but could still feel it on his toe. The touch of the deity, even in so peripheral a spot as the toe, and perhaps graciously on the toe so as not to overwhelm the mere mortal with too much bodily contact, was a profound and permanently remembered sign that he said really encouraged him in his ritual career.

I recognized this brief narrative as an ethnographic gift. The gift and its personal significance to me were enhanced by the gratification of hearing a narration of personal experience from a healer who was characteristically quite guarded in passing on any information the divulging of which might create a dangerous supernatural repercussion, a healer whom I had known for 15 years but who only now was exhibiting a degree of trust and recognition. Further, in narrating his experience of hierophany the chanter was acknowledging that my experience fell into the same category, and by reaching back to 1965 for his example he was acknowledging that such moments do not occur all that often.

I gave this as my second example not because it was more recent in my own experience but to preempt the inclination to account for my revelation in terms of suggestibility due to sleep deprivation during a long ceremony. I was not at all sleep deprived when I experienced Charismatic prophecy, and on the other hand the Navajo chanter who was my interlocutor in this instance also narrated an incident which took place on the border between sleep and waking. The altered state of consciousness is of no consequence in itself unless we consider is to be a preparation or enhancement of susceptibility to a disposition, convention, or sensibility rather than its creation.

In sum, my experience was constituted by a transmutation of sensibilities insofar as my sense of performative presence and power was spontaneously manifest in a culturally appropriate form. Although its subsequent narration created an intersubjective bond with my interlocutor the chanter, a bond that can be glossed as empathic, the revelation itself was not empathy. Transmutation of sensibilities can be a vehicle of empathy or intuition as in this or the Charismatic episode. But to say it is empathy for the ritual system and the performance instead of reserving the term empathy for a bond with other persons would be an abuse of language. We are better off referring as I have done to the incorporation of performative conventions and inculcation of performative dispositions.

★★★★★

My final bit of evidence also comes from Navajoland, but this time takes place not in a traditional Navajo ceremony but in a meeting of the Native American Church. Brought to the Navajo in the 1930s by members of Plains Indian tribes, the Native American Church has become an integral part of the religious landscape in the Navajo Nation. Its central ceremony, an all-night prayer meeting, has been adapted to Navajo sensibilities and is strongly oriented toward healing. Devotion is oriented toward a creator spirit sometimes assimilated to the Christian god, to whom access is granted through ritual ingestion of the peyote cactus. Peyote is at once a powerful medicine, a sacrament, and a spirit sometimes regarded as equivalent to Jesus. Chemically it includes a series of related alkaloids, the most significant of which in its effect is the hallucinogen mescaline. During peyote meetings the medicine is passed among participants several times during the night, often in both the forms of powder and tea. Proceedings are led by a healer called a road man whose function is to guide people along the "peyote road" of right living. A prayer meeting consists of alternating periods of song accompanied by rattle and drum, and periods of prayer until dawn when participants are fed a ritual meal and gradually allow the effects of the medicine to diminish so they can go about their everyday affairs.

My encounter with the shadow side took place not in the depths of the night's prayer and song, but after dawn when the sky had lightened. The morning hours after the ritual breakfast is served are typically spent lounging in the tepee, everyone tired from being awake all night but not yet able to sleep because of the peyote, joking and talking lazily as the effects of the medicine recede. On this particular morning at about 8:30 I left the tepee to go to the bathroom. While outside I recalled that my rented car was low on gas, and had the impulse to drive to the nearest gas station, which was nine miles down the road at the highway junction. As soon as I started the unfamiliar car the low fuel indicator light came on. It occurred to me that perhaps I should postpone this errand until later in the morning, when I had not only returned to a more accustomed perceptual state but had the opportunity to tell others where I was going. I remained anxious all the way to the gas station, mostly imagining how foolish I would appear to the others by driving off while the medicine was still affecting me, especially if I ran out of fuel and had to walk back.

I did arrive at the gas station without trouble. While filling the tank I noticed a pay telephone on the outside wall of the station, and decided to phone home to let my wife know I was all right after the all-night ceremony. The first thing she said upon answering the ring was that my son, who was 9 years old, had just told her his dream from the previous night. In the dream a group of people had gotten into our car and I was driving us all across a body of water to a place of freedom, where we would all have more space – apparently an underwater oasis with a swimming pool inside a bubble structure. In the dream I said we were low on fuel, and my son replied "Here, Dad, I have a gallon of gas, you can use this." I checked his container to make sure he really had gas (apparently as a dream father I did not fully trust that what he had was indeed gasoline), then put it in the tank and said "Now we can really travel." The co-occurrence of my son's experience and my own suggested that I had been the beneficiary of his dream gas in real time, and that this accounted for why I had successfully reached the gas station on an empty tank.

The impact on me of this dream narration would not have been as profound if I had not set off so impulsively without telling the others where I was going. When I rejoined them I narrated the incident to those present, and the healer's nephew translated for her into Navajo. As I spoke, it became narratively clear not only that my son's gallon is what allowed me to make it to the gas station, but that the water over which we were driving in his dream corresponded to the central symbolic role of water in this healer's personal interpretation of the peyote religion. Moreover, the Navajo word for water is "*tooh*," and the Navajo word for gasoline is "*chidi bi tooh*," or the "the car's water." In conversation, people often simply say "tooh" for both, and distinguish by context whether it means water or gas. The first thing the healer said in response to my narrative was "You better include this story in your book." The others said "Now you know for yourself how this medicine works. This is your story that you can tell."

In fact, the nature of the psychic connection between my son and me is that during that period he often felt quite unsettled when I was away traveling. To follow through on the notion of a transmutation of sensibilities, in this incident the medicine amplified and emphasized this connection in order to make a point to me. What can this mean in cultural and existential terms aside from the fact that I, like that other Thomas, am open to the persuasiveness of compelling evidence? As strong as it is, the peyote in itself does not account for the shadow side experience any more than sleep deprivation accounted for it in my second example. Again what is at issue are performative conventions and dispositions with respect to how to accommodate the effects of the medicine. This was eloquently put in two points made by one of the elders in this meeting as he spoke to me during a midnight break under the stars. In the first he analogized awareness of the peyote's effect to awareness of the wind: "How can you feel the wind is on you, the air moving against your body? How can you tell where it's coming from? How can you tell how the medicine is working, where it's coming from? It moves you." In the second he used the metaphor of peyote as a mirror: "The medicine is a mirror, it reflects what you do. If you want to be afraid it's afraid, if you want to be serious it's serious, if you want to joke around it jokes around, if you want to be macho it's macho. It matches you, your character."

These points, lessons really, capture both the alterity and identity of the sacred. In the first point, peyote is active and independent, like the wind blowing against a person, a sometimes subtle force that can be discerned and detected, and that moves one. It is an Other with which one comes into relation, both external in its transcendence and internal as it is incorporated – the wind (*nilch'i*), in Navajo thinking, is not something inanimate or totally external, because the wind/air inhabits and animates us as humans, and therefore is continuous with us. In the second lesson the medicine is a function of the person as it corresponds with, responds to, is shaped by, and matches the person's character and intentions. This image also combines identity in the sense that it brings the true self to the fore, and alterity insofar as a reflection projects from and stands uncannily outside the self, indeed is perhaps the archetype of the alterity of the self. The sensibilities of alterity and identity outlined in these lessons are neither Navajo nor Anglo, but simply human, and for me their transmutation was literally a "change in form." That is, my incorporation of performative conventions and dispositions made possible a change of existential form and interpretive frame such that intuition and empathy as already constituted were amplified within a matrix of symbolic and personal connections that I would not otherwise have made.

★★★★★

Anthropologists have a limited repertoire of ideas to discuss their personal encounters in the field. I will conclude by making several summary assertions about the usefulness of and interrelations among the principal terms I have evoked in my description of shadow side experiences. Empathy is a potentially valuable concept in this respect, since it can be a feeling in relation to a specific person, but also in relation to a way of life or mode of experience. But empathy is neither necessarily a personality trait, nor a learned/cultivated skill. It can also be a phenomenon of immersion in a cultural milieu.

Empathy is a specific case of intuition, one that has to do with feeling for and with another person. Intuition can be impersonal, both in the sense of not requiring a sense of caring for and in the sense that it can pertain to situations that do not involve other humans and may be about nature or inanimate objects. Empathy is eminently and perhaps obviously a phenomenon of intersubjectivity but, I would argue, so is intuition. This, pushing the argument, might even be said to be the case where intuition has to do with so-called inanimate objects.

Without adopting an overtly animist position, to the extent that even our inanimate objects participate in a world of human sensibilities, it is not going too far to invoke intersubjectivity in all instances of intuition insofar as intuition is constituted by immediate recognition of being enfolded in what Merleau-Ponty called the flesh of the world. This is perhaps easiest to see when the inanimate objects are elements of culture: artifacts, ideas, dispositions, modes of thought. Along these lines, empathy for a way of life is equivalent to intuition about a way of life, though intuition in this sense would have a more neutral evaluative valence than empathy. That is, empathy connotes fellow-feeling and kinship, being on the same side. Intuition can imply canny insight without precluding an underlying hostility.

When instances of intuition and/or empathy occur spontaneously, it is fair to call them revelation whether or not they occur within a ritual or religious setting. The instances I have recounted in this chapter were striking in part because of their spontaneity, and their spontaneity was in turn likely a product of the cross-cultural dynamics of the situations in which they took place. It is likely that the term transmutation of sensibilities describes the process of empathy, intuition, and revelation even in more mundane same-culture non-ritual settings. Nevertheless, the ensemble of performative conventions and dispositions that are brought into play to achieve the transmutation are more readily discerned in such instances as I have narrated here. And this is perhaps one of the services to ethnography that can be rendered by paying attention to its shadow side.

Part III
Epistemic Shadows

Chapter 5

Shining a Light into the Shadow of Death: Terminal Care Discourse and Practice in the Late 20th Century

Jason Szabo

Incurable illness has long been the *noli me tangere* of medicine. Nineteenth-century doctors did occasionally celebrate the personal satisfaction of palliating incurables (Coriveaud 1885); generally speaking, however, "hopeless cases" were a source of embarrassment, humiliation, and shame (Carol 2004:29–33; Szabo 2004:228–235). As for the dying process, doctors' main interest long remained its physiological aspects, rather than its personal and social consequences (Carol 2004:13, 128–179). Tellingly, there was only one French "proto-ethnography" of death and dying published during the long 19th century (Lauvergne 1842). The pickings were equally slim in the Anglo-American world, as only a handful of short texts on the care of the dying appeared during this same period (Munk 1887; Browne 1894).

This all began to change in the post-WWII years. After starting as a trickle in the 1950s, a rapidly expanding literature on death, dying, and terminal care appeared alongside a remarkable new socio-medical movement – "hospice." This essay explores the evolution of terminal care discourse before examining the "fieldwork" of two remarkable women generally credited with single-handedly launching this "revolution" – Elisabeth Kübler-Ross and Cicely Saunders. A unique blend of closeness and compassion allowed them to speak on behalf of the dying; in their name, they put forward an influential vision of the "good death." Our examination of the form and substance of their efforts serves as a prelude to discussing their fieldwork's ambiguous legacy and shadowy side. This paper's overarching aim, in fact, is to show that the personal convictions and professional investment which made the late 20th century "science of dying" so compelling also represents its Achilles' heel. This analysis concludes by discussing the lessons this case study offers social scientists interested in the positive and negative effects of being "too close" to the people or the cause they seek to understand.

The Postwar Discovery of Death

It is presumably no accident that three books on the dying process all appeared the same year (1955); one examined the question of medical secrecy (Standard and Helmuth 1955), while the others explored the psychodynamics of terminal illness (Eissler 1955) and the taboos around death in modern Western societies (Gorer 1955). These works, which ranged from pragmatic to provocative, grappled with several issues that increasingly preoccupied a small but influential group of researchers and reformers. Reflecting their training and inclinations, they struggled to answer three questions: What role does death and death awareness play in framing our lives? What impact do social norms have upon the (terminal) illness experience? Finally, how good a job is contemporary medicine doing at addressing the needs of the dying?

A few short years later (1959), three other noteworthy publications saw the light of day. The first was an ambitious, multidisciplinary volume on death, edited by a clinical psychologist named Hermann Feifel (Feifel 1959). Among other things, this work drew attention to a process they called "death denial," understood as a maladaptive response to an *état d'âme* termed "death anxiety." The other works, for their part, laid out the two distinct, and distinctly late-modern, responses to the challenge of incurability. The first, by a young sociologist named Renée Fox, explored the social dynamics and therapeutic ethos prevailing on a "Metabolic Ward," struggling to discover a Miracle Cure for a variety of devastating illnesses (Fox 1959). The others were a series of six short articles in the *Nursing Times* written by an obscure physician named Cicely Saunders, an event marking her debut in a field she eventually defined and dominated – modern palliative medicine (Saunders 1959, a–f). Though they seem worlds apart, these two institutional cultures have more in common than meets the eye. Each catered to the most difficult and unattractive of cases, those dismissed elsewhere as "hopeless." They also mark a watershed moment in the history of medicine, ushering in an era of growing concern with an experience that doctors had traditionally passed over in silence.

Much of the research carried out in the decade and a half which followed does not make for edifying reading. Among reformers' main targets was modern medicine's "cure at all costs" philosophy whose twin pillars were technology and deception. Critics increasingly insisted that prevailing practices were driven less by concerns with the patient's wellbeing than doctors' desire to avoid confronting "failure." Concerned by the pervasiveness of this ethos in American hospitals, Barney Glaser and Anselm Strauss spent several years studying the social dynamics of terminal care and its impact on patients, families, and caregivers.

Their influential work, *Awareness of Dying*, introduced the concept of "awareness contexts" into contemporary parlance (Glaser and Strauss 1965). The concept grew out of repeated observations showing that the way information was (not) shared determined the resulting patterns of behavior. They concluded that there were four awareness contexts prevailing in American health care facilities. The first, the "closed context," existed when the doctor alone knew that a case was hopeless, at most letting the nurse and the family in on "the secret." Those in the know, in turn, continued to present the patient with the official version of the truth. Should increasingly unwell patients begin to have doubts despite everyone's best efforts, a "suspicious awareness context" had emerged. The "mutual pretence context" existed when doctors and patients both "knew" and "knew that they knew," but behaved as though the other was unaware. The final variant was the "open context" wherein diagnostic and prognostic information was freely and openly communicated, even to the patient.

Beyond carefully describing the interpersonal and institutional mechanics underpinning these different (non) communication patterns, this work included an unusually sophisticated discussion of the social dynamics of terminal illness. Among its most compelling claims was that both doctors and "the system" had a vested interest in preserving the status quo, i.e., closed awareness. Doctors were afraid of "getting involved"; institutions preferred unsuspecting patients because they apparently cooperated more readily with hospital routine (Glaser and Strauss 1965:45).

More than anything, this work was an unusually sophisticated manifestation of changing Anglo-American attitudes toward "medical paternalism." In the decade which followed, people increasingly spoke disparagingly of the "medicalization" of daily life, including the medicalization of death. Enunciated most convincingly by the historian Philippe Ariès (1981[1977]: 563–572), this was a two-part argument which assumed, firstly, that "traditional societies" had a wholesome attitude toward death, banding together to assist the dying via certain situation-specific rituals and norms. The dying process, in this context, was apparently both edifying and natural. The second and related assumption was that something highly undesirable began happening in the late 19th century, as doctors and hospitals increasingly took center stage. Rather than dying at home as they had for centuries, people increasingly died in the hospital surrounded by strangers. Technological and technocratic, death had become taboo, foreign, and alienating.

If this meta-narrative played an important role in vindicating the "hospice" approach, technology's function was actually more complicated than many contemporaries realized. For the same people that attacked modernity often simultaneously insisted that untreated pain and suffering was a scandalous affront to human dignity. In retrospect, technology was both culprit and solution, as innovations in surgery, medicine, and pharmacology dramatically increased medicine's palliative capacities. As will now be seen, this was one of several paradoxes left unexplored by the hospice movement's two "founding mothers," Elisabeth Kübler-Ross and Cicely Saunders. Instead, they saw themselves as championing a return to the "good old days" when people apparently did more than simply live to fight another day.

Elisabeth Kübler-Ross, Cicely Saunders, and the Cultivation of Closeness

Like many pioneers in the field of death studies, Elisabeth Kübler-Ross was a psychiatrist. Swiss-born, she focused her attention on the psychodynamics of terminal illness after emigrating to the United States. Sharing the belief that contemporary social mores and "taboos" increased isolation and suffering, she put forward an ambitious agenda for combining research and teaching. In 1965, she began a weekly seminar which took the form of a loosely structured, hour-long, interview with an incurably ill cancer patient in front of a two-way mirror. This testimony was then used to expose frustrations and settle differences between patients, families, and staff.

From humble, informal, beginnings, these sessions attracted growing interest and recognition. Rich with the experience of 200 interviews over several years, she wrote a book summarizing her research. *On Death and Dying* (1969) was radically different from anything which had appeared before in the clinical literature. Mixing transcripts with analytical insights, her work had three objectives: Firstly, to identify the mechanisms cancer patients used to deal with their feelings. Secondly, to encourage health care workers to recognize that their attitudes toward the terminally ill tended to be less than disinterested. The third and overarching aim, it seems clear in retrospect, was to reconfigure the "communication system" between the worlds of the dying and the living in order to unleash its therapeutic potential. Whatever its merits and shortcomings, *On Death and Dying* clearly struck a nerve, selling several hundred thousand copies in the decade and a half following its publication. On the strength of this now canonical text, Kübler-Ross went on to become both a respected spokeswoman for the American hospice movement and something of a mini-industry.

For various reasons, Cicely Saunders has enjoyed a more lasting fame than her American counterpart. Born into the English upper class, her personal and career trajectory combined the conventional and the idiosyncratic. Having seen her nursing career cut short by injury, she worked for a number of years as a social worker before taking up medicine. Some years before her final career switch, she worked as a volunteer at an institution for incurables staffed and run by Catholic nursing sisters. By her own account, she was as impressed by their aggressive approach to controlling pain as by the sisters' care and devotion. Upon graduating, she became the attending physician at another Catholic hospice. Juggling the demands of clinical care with research on the use of analgesics in advanced cancer, she published a number of papers chronicling her experiences. Less than a decade later, she founded Saint Christopher's Hospice (1967), an institution widely credited with pioneering something known as "total person care." A multidisciplinary "team" approach, Saunders presciently realized, would help diminish health care professionals' distaste for terminal care.

Despite their many differences, Saunders and Kübler-Ross shared certain qualities which partly explain their prominence in discussions of the early history of the movement. Most obviously, they had the energy of "true believers" and apparently shared a remarkable gift for public speaking, reimagining the "cancer narrative" using the language and imagery of Romanticism. The importance of touching stories of redemption cannot be overstated. Beyond the propaganda-value in the battle to promote hospice as a wholesome alternative to euthanasia, Saunders's and Kübler-Ross's accounts of the "good death" reminded everyone that life's ultimate journey was something edifying, not humiliating.

It was undoubtedly their willingness and ability to become embedded with the dying which gave Kübler-Ross's and Saunders's accounts power and credibility. By linking intimacy and compassion with observation and action, they provided a receptive society with a new and powerful "science" of death and dying. They emerged as the leading spokespeople for and the public face(s) of the hospice movement; in other words, because they weren't content with criticizing the status quo, they also put forward an optimistic blueprint for change. In their compelling, complementary, accounts of what could be accomplished in the "dying space," they outlined the key components of total care. Even as doctors and nurses palliated physical and emotional suffering, the entire team worked to sustain the patient's failing sense of self. No matter how grim things seemed or became, the dying would find comfort in the idea that everything possible would be done. Despite what was happening to their bodies, hospice-style total care allowed the dying to remain fully alive while encouraging the pursuit of self-knowledge, meaning, and "closure."

Their efforts went neither unnoticed nor unrewarded. In the 1970s, hospice-care emerged as a dynamic, high profile issue whose impact on Anglo-American health care cultures has been substantial. Though effective leadership obviously played a role, their success also reflected the perfect fit between ideas and changing social circumstances. Terminal-care reform, in other words, would never have come about if Kübler-Ross and Saunders hadn't been preaching to people ready to be converted.

Though the 1950s were marked by a degree of conformity, this was also a time of creeping introspection, self-doubt, and activism. In both a positive and negative sense, the era of McCarthyism paved the way for a widespread, far-reaching, and many-fronted assault on "authority." Though obviously one of many, terminal care became an important focus of reformist zeal. Partly this reflected cancer's rising prominence, both demographic and social. Changing disease ecologies, in turn, set the stage for the discovery of an "epidemic" of unassuaged misery, both at home (Marie Curie Memorial Foundation 1952) and in institutional settings (Hughes 1960). Yet the prominence of "death and dying" also reflected a malaise that was rather less focused. Those coming of age in the immediate postwar period inhabited a world where death cast an extremely long shadow. Beyond the millions of casualties from the world wars, two seminal events – Auschwitz and Hiroshima – raised disturbing existential questions. In the postwar era, fears about the future arguably became ever more acute. Though the process was complex, death was an unusually prominent fixture of the Cold War era psyche.

There was more to this period than anxiety, however. WWII also created educational and economic opportunities of a nature and scale never seen before. The GI bill and a protracted economic boom set the stage for the emergence of a well-educated, native-born (largely white) middle class with health insurance. The role of such trends in terminal-care reform goes almost without saying. Growing wealth raised both health care spending and public expectations. Equally importantly, a burgeoning middle class supplied both the lion's share of hospice volunteers and hospice patients. A broad array of trends, within medicine and society at large, set the stage for the meteoric expansion of hospice services in the late 20th century.

Yet as will now be seen, the claims and practices put forward in the early years were neither wholeheartedly nor uncritically accepted. Just as the "death awareness" and hospice movements were gaining traction in the late seventies, individuals began expressing concern about the practices and principles of "hospice." Rather than dissipate in the face of the movement's growing legitimacy, concerns about its objective benefits and limitations have intensified. Catalyzed by a growing AIDS crisis and budget-conscious governments' increasing fixation with "cost-effectiveness," both the rhetoric and substance of hospice have come to be scrutinized. Strikingly then, a counter-movement whose success was based partly on a careful examination of half-conscious motives and a rejection of unthinking complacency now finds itself increasingly under the microscope. And, just as with the "ethos" and practices which prevailed in the immediate postwar period, some of the strengths, weaknesses, and subjectivities of the postmodern science of dying are slowly being examined and discussed.

Still a Few Bugs in the System? Controversies in the Era of Hospice

Despite the obvious appeal of its reformist agenda, concerns about both the substance of the modern science of dying and its repercussions quickly began to surface.[1] With the benefit of hindsight, this was probably inevitable. For if Saunders's and Kübler-Ross's brave forays into the world of the dying gave a remarkable power and authority to their narratives, one sees their particular fingerprints all over the truths they brought back with them from this netherworld. Were that not enough, as more and more adepts applied their methods it became clear that hospice's response to "the dying problem" was nearly as value-laden and arbitrary as the system it had worked to overturn. Rather than receding with time, these concerns were supplemented by another, arguably more seditious, line of questioning: are patients necessarily better off when handled according to hospice/palliative care principles; in other words, does the hospice approach actually work?

Even as its influence was peaking in the early 1980s, some of the basic tenets of the new school of terminal care were being called into question. Among the prime targets was Kübler-Ross's ambitious "stage theory" which claimed that there existed a "natural history of dying" wherein terminally ill patients passed progressively through five stages – denial, anger, bargaining, depression, and acceptance. The Kübler-Ross method, in turn, consisted of exploring patients' personal histories and personality structures in order to help them make peace with themselves and those around them.

Despite some early criticism of both her observations and her methodology (Schulz and Aderman 1974:137–143), "stage theory" was enormously influential for over a decade. Seduced presumably by its conceptual simplicity and therapeutic potential, well-meaning caregivers worked hard to help patients along the road to acceptance. If one Philadelphia-area psychiatrist is to be believed, this was at times done rather indiscriminately. Writing in 1982, just as enthusiasm for her ideas was beginning to wane, Michael A. Simpson observed how there has been, in this area, as in other areas of psychosocial inquiry, a sinister slide from *descriptive* to *prescriptive* models; from descriptions of what some people appear to do, to prescriptions of what everyone ought to do. This can lead to obscene practices, like the School of Nursing I encountered, where the junior nurses were given a half-hour lecture on the Kübler-Ross five, and were then sent out to the bedsides of terminally ill patients with the instruction to "get them through to acceptance" in an hour. God protect us from crude amateur meddling – especially by professionals. [Simpson 1982: 259. Emphasis in original]

Lest one be tempted to dismiss this as a case of professional condescension, one of America's leading nurses similarly spoke of her colleagues' disillusionment with "nursing's simplistic acceptance and interpretation of the (Kübler-Ross) theory" (Germain 1980:52).[2] By the early eighties, an increasingly influential community of researchers and practitioners were insisting that dying patients' emotional lives were both dynamic and unpredictable. For many, if not most, patients skipped one or more stages when they weren't moving backward and forward between them, suggesting that the process was neither invariable nor universal.

While Kübler-Ross was perhaps so deeply drawn into dying people's struggle for an existential foothold that she saw a consistent pattern to it, her harshest critics insisted that she had imagined/created an artificial model in which their experiences were the product of what she hoped and assumed should happen. Invoking the truism that beliefs shape both perceptions and behavior, George Kuykendall spoke for a growing constituency when he wrote in 1982 that "Kübler-Ross' five-stage paradigm is not drawn from her observation of dying patients. She has imposed that paradigm on their experiences. Her paradigm expresses not their experiences, but her own world-view" (Kuykendall 1981–82:41).

A number of factors shaped the "world-views" and attendant therapeutic agendas of the world's leading authorities on terminal care. Among the most influential were firsthand experiences with people who had died what they considered a "good death".[3] *On Death and Dying*, for example, opens with an account of the passing of a humble Swiss farmer, a family friend who died when Kübler-Ross was a child. Seriously injured in an accident, he took leave of those around him in the most exemplary of fashions, dying (apparently) peacefully at home surrounded by loved ones (Kübler-Ross 1969:5–6). In what was to become hallmarks of her therapeutic ideal, he was spared the agony and dilemmas she associated with modern technology even as both he and those around him quietly accepted the inevitable. Clearly profoundly affected by this experience, Kübler-Ross appears to have devoted most of her professional energies to re-creating it.

In Saunders's formative experiences, on the other hand, the prosaic and the mystical intertwine. In both her own accounts of the founding of St. Christopher's and her official biography, allusion is made to her special relationship with two dying patients, David Tasma and Antoni Michniewicz. While acting in her capacity as hospice social worker (Tasma) and, later, hospice physician (Michniewicz), Saunders apparently fell in love with these two strangers while they were on their deathbeds (Du Boulay 1984:55–59, 104–115). This love, it should be stressed, was not physical *per se* but an etherealized union of the mind and the heart. Her evocative claim that dying patients were so beautiful that one could fall in love with them came to be both a therapeutic ideal and a call to arms for Saunders and her nascent movement. If one brought enough loving feelings, it was consistently implied, the burdens of care were incommensurably lighter.

For her many admirers, Saunders's expansive embrace of suffering humanity was the essence of her special gift. Yet skeptics warned that such emotionally demanding and highly personalized care was not without its perils. In 1981, E. Mansell Pattison bemoaned the fact that, since the spread of hospice, researchers had all but stopped paying attention to physicians' emotional responses to the terminally ill. Based on his long experience, he felt that "detached compassion," i.e., productively responding to dying patients' needs while maintaining a healthy distance, still eluded many medical trainees. Those indifferent to thanatology's insights continued to view the dying process as just another professional quandary, "manageable" using the tools of medical science. Equally worrisome, in Pattison's mind, was the increasing tendency of some medical students to display an "exaggerated compassion." For him, the new care paradigm promoted by "influential public figures in thanatology" had encouraged a maladaptive psychological response in certain susceptible individuals wherein:

> instead of withdrawal from the dying, there is psychological fusion with the dying. I have seen these students not only personally identify with the dying person, but seek in their professional care of the dying to undo their own past guilts, relieve past shame, restore personal self-esteem, re-work their own prior death experiences, and anticipate their own death anxieties. [Pattison 1981:54]

Recognizing both its demanding nature and its potential appeal to those grappling with "unresolved issues," some authorities have stressed the need to carefully screen aspiring hospice personnel and volunteers. Seconded by the spirit of mutual support which prevails in most programs, such efforts have almost certainly helped. Yet for all that, staff "burnout" has been and remains a prominent concern.

That the movement has thrived at all speaks volumes about the commitment of its advocates. An examination of their profiles, especially those of volunteers whose unpaid work has been critical to the survival of most programs, allows for some tentative statements about their motives. A number of studies of volunteers indicate that they are overwhelmingly white and female, with an above-average level of education and, often enough, an above average income. For most, the death of a loved one from cancer appears to have prompted a desire to help others. The importance of having lost a loved one from cancer clearly goes further, though. Being able to say "I understand what you're going through" encourages and sustains a mutually satisfying complicity between caregivers and the cared-for.

Religious or spiritual convictions appear to be an equally important source of motivation and strength for many. From the strikingly high frequency of some sort of "religious affiliation" in certain studies of hospice volunteers (Hughes 1988:38–47) to the prominent role accorded chaplains and ministers in hospice programs, terminal care remains a branch of medicine in which secularization is at most only partial. In Britain, where her influence on the evolution of terminal care has been profound, it has been said that the hospice "in general is a Christian institution that reaches out to dying people of many faiths and makes no apology for its Christianity" (Ley and Corless 1988:105).

In the United States, on the other hand, spirituality has arguably been given short shrift. This may in part reflect the relative importance of the medical model in North American palliative medicine. Most people, however, blame public policy. Since the government first began providing hospice benefits in the early eighties, its reluctance to cover spiritual services has consistently been cited as the cause of hospices' failure to "adequately" address dying patients' spiritual needs. Yet even in North American hospice circles, spirituality is taken seriously both as a subject of learned discussion and as a therapeutic tool (cf. Wald 1986).

The power of spiritual and religious beliefs in offering meaning and comfort to dying patients and their caregivers requires little explanation. Yet deep-seated convictions, both spiritual and moral, also probably explain the acute sense of purpose that has long been one of the movement's hallmarks. Critical of a society in which people had all but "forgotten how to die" and confronted with the Supreme Court's recognition of a "woman's right to choose" and a renascent euthanasia movement, hospice has been as much a moral crusade as a therapeutic revolution. Particularly in the early years when it was struggling for legitimacy, some followers' single-minded devotion to "the cause" raised more than a few eyebrows. Even as one American observer insisted that there was something disquieting, almost cult-like, about the Kübler-Ross phenomenon (Klass and

Hutch 1985:102–104), Saunders admitted to having to constantly resist being turned into a "cult figure" (Du Boulay 1984:231). Strikingly, on at least one occasion, she had to rebuke an admirer for whom touching her constituted an act of veneration (Du Boulay 1984:149).

Terminal care, it seems clear, was never "just another" realm of clinical medicine. Yet while serving as a critical wellspring of vitality, the combination of strong personal convictions and formative life experiences probably also partly accounts for the difficulty in integrating dying AIDS patients into the "hospice family."

As with all complex and heterogeneous organizations, the responses of individuals and institutions to AIDS varied considerably. As two knowledgeable North American authors aptly observed in an article entitled "Spirituality and hospice care" (1988): "the response of some in the hospice world has been immediate, compassionate, and innovative. Other hospice programs have refused to accept AIDS patients" (Ley and Corless 1988:108). This observation suggests a stark dichotomy; in fact, there appears to have been at least three distinct behavioral-attitudinal clusters.

In 1985, Mother Theresa persuaded reluctant community groups in Greenwich Village to use the rectory of St. Veronica's Church to house dying AIDS patients, insisting that "each of them is Jesus in distressing disguise" (Anonymous 1986:8–9). That same year, the official organs of the hospice movement in America – the American Society of Hospice Care and the National Hospice Organization – emphatically endorsed the admission of AIDS patients into hospices. Two years later, an NHO-sponsored study showed that 16 percent of hospice programs had already cared for at least one patient with AIDS. Kübler-Ross was probably the highest-profile American advocate for those afflicted with what she called "the ultimate challenge" (Kübler-Ross 1987). In both words and actions, she displayed an acute sensitivity to AIDS patients' plight even as she strove to de-stigmatize the disorder which, she felt, should be viewed no differently than cancer.

Notwithstanding such leadership, many hospice programs had difficulty living up to the NHO's lofty principles. Concerns about contagion, still widespread in the late eighties, always figured prominently. Other observers stressed the unique challenges of dealing with AIDS patients, including their youth, neuro-psychiatric problems, "untraditional" social networks, or unwillingness to abandon aggressive treatments (Clark et al. 1988:851–862). In more than one instance, however, the objections appear to have been rather less principled. At a two-day conference from 1988 in San Francisco entitled "The Hospice Response to AIDS," an observer noted that many delegates expressed "frustrations about dealing with the fears and homophobia of hospice staff and community founders. One participant stated that most of her hospice's community funding would be withdrawn if the rural community learned that the hospice accepted AIDS patients" (Gardner 1988:198). Such concerns were certainly not wasted on hospital administrators; one California-based executive, Claire Tehan, summed up their collective concern with the elliptical observation that "the funding community is relatively conservative" (Lutz 1987). The fears and disapproval of some hospice staff, benefactors, families, and patients are a vivid reminder that, in the eighties, what wasting disease you were dying from now loomed as large as the traditional dying/not dying dichotomy.

In responding to AIDS, Cicely Saunders staked out an ambiguous *via media*. She was quite ready to acknowledge the disease's terrible suffering and agreed with those who argued that hospice's core concerns (quality of life, symptom control, supportive total person care) were just as applicable here as with cancer. Despite this, she initially showed little enthusiasm for allowing them into St. Christopher's. She justified her reticence partly on clinical grounds, arguing that hospice physicians (many of whom were trained in oncology) lacked the knowledge needed to manage the disease and to reliably decide when a given case was purely palliative. Besides, she reminded everyone, St. Christopher's mandate was to serve cancer patients and it was barely keeping up with existing demands.[4] Perhaps sensitive to the reaction that a policy of permanent and outright exclusion might provoke, St. Christopher's eventually adopted a policy of admitting AIDS patients who were dying of cancer (Saunders 1987:7–8), though as she was quick to remind a *Time Magazine* reporter in 1988 "hospice didn't set out to look after everyone in the world who was dying of everything" (Brand 1988:58).

While Saunders's stance presumably influenced some, the attitude of a single person cannot alone account for the emergence of a parallel AIDS hospice infrastructure with its own distinct and largely separate community of patients, physicians, staff, and volunteers. Though imputing motives is always a bit dicey, the relative inertia of elements of the hospice movement toward AIDS clearly speaks to something. Perhaps it was simply differences in life experiences and world-views which made it so difficult for these two communities to come together. For even in settings in which the ambient culture was relatively permissive, there was clearly an awkwardness in bringing together patients whose "otherness" – biological, social, and sexual – was so striking and manifest. That is not to say that the AIDS community took nothing from hospice; it appears to have readily embraced many of its practices and elements of its care philosophy. AIDS activists also paid the movement's founders a compliment by imitating their *modus operandi*, carefully dissecting the failings of the system/culture they hoped to reform. Yet the ingredients for an intimate collaboration, grounded on a sense of shared community and mutual identification, were generally not there. The relatively open embrace of active euthanasia by many AIDS patients and AIDS care-providers during the epidemic's darkest years is perhaps most telling of all. For beyond suggesting that identity politics played themselves out even on people's deathbeds, it constituted another dramatic symbol of the divide between the AIDS subculture and hospice orthodoxy.

And lest one assume that trouble "fitting in" was exclusively limited to those with AIDS, visible minorities also appear to have had issues of their own. Recent studies continue to point to a longstanding phenomenon; African Americans and Hispanics are significantly underrepresented among hospice staff and patients (Colon and Lyke 2003). While structural barriers have clearly limited their access to palliative care, just as with most other medical services, it has been pointed out that African Americans have a "cultural mistrust" of hospice care (Cort 2004). Just as with AIDS, the relative racial and social heterogeneity of hospice personnel and hospice patients raises a fascinating and heretofore largely unexamined question: what elements of the movement's philosophy, institutions, and practices transcend the particular and which are so culturally and socially bounded to resist dissemination outside of its original cultural subsoil?

Conclusion

Since the early nineties, the palliative care movement has been active on two important fronts. On the one hand, it has compellingly argued that the "hospice way" is not somehow cancer-specific, but appropriate for all chronic, debilitating, illnesses. On the other, it has struggled to adapt to changing times, forced to defend its practices in an era when "cost-effective" and "evidence-based medicine" have become the new idols. Several researchers, despite the obvious constraints, have made a spirited effort to measure up using such yardsticks (see for example, Robbins 1998; Abu-Saad 2001). Yet in doing so, they have run up against evidence which on the surface appears to undermine the claim that hospice patients are always objectively better off.

While on the whole favorable, studies of the clinical effectiveness of hospice care yield less clear-cut results than one might perhaps think. A number of them, using various indicators including patients' perceived quality of life, have shown no significant differences between hospice-style and "standard" care. Even if one accepts that, in the aggregate, the dying are better off when every aspect of their "total pain" is addressed, there remains the dilemma of the difficult case. For optimistic assertions made by some in the early seventies that hospice's system of relieving pain and suffering was foolproof (Lamerton 1973:48) have given way to more sober discussions about what to do for those terminally ill people unable to die comfortably and well despite everyone's best efforts.

The challenge to demonstrate the effectiveness of terminal care has also made manifest certain important methodological dilemmas inherent in evaluating suffering and relief. Some interesting work has shown discrepancies, both over- and under-estimations, between what dying patients claim they feel and what those around them – family, nurses, physicians – think that they are experiencing.[5] Interestingly, caregivers' impressions appear to be unstable over time, as their assessment of what patients "went through" changes in the months after the patient's death (Higginson, Priest, and McCarthy 1994:553–557). That such important issues continue to plague this field highlights the elusiveness of the dying experience. It also demonstrates that, despite the efforts of terminal-care reformers to give dying patients a voice, this realm remains something of a black box.

Arguably the most important "distorting mirror" is inseparably linked to the feelings which drove people to get involved in the first place: outrage in the face of a situation that made a mockery of deeply-felt beliefs and principles. In defending the importance of a good death to a good life, social scientists and practitioner-theorists acted on the conviction that what they were championing was not a social virtue, but a fundamental, transcendent, human truth. The principal risk when certainty is underpinned by conviction, of course, is that it can make people immune to self-doubt. Observing the paucity of proof demonstrating its superiority, those behind the 1979 study showing a dramatic change in physicians' attitudes to disclosing a cancer diagnosis hit it right on the head when they pointed out that "our data suggest that, as in Oken's 1961 study, the present policy is supported by strong belief and emotional investment in its being right" (Novack et al. 1979:900).

Another thing encouraging people to "see what they are inclined to see" that is particularly pronounced in this setting and potentially even more refractory is that death narratives and practices have nearly as much to do with the needs of "survivors" as of patients. As Margaret Robbins observed in one particularly insightful passage: "to an extent, the account of terminal illness and death and the feelings attached, constitute a story made up and rehearsed by the home carers, the patient before death, and also the health care professionals in contact with the family before and after death" (Robbins 1998:72). Arguably, this is a necessary, even inevitable, tradeoff that helps loved ones and professionals overcome an aversion to suffering. Yet soothing stories, like deep-seated convictions, can engender complacency.

To their credit, leaders within the palliative care community seem cognizant of the pitfalls and genuinely committed to allowing patients to set the agenda as much as possible. The movement also continues to attract and embrace interested outsiders from disciplines like sociology and anthropology, protecting it against insularity while remaining attuned to the impact of changing circumstances on the dying experience. A number of the movement's most prominent spokespeople have also stressed the importance of embracing social, cultural, and ideological diversity.

Ultimately, the intimate connection that practitioner-theorists forged with the dying, while exposing some of the subjective "baggage" shaping the illness experience, by no means eliminated it. Acquiring conceptual knowledge through a close familiarity with the dying and their world, it would seem, is a bit like finding one's way out of a forest by leveling the obstacles blocking one's path. While allowing in some light and opening up a trail, the falling of mature trees gives seedlings all the more room to grow. This, I would argue, in no way calls into question the hospice movement's notable accomplishments or its commitment to the humane ideals it has so consistently championed. Rather, by showing that subjective, value-laden judgments continue to affect how we perceive and respond to the "dying problem," this essay hopes to carry on the work of those who first drew attention to the plight of the dying nearly a half-century ago. If the neglect of the dying remains a problem, we should also be wary of uncritically embracing the idea that there is some universally desirable "death worth dying." Perhaps the best that we can hope for is a renewal of interest among social scientists in a vitally important issue that, for all the progress that has been made, should perhaps always remain a work in progress.

Acknowledgments

I would like to thank the editors, Thomas Schlich, and William Seidelman for their helpful suggestions on an earlier version of this paper, as well as Charles E. Rosenberg and George Weisz for their careful reading of a late draft.

Notes

1 It should be stressed that thanatologists and physician-reformers were convinced that their methodology was scrupulously scientific and that their reformist ambitions grew out of their observations rather than the other way round.

2   It is important to stress that there is no evidence that such normative pressures were universal and it would be wrong to suggest that people as sophisticated and well-intentioned as Saunders or Kübler-Ross would have condoned
such awkward, heavy-handed, practices.

3   Strikingly, an equally decisive death experience (albeit usually of a particularly
unpleasant and alienating death) appears to be a constant among those with
an equally fervent and lifelong commitment to the euthanasia movement.

4   Letter dated November 11, 1986 from Cicely Saunders to the Archbishop of
Canterbury (Clark 2006:287–288). That the foundation's first duty was to
serve cancer patients was repeated in a letter dated February 23, 1987 (Clark
2006:295).

5   Summarizing one of the largest such studies, Margaret Robbins noted that
"staff members rated pain as less severe than patient or family member, that
patients rated their own anxiety as much less extreme than either team or
family member, and that family members perceived more problems than either
staff or patients" (1998:73).

6   One recent example is the article by Karen E. Steinhauser et al. (2000), which
showed that, while there was broad concordance, physicians tended to ascribe
less importance to issues like "not being a burden" or "coming to peace with
God" than their dying patients.

7   Without wanting to alienate some of its staunchest supporters, one prominent
physician recently called for a Rawlsian-style reform of the rhetoric of terminal
care, proposing to dispense with its explicit religious references in favor of a
more universally palatable secular humanism (Kissane 2004). In a spirit of
cultural rapprochement, another internationally respected spokesman, Balfour
Mount, invokes the attitudes toward death of various "knowledge traditions"
in his lectures on palliative care rather than a narrowly Christian one. Such
public pronouncements, while tacitly acknowledging the increasingly diverse
societies in which the movement now operates, have the added benefit of emphasizing the transcendent and universal appeal of its core principles.

References

Abu-Saad, Huda
   2001   Evidence-Based Palliative Care Across the Life Span. Oxford: Blackwell
   Science.
Anonymous
   1986   News Briefs – Mother Theresa Boosts Hospice Program for AIDS
   Victims. The American Journal of Hospice Care 3(2):8–9.
Ariès, Philippe
   1981 [1977]   The Hour of Our Death. Helen Weaver, trans. New York: Knopf.
   The original work (1977) was entitled L'homme devant la mort, Paris: Seuil.
Brand, David
   1988   Dying with Dignity. Time 132(2), September 5:57–58.

Browne, Oswald
   1894   On the Care of the Dying. A Lecture to Nurses. London: George Allen.
Carol, Anne
   2004   Les médecins et la mort: XIXe–XXe siècle. Paris: Aubier.
Clark, Christina, Alice Curley, Anne Hughes, and Rachel James
   1988   Hospice Care: A Model for Caring for the Person with AIDS. Nursing
   Clinics of North America, 23(4):851–862.
Clark, David, ed.
   2006   Cicely Saunders – Founder of the Hospice Movement. Selected Letters
   1959–1999. Oxford: Oxford University Press.
Colon, M., and J. Lyke
   2003   Comparison of Hospice Use and Demographics among European
   Americans, African Americans, and Latinos. American Journal of Hospice and
   Palliative Care 20(3):182–190.
Coriveaud, Adrien
   1885   Le Médecin en face des maladies incurables, son rôle et ses devoirs, dis-
   cours prononcé à l'assemblée de l'Association des médecins de la Gironde, tenue
   à Bourg le . . . 31 mai 1885. Bordeaux: Gounouilhou.
Cort, M. A.
   2004   Cultural Mistrust and Use of Hospice Care: Challenges and Remedies.
   Journal of Palliative Medicine 7(1):63–71.
Du Boulay, Shirley
   1984   Cicely Saunders. Founder of the Modern Hospice Movement. London:
   Hodder and Stoughton.
Eissler, Kurt Robert
   1955   The Psychiatrist and the Dying Patient, New York: International
   Universities Press.
Feifel, Herman
   1959   The Meaning of Death. New York: McGraw-Hill.
Fox, René
   1959   Experiment Perilous: Physicians and Patients Facing the Unknown.
   Glencoe IL: Free Press.
Gardner, Karen
   1988   The Hospice Response to AIDS. Quality Review Bulletin 14(6):198–
   199.
Germain, Carol P.
   1980   Nursing the Dying: Implications of Kübler-Ross' Staging Theory. The
   Annals of the American Academy 447:46–58.
Glaser, Barney G., and Anselm L. Strauss
   1965   Awareness of Dying. Chicago: Aldine.
Gorer, Geoffrey
   1955   The Pornography of Death. Encounter 5:49–52.
Higginson J., P. Priest, and M. McCarthy
   1994   Are Bereaved Family Members a Valid Proxy for a Patient's Assessment of Dying? Social Science and Medicine 38(4):553–557.

Hughes, Brigadier General Glyn
  1960   Peace at Last – a Report to the Calhouste Gulbenkian Foundation.
Hughes, Marsha Magnusen
  1988   Perceptions and Services of Hospice Volunteers. An Evaluation of Wisconsin Hospices. American Journal of Hospice Care 5(3):38–47.
Kissane, David W.
  2004   Discovering Meaning in Illness and Suffering. The Seventh Annual Sandra Goldberg Lecture, McGill University, Montreal, May 4.
Klass, Dennis, and Richard Hutch
  1985   Elisabeth Kübler-Ross as a Religious Leader. Omega 16(2):89–109.
Kübler-Ross, Elisabeth
  1969   On Death and Dying. New York: Macmillan.
Kübler-Ross, Elisabeth
  1987   AIDS. The Ultimate Challenge. New York: Collier Books.
Kuykendall, George
  1981   Care for the Dying: A Kübler-Ross Critique. Theology Today 38:37–48.
Lamerton, Richard
  1973   Care of the Dying. London: Priory Press.
Lauvergne, Hubert
  1842   De l'agonie et de la mort dans toutes les classes de la société, sous le rapport humanitaire, physiologique, et religieux, Tome I-II. Paris: Baillière.
Ley, Dorothy C. H., and Inge B. Corless
  1988   Spirituality and Hospice Care. Death Studies 12(2):101–110.
Lutz, Sandy
  1987   Hospices Seen as Alternative for AIDS Care, but Executives Fear Possible Ramifications. Modern Healthcare, April 24.
Marie Curie Memorial Foundation
  1952   Report on a National Survey Concerning Patients with Cancer Nursed at Home.
Munk, William
  1887   Euthanasia: or, Medical Treatment in Aid of an Easy Death. London: Longmans, Green and Co.
Novack, Denis, R. Plumer, R. L. Smith, H. Ochtill, G. R. Morrow, and J. M. Bennett
  1979   Changes in Physicians' Attitudes Towards Telling the Cancer Patient. JAMA 241(9):897–900.
Pattison, E. Mansell
  1981   Detached Compassion and its Distortions. *In* Thanatology. Bernard Schoenberg, Arthur C. Carr, Austin H. Kutscher, Lester C. Mark, Robert DeBellis, David Peretz, and Irwin Gerber, eds. Education of the Medical Student in Thanatology. New York: Arno Press.
Robbins, Margaret
  1998   Evaluating Palliative Care. Establishing the Evidence Base. Oxford: Oxford University Press.

Saunders, Cicely
1959a   Care of the Dying 1. The Problem of Euthanasia. Nursing Times, October 9:960–961.
Saunders, Cicely
1959b   Care of the Dying 2. Should a Patient Know . . . ? Nursing Times, October 16:994–995.
Saunders, Cicely
1959c   Care of the Dying 3. Control of Pain in Terminal Cancer, Nursing Times, October 23:1031–1032.
Saunders, Cicely
1959d   Care of the Dying 4. Mental Distress in the Dying, Nursing Times, October 30:1067–1069.
Saunders, Cicely
1959e   Care of the Dying 5. The Nursing of Patients Dying of Cancer. Nursing Times, November 6:1091–1092.
Saunders, Cicely
1959f   Care of the Dying Care of the Dying 6. When a Patient Is Dying. Nursing Times, November 19:1129–1130.
Saunders, Cicely
1987   Hospice for AIDS Patients. American Journal of Hospice Care 4(6):7–8.
Schulz, Richard, and David Aderman
1974   Clinical Research and the Stages of Dying. Omega 5(2):137–143.
Simpson, Michael A.
1982   Therapeutic Uses of Truth. *In* The Dying Patient. The Medical Management of Incurable and Terminal Illness, Eric Wilkes, ed. Ridgewood, NJ: George A. Bogden and Son.
Standard, Samuel, and Nathan Helmuth, eds.
1955   Should the Patient Know the Truth? A Response of Physicians, Nurses, Clergymen and Lawyers. New York: Springer.
Steinhauser, Karen E., Nicholas A. Christakis, Elizabeth C. Clipp, Maya McNeilly, Lauren McIntyre, and James A. Tulsky
2000   Factors Considered Important at the End of Life by Patients, Family, Physicians, and Other Care Providers. JAMA 284(19):2476–2482.
Szabo, Jason
2004   Suffering, Shame, and the Search for Succour: Incurable Illness in Nineteenth-Century France. Ph.D. dissertation, McGill University.
Wald, Florence S., ed.
1986   In Quest of the Spiritual Component of Care for the Terminally Ill. Proceedings of a colloquium, Yale University School of Nursing, New Haven, May 3–4.

Chapter 6

The Hidden Side of the Moon, or, "Lifting Out" in Ethnographies

Annette Leibing

Prelude: The Hidden Side of the Moon

> *Seht ihr den Mond dort stehen?*   *Do you see the moon there?*
> *Er ist nur halb zu sehen,*   *It is only half visible*
> *Und ist doch rund und schön!*   *And yet it is so round and fair.*
> *So sind wohl manche Sachen,*   *Thus it is with many things:*
> *Die wir getrost belachen,*   *We thoughtlessly mock them*
> *Weil uns're Augen sie nicht sehen.*   *Because we cannot see them.*
> *[3rd strophe of Matthias Claudius' [1740–1815] Abendlied [Evening song]; set to music by Franz Schubert and others]*

When I first started to think about the topic of the invisible – the data in the shadow – the above-cited "Abendlied" from my childhood always sprang to mind.[1] In its third strophe, the hidden side of the moon is a metaphor for someone's ignorance when judging or ridiculing something on appearance. The moon, and its light, could easily be perceived to be cold or frightening. The author Matthias Claudius, however, was a happy family man steeped in texts stemming from German romanticism – he sensed the moon as beautiful. What bothers him is the totality of sensing – part of the problem I want to elaborate in this article.

I was visiting Berlin the summer I began thinking about the data in the shadow, and there I bought a small book written by Walter Benjamin called "Childhood in Berlin around Nineteen Hundred." One of this book's *Märchenphotographien* (fairy tale photos), to use Theodor Adorno's term for Benjamin's miniature texts made of memories and melancholy, carries the title *The Moon*. In this text, the moon illuminates a second or parallel world ("Nebenerde," p. 75) that does not exist during the day. One has to wait for the right moment of the moonlight in order to be able to see.

> When it [the moon] was standing in my room and I woke up, I did not seem to exist anymore in that room . . . At that moment, the first thing I set my eyes on were the two cream-colored sinks . . . During the day I never even thought of looking at them. However, in the moonlight the blue garland on the rim of the sink . . . became a nuisance. (. . .) With surprise I found that nothing could urge me to think the world. Its nonexistence would not have been any bit more questionable than its existence, which seemed to wink at its nonexistence. [Benjamin 1987:74 and 75; trans. A.L.]

In the fall of that same year, I saw in Montreal Robert Lepage's movie *La face cachée de la lune*. The story is about the struggling philosopher Philippe, who is able to see himself in a different light after his mother's death, which had evoked scenes of his childhood and, as a result, caused him to reflect on the absurdity of his and his brother's present life. Here, the hidden extant in a parallel world is, in reality, the complement of, or in dialogue with, the world in the foreground.[2] Like Walter Benjamin, who is writing about his childhood in Berlin, sensing that he probably would not see the city again, Robert Lepage's Philippe is only able to see hidden aspects of his life through the passage of time, triggered by a major event (for Benjamin it was the shadow of Hitler's regime, for Philippe the loss in a mother's death). The backward glance provides a new emotional coloring of the past, which reflects on the present – a temporal, and often spatial, distance that potentially enables the viewing of details in a different light: completely new elements can emerge, while others slip away into a new distribution of darkness.

What does all of this have to do with my own "blurred borders between ethnography and life," the subtitle of this volume? The reason I became interested in writing about the topic of the invisible, the shadow, was my own increasing awareness of the emotional coloring of my perceptions of the world in which I was living and doing research. It is an autobiographical inquietude that is the source of this article, as is the case for most of the authors' works in this volume. I do use my own areas of invisibility in fieldwork as a starting point, but I rely only initially on this kind of personal data. My goal here is more technical: to discuss a possible approach toward data in the shadows, which in the following will be called "lifting out."

Interlude: Emotional Categorization

After I had lived for more than ten years in Brazil, moving to Quebec seemed easy. Brazil is often called the "country of contrasts" (Bastide 1979; see also Leibing 2001) – the overwhelmingly noisy, colorful, tender, and cruel place of living and doing fieldwork. Conversely, in many respects Quebec is not so different from Germany, my country of origin. Quebec I would describe in more pastel colors, with a greater interiority and where Schubert *lieder* might go with some of its emotional landscapes instead of sounding like Fitzcaraldo's operas in Werner Herzog's film, as they did in Brazil. But the move wasn't so easy.

When describing my life in Brazil in the most general terms, it is easiest to name three periods. First there was a period of fascination in which I idealized Brazil with its smiling faces, easy communication, and sensuality. This was followed by a second period of disenchantment and deception with Brazil's everyday violence (not only in the form of firearms). In the third period I more carefully mediated between my values as a modified German and the Brazilian reality. A similar, but less delineated and much quicker, process happened in Quebec.

Now, as I look back and reflect on my process of partially "nativizing" in Brazil and Quebec, I notice the strength and influence of an emotional fluctuation in the way in which I was able to see and to interpret my life, the country in which I was living, and my research data. I was unable on several occasions to feel or to see "the hidden side of the moon." On a personal level this might have no implications. With respect to ethnographic data, this kind of "blindness," however, invokes a major conundrum in science: the fact that truth claims are anchored in worldviews, paradigms, or moodiness. The corollary of this conundrum is the question of how any data, once having become a scientific text, a fact, or general knowledge, can be eventually "denaturalized" – that is, have its layers of the taken-for-granted uncovered. I suggest here that "seeing the past," as I will describe it later on, is a first step in a critical dialogue with data previously collected.

When I began my research in Brazil, it was the other, the exotic, at the foreground of my interest. For my master thesis, for example, my research took place in a small village. I studied the interplay of psychiatric medications (and individualizing biomedical concepts) with local healing ceremonies that blurred the boundaries of the individual body through the incorporation into the healing process of other community members. The longer I stayed in Brazil, the more I turned my gaze to urban phenomena, closer to my own everyday life, although still mostly linked to psychiatry.

This is part of a general tendency in anthropology – a growing interest in studying one's own culture rather than the exotic other (e.g., Marcus 1999). However, I did not study Germany; Brazil had become a (partial) home to me. I became a researcher of an otherness that – through the deeply emotional and conflictful process of engaging with that country as a home – resulted in an epistemological privilege (see Labaree 2002) – a privilege that at the same time undermined those details that had become commonsense, everyday life and which were often smashed between home-sickness and idealization or the need for normality.

I have been speaking of the role of emotions – or, better, "moodiness" – as inevitable in approaching data of any sort. My arguments go beyond the personal level of emotions, or what Paula Saukko calls "emotional subjectivism" (2002:247ff.): the exploration of intimate experiences in autobiographies. These autobiographical explorations, although revealing additional layers of data when compared to more descriptive texts, risk becoming a "'talk-show dilemma' of uncritically rehashing familiar tropes . . . as 'authentic' experience" (Saukko 2002:248). Emotionality or moodiness, as conceived in this article, and the notion of ideology are similar in that both describe the way people relate to their world; emotions can be defined as embodied ideologies. "Ideology," for Louis Althusser (2001:9), is "a representation of the imaginary relation of individuals to the real condition of existence." This is a material relationship because "an ideology always exists in an apparatus, and its practice, or practices" (ibid.:12). These practices exist in and lead to the formation of categories, that not only help to order the world one lives in, but without which this reality would be a chaos and unliveable. A category, "something . . . in-between a thing and an action . . . , historical and political artifacts" (Bowker and Star 2002), is infused with deeply emotional ideologies. The emotional quality of understanding the world and looking at the past might be crucial to thinking about data in the shadow (e.g., Crapanzano 1986). In other words, a dialogue with the past does not mean the discovery of a final truth or an archaeology of the inner self, but a process of sensibilization towards one's own and others' categorizations of the world.

What is at stake here is not so much *that* emotions (or ideologies) form the way one is able to understand and be in the world, but the implications and impact of that fact, that is, often unrecognized relations of power[3] that can lead to conflict, suffering, and prejudice. I want to situate my arguments between the emotional categorization of ethnography and the act of looking back as a tool for getting in contact with the invisible – be it the hidden, the unconscious, the denied, or the forbidden. An example of this can be found in two publications by medical anthropologist Nancy Scheper-Hughes and their reception in the countries in which the fieldwork was conducted. On the back cover of her 1972 ethnography about schizophrenia in rural Ireland, the *Irish Times* is quoted: "It is easy *to question* and even *to disagree* with some of the inferences drawn from the results" (emphasis added). Likewise, Scheper-Hughes' book *Death without Weeping* (1992) received harsh critiques from Brazilian intellectuals. The book, which has never been translated into Portuguese, is about the difficulty of mothers living in a *favela* in the state of Pernambuco: difficulties related to extreme poverty, high infant mortality, and the provision of care for infants. The book has been criticized, for example, by the Brazilian anthropologist Lygia Sigaud (1995) who writes that Scheper-Hughes:

> was selective in relation to the mothers' behavior toward their babies and the behavior of the other inhabitants of that neighborhood in the face of poverty. The selection criterion seems to have been whether the behaviors were shocking to her (. . .) [The questions the author asks in this book] only make sense if one begins with the assumption that there exist "natural" or "normal" behaviors of mothers toward their babies, and of poor people toward poverty. [p. 170f.; trans. A.L.]

One could argue that Scheper-Hughes held up the mirror to taboos in both Ireland and Brazil, so that people of the respective countries found it difficult to deal with those parts of reality excluded from public discourse. But also the contrary might be argued: Scheper-Hughes has been so involved in what she calls "militant anthropology" (1995) that she was selective in her observations and filtered them through ideologies associated with militancy. As the Brazilian anthropologist Luís R. Cardoso de Oliveira (2004) argued, ". . . this kind of militancy seems to have negative ethical-normative implications, in that it leads to an excessively selective attitude in relation to the native point of view, which is transformed into an appendix of the good ideas and solutions of the illuminated anthropologist" (p. 12; transl. A.L.). But neither argument is to be made here, as the focus is on those in-between spaces that only the accusations and defenses can reveal. This involves looking at the way arguments are made based on emotional categorization: the arguments concerning *Death without Weeping* point to certain taboos in Brazil, for instance the criticism of a mother (conceived as a saint) or the criticism of the general myth of a child-friendly society. Conversely, the arguments also point to certain taboos in North American militancy, namely the perception and presentation of data that might contradict or mitigate a call to action.

But, then, how to get closer to these in-between spaces, the "hidden side of the moon"?

Approaching Data in the Shadow

The search for knowledge is therefore an exercise in reminiscence. [Avishai Margalit 2002:2, writing about Plato]

Symptoms are meaningless traces; their meaning is not discovered, excavated from the hidden depth of the past, but constructed retroactively. [Slavoj Žižek 1991:188–189]

Visuality

The majority of things about which we write as anthropologists have been observed through the human eye. However, this observation is often made with the help of technologies, creating various visualities. Joseph Dumit (2004) has argued that in the case of technologies of seeing, images become "recaptioned, decontextualized, and recontextualized," something he calls "visuality" or "visual truth" (p. 17). Faith in science and its technologies – and this includes anthropological training in data gathering – is but one solution for the hope of being able to see. Good examples for explaining visuality are technologies which are visual enhancers, such as the PET Scan (Positron Emission Tomography) or MRI (Magnetic Resonance Imaging) in medicine, the telescope in astronomy, or the microscope in biology and medicine, which provide valuable information through images, revealing what was once invisible. But it might take centuries to develop the technology to see what is hidden in a particular instance, and, as several scholars have argued (e.g., Thomas Kuhn, Ludwik Fleck), a breakthrough additionally needs to fit into the general knowledge of that time in order to become true (see also Maseri 1997:1014).[4] Further, many of these images have to be "read" – or decontextualized (Dumit) – by specialists, and as a result, the same visualizing technology can show different realities, depending on the way it is being integrated into expertise (Dumit 1995).[5]

Lynn Gamwell argues, in her article about the history of the microscope, that the evolution of this instrument not only meant increasingly sharper images of ever smaller parts due to advances in technology, but also resulted in new ways of conceptualizing seeing in the general contemporary culture. For example, at the end of the 19th century, French symbolist Odilon Redon drew an analogy between his subjective moods and microorganisms he saw through the microscope, "both hidden and potentially morbid" (p. 49); and late-19th-century architects created spaces resembling cells or slices of tissue prepared for the microscope. Not only the world one lives in shapes the way one is able to see, but also what one sees shapes the world (see also Brecht and Nikolow 2000). In short, images are "the result of a collective disciplining process," including regulatory guidelines and more informal arrangements (Cambrosio and Keating 2000:249).

Ethnographies generally depend on the anthropologist's capacity to observe and the anthropological training can be perceived as a technology of seeing. This, however, is often a solution embedded in ocular epistemology – a model of inquiry "assert[ing] that accurate representations of the world can be produced [to] . . . map the worlds of real experience" (Denzin 1997). It is revealing that Claude Lévi-Strauss, at the beginning of his well-known book *Tristes Tropiques* (1976), describes New York poetically; he compares New York's streets to shady valleys in which colorful cars look like flowers. He then describes his arrival in Rio de Janeiro, comparing its famous hills to stumps in a toothless mouth. While in the United States the (expected) modern world is experienced as beautiful, in Brazil the urban world is described as ugly. It is the good savage he is prepared to see in Brazil. Although he *sees* and is shocked by the misery he finds in Brazil's remote native communities, the people and the surrounding nature are perceived and described as beautiful and authentic, permitting Lévi-Strauss to write again in the most poetic of metaphors.

Befindlichkeit

If visuality reveals but also hides, what other approaches can be "envisioned"? What has been critically called "ocular epistemology" refers to the illusion of observing reality in its complexity through seeing. Nevertheless, in English "seeing" can also mean a much deeper process of understanding, for example in the expression "you see?," meaning "do you understand what I mean?" (see Leibing, in press). In this sense, seeing is the result of arriving at a conclusion; it can involve all senses, not just the eyes. Thus "seeing" involves "the multisensory modes of constructing and experiencing the world that all cultures possess" (Howes 2003:45; see Zimmerman 2001 on the struggle of 19th-century German anthropologists to ban subjectivity from their looking at objects).

Another angle from which to view this theoretical problem is to use the notion of *Befindlichkeit* in the sense given to it by the German philosopher Martin Heidegger. The German verb *sich befinden* means both to be located somewhere and a state of feeling a certain way; *sich finden* means to find oneself. In *Being and Time* (1962), Heidegger describes sensing as emotional or "moody" and notes how sensing forms perceptions of the world that cannot be reduced to ocular "seeing":

This is shown by bad moods. In these, Dasein [Being; A.L.] becomes blind to itself, the environment with which it is concerned veils itself, the circumspection of concern gets led astray. States of mind [=Befindlichkeit; also translated as attunement; see King 2001] are so far from being reflected upon, that precisely what they do is to assail Dasein in its unreflecting devotion to the "world" . . . A mood assails us. It comes neither from "outside" nor from "inside," but arises out of Being-in-the-world . . . Having a mood is not related to the psychical in the first instance . . . It is precisely when we see the "world" unsteadily and fitfully in accordance with our moods, that the ready-to-hand shows itself in its specific worldhood, which is never the same from day to day. (. . .) Yet even the purest theory has not left all moods behind; even when we look theoretically at what is just present-at-hand . . . [B]ut pointing this out is not to be confused with attempting to surrender science ontically to "feeling." [p. 177f.; emphasis added]

Getting closer to the invisible through awareness of *Befindlichkeit* might overcome some of the limitations of "visuality" by including and thematizing the unsteadiness of sensing the world due to emotions. This is not the space to critically discuss the concepts of *Befindlichkeit* and *Dasein* (see, for example, Wenning 2002). It suffices to say that, according to Heidegger, overcoming the "blinding" of sensing the world through moods is never completely possible. For the moment, I discuss a possibility for approaching this kind of "veiled" data that is tightly linked to *Befindlichkeit*. I call this possibility "lifting out," after philosopher and psychologist Eugene Gendlin.

Lifting out

Some authors think that Heidegger's *Befindlichkeit* is a passive state because of another of his notions, *Geworfenheit*, "to be thrown into the world" (e.g., Lübcke 1992). For Eugene Gendlin (1978), though, *Befindlichkeit* is an active state and a positioning towards and within the world, not necessarily an interior state.

This understanding is active . . . We have had some part in getting ourselves into these situations, in making the efforts in response to which these are now the facts, the difficulties, the possibilities, and the mood has the implicit "understanding" of all that, because this understanding was inherent already in how we lived all that, in an active way. [Gendlin 1978:44]

Gendlin describes a process of naming (or "lifting out") through which elements sensed as problematic are recontextualized. This is an act that creates new perspectives on a given situation. He gives the example of a woman in psychotherapy and explains her step-by-step transformation by paying attention to "lifting out" within each step.

> In this example one can see what I call "content mutation." . . . In retrospect the steps can make a chain of thought, but moving forward *each step comes by contradicting the previous one.* What does this contradicting? It is the "sensing" that happens during the silences between. She has the "feel" of it, and this feel is each time different than what she has said. [ibid.; emphasis added]

When this process has been successful, the result is the revelation of data that had previously been eclipsed in the shadow. This process is first of all *felt*, and only subsequently becomes cognicized. "To go back into how one has been living is a forward-moving step," writes Gendlin (ibid.).

Neo-Lacanian Slavoj Žižek makes a similar point to Gendlin. In his article "The truth arises from misrecognition" (1991), Žižek calls attention to the importance of misrecognition (Gendlin would call this "contradicting") in the approach toward a truth lying beyond the most obvious data. He warns that "if we want to spare ourselves the painful roundabout route through the misrecognition, we miss the truth itself" (p. 196). Žižek uses the example of Elizabeth and Darcy, the main characters in Jane Austen's novel *Pride and Prejudice*, whose misrecognition of each other (through pride and prejudice) is what above has been mentioned as the incapacity to see "the hidden side of the moon"; it is "only the 'working through' of the misrecognition which allows us to accede to the true nature of the other and at the same time to overcome our own deficiency" (idem). It is the interconnectedness of Darcy's pride and Elizabeth's prejudice and the disturbing clash that reveals the falsity of the protagonist's characters (e.g., Elizabeth is a not a pretentious empty-minded woman by herself, but she is this through Darcy's eyes). Several circumstances in the story enable the protagonists' discovery of the real nature of the other and, as Žižek argues, lead to a "true love." Had they stayed together at the beginning of the story, within the context of pride and prejudice, their love might only have been rather shallow. This enlightening discovery, achieved only through disharmony – something Gendlin would call "lifting out" – can be found in the work of various other authors as well.

Paula Saukko (2002) makes a similar point when she discusses "agonistic dialogues" that emphasize differences. She opposes these dialogues to dialogical methodologies or triangulation that involves the negotiation of a common reality.

> The trouble with these consensual or amalgamating programs [of negotiating a shared reality] is that it threatens to muddle the specificity of the perspectives [and] . . . this may undo the original quest to capture different views . . .

> Agonistic dialogues . . . underline the distinctive nature of each perspective, deriving from the fact that each individual approaches the world from a slightly different location/angle . . . [T]he aim of the agonistic model is to bring different perspectives into an egalitarian political dialogue, which *alters the individual perspectives* and changes the course of the history . . . [p. 255; emphasis added]

Saukko's suggestion is akin to "lifting out" in that a disturbing element – the perspective of a differently positioned person – brings into question the taken-for-granted and eventually leads to the perception of a reality that had been in the shadow. It is not the case that a new narrative replaces the former one, but that the gap and the divergences between these narratives provide new material for reflection.

Another example is Marilyn Strathern's suggestion that gaps and differences should be at the center of ethnographic studies. This centering helps to avoid pitfalls such as naturalizing those gatekeeping concepts (such as community versus individualism) anthropologists invented to describe "the other"; concepts that when used in comparisons highlight certain cultural features and overshadow others. Instead of denying or inverting such gatekeeping concepts, Strathern suggests exposing them, and thus the noncomparability of cultures, through a "disturbing encounter" (Strathern gives the example of an encounter of Melanesian Highland men and women with Western feminists), which forces the anthropologist (through lifting out, we would say; or through astonishment; see Leibing 2004) to mediate between the two positions.

> This would require being open to a form of negation that did not just deny one proposition in favor of another, by reversing its terms, but refused to "see" that a proposition had been put forward at all. A distinction between gift and commodity economies would, after all, carry little weight if one's interest were in men and women's respective power over the manipulation of things. [p. 95]

Coming back to the example of Elizabeth and Darcy in *Pride and Prejudice* – the new vision of the loved one does not make Elizabeth or Darcy only good and noble persons. The former vision that was wrong in its *totality* is still valid, although having lost its importance due to a richer perception of the other. Only the consideration of *both* visions enables to shed light on, for example, the incorporation of class relations (they belong to different classes) or gender-specific clichés. Lifting out can be accidental and circumstantial as in the case of Jane Austen's novel. It can be forced or fostered through techniques such as artificial encounters (Strathern) or agonistic dialogues (Saukko). It is most often the act of looking back

– seeing the past as incongruent with the present – that enables the formulation of new insights and new positionings. It is though problematic that Gendlin in the end looks at understanding through *Befindlichkeit* as an individual process for psychotherapy (though less intrapsychic in its approach than most psychotherapies). The individuals in his model ideally reaches an insight, which is perceived as total, a "successful psychotherapy" (Žižek's "true love" could be easily understood as final, as well); I want to argue instead in favor of a partial view (see Haraway 1995), of the partial and situated "lifting out".

Reflections on seeing the past

Upon the release of another edition of her book on schizophrenia in Ireland, Scheper-Hughes added a longer preface (2001) and published an article (2000). In these she discusses a conflicting encounter with the people of the village she had studied 20 years earlier. Beside the fact that anthropological approaches have changed, a recategorization of her perceptions of the world – her own and the one of the community she had studied – could happen, because she reacted to the criticism stemming from the people she had described in her book. Like Carolyn Ellis (1995) who perceived her earlier fieldwork under a different light after being confronted by the angry community she had written about,[6] Scheper-Hughes (2000) describes, as an accusation of "blindness," the hostility from the community members and other Irish communities who reacted to her book. For example, Scheper-Hughes argues that a journalist from an Irish Catholic journal "charged me with religious bias[,] suggesting that I was 'strangely insensitive to the religious idealism of the people' and that my 'hostility . . .' had made me tone deaf in my interpretation of religious phenomena" (p. 126). Scheper-Hughes then describes the positive side of the community she had previously painted in dark and "maddening" colors, due to her earlier assumptions (following Foucault) that a culture can largely be defined by what it excludes. Her new (2000) description is also distinctly emotional and plays with different lights and shadows. Although Scheper-Hughes was expelled from the community after her return, and no common ground of understanding has been found, changes in both community and anthropologist can be observed and articulated (like a more conscious child-raising in that community, something which had been criticized in the book). A further rewriting of Scheper-Hughes' text could be imagined, when the author one day meets the community under different circumstances.[7]

Lifting out is therefore about the complexity of positioning oneself and taking a critical stance toward changing categorization. This foremost provides a possibility to rethink the once perceived in a new light through which a new text about a certain topic might eventually emerge. This is a process that involves the author, but is not about the author herself, nor does she have to appear in the new text, except when this is explicitly the topic.

The film *Blind Spot – Hitler's Secretary*, by André Heller and Othmar Schmiderer (2002), is a further example for this kind of positioning. The film shows the late Traudl Junge, who worked for Adolf Hitler as a secretary until his suicide in 1945. Mrs. Junge tells of the everyday life in the bunker and is unable to forgive herself for the naivety of having liked Adolf Hitler, who to her was something like a father figure. She lived too close to him, blinded by the apparently friendliness and care of the (admittedly) bizarre man. "I thought I would be at the source of all information. But I was really in a blind spot," she said in front of the camera. But there is an additional narrative in the film that reveals a new perspective: the film also shows Traudl Junge watching herself in the first raw version of the film, telling her story. At this point she is able to see and to comment on some of her what psychologists would call "defense mechanisms" while trying to explain herself. Through this act of lifting out she approaches her life from a different perspective.

Also Paul Rabinow, in his book *Reflections on Fieldwork in Morocco* (1977), includes in his analysis the factors "time" and "change." Rabinow elucidates his rethinking and repositioning during and after fieldwork; he notes that he needed a long time to come to an understanding of a variety of aspects of the Moroccan way of life. It is his own changing perspective – resembling Gendlin's steps through lifting out – which is at the core of his analysis. However, it is neither the Freudian psychological self nor the cogito of the Cartesians (p. 6) that is at the core of this kind of analysis, but the author as "the culturally mediated and historically situated self . . ." (ibid.). Rabinow lucidly describes not only his own alterations within the process of understanding, but also those of his informants who are forced to objectify their everyday life in order to explain it to the anthropologist. Rabinow does not reach a "final truth" in this book. His accumulated knowledge is always unfinished and thin. And each time it results in a new and potentially thick positioning of the anthropologist who feels the world around him in a specific way, perpetually reevaluating earlier data.

Like Gendlin, who talks about "contradictions" or "elements that are sensed as problematic" and that lead to change (see above), Rabinow speaks of eruptions and interruptions of communication. When the emotional chaos following these interruptions can be integrated into the wider context, understanding occurs and a new feeling towards the other arises.

Whenever these breaks [of communication] occurred . . . , the cycle began again. This cross-cultural communication and interaction all took on a new content, often a new depth. The groundwork we had laid often seemed to fall away from under us and we scrambled somewhere else. More had been incorporated, more could be taken for granted, more could be shared. (. . .) Fieldwork, then, is a process of intersubjective construction of liminal modes of communication. [Rabinow 1977: 154f.]

As my initial reflections suggest, time (here: looking back) might be an important factor in getting closer to one's moods and formation of categories and, consequently, to data in the shadow. Rabinow, who visited Morocco in 1968 and published his book in 1977, was able to do so. I can look back now to my life in Brazil, especially after having lived a parallel experience in Québec and *see* – in the "understanding" sense given above – the coloring of these contexts according to my *Befindlichkeit*.

Finale: The Context of Lifting Out

So far I have given a number of examples which should strengthen my argument that a disturbance or contradiction in taken-for-granted narratives can lead to a reformulation of one's perception of reality, even more so after the passage of time. In all examples the authors use some concept of otherness to describe the "shadow" that is clearly delimited in both its falseness and its correctedness. This is also the case when the newly achieved state of knowledge is considered unfinished, as Rabinow does.

When thinking about my fieldwork in Brazil, I came to question this kind of bounded otherness as too simple and culture-bound. In cultures where the perception of reality is linked to fusion and inversions[8] as I have described it in a recent article on the difficult notion of "good" and "bad" in urban Brazil (Leibing 2001, 2004), the new that emerges is generally less clear-cut in relation to the previous perception. It is revealing the way Roger Bastide's perception of Brazil, in the introduction of his book *Brésil, Terre des Contrastes* from 1957, reinforces the image of harmony through the fusion of contrasts (Lévi-Strauss's definition of structuralism, the "search for unsuspected harmonies" comes to mind).

All notions which [the sociologist] has learned from European or North American countries do not count here. The old gets mixed with the new. The historical epochs get entangled. The same terms like "social class" or "historical dialectics" do not have the same significance, did not receive the same concrete realities. Instead of rigid concepts, it is necessary to discover notions which are in a certain way liquid, capable of describing phenomenon of *fusion* . . . of interpenetration . . . The sociologist who wants to understand Brazil often has to transform himself into a poet. [p. 15; emphasis added]

While Donna Haraway has remarked that "[f]usion is a bad strategy for positioning" (1995), it is not necessarily the fusion of contrasting perceptions that can be at the heart of analyses of Brazilian culture, but is rather the interchangeability of these perceptions. Take Maria Isaura Cavalcanti's description of the famous samba schools in Rio de Janeiro (1997). In these schools, the "good and bad walk hand in hand." Many schools are financed by the bosses (or bankers, *banqueiros*) of the illegal "animal lottery" (*jogo de bicho*) which moves an enormous amount of money in the city. At the same time, the schools legitimate the bosses' actions by helping the poorer populations, which are the main clientele of the lottery. By helping the samba schools, the bosses can translate the prestige of a victory or a first-place win in the annual carnival competition in Rio de Janeiro ". . . into the recognition of the positive social value of the bankers of the animal lottery in Rio de Janeiro's life" (p. 153f.). Cavalcanti's analysis shows a radical positionality by describing illegality (and sometimes violence) as part of the *double* discourse on new, strong samba schools; modernization and mercantilization are tied to old values of patronage such as "honor, authority, loyalty," without either discourse acknowledged as predominant. Likewise, rule-breaking in Brazil is simultaneously immoral and, through the concept of *jeitinho* (meaning something like creatively and playfully avoiding trouble), a positive value (see Leibing 2002; Barbosa 1992).

Boundaries of good and bad are much more flexible in Brazil; this makes lifting out something more fragile and disturbing, especially for someone whose values are more absolute and dichotomous. This kind of reality entails a fluctuation of values depending momentarily on the observer's eye. Here, a "contradiction" as an opposition, as Gendlin described the trigger for "lifting out," is sometimes hardly perceivable. The "ambivalent language of the double-bind message of the Brazilian culture," to use the terms of anthropologist Luiz Eduardo Soares (1999) for the contradicting values in Brazil, nevertheless relies – as everywhere – on notions, which are often unperceived and taken for granted. For instance, only after the emergence of a new phenomenon at the end of the 1990s, the appearance of young gangsters stemming from the middle class instead of the general notion of bandits emerging from the poorer classes (Leibing 2002; Fiuza 2004), did a discussion in Brazil start about the origins of violence in the country and the contradictory role of key persons like policemen, who are often involved in crime.

Perhaps the search for the hidden side of the moon needs to acknowledge that "lifting out" is as culture-bound as the values and categories it aims to illuminate.

Notes

1   This association did not happen by coincidence – Schubert *lieder* have accompanied me for a long time. They were important tools for dealing with questions of identity and homesickness when I lived abroad (see Leibing in press). As it often happens when the genesis of a paper extends through time (here, after Athena McLean's invitation to participate in this project) until the final writing down of this text – almost one year later – the first association develops in its own right. Because of a selective perception of reality, it was as if all of a sudden a number of texts about the moon crossed my way. I decided to keep this chain of almost free association as a prelude to this article because it illustrates several aspects of the problem taken up in the paper's discussion.

2   In an interview, Robert Lepage links the other (here the discovery of new places like the moon) to narcissism: "By going to the moon, one looks for a new earth. The same thing with Mars. One looks for another part of the universe to look at oneself: all this is narcism" (Perreault 2004:3; trans. A.L.).

3   Power is here understood in the Foucaldian sense as "the relational environment in which actions take place, and so is the sum of influences on actions . . ." (Prado 1995:162).

4   In the article "Inflammation, Atherosclerosis, and Ischemic Events – Exploring the Hidden Side of the Moon," Attilio Maseri comments that ". . . it is easier to study the details of accepted paradigms than it is to develop new hypotheses, just as it was easier to map the visible face of the moon than it was to explore its hidden side" (1997:1014).

5   Lynn Gamwell (2003) describes the evolution of visuality within the history of the microscope that, when invented in the 17th century in Holland, delivered images with chromatic distortions, something that disappeared once the achromatic lens was developed in 1830. Fascinating dimensions of life became visible, like microbes, leading to Louis Pasteur's and Robert Koch's revolutionary theories. Likewise, at the beginning of the 20th century, Alois Alzheimer, who was described by his biographers as someone who only believed what he saw and was not influenced by fashionable theories, was able to describe the typical plaques and tangles in the brain as the major biological markers for Alzheimer's disease with the help of his microscope and new cell-staining methods (Maurer and Maurer 1998; Leibing 2006).

6   "When some details didn't fit into a pattern [during the fieldwork for the book], I explained it away as an 'exception' or defined it as an indicator of social change . . . I convinced myself of the accuracy of what I said by pushing and squeezing all the details into my emerging categories . . . Was the breakdown of loyalty within this family that I experienced in 1989 a product of Fishneckers

having more contact with mainstream society . . . ? Or had I been wrong about this phenomenon all along because I had not been privy to deep emotion? . . . I didn't 'know' them from inside as I did now . . . Now my understanding came from more than observation and detachment; it came through emotional sensitivity and involvement" (Ellis 1995:92).

7 Scheper-Hughes speaks here about a "highly disciplined subjectivity" as the task of any anthropologist in the field (p. 132).

8 "The concept of 'fusion' describes local practices of melting down notions which once were separated, notions of contrasts and oppositions and which nevertheless are embedded in a wider political and economic context. 'Inversions', on the other hand, while linked to fusion, turn common sense values upside down, reverse them and through this kind of confusion split off certain practices from a wider moral economy" (Leibing 2001:51f.; trans. A.L.).

References

Althusser, Louis
  2001   Lenin and Philosophy and Other Essays. Ben Brewster, trans. New York: Monthly Review Press.
Barbosa, Lívia
  1992   O Jeitinho Brasileiro, A arte de ser mais igual que os outros. Rio de Janeiro: Campus.
Bastide, Roger
  1979 [1957]   Brasil, Terra de Contrastes. M. I. P. Queiroz, trans. São Paulo: Difel.
Benjamin, Walter
  1987   Berliner Kindheit um neunzehnhundert. Frankfurt am Main: Suhrkamp.
Bowker, Geoffrey C., and Susan Leigh Star
  2002   Sorting Things Out, Classification and its Consequences. Cambridge: The MIT Press.
Brecht, Christine, and Sybilla Nikolow
  2000   Displaying the Invisible: *Volkskrankheiten* on Exhibition in Imperial Germany. Stud. Hist. Phil. Biol. & Biomed. Sci. 31(4):511–530.
Cambrosio, Alberto, and Peter Keating
  2000   Of Lymphocytes and Pixels: The Techno-Visual Production of Cell Populations. Stud. Hist. Phil. Biol. & Biomed. Sci. 31(2):233–270.
Cavalcanti, Maria I. V. C.
  1997   Violência e Cordialidade na Cultura Brasileira, O jogo do bicho e o carnaval carioca. *In* O Mal à Brasileira. P. Birman, R. Novaes and S. Crespo, eds. Rio de Janeiro: Eduerj.
Crapanzano, Vincent
  1986   Hermes' Dilemma: The Masking of Subversion in Ethnographic Description. *In* Writing Culture: The Poetics and Politics of Ethnography. James Clifford and G. E. Marcus, eds. Berkeley: University of California Press.

Denzin, Norman K.
  1997   Interpretive Ethnography, Ethnographic Practices for the 21st Century. Thousand Oaks: Sage.
Dumit, Joseph
  1995   Twenty-First Century PET: Looking For Mind and Morality Through the Eye of Technology. *In* Technoscientific Imaginaries, Conversation, profiles, and memoirs. G. E. Marcus, ed. Pp. 87–128. Chicago: University of Chicago Press.
Dumit, Joseph
  2004   Picturing Personhood, Brain Scans and Biomedical Identity. Princeton: Princeton University Press.
Ellis, Carolyn
  1995   Emotional and Ethical Quagmires in Returning to the Field. Journal of Contemporary Ethnography 24(1):68–98.
Fiuza, Guilherme
  2004   Meu Nome não é Johnny, A viagem real de um filho da burguesia à elite do tráfico. Rio de Janeiro: Record.
Gamwell, Lynn
  2003   Beyond the Visible – Microscopy, Nature, and Art. Science 22(5603): 49–50.
Gendlin, Eugene T.
  1978/79   Befindlichkeit: Heidegger and the Philosophy of Psychology. Review of Existential Psychology & Psychiatry 16(1–3):43–71.
Haraway, Donna
  1995   Situated Knowledges, The Science Question in Feminism and the Privilege of Partial Perspective. *In* Technology and the Politics of Knowledge. A. Feenberg and A. Hannay, eds. Bloomington: Indiana University Press.
Heidegger, Martin
  1962   Being and Time. John Macquarrie and Edward Robinson, trans. San Francisco: Harper.
Howes, David
  2003   Sensual Relations, Engaging the Senses in Culture and Social Theory. Ann Arbor: The University of Michigan Press.
King, Magda
  2001   A Guide to Heidegger's Being and Time. John Llewelyn, ed. New York: State University of New York Press.
Labaree, Robert V.
  2002   The Risk of 'Going Observationalist': Negotiating the Hidden Dilemmas of Being an Insider Participant Observer. Qualitative Research 2(1):97–122.
Leibing, Annette
  2001   Marcinho et Mauricinho, Violence et les nouveaux héros de Rio de Janeiro, Brésil. Anthropologie et Sociétés 25(3):51–68.
Leibing, Annette
  2002   Flexible Hips? On Alzheimer's Disease and Aging in Brazil. Journal of Cross Cultural Gerontology 17:213–232.

Leibing, Annette
2004 Préface – Enregistrer le vrai (Taping Truth). *In* Pouvoir Guérir, Savoirs humanitaires et autochtones. Julie Laplante, ed. Pp. xi–xvi. Quebec: Les Presses de l'Université Laval.

Leibing, Annette
2006 Divided Gazes: Alzheimer's Disease, The Person Within And Death In Life. *In* Thinking about Senility – Culture, Loss, and the Anthropology of Senility. A. Leibing and Lawrence Cohen, eds. New Brunswick: Rutgers University Press.

Leibing, Annette
In press Seelige Erinnerungen – ein Essay über verkörperte Memoria. *In* Verführerische Leichen – verbotener Verfall, "Körperwelten" als gesellschaftliches Schlüsselereignis. Liselotte Hermes da Fonseca and Thomas Kliche, eds. Lengerich: Pabst Science Publishers.

Lévi-Strauss, Claude
1976 [1955] Tristes Tropiques. Paris: Plon.

Lübcke, Poul
1992 Martin Heidegger: Philosophie als radikales Fragen. *In* Philosophie im 20. Jahrhundert. Vol. 1. A. Hügli and P. Lübcke, eds. Reinbek: Rowohlt.

Marcus, George E.
1999 Critical Anthropology Now: An Introduction. *In* Critical Anthropology Now: Unexpected Contexts, Shifting Constituencies, Changing Agendas. G. E. Marcus, ed. Pp. 3–28. Santa Fé: SAR Press.

Margalit, Avishai
2002 The Ethics of Memory. Cambridge: Harvard University Press.

Maseri, Attilio
1997 Editorial: Inflammation, Atherosclerosis, and Ischemic Events – Exploring the Hidden Side of the Moon. The New England Journal of Medicine 336(14):1014–1016.

Maurer, Konrad, and Ulrike Maurer
1998 Alzheimer, Das Leben eines Arztes und die Karriere einer Krankheit. München: Piper.

Oliveira, Luis R. Cardoso de
2004 Pesquisas *em* versus Pesquisas *com* Seres Humanos. *In* Antropologia e Ética. O Debate Atual no Brasil. Víctora, Ceres et al., eds. Pp. 33–44. Niterói: Ed. UFF.
Online. http://www.unb.br/ics/dan/Serie336empdf.pdf, accessed January 2005.

Perreault, Luc
2004 Le Québec est sorti de sa coquille. La Presse February 09: "Arts et Spectacles," p. 3.

Prado, C. G.
1995 Power. *In* Starting with Foucault: An Introduction to Genealogy. Boulder: Westview.

Rabinow, Paul
   1977   Reflections on Fieldwork in Morocco. Berkeley: University of California
   Press (Quantum Book).
Saukko, Paula
   2002   Studying the Self: From the Subjective and the Social to Personal and
   Political Dialogues. Qualitative Research 2(2):245–264.
Scheper-Hughes, Nancy
   1992   Death without Weeping, The Violence of Everyday Life in Brazil.
   Berkeley: University of California Press.
Scheper-Hughes, Nancy
   1995   The Primacy of the Ethical: Propositions for a Militant Anthropology.
   Current Anthropology 36(3):409–420.
Scheper-Hughes, Nancy
   2000   Ire in Ireland. Ethnography 1(1):117–140.
Scheper-Hughes, Nancy
   2001 [1979]   Saints, Scholars, and Schizophrenics: Mental Illness in Rural
   Ireland. Berkeley: University of California Press.
Sigaud, Lygia
   1995   "Fome" e Comportamentos Sociais: Problemas de explicação em antro-
   pologia. Mana 1(1):167–175.
Soares, Luis Eduardo
   1999   *"A Duplicidade da Cultura Brasileira." In O Malandro e o Protestante, A
   tese Weberiana e a singularidade cultural brasileira.* J. de Souza, dir. Brasilia: Ed.
   UnB.
Strathern, Marilyn
   1988   Commentary: Concrete Topographies. Cultural Anthropology 3(1):
   88–96.
Wenning, Mario
   2002   Heidegger and Adorno: Opening Up Grounds for a Dialogue. Gnosis
   VI(1):online   version.   http://artsandscience.concordia.ca/philosophy/gnosis/
   vol_vi/heidegger_adorno.html.
Zimmerman, Andrew
   2001   Looking Beyond History: The Optics of German Anthropology and the
   Critique of Humanism. Stud. Hist. Phil. Biol. & Biomed. Sci. 32(3):385–411.
Žižek, Slavoj
   1991   The Truth Arises from Misrecognition. *In* Lacan and the Subject of
   Language. E. Ragland-Sullivan and M. Bracher, eds. New York: Routledge.

Part IV

The Politics of Ethnographic Encounter:
Negotiating Power in the Shadow

Chapter 7

The Gray Zone: Small Wars, Peacetime Crimes, and Invisible Genocides

Nancy Scheper-Hughes

Preamble: The View from the Barrio

In this chapter I want to trouble distinctions between visible and invisible, public and private, legitimate and illegitimate forms of violence in times of war and in times of relative peace. Anthropologists are well positioned to do so insofar as our craft requires a surrender of ordinary life, native habits, familiar habitats, and personal attachments to engage in long and intense periods of living among strangers and bearing witness to human lives and events lived in less well-lit, certainly less visible, and often marginalized spaces of the world. Anthropology's constituting interest in otherness demands close attention to people often overlooked, to peoples "without history," as Eric Wolf (1982) described populations existing prior to and outside the orbit of Western "civilizations." Anthropology attends to the minutia of everyday life and to "small things forgotten" and "no-account" people – "*gente pequena*" as my friends in Northeast Brazil often disparagingly refer to themselves – whose lives and deaths go unnoticed.

The following essay concerns "small wars and invisible genocides" (see Scheper-Hughes 1996a), the everyday forms of violence that precede, make possible, and make thinkable extraordinary violence – world wars, genocides, and ethnic cleansings. Small wars also refer to states of indeterminacy in-between and after wars that are not war, but yet not peace.

Ground Zero

In the months following 9/11, we found ourselves in a state of shock and raw grief, feeling deeply wounded. We began to behave like a nation of trauma victims. Indeed, the language of post-traumatic stress disorder permeated everyday conversation, just as the once alien terms "neurotic," "manic-depressive," and "obsessive compulsive" began to be discussed in working-class homes of NYC in the 1950s. Clinical psychiatry – the view from within – gave us a way to understand and critically reflect on ourselves. Anthropology – the view from afar – provides different tools for critical reflection.

The events of 9/11 were to a certain extent over-determined, even predictable, had Americans been more alert and more attentive to the way that "we," the passive beneficiaries of global affluence, were perceived from below – "the view from the barrio," the refugee camp, the *favela*, the shantytowns and squatter camps where most of the world's populations live. While not discounting or minimizing the real dangers of international terrorism, we do need to question our national self-perception as innocent victims and explore our parallel role as passive and complicit "bystanders" to the world's misery. This is not to suggest that Americans "deserved" 9/11 but to caution against nurturing a perception of national "woundedness." Sentiments of misplaced victimhood – as the history of genocide and the current war in Iraq most painfully exemplify – are extremely dangerous.

After 9/11 I found myself returning to a few key texts: Gabriel Garcia Marquez's *Chronicle of a Death Foretold* (1982) [How could we not have read the signs?]; Hannah Arendt's *The Human Condition* (1958) and *Eichmann in Jerusalem* (1963) on the utter banality of evil [Eichmann was so *ordinary*, so perfectly normal, a hardworking bureaucrat doing his best to rise up the ranks of his institution]; to W. B. Yeats' (2004) *Second Coming*: ["Things Fall Apart/ The Center Cannot Hold/ Mere Anarchy is loosed upon the world [. . .] The Best lack all conviction, while the worst/ Are full of passionate intensity"]. Finally, I returned to René Girard's (1986, 1987) writings on sacrificial violence and the surrogate victim, the ritual scapegoat, the one whose death helps to resolve terrible, unbearable conflicts, difficulties, and unconscious collective anxieties and angers. The victims of the attack on the World Trade Center were certainly "ritual scapegoats," but so were the airborne suicide terrorists whose lives were held hostage to fundamentalist convictions and whose bodies were given up – *sacrificed*, that is – by their own leaders, in some cases by their own families. Iraq and its uncounted, unacknowledged civilian casualties – estimated to have surpassed 100,000 deaths (Roberts, Lafta, Garfield, Khudhairi, and Burnham 2004) are likewise surrogate victims and ritual scapegoats, punished for an atrocity (9/11) in which they played no part.

There are two paths to explore – first, a genealogy of violence and genocide exploring the links between mass violence and everyday violence, between war crimes and peacetime crimes; second, "'making sense'" of violence as a first step toward "'un-doing'" evil and remaking a shattered world. While settling on the first I will include a few thoughts on the second.

The Anthropology of Violence

In the introduction to our edited volume, *Violence in War and Peace* (Blackwell 2004b: 1–31), Bourgois and I have developed a theory of violence linking everyday and structural forms of violence with military and political violence. We argue that violence is a slippery concept – non-linear, productive, destructive, *and* reproductive. Violence is mimetic, like imitative magic or homeopathy. Like produces like, that much we know. Violence gives birth to itself. So we can rightly speak of chains, spirals, and mirrors of violence – or, as I prefer – a *continuum* of violence. We know, as though by rote, that wife beaters and sexual abusers were themselves usually beaten and abused. Repressive political regimes resting on terror/fear/torture are often mimetically reproduced, later, by the same revolutionary militants who overthrew the dictators.

Structural violence – the violence of poverty, hunger, social exclusion and humiliation – inevitably translates back into intimate and domestic violence. Political torture is amplified by the symbolic violence that trails in its wake, making the tortured feel shame for their "weakness" in betraying their comrades under duress. Rape survivors – especially when violated with genocidal or sadistic political intent during civil wars – often turn into living-dead people, refusing to speak of the unspeakable, and are often shunned by kin and community, even by their husbands and lovers.

Violence cannot be understood solely in terms of its physicality – physical force, assault, or the infliction of pain. Violence also includes assaults on the personhood, dignity, or sense of worth or value of the victim. The social and cultural dimensions of violence give violence its power and meaning. Focusing exclusively on the physical aspects of torture/terror/violence runs the risk of degenerating into a theater – a pornography of violence – where the voyeuristic impulse subverts empathic witnessing, let alone critiquing, writing, and working against violence.

Violence cannot be objectified and quantified so as to allow clear and positive criteria for defining any particular act as violent or not. Of course, police, social workers, therapists, and judges *must* decide whether spanking a child with a hand, a hairbrush, or a leather strap, or throwing a child across a room, or slamming him or her against a wall is a violent act or a culturally defined and legitimate expression of parental authority and responsibility. World courts must decide whether to include "dirty wars" and "ethnic cleansings" under the legalistic rubric of genocide. But violence itself defies easy categorization.

Violence can be everything and nothing; legitimate or illegitimate; visible or invisible; meaningful or useless; gratuitous or utterly rational and strategic. Revolutionary violence, community-based massacres, and state repression are often painfully graphic and visible. The everyday violence of infant mortality, slow starvation, infectious disease, despair, and humiliation that destroys humans with even greater frequency is usually invisible or misrecognized. What constitutes violence is always mediated by an expressed or implicit dichotomy between legitimate or illegitimate, permissible or sanctioned acts. Most violent acts consist of conduct that is socially permitted, encouraged, or enjoined as a moral right or a duty. Often, violence is not deviant behavior, not disapproved of, but to the contrary is defined as virtuous action in the service of conventional social, economic, and political norms. The "'legitimate'" violence of the militarized state is invariably differentiated from the unruly, illicit, violence of the mob, the dissenters.

Depending on one's geo-political–economic position in the world order, particular acts of violence may be perceived as "depraved" or "glorious" as when Palestinian suicide bombers are alternatively viewed as terrorists or as martyrs or when U.S. military forces in Afghanistan or Iraq are viewed as liberators or oppressors. Violence (like power) is said to corrupt absolutely, except when it is said to ennoble or liberate the perpetrator, like the colonized subjects Jean-Paul Sartre (1964) argued could only regain their humanity through revolutionary violence. Perhaps the most one can say about violence is that like madness, sickness, suffering, or death itself, it is a human condition. Violence is present (as a capability) in each of us, as is its opposite – its rejection. We are profoundly social creatures and our cultures, social structures, ideas, and ideologies shape all dimensions of violence, its *expressions* and its *repressions*. Torturing and killing are as cultural as nursing the sick and the wounded or burying and mourning the dead. *Brute* force is a misnomer; violence wears a very human face. Most violence is not "senseless" at all.

Missing the Genocide

Violence is not a natural topic for anthropologists who are trained to behave like inverse bloodhounds, following the trail and the scent of "the good." A basic premise guiding modern anthropology was, quite simply, to see, hear, and report no evil (and very little violence) from the field. The work of anthropology demands an explicit ethical orientation to "the other." Traditionally, this meant maintaining a respectful distance and a reluctance to name wrongs, to judge, to intervene, or to prescribe change, even in the face of considerable human misery.

We knew, of course, how often well-meaning but uninvited interventions were used against traditionalist, nonsecular, and communal people who stood in the way of the Western civilizing project and its notions of freedom, rationality, and liberal democracy. And we understood that if anthropological work *was* to be in the nature of an ethical project, it had to be transformative of the self, while putting few demands on the cultural "other." Thus, cultural (and moral) relativism evolved as the anthropologist's sacred oath. But in times of genocide and mass violence, cultural relativism led to moral blindness.

In *After the Fact*, Clifford Geertz (1995) notes with some chagrin that he often had the uncomfortable feeling of arriving either too early or too late to observe the significant political events and upheavals that descended on his respective field sites in Morocco and Java. In fact, however, he consciously avoided the conflicts by moving back and forth between his field sites during periods of relative calm, thus managing to "miss the genocide." Thus, nothing in Geertz's ethnographic writings hinted at the "killing fields" that were beginning to engulf Indonesia soon after he had departed from the field, a massacre of suspected Communists by Islamic fundamentalists in 1965 that rivaled recent events in Rwanda. The only mention of that extraordinary blood-bath – a political massacre of some 60,000 Balinese following an unsuccessful Marxist-inspired coup – is buried in a footnote in which Geertz draws a parallel between the highly stylized and folkloric Balinese cock fight and the religious massacres. He wrote: "if one looks at Bali – as the Balinese themselves do – through the medium of the cock fight, the massacres that occurred seem if not less appalling at least less like a contradiction to the laws of nature" (p. 452).

In my case, it took me more than two decades to confront the question of political violence which, given my choice of early field sites – Ireland in the mid-1970s, Brazil during the military dictatorship years, and South Africa on the cusp of the first democratic elections – must have required a massive dose of denial. While studying the madness of everyday life in a small, quiet peasant community in western Ireland, I was largely concerned then with *interior* spaces, with the small dark psychodramas of scapegoating and labeling within traditional farm households that was driving so many young bachelors to drink and to bouts of depression and schizophrenia. I paid scant attention then to the political activities of little Matty Dowd, from whom we rented our cottage in the mountain hamlet of Ballynalacken, and who used our attic to store a small arsenal of guns and explosives that he and a few of his Sinn Fein buddies were running to Northern Ireland. Consequently, I left unexamined until recently the links between political violence in Northern Ireland and the tortured family dramas in West Kerry, with their own violence.

In the bucolic countryside and family farms of West Kerry I found evidence in the 1970s of structural and symbolic violence toward the later-born sons whose role as farm heirs excluded them from matrimony and child-bearing and consigned them to a monkish existence serving their so-called "sainted" elderly parents. As a village demographer and "clerk of the records" there, I had gathered enough stories and been present at enough family and community crises to know what a great many ordinary villagers knew without ever going to university – that something was gravely amiss. There were too many psychological tragedies to account for – some taking the form of madness ("schizophrenia"), a greater number expressed in deep clinical depressions and, in more recent years, a shocking number of young adult suicides. There was trouble in the system, a very "nervous system," indeed (see Taussig 1992).

Beneath the quaint thatched roofs of the rural farm households an extraordinary drama of masked violence and ritual sacrifice was taking place. Up through the 1950s, when family farming was still a valued and productive way of life, the firstborn son would have inherited the farm, but by the time I arrived in "Ballybran"/An Clochan the firstborn were being reared for export. And rural parents were faced with a new problem – how to retain at least one son for the farm and for the care of themselves in their dotage. The new family "selections" paradoxically privileged the firstborn children by "disinheriting" them, thereby allowing them to leave the village with honor, and victimized the designated heirs in relegating them to the status of pathetic "leftovers" and stay-at-homes, "good enough" for the village, a place not then generally thought of as very good at all.

This family dynamic involved considerable symbolic violence – a cutting down to size of the designated farm heir; a sacrifice of manhood and reproductivity to permanent celibacy, and exploitation of his labor. This was accomplished through considerable shaming and ridicule toward these captive men. The moral economy of farm inheritance constituted what Pierre Bourdieu (1977) would have called a "bad faith economy," based on lies and secrets, and concealing the true state of affairs. In fact, the situation I describe here was very similar to one described by Pierre Bourdieu (1962) with respect to the bachelor peasants of Béarn, his own home region of France. Bourdieu (2004) recalled a "simple" village scene – a small dance on Christmas Eve in a rural tavern – that haunted him for more than 30 years. Later, he reflected: "I witnessed a very stunning scene: young men and women from nearby towns were dancing in the middle of the ballroom while another group of older [local village] youths, about my age at the time, all still bachelors, were standing idly on the sides. Instead of dancing, they were intensely scrutinizing the hall and unconsciously moving forward so that they were progressively shrinking the space used by the dancers." The resentment of the village bachelors, sidelined at the dance (as in life), spilled over into their angry, nonverbal challenge to the "townie" dancers.

The spurned farm heirs of Béarn, like the bachelor farmers of An Clochan, were fated to permanent bachelorhood and virtually "forbidden" to reproduce. The aggressive behavior of the village bachelors at the tavern dance was, in effect, a symbolic protest against the new "matrimonial market" that had emerged among the "emancipated" factory workers from nearby towns. The older, rural system of match-making, controlled by the elders, had since given way to a "free market" where young men were expected to manage their own marital and reproductive affairs, counting on their personal assets and "symbolic capital": the ability to dress, to dance, to present oneself, to talk to girls, and so on. This courtship transition had almost completely disenfranchised the rural class of shy bachelors who had always depended on intermediaries to arrange their personal and romantic affairs.

The transition from arranged marriages to "free exchange" signaled the demise of an entire class of small peasant farmers which the French state was trying to eliminate through various "modernization" projects soon after World War II (Bourdieu and Waquant 1992:165). Although this "war" on the class of peasant farmers was accomplished without overt violence and bloodshed, the brutality of the process was grasped intuitively by the young anthropologist who observed with mounting horror the shame and impotent rage of the bachelor wallflowers sidelined at that poignant Christmas Eve dance in Béarn.

In a nutshell this was also the situation of the young, angry bachelors of An Clochan. While some bachelor farmers adjusted to the new system, making their daily little accommodations to it without complaint, others could not bring themselves to do so, and over time grew into angry, isolated, hurt, and bitter individuals, cut off from the flow of human life. Some became the depressed and alcoholic bachelor farmers who populated the several village pubs that catered to the village. There, on many long and dark winter nights, they wept quietly for everything they had missed in life. Others become the saintly hermits who retreated to their barns and sought companionship in their dogs and cows, and still others became the long-term mental patients at St. Finan's hospital in Killarney, men obsessed with fears of bodily encroachment and possessed by unfulfilled and unruly sexual and generative needs and fantasies. This social tragedy was masked by a family myth of social and mental incapacity so that community needs were served at the expense of solitary victims.

Since then, I have continued to study other forms of "everyday" violence: the abuses of medicine practiced in bad faith against the weak, the mad, and the hungry, and the social indifference to child death in Northeast Brazil that allowed political leaders, priests, coffin makers, *and* shantytown mothers to dispatch nonchalantly a multitude of hungry "angel-babies" to the afterlife. In Brazil I did not begin to study state violence until in the late 1980s when the half-grown sons of some of my friends and neighbors in the shantytown of Alto do Cruzeiro began to "disappear" – their mutilated bodies turning up later, the handiwork of police-infiltrated local death squads.

Today, the world, the objects of our study, and the uses of anthropology have changed considerably. And those privileged to observe human events close up over time and privy to local, community, and state secrets that are generally hidden from view until later, much later, after the collective graves have been discovered and the body counts made, are beginning to recognize an obligation to identify the sources, structures, and institutions of mass violence. This new mood of political and ethical engagement has resulted in considerable soul-searching. But given our insistence on appreciating difference and divergent ethical principles, what form(s) could this soul-searching possibly take?

In the following I argue that everyday violence – "peacetime crimes" – make mass violence and genocide possible. My contribution lies in weaving together disparate threads of daily practice that seem to allow genocidal-like behaviors toward certain classes of "dispensable" people. I end with a painful personal vignette showing that anyone – including the vigilant anthropologist – is capable of being a bystander and complicit with structural violence, even when it is directed against those we most love. Here we reach the most deeply protected of all public secrets – the violence of everyday life.

A Genealogy of Genocide

With the shocking reappearance of genocides and other forms of state and terrorist mass killing in the late 20th century we have witnessed what many people had believed – following the Holocaust – could never happen again. Holocaust scholars have emphasized the "modernity of genocide," its link to a specific level of state formation, technological efficiency, rationality, and subjectivity. Zygmunt Bauman (1989) views the Holocaust as a kind of mad triumph of rational efficiency, a distorted byproduct of the increasing rationalization of social life. More recently, Georgio Agamben (1999) identified the concentration camp as the prototype of late modern bio-politics with its production of a population of "living dead," those whose bodies could be taken by the state at will, neither for the purpose of sacrifice nor as a punishment for crimes, but merely because of their "availability" for execution. Thus, the Holocaust is something of a misnomer; it was neither about religion nor about bodies "sacrificed" as "burnt offerings." If Agamben is correct, late modern genocide is about actualizing a social and technological capacity to exterminate, cleanly and absolutely.

What kinds of modernity do the genocides in Cambodia, Rwanda, and Burundi represent? Characteristic of all of them is an obsessive focus on the body – on bloodlines and genealogy and on phenotypes and body types – the particular shape and length of heads, arms, legs, buttocks, hair, and lips. Perhaps it captures the race-mad corporeal imaginary of the late modern Western world. But the "dirty wars" and "social hygiene" projects of military governments of Brazil, Argentina, and apartheid South Africa relied on techniques of torture and mass killing that could hardly be described as "modern." The apartheid government's security forces "reinvented" witch burnings; they discarded some political enemies by burning them – even while still alive – over barbeque pits. The Brazilian and Argentinean military governments' tool kit of tortures resembled nothing so much as the crude techniques of the Inquisition. Even political "disappearances" call to mind ancient rumors of body snatching, blood libel, and ritual killings.

Once again, we are forced to revisit the question that so vexed a generation of post-Holocaust social theorists: *What makes genocide and mass violence possible?* What are the limits and capacities of anthropos? How do we explain the complicity of ordinary, "good enough" people to outbreaks of genocidal violence? Adorno and the post-World War II Frankfurt School suggested that participation in genocide requires a strong childhood conditioning that produces almost mindless obedience to authority figures. Daniel Goldhagen (1996) argued to the contrary that thousands of ordinary Germans participated willingly, even eagerly, in the Holocaust, not for fear of punishment by authority figures but driven by race hatred alone.

Genocides and mass killings rarely appear on the scene unbidden. They evolve. There are identifiable starting points or instigating circumstances. They are often preceded by social upheavals, by a precipitous decline in economic conditions, political disorganization, or by radical social change leading to a state of anomie. Conflict over scarce material resources – land and water – can escalate into desperate mass killings when combined with social sentiments that question the humanity of the opposing group. Extreme forms of oppositional thinking – us versus them – can result in a social self-identity predicated on a notion of "the other" as enemy.

The Holocaust alerted a generation of post-WWII scholars to the dangerousness of social conformity and the absence of dissent. [Hence the popular slogan: "Question Authority!"] The conflicts in the Middle East, in the former Yugoslavia, and in sub-Saharan Africa suggest that a past history of social suffering and *woundedness*, especially a history of ethnic, religious, or racial victimization, can lead to a predisposition to mass violence. A continuous and unresolved, inter-generational traumatic stress disorder can lead to a state of hyper-reactivity that can explode into another cycle of "self-defensive" mass killings.

Ritual sacrifice and the search for a generative scapegoat – a social class or ethnic group on which to pin the blame for social and economic problems – is also a common precondition for genocide. Another precondition is a shared ideology, a blueprint for living, and a vision of the world that defines obstacles to the good life or the holy life in the form of certain people who must be removed, eliminated, wiped out. There is often the belief that everyone will benefit from the social cleansing, *even the dead themselves*.

Finally, there must be a broad constituency of *bystanders* who either (as in white South Africa) allow race-hostile policies to continue without massive civil disobedience or (as in Nazi Germany and in Rwanda) who can be recruited to participate, when needed, in genocidal acts. Less recognized is the supporting role of global bystanders, powerful nation states whose people are the passive beneficiaries of economic globalization and who can seem indifferent to the misery of the rest of the world. International and nongovernmental agencies can also play the role of global bystanders, in delaying or refusing to intervene in genocides, as in the case of Rwanda when UN peacekeepers were instructed to do nothing. The origins and evolution of genocide and mass violence are complex and multifaceted, but they are not inscrutable or unpredictable.

The Genocide Continuum

The violence continuum to which I refer is comprised of a multitude of "small wars and invisible genocides" conducted in the normative spaces of public schools, clinics, emergency rooms, hospital wards, nursing homes, court rooms, prisons, detention centers, and public morgues. The continuum refers to the capacity to reduce other humans to nonpersons, monsters, or things which gives license to institutionalized forms of mass violence.

The idea of a genocide continuum flies directly in the face of a powerful tradition of genocide studies that argues for the absolute uniqueness of the Holocaust and for a careful and restricted use of the term (see Fackenheim 1970). But if there is a risk in overextending the concept of "genocide" into spaces and corners of everyday life where we might not ordinarily think to find it, there is an even greater risk in misrecognizing genocidal sentiments enacted in everyday practices during times of relative peace.

Bourdieu's unfinished theory of violence revealed the violence and aggression that was tucked away in the minutiae of ordinary social practices – in the architecture of homes, in gender relations, in communal work, in the exchange of gifts, and so forth. Italian phenomenologist and radical psychiatrist Franco Basaglia coined the term "peacetime crimes" – *crimini di pace* – to express the relationship between wartime and peacetime, between war crimes and peace-crimes (Basaglia 1987). Basaglia's awakening occurred when he first entered an Italian *manicomio* (a traditional state mental asylum) as a psychiatric intern after WWII. He was immediately struck by a frightening sense of *déjà vu* – the odor of defecation, sweat, and death catapulted him back to the prison cell where he had been held as a member of the Italian resistance during the German occupation. That single terrifying moment was the basis of his equation of mental hospitals with concentration camps, and the links between war crimes and everyday, peacetime crimes.

International war tribunals had just been established to try those guilty of war crimes, treated for the first time as crimes against humanity. Meanwhile, Basaglia struggled to unmask the invisible and therefore unrecognized "crimes against humanity" practiced in Italian state mental asylums after the war. Some of the disturbed inmates were suffering from war-related PTSD only to encounter in the mental hospital a new battery of medically sanctioned tortures, including the same kinds of solitary confinement, physical restraint, removal of clothing, and exposure to cold, dirt, and sleep deprivation they had encountered as prisoners of war. But the men in white were now supposed to be healers when they applied therapeutic "strangleholds."

Basaglia's concept of peacetime crimes allows one to see the parallel uses of torture and rape during peacetime and wartime. One can also see the resemblances between official raids by INS agents on Mexican and Central American refugees at border crossings and earlier state-sponsored genocides of Native Americans, such as the Cherokee Indians' forced exile, their "Trail of Tears." Peacetime crimes become war crimes when they are applied systematically, institutionally, and with the legitimacy of the state behind them.

Peacetime crimes make a certain kind of domestic "peace" possible. The phenomenal growth of prisons in the United States took place in the absence of dissent. How many executions – including of the mentally ill and mentally deficient – are needed to make life feel more secure? How many maximum security prisons are needed to contain an expanding population of young Black and Latino men seen as a class of "public enemies"? Ordinary peacetime crimes, such as the steady evolution of American prisons into black concentration camps, constitute the "small wars and invisible genocides" to which I refer, as do the infant mortality and homicide rates in Oakland, California.[1] Events like these constitute invisible genocides not because they are secreted away but quite the opposite. As Wittgenstein once observed, the things that are hardest to perceive are those which are right before our eyes and taken for granted.[2]

These events evoke the analogic thinking that enabled social critics like Erving Goffman, Jules Henry, and Franco Basaglia to perceive the logical relations between concentration camps and mental hospitals, nursing homes, and other "total" institutions, and between prisoners and mental patients and allow us to see the capacity and the willingness of ordinary people – society's "practical technicians" – to enforce, at other times, "genocidal"-like crimes against classes and types of people thought of as waste, as rubbish, as "deficient" in humanity, as "better off dead" or even as better off never having been born.

The mad, the disabled, the mentally deficient have often fallen into this category, as have the very old and infirm, the sick-poor, the immigrant, the refugee, and despised racial, religious, and ethnic groups. Erik Erikson (1950) referred to "pseudo-speciation" as the human tendency to classify some individuals or social groups as less than fully human – a necessary prerequisite to genocide that is carefully honed during the unremarkable peacetimes that can precede the sudden, and only seemingly unintelligible, outbreaks of genocide.

Sacrificial Violence and Invisible Suffering: The Case of Angel-Babies

In *Death without Weeping*, based on several extensive periods of field research between 1964 and 1990[3] in the sugar plantation zone of Northeast of Brazil, I explored the social indifference to staggering infant and child mortality in shantytowns of Northeast Brazil. Local political leaders, Catholic priests and nuns, coffin makers, and shantytown mothers themselves casually dispatched a multitude of hungry "angel-babies" to the afterlife each year, saying: "Well, they *themselves* wanted to die." The doomed infants were described as having no "taste," no "knack," and no "talent" for life.

The idea of an almost instinctual mother love is deeply rooted in Brazilian culture as it is elsewhere in the West (see Scheper-Hughes 1993:357–359) but the ideology served as an effective barrier hiding the fact that in Brazil (as in the United States) only certain infants are loved and desired and brought into the circle of protective custody and care. The "letting go" of infants is silent, invisible, and documented only with difficulty in pockets of hunger, scarcity, and unrelieved loss and deprivation that lead a great many mothers to think it would be better if some of their infants had never been born or, at the very least, that they live brief lives, thus diminishing the amount of misery and suffering in the world, especially in the lives of the mothers.[4]

Medical practices such as prescribing powerful tranquilizers to fretful and frightfully hungry babies, Catholic ritual celebrations of the death of "angel-babies," and the bureaucratic indifference in political leaders' dispensing free baby coffins, but no food, to hungry families and children, interacted with maternal practices such as radically reducing food and liquids to severely malnourished and dehydrated babies so as to help them, their mothers said, to die quickly and well. Perceived as already "doomed," sickly infants were described as less than human creatures, as ghostly angel-babies, inhabiting a terrain midway between life and death. "It is better that these spirit-children return to where they came," mothers said of their wasted infants whose blank staring eyes already seemed to focus in a space beyond the known world.

What is at stake in the "extreme situation" – whether in the hungry shantytown or in the concentration camp – is the ability to retain a human status. When Primo Levi returned in 1945 after spending 22 months in Auschwitz, he described (1995) a subpopulation of prisoners called Musselman. These were "non-men who marched and labored in silence . . . who had given up responding to [the environment] at all, and who had become objects, finally reaching a point of no return." The descriptions of vacant stares, indifference to food and drink, the lethal passivity that comes with total trauma and extreme suffering resemble my descriptions of the starved and abandoned angel-babies of Alto do Cruzeiro. Both evoked strong feelings of revulsion, fear, and rejection, along with the need to declare them as nonhumans.

Thus, I gradually came to think of the shantytown angel-babies more in terms of René Girard's (1986, 1987) idea of sacrificial violence. The given-up, offered-up angel-babies of Bom Jesus seemed to me to be prototypical generative scapegoats, sacrificed in the face of terrible domestic conflicts about scarcity and survival. And that is, in fact, just how their mothers sometimes spoke of them.

"What does it mean," I asked several women of the Alto during a local Mothers Club meeting on the top of the Alto do Cruzeiro, "to say that a baby '*has*' to die, or that it dies because it '*wants*' to die?"

Terezinha was the first to speak. "It means that God takes them to save us from suffering."

"But why would God want little babies to suffer so much in dying as they do?" I asked.

"Don't ask me," answered Edite Cosmos. "But perhaps these ugly diseases are sent by God to punish us for the sins of the world. It is strange because we ourselves are the sinners, but the punishment falls heavily on them."

"Be quiet, Edite," said Severina Ramos. "They die, just like Jesus died, to save us from pain and suffering. Isn't that right, Sister Juliana?"

But Sister Juliana, a native of the dry *sertão* where babies did not die (she said) like flies as they did in the sugar zone, was not so sure that the women were right in their theological thinking. "I don't think Jesus wants all your babies," she said. "I think He wants them to live." But Sister Juliana was a nun and the Alto women didn't pay her too much attention. What could she possibly know about babies?

The ability of desperately poor women to help those infants who (they said) "needed to die" required an existential "letting go" (contrasted to the maternal work of holding on, holding close, and holding dear). Letting go required a leap of faith that was not easy to achieve. And these largely Catholic women often said that their infants died just as Jesus died so that others – especially themselves – could live. The question that lingered, unresolved, in my mind was whether this Kierkegaardian "leap of faith" entailed a certain Marxist "bad faith" as well.

The sacrificial theme appeared in many other guises, as for example in the belief that infants named after powerful patron saints often become "the first fruits" offered to them. An oft-recited folk motif in the rural Northeast of Brazil tells of a peasant who lost his favorite donkey, then his wife, and then his newborn son all in close succession. He is grief stricken until a kindly man appears who later is revealed as an apparition of St. Anthony. The visitor tells the man that God knows what He is doing. If the donkey had lived he would have thrown the peasant into a ditch where he would have died of thirst. If his wife had lived she would have become the lover of his best friend; and if his child had lived he would have become an outlaw and a bandit. Many people in the shantytown had experienced the loss of a beast of burden and quite a few men had lost their wives during childbirth, but virtually everyone has lost a baby, and many have lost several. St. Anthony's words of consolation are often repeated. "Better the child should die," Alto women say to each other, "than either you or I."

I certainly did not want to blame shantytown mothers for putting their own survival over and above that of their infants and small babies, for these were moral choices that no person should be forced to make. But in denying authorship of their acts and in blaming the deaths of their "angel-babies" on the willingness and "readiness" of their doomed infants to die, the mothers seem to be reproducing a moral climate similar to descriptions of life in the death camps.

While the fresh air of liberation theology blew away some of the cobwebs of baroque religious traditions affecting shantytown mothers and infants, in particular those concerning the celebration of angel-babies, it left a vacuum in its place. As newly trained priests and nuns came to view the unnecessary deaths of infants and small babies as a human tragedy, they discouraged mothers from falling into comfortable religious consolations provided by folk Catholicism. "Jesus never intended that the innocent should suffer and die for our sins," Sister Juliana told the bereaved mothers of the Alto do Cruzeiro. But the infants continued to die all the same. It may be inappropriate, heartless almost, to refer to those unnecessary angel-baby deaths as an invisible genocide. Lacking is any *intention* to rid the world of a specific class of people. To the contrary, infants were viewed as an unlimited, indeed limitless, supply of souls that could be constantly recirculated. This allowed the die-outs of shantytown babies – in some particularly "bad" years, as many as 40 percent of all the infants born in the Alto do Cruzeiro – to pass without comment, surprise, or grief. "Well, it's just a baby," women would say.

Maternal Thinking and Military Thinking

In the spring of 1995 I was invited to give a series of lectures in Israel. It was a relatively peaceful time but a constant state of vigilance and preparedness for war was palpable. At a talk at the Van Leer Institute of Gender Studies in Jerusalem on mother love and child death in Brazil, a woman in the audience became visibly perturbed. During the question and answer period she said that my talk had made her extremely angry because she was able to identify with the mothers in my study who "fatalistically" exposed their infants to premature and unnecessary death in the interest of self- and family survival. It made her think about how she, too, had perhaps "fatalistically" surrendered both her adolescent son and her daughter to the military, thus putting them in harm's way. She referred to the incredible fragility of mother love when it comes into contact with harsh political and economic realities.

And it was here, in particular, that peacetime and wartime, maternal thinking and military thinking, converged (see Scheper-Hughes 1996b). When mothers greet their frail and untrustworthy (because they might disappoint the mother) newborn infants as a stranger to be excluded or as an alien and invading enemy whose life is a threat to personal or family stability, they are expressing a dangerous, though all too human, sentiment that is essential to military recruitment and thinking – the idea of "acceptable death." In Northeast Brazil, "acceptable death" took the form of "holy indifference" to the death of angel-babies and a belief in a kind of "magical replaceability" which emphasizes the interchangeability of persons. One more, one less . . . there are always more where they come from. "Don't grieve, Dona Maria, *it's only a baby*. You'll soon have another."

When angels (or martyrs) are fashioned from the dead bodies of those who die young, "maternal thinking" most resembles military, especially wartime, thinking. On the battlefield as in the shantytown, triage, thinking in sets, and a belief in the magical replaceability of the dead predominate. Above all, ideas of "acceptable death" and of "meaningful" (rather than useless) suffering extinguish rage and grief for those whose lives are taken and allow for the recruitment of new lives and new bodies into the struggle.

Just as shantytown mothers consoled each other that their hungry babies died because they were "meant" to die or because they "had" to die, Northern Irish mothers, South African township mothers, and Palestinian mothers console each other at political wakes and funerals with the belief that their sacrificed and "martyred" children died purposefully and died well. I might refer to the woman's *abdication of their maternal authority* and the maternal values of "world-preserving and world repair" to the most pernicious kind of "peacekeeping" – the kind that says, "don't rock the boat, do what *the man* says. And whatever you do, don't be perceived as a troublemaker."

This kind of thinking is not exclusive to any particular class of people. Whenever humans attribute some value and meaning – whether political or spiritual – to the "useless suffering" of others they behave a bit like public executioners.

The Gray Zone

Primo Levi (1995), survivor of the IG Farben Petrochemical plant at Auschwitz, referred to the "gray zone" in human responses to "spaces of death." Concentration camp inmates – like the kidnapped, torture victims, and the starving – are often forced into a morally ambiguous space of mutual betrayal and complicity in exchange for the smallest personal advantage. The gray zone is populated by a thousand little betrayals in the desperate, covert, and continuous struggle to survive. Like Primo Levi, Brazilian peasants from the drought- and famine-plagued Northeast are keenly aware that the "good" die young and that the ability to survive disaster requires "a knack for life" and a willingness to cheat death. Survival tactics are not always the most morally edifying. Survivors of the camps, like drought survivors in Northeast Brazil, comment on their own complicity: "None of us here is innocent."

Rubbish people – Happy Valley Nursing Home

We need go no further than our own medical clinics, emergency rooms, public hospitals, and old age homes to encounter other classes of "rubbish people" treated with as much indifference as Brazilian "street kids" (Scheper-Hughes 2004a) or angel-babies on the Alto do Cruzeiro. The following vignette should suffice.

Several years ago I stepped outside "Happy Valley" Nursing Care Center to take several deep breaths before returning inside to face what was left of (*and left to*) my impossibly dear and impossibly frail parents, then approaching their nineties. A "late in life" child, I can only remember my father with gray and then with white hair. As a 5-year-old I often cried myself to sleep after reciting the requisite bedtime prayer, "Now I lay me down to sleep," full certain that it was my parents who would surely die before I woke. But in the end they fooled everyone and outlived their much younger siblings, joining that small cohort that sociologists refer to as the "oldest old." With me living 3,000 miles away and an older sibling who spent a good part of each year traveling, the once unthinkable idea of a nursing home crept up on us as my mother's strength and independent spirit began to fade away and as my father's mobility was curtailed by a broken hip and Parkinson's disease.

By the time they moved into Happy Valley, both parents were physically dependent, immobile, and incontinent, but only Dad, at 95, was able to express his frustration at his painfully reduced condition in life. Mom, suffering an advanced state of mind-loss, was by then maintained by a plastic sack of brown liquid, suspended from a moveable pole, and dripped by tubes directly into her abdomen. A victim of what medical professionals like to call Alzheimer's disease, Mom had lost language and she communicated by howling, though true to her reserved character, always gently and in a lady-like fashion. I was certain that her sounds were not meaningless and that she was protesting. When not thrashing about, she seemed resigned, but with the hopeless, open-eyed, and desperate stare of a hooked rainbow trout. Whenever Mom saw me and when – ignoring the nurse's rules – I would release her from her final hook and line and wheel her into the sunny courtyard of the nursing home, she would smile and she was attentive to the birds overhead and to the bright pink azaleas that were always one of her favorite flowers. She would hold the blossoms in her hand and try to speak. Sometimes she would even nod her head at me, but I could never convince the nursing staff that Mom was still a person and still conscious of the world around her.

Around the corner, virtually trapped in his semi-private room, which he shared with a more robust but ill-mannered bully who stole his socks and shirts, Dad was likewise maintained by three or four tins of the liquid protein-calorie *Ensure*. At every given opportunity, he would spill the sticky stuff into his wastepaper basket into which he also occasionally relieved himself because he could not, he said, always get to his bedside porter-potty on time. And so, the wise, modest, and scholarly man who taught me courage under fire ("*Nil Desperandum!*" was his lifelong motto), the self-taught organic intellectual who introduced me to multiple ways of seeing and knowing the world disparagingly referred to himself as "Little Jack Horner" (that is, stuck in his corner).

As ever-increasing numbers of the aged are both sick and poor due to the astronomical cost of late life medical care, they are at risk of spending their remaining time in public or less expensive private institutions like "Happy Valley." In these private, for-profit nursing homes, care for residents is delegated to grossly underpaid and under-trained workers who protect themselves by turning the persons and bodies under their protection into things, bulky objects that can – once a staffer gets the hang of it – be dealt with in shorter and shorter intervals. Cost-saving demands bear down on "staffers" to minimize the personal care and attention given to the residents, especially those like my parents, whose limited savings were quickly used up by the institution and who had to be supported by the state through Medicaid. My Dad saw through the sham of benevolence and he often made sport of a large poster hanging in the common room that welcomed new residents to Happy Valley's "circle of care" and informed them of their rights. But it was with the dark and double-edged humor of the gallows.

The underpaid staff needed, no less than I did, to duck out of the home as often as possible, for a smoke, a snack, or a breath of fresh air. But other work survival tactics at the Home were less defensible. Often personal names of residents were dropped and they were addressed as "you" or "that one over there." Little notice was taken of small requests so that sooner or later expressions of personal preference – to turn up or down the heat, to open or close a window, to bring a cold drink, to lower the ubiquitous TV or to change a channel – were soon extinguished. Passivity sets in. When the body is rolled from one side or the other for cleaning or to clean the sheets [body and sheets are equated], or when the resident is wheeled conveniently into a corner so that the floor could be more easily mopped, and when cleaning staff do little to suppress disgust at bodily effluvia – urine, blood, feces, nasal discharge, or phlegm out of place – on clothing, under the nails, on wheelchairs, or in wastepaper baskets, the person trapped inside the failing body comes to see themselves as "dirty," "vile," "disgusting," "out of place," redundant – in short, as an object and nonperson. An essay by Jules Henry (1966) on "Hospitals for the Aged Poor," documenting the attack on the elderly individual's dwindling stock of personal and psychological "capital" by unconscious hospital and nursing home staff, rings as true today as when it was first written.

The destruction of personhood is aided by the material circumstances of the Home. Although individualized laundry baskets were supplied for each resident, the staff refused any responsibility for lost or mix-matched clothing, even when each piece was carefully labeled. Several times I arrived as late as 11:00 in the morning to find my Dad in bed and under his sheets, completely undressed because, he would say, he had "no clothing" to wear. Arguments with staff were often counterproductive. When all personal objects – toothbrush, comb, glasses, towels, pens and pencils – continued to disappear no matter how many times they were replaced, the resident (if he or she knows what is good for him or her) finally accepts the situation and adapts in other ways. Eventually, residents (though following Goffman, inmates is perhaps the better term) were compelled to substitute other objects for those which were less available. The plastic wastepaper basket becomes the urinal, the urinal becomes the washbasin, the water glass turns into a spittoon, the despised adult diaper is used defiantly as a table napkin, and so forth. Meanwhile, the institutional violence and bureaucratic indifference are masked as the inmate's state of mental confusion and incompetence. Soon almost everything in the institution invites the resident to regress, to give up, to surrender, and to accept their seemingly inevitable fall from grace. But where are the forces of liberation or a "human rights watch" in hidden spaces of dehumanization and "invisible genocide" in such normative institutions (of caring) as these? And so, Dad stared grimly at the wall in his corner of the room and Mom howled, like "the wild boy" of Avignon staring at the moon. But both retained to the end their keen sense of justice and injustice.

How can I possibly say these things without screaming? But I *am* screaming. You see, I was unable to do the only thing that could have reversed this mad system: To run down the halls of Happy Valley Nursing Home, pulling out the tubes, detaching the liquid bags, knocking over the porter-potties, and picking up my ancient and beloved old ones and taking them home to California to live with me. But I didn't. I remained a passive bystander to their final un-doing.

On September 17, 1997 my father passed away in a hospital, but without too much labor. His final moments, at least, were peaceful. And in death his bodily dignity was restored to him. The young working-class funeral director, Vinnie, who attended to my father's remains and supervised their removal from Baltimore to our last "home" in Queens, New York, for a simple funeral executed his tasks with extraordinary care and concern for my late father's dignity. In his dark blue suit with jaunty rosebud in its lapel, his handsome white beard trimmed, my father's charisma and personhood were ultimately returned to him. A simple gift. But it is a deadly commentary on postmodern life (and on all of us) when the body we love is given greater honor and value in death than in the last years of a long, gentle, and beautifully ordinary life.

Un-doing

Peacetime crimes are so deeply inscribed in our ordinary, unexamined lifeways that no one is exempt, least of all the "critical" and "militant" anthropologist. Obviously, social and political critique must extend to self-critique, to illuminating how ordinary, everyday ways of thinking, loving, and being in the world are implicated in the violence that we are trying to understand and to overcome. The demons have not fled – we have faced the terrorist and she is us.

All forms of violence are sustained by the passively averted gaze. The critical lens moves in and out, intentionally juxtaposing the different levels of violence – macro and micro, economic, epistemic, and the deeply personal and subjective. I have tried to show a way of reading across the scales of power and of violence to allow a recognition of their connections and continuities. Mass violence and genocide are part of a continuum. Genocide is normally socially, politically incremental, and is often perceived and experienced by perpetrators, collaborators, bystanders – and even, eventually, by victims themselves – as ordinary, routine, even justified.

The preparation for mass killing is found in social sentiments and in institutions ranging from the family, to schools, churches, hospitals, and the military. The early "warning signs" include an evolving social consensus toward: the *devaluing of certain forms of human life* (pseudo-speciation, dehumanization, reification, and depersonalization); *a refusal of social support and humane care* to vulnerable and stigmatized social groups seen as social para-sites (whether "illegal aliens," "welfare queens," or hospitalized "gomers" and "nursing home elderly"); *the militarization of everyday life* (e.g., the growth of prisons, the acceptance of capital punishment; heightened technologies of personal security, including the house gun and gated communities); *increasing social polarization, fear and moral panics* (the perceptions of the under-class, street children, or certain racial or ethnic groups as dangerous and socially polluting public enemies); and finally, *reversed feelings of victimization* as dominant social groups and social classes demand strong policing to put despised subordinate or marginal groups in their proper place.

Once recognized, how can these negative social forces be transformed? I have found useful Emmanuel Levinas's (1986) notion of the "primacy of the ethical" (see Scheper-Hughes 1995) which suggests certain tran-scendent, transparent – I dare to say (as an anthropologist!) pre-cultural – first principles. Traditionally, anthropologists have understood morality as contingent on, and embedded within, specific cultural assumptions about human life. But there is another philosophical and theological position that posits "the ethical" as existing outside of, and even as prior to, culture. As Levinas writes: "Morality does not belong to culture: [it] enables one to judge it."

Some human actions and events, including genocide and mass violence, have to be exempt from the anthropologist's normally relativizing discourse. Even Derrida, the master of deconstructionism, has posited certain dimensions of human life and experience that have to exist outside the decon-structivist framework. Among these "exemptions" are, he suggests, (evok-ing Hannah Arendt's *Human Condition*) notions of justice and fairness, forgiveness, promise-keeping, and hope. One thinks, for example, of the poignant scene from Truffaut's *The Wild Child* in which the pre-socialized and barely verbal wolf-boy lashes out at his human captor screaming one of his first full sentences: "Not fair!"

The demand for justice, for mutual responsibility, accountability, answerability to the existence of "the other" – the ethical, as I define it – may be said to be *pre-cultural* to the extent that our existence as humans, as uniquely social beings, already presupposes the presence of others. While traditional anthropological relativism assumes that thought, emotion, and reflexivity come into existence with words, and words come into being with language embedded within culture, the very pre-structure of language, our uniquely human readiness for speech, assumes an interlocutor and a given relationship with another subject. I have never been able to escape the following observation: that we are thrown into existence at all presupposes a given moral relationship to an original other/mother and she to me.

"Basic strangeness" – the profound shock of misrecognition reported by some mothers in their first encounters with a newborn – is perhaps the prototype of all dangerously alienated "self–other" relations, including those leading up to genocide. As every new mother knows, the only possibility for fragile life to grow and prosper is for a sense of estrangement, what I have elsewhere called "basic strangeness," to be replaced by "basic love" which for me connotes a very minimalist notion of "love" understood as a refusal to objectify, to hate, and to kill. Martin Buber's "I–Thou that supersedes I–it relations" certainly comes to mind.

Above all, it is essential that we exercise a defensive hyper-vigilance and hyper-sensitivity to all the mundane, normative, and permitted acts of violence that are directed against certain "classes" of disqualified and despised humans. Perhaps a constant mobilization for constant shock and hyper-arousal in response to the little violences – "the small wars and invisible genocides" of everyday life – is one ethical response to Walter Benjamin's (1969) view of late modern history as a chronic "state of emergency."

Acknowledgments

Sections of this essay were previously published in Scheper-Hughes and Bourgois, "Making Sense of Violence," Introduction to our edited anthology, *Violence in War and Peace* (2004b, Blackwell Publishing). I am grateful to Philippe for our years of exciting and productive intellectual collaboration of the sort that rescues life in the academy from being little more than a lonely office off a dark corridor, bookshelves, answering machine, and a computer.

Notes

1   Eric Kleinenberg's *Heat Wave* is a brilliant analysis of the unnecessary deaths of 773 Chicago residents during the summer of 1995. Most of the victims were Black, elderly, and poor, many died alone and barricaded behind locked doors and sealed windows. They perished in the brick ovens of their single occupancy rooms and dilapidated tenements during a July heat wave. The response of public officials was appalling. They invoked nature, the hand of God (held responsible for turning up the city's thermostat to 106 degrees in the shade on July 13), while simultaneously minimizing the damage. Mayor Daley responded with the unforgettable words: "It's hot, it's very hot. We have our little problems but let's not blow it all out of proportion. We go to extremes in Chicago. And that's why people *like* Chicago . . . The city cannot be held responsible for the heat." Predictably, the victims themselves

were held accountable for their deaths. "We're talking about people who die because they neglect themselves," the Chicago Commission of Health and Human Services said at the time. The city's official report on the disaster, entitled the "Mayor's Commission on Extreme Weather Conditions," naturalized the disaster and emphasized that "those most at risk may be least likely to want or accept help from government." Assigning blame to the failures of the poor to bootstrap themselves out of dangerous neighborhoods and substandard housing was (Kleinenberg argues) a sign of public neglect endemic in American inner cities. What really happened in July 1995 was social murder.

2   In the documentary film *The Blind Spot* (see Leibing, this volume), Hitler's secretary claims that she was simply unable to perceive the evil in Hitler even though she worked with him on a daily basis and because she was too close to him.

3   I continue to work in Northeast Brazil on topics ranging from death squad violence to the killing of street children, the illegal international adoptions of poor infants, and the traffic in human organs (see Scheper-Hughes 2006a and b).

4   My writings on infant mortality and selective neglect in the backlands of Northeast Brazil are contested among scholars in Brazil and elsewhere. I have not drawn a pretty picture but I stand by my observations knowing that the people of *Alto* and the town I call *Bom Jesus da Mata* in Pernambuco do not contest my findings and interpretations, which I have studiously shared with them in dozens of base community meetings. Instead, they have used my analysis to address pressing social and political issues related to structural violence, hunger, scarcity, grief and loss, gender and sexuality, reproduction and parenting, resilience and resistance. *Death without Weeping* has never been published in Portuguese, making it unavailable for more public debate and discussion. However, a Spanish translation, *La Muerte Sin Llanto: Violencia y Vida Cotidiana en Brasil*. Barcelona: Editorial Ariel, S.A. (1997) is available.

5   In Walter Salles' film, *Broken April*, a father sends all his sons to kill and be killed, one after the other, to save the family's honor in a land conflict. Sacrificial violence is also linked at certain times and places to family honor. As the protagonist says in *Broken April*: "We have lost everything, the only thing we have left is honor" (Annette Leibing, personal communication).

References

Agamben, Giorgio
   1999   Remnants of Auschwitz, The Winners and the Archive. D. Heller-Roazen, trans. New York: Zone Books.
Arendt, Hannah
   1958   The Human Condition. Chicago: University of Chicago.

Arendt, Hannah
   1963   Eichmann in Jerusalem: A Report on the Banality of Evil. New York: Vintage.
Basaglia, Franco
   1987   Peacetime Crimes. *In* Psychiatry Inside Out: Selected Writings of Franco Basaglia. Nancy Scheper-Hughes and Anne M. Lovell, eds. Pp. 471–497. New York: Columbia University Press.
Bauman, Zygmunt
   1989   Modernity and the Holocaust. New York: Cornell University.
Benjamin, Walter
   1969   Theses on the Philosophy of History. *In* Illuminations. H. Arendt, ed. Pp. 83–109. New York: Schocken.
Bourdieu, Pierre
   1962   Célibat et condition paysanne. Études rurales 5–6 (Apr.–Sept.).
Bourdieu, Pierre
   1977   Outline of a Theory of Practice. Cambridge: Cambridge University Press.
Bourdieu, Pierre
   2004   The Peasant and his Body. Ethnography 5:579–599.
Bourdieu, Pierre, and Loïc Wacquant
   1992   An Invitation to Reflexive Sociology. Chicago: University of Chicago Press.
Erikson, Erik
   1950   Childhood and Society. New York: Norton.
Fackenheim, Emil
   1970   God's Presence in History: Jewish Affirmations and Philosophical Reflections after Auschwitz. New York: New York University Press.
Geertz, Clifford
   1995   After the Fact: Two Countries, Four Decades, One Anthropologist. Cambridge, MA: Harvard University Press.
Girard, René
   1986   The Scapegoat. Baltimore: Johns Hopkins University Press.
Girard, René
   1987   Generative Scapegoating. *In* Violent Origins: Ritual Killing and Cultural Formation. R. Hamerton-Kelly, ed. Pp. 73–105. Stanford University Press.
Goldhagen, Daniel Jonah
   1996   Hitler's Willing Executioners. New York: Alfred Knopf.
Henry, Jules
   1966   Sham, Vulnerability and Other Forms of Self Destruction. New York: Vintage.
Klinenberg, Eric
   2001   Bodies That Don't Matter. *In* Commodifying Bodies. Nancy Scheper-Hughes and Loic Waquant, eds. London: Sage.
Klinenberg, Eric
   2002   Heat Wave: A Social Autopsy of Disaster in Chicago. Chicago: University of Chicago Press.

Levi, Primo
　1995　Survival in Auschwitz. Washington: Touchstone.
Levinas, Emmanuel
　1986　Useless Suffering. *In* Face to Face with Levinas. Richard Cohen, ed.
　Albany, NY: State University of New York Press.
Marquez, Gabriel Garcia
　1982　Chronicle of a Death Foretold. New York: Alfred Knopf.
Roberts, Les, Riyadh Lafta, Richard Garfield, Jamal Khudhairi, and Gilbert
　Burnham
　2004　"Mortality Before and After the 2003 Invasion of Iraq: Cluster Sample
　Survey". The Lancet 364(9448):1857.
Sartre, Jean-Paul
　1964　Les Mots. Paris: Gallimards.
Scheper-Hughes, Nancy
　1993　Death without Weeping: the Violence of Everyday Life in Brazil.
　Berkeley: University of California Press.
Scheper-Hughes, Nancy
　1995　The Primacy of the Ethical. Current Anthropology 36(3) (June):
　409–420.
Scheper-Hughes, Nancy
　1996a　Small Wars and Invisible Genocides. Social Science & Medicine
　43(5):88.
Scheper-Hughes, Nancy
　1996b　Maternal Thinking and the Politics of War. Peace Review 8(3):353–
　358.
Scheper-Hughes, Nancy
　2000　Saints, Scholars and Schizophrenics: Mental Illness in Rural Ireland.
　New and updated edition. Berkeley and Los Angeles: University of
　California.
Scheper-Hughes, Nancy, and Loic Wacquant, eds.
　2002　Commodifying Bodies. London: Sage.
Scheper-Hughes, Nancy
　2004a　Dangerous and Endangered Youth: Social Structures and Deter-
　minants of Violence. Annals of the New York Academy of Sciences 1036:
　13–46.
Scheper-Hughes, Nancy
　2004b　Violence in War and Peace. London and Malden: Blackwell
　Publishing.
Scheper-Hughes, Nancy
　2006a　Kidney Kin: Inside the Trans-Atlantic Transplant Trade. Harvard
　International Review 27(4):62–66.
Scheper-Hughes, Nancy
　2006b　Death Squads and Democracy. *In* J. and J. L. Comaroff, eds. Law and
　Disorder in the Postcolony. Chapter 4, pp. 150–187. Chicago: University of
　Chicago Press.

Taussig, Michael
  1992   The Nervous System. New York and London: Routledge.
Wolf, Eric R.
  1982   Europe and the People without History. Berkeley: University of California Press.
Yeats, William Butler
  2004   The Second Coming. Collected Poems of W. B. Yeats. P. 158. Hertfordshire: Wordsworth Poets Library.

Chapter 8

Others within Us:
Collective Identity, Positioning, and Displacement

Meira Weiss

Introduction

"'Jane Doe'[1] was the first dead body I have ever seen," I wrote in my field notes while describing the rite of passage that I underwent when entering the morgue. "Today is the first time I saw a dead person, a body"[2] I wrote in my field journals on June 26, 1996. I refer here to my last research done at the National Institute of Forensic Medicine, located in Abu Kabir near Tel-Aviv. On that day the physician took me into the morgue on some pretext and showed me a decaying body, eaten by wild beasts, with pieces missing and falling apart. "I will never forget," I wrote in my field journals, "the first time in which I saw a really dead person, bare and exposed."

But everything has been changed now, nine years afterwards, when I was in the process of writing the book based on this research. I re-read my field journals and all the details, views, and colors of "Jane Doe's" case came to life again. So did the smell. That sweet, unique smell of human decay. I realize now that it wasn't the first time I smelled that scent. I have smelled it before. I now remember the scent taking me down memory lane . . .

As I write about "Jane Doe," I remember clearly. Actually, "Jane Doe" was not the first dead body that I had seen. The first one was an Egyptian soldier. I forgot about him completely, but now I remember him vividly, feeling the memory in my body.

Immediately after the Six Days War, in June 1967, while I was an officer in the Israeli army, we were taken – the officers of the military base – to a "victory tour" in Sinai, "to see the victory." At night, in Bir Gafgafa, when we slept outside, together with the echoes of gun shots, this horrible sweet scent came to me. . . . It was the smell of bodies decaying in the desert. The Sinai desert was full

of such dead bodies of Egyptian soldiers, parts of human flesh, teeth, and shoes.
The bodies were lying there, scattered in the sands. We passed them, those black
bodies, dismembered, of hundreds and thousands of Egyptian soldiers.

We photographed every body that we saw. They were part of our victory albums.
My album is full of dead body photographs. We did not feel anything weird or
disgusting about having our victory tour while passing those scattered bodies in the
desert. It did not occur to the organizers that they should postpone the tour until
after the bodies had been transferred (were the bodies transferred eventually?). On
the contrary: We felt it was part of the tour, and that photographing the dead
bodies was photographing our victory. We did not think that we were photographing
the horror.

I have forgotten all about that tour. I did not remember those bodies of the "enemy."
Today, when I write about "Jane Doe" and smell the sweet decaying scent again,
I remember you, the dead bodies of the "enemy." I look at the old photographs
of you. I am looking at the white background of the desert sands, and the hori-
zontal body of an Egyptian soldier, in a light-colored uniform, almost the color
of the sand, with a long face, black, dismembered body, and teeth that came out
of the face. I look at him with horror. You, the Egyptian soldier, and not "Jane
Doe" from the Institute of Forensic Medicine, you were my very first dead body.
I watched you, I smelled you, and almost ran over you with our victory tour
vehicle. We were 18-year-old boys and girls and I have "forgotten" all about you.
But you still lived in the back of my memory, brought to life again by the power
of smell.[3]

This paper is an experiment in biographical positioning.[4] I was born in
Israel, to European-born parents who came to that country when they were
themselves children. I am a child from the upper middle class who became
an officer in the Israeli military, and later a professor at the Hebrew
University, and a mother of children who also went into the military. My
life-course embodies all the "right choices." Yet it is also a course dictated to me by my country in ways I only recently came to question and
resist. Through the biographical positioning and the effort to review and
reinterpret my previous ethnographic works that ensue, I describe how
my research has set me against that chosen course.

As I "enlisted myself" to revise this article, the El-Akza Intifada (the
second Palestinian uprising) has burst out and become more and more
violent, including the horrible lynch cases out and terror attacks by individuals and the state. This is a common situation for anthropologists who
write on their own society: they are too emotionally involved. But there
is more to it. In the face of situations that threaten "the national security"
I find myself torn between being an enlisted citizen and a critical anthropologist. I feel that I share my informants' subjugation. The construction of
Israeli identity is part of my own construction.

This experiment in reflexivity is meant to throw into relief the dialectics of "positioning" as well as "displacement." In the process of writing this article I have noticed a strange symmetry between my research subject and my professional life. Like my country, I have been preoccupied with the exclusion of "harmful" or "potentially threatening" bodies of data and ideas. I argue here that the construction of collective identity involves coercive labeling (and hence exclusion) of "others." The construction of my research also involved excluding data that related, for example, to social practices of "selection."

While conducting the research I was harassed by informants and followed by the Israeli security services. This fact served as a constant reminder that I was, in terms of my research, on "the right track." But at the same time it scared me because I felt it was wrong to criticize my country in such a way. Even my academic writing was censored by myself and by the reviewers. Censoring the term "selection" (of the Israeli perfect body by state representatives) and replacing it with the more neutral "screening" is a case in point (Weiss, 2002). While I believed that the reality I was describing consisted of selection, I refrained from using the actual term so as not to construct an analogy between Israel and Nazi Germany. Some of these terms and issues will be presented here, uncensored, for the first time. This experiment hence also serves as an opportunity for professional "outing."

The Body as Social Mirror

Anthropologists have studied collective identity as a negotiated order built upon the interplay of "self" (us) and "others" (them). Arguing that a definition of "self" is always contingent on conceptualization of "others," anthropologists brought into their study an acute awareness of the personal/professional/collective dualities of "inside" and "outside," "participating" and "observing." While this assertion is quite general, the actual dynamics of collective identity are also always contextual. In this article I analyze the Israeli context, positioning myself within that context as a participant observer.

The body of work that spawned this article consists of various studies that I conducted over the years: parents' selection of their children, testing and screening of soldiers, the commemoration and bereavement of fallen soldiers, media coverage of "terrorist" bombings, and women living under the masculine script of soldiering (see Weiss 1994, 1997, 1998a,b), but mainly my forthcoming book (Princeton University Press) dealing with the politics of the dead body in Israel (via its national forensic medical institute) and my recent book, *The Chosen Body: the Politics of the Body in Israeli Society* (Stanford University Press 2002).

"The Chosen Body" is the masculine, Jewish, Ashkenazi, physically perfect and wholesome figure. This trope serves as an ideal type by which concrete Israeli bodies are screened and molded from their birth to their death. My analysis is concerned with representations of the body – or embodiments – as discursive formations, mediated through language as well as embodied practices. The focus of this article is on the symbolic administration of boundaries between "our" and "their" bodies. Such boundary-work that maintains the exclusion of bodies represents the construction of "self" vis-à-vis "others" on a social and political level. This study thus attempts to link the individual, social, and political body. The ethnographic interface where these constructs meet is the National Institute of Forensic Medicine.

The National Institute of Forensic Medicine

Located in Tel-Aviv, the National Institute of Forensic Medicine is a terminus for bodies in need of identification or examination. In the Institute, "self" and "others" are physically and symbolically mixed, processed, and separated. It is also a meeting ground for different, almost opposite approaches to the body. On the one hand, it is a scientific Institute, affiliated with the Sackler School of Medicine (Tel-Aviv University) and operating a state-of-the-art genetic laboratory. On the other, it is also closely inspected by the *Chevra Kadisha* (Aramaic for "holy society"), the religious Burial undertaking organization that, except in the army and kibbutzim, has a monopoly on burials. On the one hand, the Institute is a civil organization working under the Ministry of Health. On the other, the Institute fulfills the requirements of the military and the police. I conducted observations and interviews in the Institute since 1996.

The Institute of Forensic Medicine conducts tests in order to identify bodies and physical violence. It is the only Institute of Forensic Medicine in Israel and as such receives thousands of "cases" per year. These cases include rape, medical malpractice, the death of babies, the battering of prisoners in jail, and the death of Palestinians in security interrogations (Hiss et al. 1996). These "cases" are brought to the Institute by various state organizations that are interested in the Institute's professional opinion, such as the police, the Israel Defense Forces, the prison authority, the Ministry of Health, and private people. Autopsy is supposed to be performed only with a court's order or with the consent of the relatives.[5] Despite having been created to support the state authorities, the Institute also operates as a guardian of human rights, often in the context of male and female minorities (e.g., prisoners, Palestinian "terrorists," infants, the elderly, and victims of rape).

From an anthropological point of view the Institute provides a unique meeting ground for the personal body and the social order. The cases examined in the Institute, the nature of its practice and the applicability of its findings, are directly connected to breaches in Israeli society, in particular to nationalistic, religious, and ethnic breaches. The Institute maintains (often unwillingly) differences between Jews and non-Jews, Palestinians and Israelis, soldiers and non-soldiers. These differences have received a lot of sociological attention, but never in the context of forensic medicine.

One of my most startling findings was that the handling of bodies in the Institute reflected the boundaries of collective identity in Israel. Jews versus non-Jews was the first dichotomy according to which bodies are handled. Three procedures – circumcision, tattoo removal, and tissue burial – were performed only for Jews. The second and more stringent dichotomy is between soldiers and non-soldiers. The bodies of soldiers are kept apart and handled almost ceremonially. It is forbidden, under all circumstances, to take body tissues from soldiers. It is forbidden, for example, to harvest skin for the skin bank from the corpses of fallen soldiers, or to practice on them for the purpose of developing medical skills. Previously, skin was harvested from Israeli-Arabs and Palestinians. I was told – off the record – that the times of the first Intifada (the first Palestinian uprising, 1987–93) were especially good for harvesting. Recently, new immigrants and foreign workers from Eastern European countries have replaced the Palestinians as a source of skin. The national skin bank in Hadassah hospital, which is designed to cater to military needs, similarly does not receive any of its skin from soldiers' bodies. In 1999–2000 there was an upsurge of reports in daily newspapers[6] concerning organ trafficking and medical practicing on corpses allegedly taking place in the Institute. The interesting point is that the reports did not criticize this phenomenon in general, but rather accused the Institute of using the corpses of fallen soldiers for such purposes. In other words, the newspapers – even those with a leftist and liberal orientation – fought to preserve the integrity of the "chosen body."

The Children of Yemen

Since 1996, a new social issue has become a major task in the Institute's agenda. Dubbed the case of the "missing Yemenite children" by the media, the issue involved reports on large-scale and systematic kidnapping of the children of Yemenite immigrants during the early 1950s, and their being put up – without their parents' knowledge or consent – for adoption by Ashkenazi families. Many immigrants from Arab countries were flown to Israel after its establishment in 1948. Among these were Yemenite Jews who were gathered in transition camps. Following many complaints regarding the disappearance of Yemenite children (currently estimated around 1,000) from hospitals and schools within these camps, a state commission of inquiry was established in 1995 to look into the affair. It authorized the Institute of Forensic Medicine to open the graves of adopted children and conduct DNA analysis in order to establish the corpses' "real" lineage, i.e., the match between them and their alleged Yemenite family. The process of exhumation and identification began by taking blood samples from ten chosen families and comparing it with mitochondrial DNA produced from the corpses.

I am interested in the Yemenite children affair as another example of the Israeli discourse on the "chosen body," and particularly the move from one, collective, interchangeable body to many different, ethnic bodies.[7] The Yemenite children affair was constructed as a burning ethnic issue, which threatens to dismantle the integrity of the "body politic" of the state and its (Ashkenazi) elites. The protest of Yemenite activists, and the forming of a state commission of inquiry in response to that protest, imply that what could happen in the early 1950s – the time of the melting-pot doctrine, of high collectivism, of Ben Gurion's statism – is de-legitimized today. The story of the coerced adoption of the Yemenite children is revolting evidence of the "melting-pot" doctrine, which aimed to assimilate all Jews of different origins at the expense of effacing ethnic traditions and subjecting them to Ashkenazi hegemony.

During my sabbatical in the USA, I was approached a few times by Yemenite families from Israel and representatives of the Jewish Yemenite Federation there. They saw me as a potential go-between, an established Ashkenazi professor who is also prepared to be on their side. One of the heads of the Yemenite Federation told me there is a reason why the State of Israel has refrained from opening the graves of the alleged Yemenite children for so long. According to him, this would have exposed the fact that these children were subjected to horrible medical experiments in the 1950s. The children died because of official medical experiments.[8] Shocked, I asked some of my (rather critical and reflexive) Israeli colleagues what they think about this claim. Their first reaction was, "do not publish this. You would jeopardize the country." When my husband goes to pick up material from a Yemenite representative in Israel, I ask him to park his car a few blocks away from her home, so that the *Shaback*

(GSS – General Security Service) will not register the car's number. He does not listen to me. When I meet again with my contact person in the USA, he tells me that the *Shaback* (GSS) knows about my involvement.

My sister Ofra died as a young girl from polio in the 1950s. Almost 50 years later, during a conversation with the spokesperson of the Yemeni leader, I tell her I was always told how she was "a healthy child in the morning, and dead in the evening." There are similar stories about the dead/missing Yemenite children. The spokesperson told me that there can be no such thing as hospitalization and death on the same day. Polio takes at least ten days, she said. In the 50s, the spokesperson said, the hospitals were crooked. Don't believe them; the doctors took your sister like they took the Yemenite children. She is probably alive. Give me all the details, her identification number, and I will ask our computer experts to look her up for you. You have a sister.

I didn't know what to do about this conversation. I asked my father if he saw Ofra's body. No, he said, but I have one memory of her in the last days: I came to visit her, in the hospital, and they didn't let me in. I had to push my way into the room. I saw her, alone, sad, and when she saw me she began to smile. Then they took me out. Brutally. When she saw I was leaving the room, she looked at me with a face that knew she was losing me forever. I will not forget that look.

He told me about this 50 years after it happened. Not a minute sooner.

At this point I think about the parents of the Yemenite children; how their children were separated from them, how their children became sick and were taken to the hospital and remained there until the death notice was issued. I think about the brutality of the medical establishment, which didn't allow parental visits because of some "risk of contamination" or "lack of order." I realize the strength of that establishment, the medical establishment, in relation to individuals, even hard-headed Ashkenazi individuals like my father. I think how tempting it must be to believe that your kith and kin are alive. I remember how I used to daydream for hours that my sister would appear again. I used to play with paper dolls, dress them up and hope they'd come to life and be Ofra. I am almost tempted to give Ofra's details to the spokesperson.

From my personal diary:

Tami, my daughter, is undergoing an officer's course in the Israeli Army. I am ambivalent; on the one hand, worried sick, recalling my own experience of ordeal on that course, when my body refused to act, thus expressing its resistance; on the other hand, happy for her, and in a strange way very proud and anxious to see her through. I wait for her at home at the weekend, wondering what she'll look like. Hoping that she'll come in the door, radiant, and say how good she's feeling. I'm afraid of her weakness and of my impotence. You raise a child for 18 years, and one day they take her away from you. Just like that. And all sorts of 19-year-old children decide what will happen to her. If she's fit or not. When she gets sick, you cannot take care of her. You cannot even take her to a doctor. Nobody wants to hear from you. She's a soldier. What do you mean she's a soldier . . . She's my daughter, isn't she? I feel bad. I feel bad for Tami. I don't want her to suffer in the army like I did. I'd like to fall asleep for the entire summer, and wake up when the course is over.

The letters I send out are cheerful and happy. The following one, a typical letter, was written and sent after a visit in the camp where Tami was. During the visit I felt sick and nauseous. My body remembered my harsh experience in the Israeli Army. But the letter was happy:

> Hi Honey . . . It's really difficult, but I'm sure you can handle it. I saw you yesterday and it made me calm down. I understood what a great daughter I have. I have complete faith in you. But with all due respect, an officer or not, even if you won't finish this course, I know what you're worth. Not making it is not the end of the world.

Reading back through these letters, I feel what Simon de Beauvoir called a sense of dédoublement, of being double. My body remembers the pain, while my mind is rationalizing. I am nauseous, but take the ride again, despite all the alarms. I am mother #X; just like one of my respondents, taking part in the cult of the "chosen body," speaking in two languages, the passive and the active. The only difference, I think to myself, is that I write, too. But does writing make a difference?

I am at Berkeley (1996–97), on sabbatical, working on the material that provided the basis for this article and my 2002 book. I summarize my field notes about the exhumation of Yemenite children. I have a few questions about the process of mitochondrial DNA identification. I'll call the Institute tonight. Later, when I call home I hear from Shay, my son, about a suicidal terrorist bombing in the marketplace. Suddenly my whole body hurts. I call the Institute of Forensic Medicine, where all the victims are brought for identification. No questions about DNA and the Yemenite children. Irrelevant now. I ask about the bombing. I then call a colleague at the Hebrew University, who tells me, it's not anyone we know. A few minutes afterwards the telephone keeps ringing. The Israelis here at Berkeley want to know if everything is all right at home. My mother is calling, trying to convince me not to publish my book in order not to hurt Israel. My conversations with my mother are not conversations dealing with familial issues.[9] The Nation, through my mother, is warning me. The American anthropologist does not share my dilemmas. The American anthropologist is committed to uncover-

ing others' misdeeds, others' violence.[10] *For the Israeli anthropologist, the quest for collective identity begins in the others within us.*

Suicide bombers' attacks ("Piguiim")

If the soldier's body is the "chosen body" and the apex of collective Israeli identity, then the body of the Palestinian suicide bomber ("terrorist") is the ultimate other. The following analysis sets out to examine this claim.

"Terror attack" (*Pigua*, in Hebrew) is an integral part of my research as well as my life in Israel. Approximately two to four hours after the *Pigua* (the "terror" attack) – the exact timing depends on the attack's distance from the Institute – the bodies and their severed parts start to arrive. Religious demands in Israel require the identification process to be completed in the shortest possible time, as burial must not be delayed.[11] This requirement becomes particularly demanding in mass disasters, due to the sheer number of casualties who are often disfigured or fragmented as a result of the explosions. The Institute takes pride in succeeding in identifying the casualties of the 18 terrorist bombings that occurred in Israel between 1993 and 1996 within no more than 24 hours (Kahana, Freund, and Hiss n.d.:2). The efficient and rapid completion of identification is enabled by a variety of techniques as well as the interdisciplinary collaboration of several agencies within and without the Institute. Genetic matching has proven extremely useful in identifying torn body fragments of the victims, as well the suicide bombers, who are not reported as missing by their families.

The scientific and sterile language conceals a difficult political reality. In the Jerusalem bombings and other cases, the Institute has provided the scientific technology that allowed the *Shaback* (the Israeli General Security Service), aided by the Israel Defense Forces, to successfully identify the suicide bombers. Positive identification of the suicide bombers was made possible following a request by the General Security Service to the Palestinian Authority to allow the parents of the suspected bomber to submit to DNA testing.[12] The tests were brought to the Institute, where the remains of the bomber had been transferred following the attack. The procedure developed in the Institute received official recognition in the form of the Ministry of Internal Security 1998 Award for research and development. The importance of identifying the suicide bombers is, according to military sources, not in learning their names, but in the lead the identities provide to uncovering other potential bombers. According to security officials, *Hamas* usually misinforms families about the death of their sons in suicide bombings. *Hamas* activists allegedly notify families immediately after the attacks by sending them regards from their sons. The families of the bombers always express disbelief and amazement on hearing the news. This is supposedly done to avoid families setting up mourning tents and to try to keep the bombers' identities secret. This explanation, however, may also be part of Israeli propaganda.

Dr. Angels, who was critically injured 25 years ago in a terror attack, is the head of the biology lab in the Institute and is responsible for DNA matching. In a personal interview she told me that "DNA matching is something we usually do in case of bombers. Because there is no ante-mortem file, I do not see people or files . . . Only test results of genetic markers. This is the most scientific part of the Institute. Pathologists may think the most fragmented body is likely to be the bombers. But such inference can be misleading. I do not make mistakes. However, I can only confirm identification, not reach it by myself. I depend on the *Shaback* (the General Security Service (GSS)) for identification. In previous years, terrorist organizations proudly announced the identity of the bombers. The General Security Services (GSS) would immediately bring blood tests from the family. I would verify the match, and the GSS would demolish the family's house. Today, the terrorist organizations have become smarter. They don't give us free information any more. Now the General Security Services (GSS) usually provide me with several blood tests, and I make the comparisons."

Following positive identification, the Israeli General Security Service (*Shaback*) usually seals the house of the bomber's family or ruins it. This act of intimidation is an official Israeli policy. Some of the Institute's workers, who are involved in the process of DNA matching, are politically associated with the Left (the Peace camp). When asked if they reflect on their involvement in what leads to the sealing of Palestinian homes, they told me that their response is not to reflect but to deny. I was told by lab workers and by statisticians (responsible for assessing the statistical probability of error in identification) that they disengage themselves, emotionally and mentally, from the work they conduct. I did not publish these interviews earlier, because their analysis reminded me too much of the case of the Nazi doctors. I sympathized with these people because, like me, they denied and excluded an inner dissonance that could potentially undermine national security.

Kuna Wants to Kill Ariel Sharon

I began with Jane Doe's case, and will close with the following story which was also latent for many years.

From my personal diary

Today, February 7, 2001. It is one day after the elections, and at midnight we found out that Ariel ("Arik") Sharon was the elected prime minister of Israel. During all that night I had nightmares of Arik. In my dream I speak to Kuna, Nisho's father, from the 1973 October War. Both of them are dead. Yeti, Nisho's mother, is dead too. I open my field journals, written for my thesis on bereaved parents from the 1973 October War. I came to Yeti and Kuna towards the end of the war. They were two of my respondents, and I came to their poor apartment in Pardes Katz. They were new immigrants who emigrated from Romania three years before that. Nisho, their son, was declared MIA. At first there was hope that he was alive, but when the Israeli captives returned after a month, Nisho was not among them. The captives said that an Egyptian soldier killed Nisho. Kuna then embarked on a never-ending journey of questioning the captives, commanders, and soldiers. He had become an expert on the October War regarding everything that concerned his son's death.

Nisho was killed in "Missouri" (a fighting site in Sinai) on October 21, 1973. Two days before that, so Kuna found out, Sharon had received an order to capture the Missouri. Although he did not agree with the order, he committed himself to execute it. In addition he was told that hundreds of warriors were scattered around the area and that he should gather them. Despite his resistance (given his desire to save all his force for the Suez Canal crossing), Sharon promised to follow this order too.

The battle of the "Missouri" began with a tiny force of tanks sent by Sharon to the area. This tiny force began fighting, knowing that the major portion of the forces had not yet arrived but that it would be arriving at any moment. The troops did not know that Sharon had decided not to send the reinforcements. One after the other, the tanks were hit and caught fire. Nisho jumped from his tank and broke his leg. He was lying on the sand and couldn't move. Two officers ran backwards in order to join the Israeli forces. One of them was shot by the Egyptians and later received a medal of honor. The other reached the Israeli forces a few hours later.

The troops that remained in the field – soldiers with no officers who found themselves alone – decided to flee backwards too, but then they received an order through the radio: "Stay where you are. Do not move. Arik's battalion is on its way toward you. Be in contact with him." The troops remained in their position. They did not have enough water. A few hours passed. No one arrived. The group tried to contact Sharon. His network was closed. Hysterical, they were calling him again and again, but his net was still closed and sealed. They called their unit, asking for instructions, and were told again to hold their position and wait for Sharon. The sun began to set. The troops in the field heard voices speaking in Arabic. The radio was silent. The Israeli soldiers began to panic. The sun set. Egyptian soldiers surrounded the Israeli soldiers and they were called to surrender. The Israeli troops surrendered but while raising their hands, one of them shot an Egyptian solder and killed him. The Israeli soldier was killed by the Egyptians. He later received a medal of honor.

The Egyptians organized the group of Israeli captives to start moving. Nisho was lying in the sand, with a broken leg. He screamed: "Don't leave me . . ." The other captives were too afraid to approach him. Someone who finally dared to, told him: "do not be afraid, Arik is coming for you." Nisho kept screaming: "Don't leave me here." One of the Israeli soldiers, who understood Arabic, heard the Egyptians planning to shoot Nisho. He was asking them not to do it and they warned him to shut up. Another Israeli soldier walked toward Nisho and tried to help him but the Egyptians shot him in the legs. The Israeli captives started moving. The Egyptian soldiers shot Nisho and killed him.

When the Israeli captives came back to Israel, they told their story about the terrible waiting for Arik Sharon. When the officer who ran towards the Israeli forces and managed to escape was telling Kuna that story, the officer soiled his pants.

"I had to be there with Nisho," Kuna told me when the questioning was over. "Why did I bring him to Israel?" Yeti, Nisho's mother, asked me when we returned to their home.

After a while, following many futile attempts to bring Sharon to trial, 56-year-old Kuna died of a heart attack. Yeti joined him shortly afterwards.

But the story does not end there. There are many ends, endless ends.

A short while before his death, when I arrived in Kuna and Yeti's apartment, Kuna told me: "This is it. I tried everything. If I cannot bring Sharon to trial, I will kill him." Kuna opened a drawer, pulled out a gun and showed it to me: "I bought it today. I am going to kill him."

I went out of the house. It was dark already and I sat on the pavement. I did not know what to do. I was only a young woman, 24 years old or so. I understood that I had just been told by someone that he was going to kill Arik Sharon. Maybe I should go to the police? I decided to stay there, watching. If he goes out, I told myself, I will stop him. After a few hours, when nobody came out of the house, I came to the conclusion that Kuna would not kill Sharon that night. But I was not certain. Around 5 AM I reached my house.

When the first Lebanon War broke out in 1981, a few years after Kuna's death, and Arik Sharon was the one who led the Israeli forces, this event with Kuna came back to me. The Lebanon War affected me and my body. I dreamt about buildings falling down in Lebanon. I was constantly tired as if my strength leaked out of my body. After Tami, my daughter, said in class that the Lebanon War was futile, I was denounced as a traitor by my neighbors. Surrounded by the public consensus regarding the war, I felt physical weakness. People who met me asked if anything was wrong – meaning if I had lost anyone in battle. I replied no, but when in the middle of the war we celebrated the birthday of my son Shay in the kindergarten, I remember one of the neighbors asking us not to sing aloud because the funeral procession of a soldier was taking place in the street. I remember looking around and asking myself how many of these kids in this kindergarten will be killed at war when they are 18 years old. The war fills my body. I hate this war.

The Lebanon War shattered everything and so many young men died. During those nights, I dreamt about Kuna, and talked to him, asking the dead person: "Why, eventually, didn't you kill Sharon? Why did I try to convince you not to kill Sharon? You died anyway a short while afterwards, and we would have saved so many people." I know I shouldn't be thinking like that, especially today after Rabin's assassination. But the thought is there. Thoughts have no limits. I bear this story with me. I have carried its weight all these years.

I still haven't written down Kuna's story in full. I'm sure I'll do it in the near future. But in what I have written, there was never a mention of that night. I had "forgotten" that night with the gun. I remembered it only years afterwards, when the Lebanon War broke up and I had a little son who, I understood, was also going to be a soldier.

Epilogue

July 2001 was a particularly hectic month for the Institute of Forensic Medicine's staff. Seven cadavers, allegedly belonging to Palestinian "terrorists," piled up in the refrigerators, awaiting their autopsies. The staff were waiting for the court order mandating autopsy, which had been delayed. When the order finally arrived from a military court, the autopsies were further delayed by the families' demand that the autopsies were to be conducted only in the presence of the families' representative. Dr. Lisser (the senior forensic doctor) agreed to the families' demand as long as the representative was a physician. The families' lawyer replied that a physician had already been chosen and that he would be arriving from abroad. At this point, Lisser declared that no autopsy would take place until scientific identification had been made in regard to the cadaver. The cadavers had been identified by the *Shaback* (the General Security Service) based on its sources of information regarding missing people in Palestinian villages, Lisser explained; this was not a scientifically valid identification (i.e., based on fingerprints or DNA). I asked Zilpa, the admissions clerk, why not use the Palestinian families (that appealed regarding the autopsy) for the purpose of identification. Zilpa's answer was that "we've already tried to do that in the past, but these families – although they are probably the families we're looking for – always refuse to confirm the identification because they are afraid that the General Security Service will demolish their houses, as it usually does in such cases." If the families do not appear and the cadaver remains unidentified for a certain period of time, the cadaver is legally regarded as a "John Doe" and the court mandates its autopsy.

In the following days, a "neighbor" of the families from the Palestinian town of Jenin arrived at the Institute for the purpose of identification. He was escorted by a convoy composed of lawyers, a photographer, Dr. Paul Lance (from the Institute of Forensic Medicine in Ireland), and men from the General Security Service. The convoy was brought into the library room and treated with refreshments. The "neighbor" was escorted to the morgue, where he identified one of the cadavers as Machmud Halil.[13] Following identification, Halil's cadaver was prepared for the autopsy. Lying on the dissection table, the cadaver appeared to be in good shape, except for the holes left by the bullets. Halil was a young guy, rather dark, and bearded. His face lacked a chunk around the left eye, probably due to the shooting.

The cadaver's file (number 1,137) contained the following description which was relayed by military authorities: *"In July 11 2001, a military ambush of the Israeli Defense Forces encountered several terrorists in the Jenin area and engaged them in battle, killing two terrorists and capturing weapons."* A separate sheet inside the file contained a press release (source: AP) stating that *"in July 11 2001 two Palestinians were arrested by Israeli soldiers near Jenin."* The sheet also contained a request for more information from the Institute based on the autopsy. The Institute, I thought to myself, was once again entangled in a messy situation. It had the authority to decide between two versions, one validating the military's claim that armed Palestinians were shot in battle, the other corroborating the claim made by Associated Press, namely that the Palestinians were captured alive, cuffed, and then killed. This was a forensic decision, but it also had many military, political, and even social implications.

As I was thinking, Dr. Paul Lance was conducting his own external examination. He observed the cadaver from all sides while talking into a small tape recorder. He then photographed the shot holes in the front part of the neck. So far everything was relatively calm. Suddenly, Dr. Lance pointed at the shot holes in the front of the neck and said to Dr. Lisser: "These should be the entry wounds, correct?" "Yes," was the answer. The Israeli pathologists suddenly became very quiet. One of the Israeli pathologists moved towards the corner and whispered to me in Hebrew: "It's good for us that he thinks the entry wounds are in the front. Everyone with a little experience in forensic medicine can see that the entry wounds are in fact in the back." If the entry wounds were in the back, this would mean that the Palestinians had been shot from the back, rather than in battle. This would increase the likelihood of the foreign press release being correct. The Israeli pathologists showed me the hat that was worn by the Palestinian. The back of the hat was torn. The shirt of the Palestinian was also torn in the back by what appeared to be bullet holes. However, the Israeli physicians did not show these artifacts to Dr. Lance.

For a few minutes afterwards I was completely puzzled. I was genuinely relieved that the observer has apparently failed to realize that the shooting was done from the rear. But at the same time I criticized myself for feeling that way. Was I also conscripted? I felt that I strongly agreed with the Israeli pathologists and that Dr. Lance's misunderstanding was indeed good for us. But then I also asked myself silently what and who is this "us"? In the following minute, I also felt ashamed by observing what appeared to be the demise of scientific neutrality.

My thoughts were stopped by a comment from Lisser: "The Palestinians think we have tortured the terrorists. The Israeli forces admit to the shooting. The question in front of us is whether we've tortured him." As I was thinking to myself, *"Why is Lisser saying, 'we have tortured'?"* the external examination was already over and the autopsy had begun. The pathologists used x-rays to locate bullet fragments, and then patiently cut through tissues and organs to find the fragments and store them in plastic bags. Dr. Goldshtein, the forensic anthropologist, had already taken fingerprints and was now doing the teeth. "He visited the dentist recently, had a temporary filling," she commented to us. "Well, I guess he will not have to go back with it to the doctor," Lisser replied. I noticed that Dr. Lance was now examining the "terrorists" clothes, writing something in his notebook. I imagined that he could not miss the entry signals. Perhaps his earlier question only pretended to be naive?

My meandering thoughts clicked into focus again at the sight of Dr. Lance, now moving the body in order to examine the thigh more closely. Directing his attention to a purple bruise apparently caused by a bullet, Dr. Lance asked Dr. Lisser if this could be a torture bruise. Lisser replied that it was a "passage bruise" caused by a passing bullet. As Dr. Lance was scribing and drawing in his notebook, apparently in relation to the thigh bruise, Dr. Mirsky (one of the house pathologists, a new immigrant from Moscow) became annoyed and said to us in Hebrew: "This is a provocation, can't you see this is a provocation?" Later I heard from the Palestinian lawyer who came to the Institute that Dr. Lance reported that a bruise on the thigh was probably caused by torture.

Autopsies like the one just mentioned might appear extraordinary to the Western reader, but they are part of the daily routine of the Institute. Furthermore, this "case" exemplifies the unique mixture of security, nationalism, and forensic medicine, which is so characteristic of the Institute and of contemporary Israeli society in general. This case exemplifies the politicization of how terrorism is perceived, and the social construction of boundaries connected to terror – not just territorial boundaries, boundaries between Palestine and Israel, but also symbolic boundaries between us and them, as well as between participation and observation, objectivity and commitment. In the case of Halil the need to identify the body illustrates how terrorism is enlisted for the purpose of boundary construction. Although it was not clear whether Halil was a terrorist or "just" a Palestinian who was shot by Israeli soldiers, he was presented by the Israeli forensic team as a terrorist.

This presentation constructed a boundary between "us" and "them." It was possible to feel this boundary-work in the negotiation that took place between Dr. Lisser and Dr. Paul Lance. This boundary also became very tangible in a territorial context, whenever the military authorities had to confirm and allow passage from Palestine to Israel for the purpose of identification. I chose to conclude with this case because it poses a question mark that looms large over the discussion. Until now I have argued that terrorist events highlight the essential, practical, and symbolic linkage between the private and public body, the personal body and the body politic. The case of Halil illustrates how taken for granted this linkage has become, and how conditioned are the reflexes of the Israeli collectivity. I chose this case for the conclusion precisely because of the light it casts on our social reality. One of the roles of anthropology is to remind us that our cultural premises, which seem to be taken for granted, are based on social scripts. In our case, terrorism exists and it creates boundaries between "us" and "them." I would like to remind us that the opposite process also takes place. Once these boundaries are put in place, they already construct a reality which is committed to terrorism and fighting terror.

The "case" of Halil was presented by me, for the first time, in my lecture at UC Berkeley on January 30, 2005. Before presenting this "data" I got the following e-mail:

Professor Weiss

I am Lieutenant Wing from the Campus Police Department and I oversee special events. I understand that Prof. Weiss is scheduled to give a talk Monday, at 4 p.m. at 160 Kroeber about her book, The Chosen Body. I also understand that there has been some controversy surrounding Prof. Weiss' research and that there is some media attention focused around this lecture. I also understand that Prof. Weiss has been labeled anti-Semitic and has received death threats due to her research.

I am in no way making any comments regarding Prof. Weiss' research, but I need much more information regarding tonight's lecture so that I can make an assessment regarding safety and security. Please call me as soon as possible so we can discuss the particulars of this event. My goal in this is to assist you in having a safe and productive event.

Yours,
Lieutenant Wing.

Notes

1   "Jane Doe" was a body found in the zone between Jerusalem and the Palestinian Authority. Its identity remained unknown for several months.

2   Jewish bodies are not presented in funerals and Jews are not supposed to observe the dead body. In some of my previous studies I have seen dead bodies in hospitals but this was very brief and soon after death. In the Institute I was exposed to the "real" dead body and this exposure carried with it symbolic meaning of initiation (see Weiss, forthcoming in Princeton University Press).

3   Today, writing a book on the Institute of Forensic Medicine, I understand that the body of "Jane Doe" that Dr. Levin showed me as part of my initiation . . . also released the hidden memories of the Egyptian soldiers.

4   Richardson 1997:10; Weiss, 2001, 2002. A few sections of the current paper appeared earlier in Weiss 2001, 2002. Most of the names and details are fictitious (in order to maintain confidentiality).

5   Jewish laws of conduct (the *Halacha*) generally prohibit the option of autopsy, which is regarded as compromising the "honor" (integrity) of the dead. Representatives of "the Holy Society" and the Army Rabbinate are present daily in the Institute in order to keep the Jewish law. Autopsies are never automatic but require permission and negotiations. Another conflict between Jewish religion and the Institute transpires in the context of identification. According to the *Halacha*, visual identification by a relative is valid and sufficient; in the eyes of the Institute's staff, such identification is not scientifically valid.

6   For example Esti Aharonovitz, "the grand body theft," Ha'ir 11/12/99.

7   This study is based on interviews, observations, and textual analyses, which took place between 1996 and 1998. I have interviewed 20 family relatives whose children were allegedly abducted in the Yemenite children affair. These people were approached by myself at the National Institute of Forensic Medicine, where they arrived for blood drawing and DNA testing. I observed the ten exhumations that followed and conducted further interviews with the Institute's staff. Additional key informants in the Yemenite group were interviewed separately. All interviews were conducted in Hebrew. Textual analysis for this study focused on some 61 hours of protocols of

testimonies given before the official commission of inquiry set by the Israeli government in 1995 to look into the disappearance of Yemenite children. Additional texts included official records and documents pertaining to medical treatment of Yemenite immigrants in the transit camps and official letters sent to families regarding their missing child. These texts were part of the material presented before the committees and before the Israeli Court of Justice.

8 This accusation brings to mind the World War II plutonium experiments in the USA, in which medical researchers injected hospital patients with radioactive plutonium in order to learn its effects on the body (see Kaufman 1997).

9 In contrast to other anthropological reflections, for example Ruth Behar's. Other personal accounts of anthropologists that have influenced my writing include the reflections of a woman anthropologist written under the pseudonym Manda Cesara (1982; see also Poewe 1988, 1999), and in the Israeli context, Kunda's (1992) illuminating critique of the exclusion of the political from Israeli ethnography.

10 Ultimately it will be important for anthropologists in the USA and elsewhere to confront the kind of "agony" I am trying to pinpoint. Living with a sense of real concern about our role as public critics of our/other societies should be relevant to anthropologists everywhere. Writing culture from within "a bind" will increase before it can (ever?) diminish. This paper might encourage many anthropologists, not only Americans, to think about the intrusion of their own nationalism into their work.

11 This requirement holds in regard to Jewish bodies and particularly fallen soldiers. However, bodies of Palestinians are sometimes kept for a long time, especially in the case of terrorists. Dr. Lisser told me (personal interview) that although the Institute strives to maintain the honor of the dead, this does not apply to "terrorists" who are usually denied burial.

12 "Allowing families to submit to blood testing" is the official phrasing. In reality, blood testing is often enforced on Arab-Israeli or Palestinian families regardless of their cooperation. There is no legal procedure at work here. Although blood testing without consent is illegal, it is overlooked by Israeli courts, being the only way of ascertaining the bomber's identity.

13 This name, like the other names referred to in the present article, is a pseudonym.

References

Cesara, Manda
    1982   Reflections of a Woman Anthropologist: No Hiding Place. NY: Academic Press.
Hiss, Jehuda, and Tzipy Kahana
    n.d.   Suicide Bombers In Israel.

Hiss, Jehuda, and Tzipy Kahana
    1995   Medicolegal   Investigation   of   Death   in   Custody: A   Post-Mortem
    Procedure for Detection of Blunt Force Injuries. American Journal of Forensic
    Medicine and Pathology 17(4):312–314.
Kahana, Tzipy, Maya Freund, and Jehuda Hiss, n.d. Suicidal Terrorist Bombings
    in Israel – Identification of Human Remains.
Kaufman, Sharon
    1997   The   World   War   II   Plutonium   Experiments.   Culture,   Medicine   &
    Psychiatry 21:161–197.
Kunda, Gideon
    1992   Criticism   on   Trial: Ethnography   and   Cultural   Critique   in   Israel.
    Te'oria U'bikoret 2:7–25 (in Hebrew).
Poewe, Karla
    1988   Childhood   in   Germany   during   WWII: the   Story   of   a   Little   Girl.
    Lewinston: The Edwin Mellen Press.
Poewe, Karla
    1999   No Hiding Place: Reflections on the Confessions of Manda Cesara. *In*
    Sex, Sexuality and the Anthropologist. F. Markowitz and M. Ashkenazi, eds.
    Pp. 195–207. Urbana: University of Illinois Press.
Richardson, Laurel
    1997   Fields   of   Play: Constructing   an   Academic   Life.   Rutgers: Rutgers
    University Press.
Weiss, Meira
    1994   Conditional Love. New York: Bergin & Garvey.
Weiss, Meira
    1997   War   Bodies,   Hedonist   Bodies: Dialectics   of   the   Collective   and   the
    Individual in Israeli Society. American Ethnologist 24 (4):1–20.
Weiss, Meira
    1998a   Engendering Gulf War Memories: Israeli Nurses and the Discourse of
    Soldiering. Journal of Contemporary Ethnography 27(2):197–218.
Weiss, Meira
    1998b   Narratives of Embodiment: The Discursive Formulation of Multiple
    Bodies. Semiotica (118–134):239–260.
Weiss, Meira
    2001   "Writing   Culture"   Under   the   Gaze   of   my   Country.   Ethnography
    2(1):77–91.
Weiss, Meira
    2002   The Chosen Body: The Politics of the Body in Israeli Society. Stanford:
    Stanford University Press.
Weiss, Meira
    In press   From the Heart of Darkness: Power and Knowledge at the Israeli
    National Institute of Forensic Medicine. Princeton: Princeton University Press.

Chapter 9

Falling into Fieldwork: Lessons from a Desperate Search for Survival

Rose-Marie Chierici

Cheche lavi, detwi lavi [1]

This is the story of Mathias Exavier, a strapping young man from a coastal village in northern Haiti. With great courage and some trepidation, Mathias left family and kin one fateful morning in 1992 and boarded a crowded, rickety boat bound for the USA to *cheche lavi*, to search for a better life. Like any 18-year-old embarking on the adventure of a lifetime, he was brimming with hope and youthful enthusiasm, never suspecting that his dreams would end abruptly a few months later and that he would die in a hospital in upstate New York. This migration story is also in small part my story, that of a Haitian émigré whose urban, upper-class Haitian family was among an earlier wave of immigrants who came to the US in the early 1960s. Although Mathias and I shared a national origin and history, we were also separated by social class and geography and most likely never would have met in Haiti. However, our paths crossed under unusual circumstances and for three weeks we shared intense moments as I witnessed his suffering and untimely death.

Mathias was born on September 26, 1973 in Pillate, on the northern coast of Haiti. Pillate is a poor village where fishermen bring in small catch, farmers coax reluctant crops from the impoverished land, and very few villagers read and write. It is linked to other villages and market towns by a nearby road and mountain paths. Port-au-Prince, the capital, seems so far away. To get there one has to cross mountains on foot or muleback or venture on a long and expensive truck ride over gullied roads. However, the ocean offers a straight and clear way out of Haiti toward the mythical place called *Miyami* (Miami). In *Miyami*, Haitians say, there are jobs; one can prosper and become someone. The arms of the police, the army, secret societies, and the *attache* (paramilitary forces) do not reach that far. Social hierarchies which keep peasants "in their place" do not exist in *Miyami*. No one is killed for political beliefs and the government does not tax the poor to support the rich. There are large cities, roads are paved, and there are no weeds or rats. Migrants who can *jambe dlo* (cross the ocean) will be able to get a job and send money home to support the extended family. It is no wonder, then, that so many risk taking a *kante*[2] (sailboat) and head for the unknown. Paradoxically, the people of Pillate have more contact with Florida than with Port-au-Prince. If communication with the capital is not possible, audio cassettes as well as remittances and other gifts link the villagers to migrant communities in the US which themselves occupy a precarious position in the foreign land.

Mathias believed in the myth and left home to follow a dream. However, his dream collided with reality; he was barely 19 when he died in Rochester, NY on August 31, 1992.

In relating Mathias's story, I look back at an experience which compelled me to explore some important issues, both personal and professional, that brought into sharper focus the quest for meaning which is at the heart of the anthropological enterprise. I use Mathias's short life history to lift the veil of anonymity that silenced one victim in order to both personalize anthropology and situate his local tragedy within the context of other global catastrophes. My role as an ethnographer is to "give[s] voice . . . to those who have been silenced . . . by political and economic oppression and illiteracy . . . as have their children by hunger and premature death" (Scheper-Hughes 1992:28).

In this essay, I draw on my own experience as Haitian and immigrant to describe and explore how globalized racism and structural violence shaped Mathias's options and continue to reproduce inequality and silence the poor. I side with Farmer (2003) in observing that there is something wrong in a world where the suffering of the powerless is ignored. We anthropologists must not only bear witness to the suffering of the poor but must advocate on their behalf.

I am drawn to question anthropology's claim to objectivity which prevents practitioners from expressing personal anguish when encountering human tragedy in the course of fieldwork. I have come to realize that through sharing the pain of our informants we begin to understand the suffering we observe and write about – suffering that forms the canvas of so many lives. It is also at this juncture that we convey our understanding to others and share our humanity. "Anthropology that does not break your heart just isn't worth doing" (Behar 1996:177). As I tried to find some meaning in Mathias's tragedy I also struggled to understand how being an anthropologist influenced the way I approached this experience. Meeting Mathias, under circumstances which I will describe, invited me to reflect on the precarious balancing act that we, anthropologists, perform when we do fieldwork, or "fall into it" as in my case. We are observers yet participants. We collect life histories and other data from individuals, analyze them and construct theories which "absorb" our informants' stories into the larger context of human experience. Yet we also glimpse the private worlds of others, share their pains and struggles and at times espouse their causes. I wonder, though, why even we sometimes choose to ignore or avert our eyes from certain suffering.

Mathias's tragedy is also the plight and the suffering of Haiti. Haiti had a glorious beginning as the first nation where slaves earned their freedom by defeating a powerful colonial army. Yet Haiti has gone from being the richest colony of France to its current status as the pariah of the Caribbean and the poorest country of the western hemisphere. Its history of political instability, sporadic violence, and perceived inability to govern itself has been used to legitimize foreign intervention and meddling in its internal affairs.

In 1991, a few months before Mathias left home, American forces landed on Haitian soil to contain civil unrest that followed a military coup d'état that toppled democratically elected President Aristide's first government. They returned in 2004 when Aristide was once again "removed" from office, barely a year after elections that had been certified legitimate by international observers. Haiti finds itself at yet another impasse – a potentially bloody upcoming election, hunger, ecological degradation, unemployment, lawlessness, dire poverty, and neglect fuel violent reprisals and send waves of migrants to seek relief elsewhere. The country has also been profoundly affected by false accusations that AIDS originated in Haiti and that Haitians were responsible for bringing it to the US (Farmer, 1991). By the time the United States' Centers for Disease Control and other health organizations had set the record straight, Haiti's fledgling economy and tourist industry were destroyed. Haitians working and living abroad were ostracized, shunned, and stigmatized as AIDS-carrying, disease-ridden undesirables. Many lost their jobs; others were harassed and hunted down.

Haiti's turmoil catches our interest for a while, and then blends into the daily fare of customary violence and terrorism, famines and natural disasters, mass migrations and wars elsewhere in the world. For many of us these events remain distant, confined to fleeting images and newspaper accounts since we seldom encounter the individuals, like Mathias Exavier, whose drama and suffering we watch or read about.

Mathias's life belongs in the global ethnoscape that Appadurai describes as a "landscape of persons who make up (the) shifting world in which we live, tourists, immigrants, refugees, exiles, guest workers, and other moving groups" (1991:192). Mathias also lived at the periphery of the West Atlantic System: what happens in his village is controlled by what happens at the center of global power, i.e., the US.[3] Mathias was also a transmigrant whose actions, decisions, and identity were "embedded in networks of relationships that connect (migrants) simultaneously to two or more nation-states" (Basch, Glick Schiller, and Szanton Blanc 1994:7).

Mathias left Pillate on December 26, 1991 aboard a sailboat built in his village. His decision to leave Haiti was a difficult one, influenced by political as well as economic factors. People in his village were staunch supporters of Aristide and had voted for him in December 1990. Following the coup that sent Aristide into exile on September 30, 1991, the military repeatedly conducted retaliatory raids in the area. Several people were killed at random or were abducted and never returned. According to international human rights observers, more than 3,000 Haitians died after the coup in urban areas alone, not to mention unreported persons from "unobserved" rural areas.[4] Mathias and his family rightly feared for his life. There was nothing for him in Pillate – no future, no prospect of work, no peace. A *kante* was ready to leave and Mathias's brother-in-law urged him and his sister, Virginie, to "go for it." Since he was young and strong they felt that he had a good chance to survive the escape and succeed abroad. They invested all their resources to finance Mathias's trip in hopes of a better future for the extended family. The family recounts this drama on the cassette they sent me, his mother begging him not to go and holding onto him as he boarded the *kante* at daybreak.

The events which led to Mathias's departure are closely linked to political tensions influenced significantly by Haitian class politics and ideology. Even though Aristide had been duly elected in 1991 with strong support from the poor and disenfranchised, his government was threatened from the outset. Drawing on Liberation Theology and peasant metaphors, Aristide's popular *ti legliz* (people's church) movement threatened the sacred cows of Haiti: the ruling class, the military, and the Catholic Church. He preached that a popular struggle could be successful, that poverty should not be a stigma that keeps the poor in an inescapable caste-like hierarchy. Poverty, Aristide told the poor, results from socioeconomic pressures and class oppression and can be changed. The poor can become agents for change and work to narrow the gap between social classes.

The ruling classes found these ideas unsettling and labeled him a "communist." Aristide challenged the professional and merchant elite's position and status in ways that even Duvalier[5] had not done. He also confronted the military and exposed its record of oppression. The Catholic

Church, which has strong ties to the upper class, also felt the pressure. Liberation Theology and Aristide's *ti legliz* ideologies put the Church at the center of a political struggle and reform movement it was not prepared to join.

There were attempts to bridge the differences through proposed reforms, but elites who considered some concessions withdrew support when they realized that these would cut deeply into their power. The military tempered its conciliatory stance when it became clear that Aristide really meant to curb illegal activities. The Church could not tolerate this so-called Marxist in its ranks. Traditionally hostile factions of Church and military joined forces to preserve the status quo. Publicly, the coup that toppled Aristide seemed justified in order to reestablish law and order.

During my visit to Haiti in March 1991, I saw two distinct camps with divergent ideologies. In the countryside people talked of Aristide as their spokesman, their savior. They had given him a mandate and felt strongly that he would fulfill his promises to give them a voice and bring them out of misery into poverty, a slight improvement but a definite step in the right direction. The disenfranchised were willing to work for change and knew that the process would not be easy.

In Port-au-Prince feelings were very different. The wealthy feared for their safety, they talked of sending their children abroad until the situation was "normalized." They were not comfortable with the new administration and the social conflicts that generated violence and threatened business and property. Although they never showed any interest in the state, the elite has always used its resources freely. Trouillot[6] suggests that the professional and commercial elites are no more nationalist than foreign merchants and Farmer (1988) adds that the Haitian state is against the nation: ". . . the state and the nation are not one and the same. The State in Haiti has chosen to ally itself not with the nation, but with capital, regardless of its provenance" (p. 97). Until Aristide, the Haitian poor had no link to the state, no protection from it, and no stake in it; they only financed it.

Mathias and his family knew that no aid would come from the government; they were so far removed from the centers of power that no one would ever care what happened to them. This is nothing new. In Haiti the peasants have been on the margins of society since the War of Independence. Their labor has always supported the state yet they never had a voice in its affairs. When Aristide offered to speak for them, there was a glimmer of hope which was ruthlessly dashed. The lack of freedom, power, and resources, together with poverty, misery, senseless random acts of violence, and disrespect for human life explain the despair, the feelings of rejection, and the need to look elsewhere for solutions. When Mathias left

Haiti, he was fleeing from the State. His act was a vote of no confidence for the repressive government that had taken power from "his" president.

Levine paints a chilling "image of stateless people – people on boats between two states, neither of which wants them, people who arrive on land often only to remain bureaucratically afloat" (1982:4). This snapshot encapsulates Mathias' experiences. In the early hours of December 26, 1991, by the beach his mother was holding onto Mathias, her youngest child, fearing for his life. That morning over 200 people crowded into a wooden sailboat built for considerably fewer and sneaked away under the cover of darkness. They carried a few chickens, some rice and water, as well as their hope for a better future. They expected the trip to last only a few days. Mathias told me of the rough seas and storms that rocked their boat and of his fears when a Coast Guard helicopter flew over them, churning the waters and spinning them around. He did not know about helicopters and the sight was a harbinger of the frightful things he was to encounter in the new places he would visit. By the time they reached Guantanamo, less than a hundred miles away, several people had died. Those who survived were taken to the detention camp where, on January 1, 1992 they joined thousands of other refugees in a depressing tent city. Mathias spoke kindly of those who rescued him and saved him from the ocean. Several days later, after long hours of testimony, medical check-ups and shots, he and his older sister were photographed, finger printed, and issued a document which identified them as "parolees".[7] As parolees Mathias and his sister entered a network of governmental and voluntary agencies that would monitor their resettlement process. On January 22, they were released from the camps and boarded a flight for Miami. Mathias's account of that short trip was very vivid. He was fascinated and frightened as the plane soared through the clouds and he watched the sea speeding under him.

I heard the account of this journey when I met Mathias at the hospital in Rochester. Mathias was in a bureaucratic limbo, alone and utterly frightened. He was still dazed and confused by all that had happened to him, most of which he could not understand. I was called to assist his physicians' attempts to communicate with him, Mathias spoke only Haitian Creole. The physicians needed to explain to him that he was suffering from acute liver failure as a result of medication he had received in Miami upon his arrival from the Guantanamo Detention Camp. They wanted me to tell him point blank that he was dying, that his ammonia levels could not be controlled, and that his kidneys were not filtering the poison from his system. I refused. I knew no Creole words for ammonia levels, prolactin, bilirubin, or dialysis and Mathias had no tools to process this kind of information. Instead we talked of home. I remember the excitement in his eyes when finally someone could understand and answer some of his questions.

Upon his arrival from the detention center, Mathias was administered a standard Tuberculin skin test. His skin test was positive because, like most Haitians, he had been exposed to the bacillus, so he was given Isoniazid, an anti-tuberculosis drug, as prophylaxis; chest X-rays later showed that Mathias never had TB. Mathias developed an unusual allergic reaction which slowly escalated, undetected, into the liver and kidney failure which ultimately cost him his life only seven months after his arrival in the US. Although Isoniazid is administered routinely to immigrants from countries like Haiti where tuberculosis is endemic, liver enzyme levels have to be closely watched during the course of treatment,[8] but nobody monitored Mathias's levels.

I don't know if follow-up visits had been scheduled and Mathias did not keep his appointments, or whether he did not speak enough English to follow instructions properly. But by the time he was taken to the hospital in Rochester that August he was suffering from an acute case of jaundice; his liver and kidneys were no longer working. Already ill, Mathias left Florida in the summer with a group of Haitian migrant workers hoping to find better opportunities for employment in upstate New York. He tried to ignore the symptoms of his disease, the headaches, chills, and bouts of dizziness. After all, he had to keep working to support his family; they depended on the remittances he would send. To make matters worse, $164.00 he had so painfully saved were stolen. Mathias finally collapsed while harvesting apples in an orchard. He could no longer manage and had to stay in bed. As he became more and more lethargic a friend brought him to the Emergency Room of the local hospital. His condition had already progressed beyond what they could do for him there and shortly after his admission he was transferred to the Intensive Care Unit at the Rochester hospital.

For the next three weeks I visited Mathias every day and became his window into this strange new world. I called on my family and other Haitians and contacted friends who had been to Haiti to help and support him. I stayed with him through ultrasound and dialysis sessions because he was so afraid. One morning the hospital called and asked me to come as soon as possible because Mathias was not well. His body was rigid; his wide-opened eyes stared unblinking. I tried to talk to him but he would not respond. I was told that this situation started when Mathias returned to the ward after an MRI (magnetic resonance imaging). I could easily imagine how frightened he must have been in this stainless steel coffin-like machine, having no clue of what was happening since no one had explained the procedure in his language. He must have thought that he had died. When he finally emerged from this catatonic state, I promised him that I would not let him go alone for tests and requested that I be informed when he was scheduled for procedures.

Instead of just interpreting for the medical team, I became involved in Mathias's care and requested explanations. I discussed his treatment with the attending physicians and other specialists involved in his case and relayed the information to his sister in Florida. A liver transplant presented the only glimmer of hope, but since Mathias was neither an illegal alien nor an immigrant no one knew exactly how to arrange this. As the hospital administrators debated over who would pay for his treatment and the County tried to find money to pay for a bus ticket to send him back to Florida, and transfer the problem elsewhere; a pro-bono lawyer was frantically contacting Social Services, tracing immigration records, and tracking down witnesses who could testify that Mathias had worked in Wayne County and was therefore eligible for health benefits. By the time the attorney completed an affidavit which contained the necessary information we had run out of time; three weeks had whizzed by.

As day broke on Monday, August 31, 1992, Mathias died. He began hemorrhaging during the night and was transferred to the Intensive Care Unit. I was told that in his delirium he might have pulled the fistula left in place in his groin for dialysis access and the bleeding that ensued could not be stopped. The hospital called to let me know that he did not have long to live and to hurry. When I arrived shortly thereafter the nurse cautioned that Mathias did not "look like himself" but was not in pain. Indeed, what I saw was worse than I could have imagined. The body lying in the bed seemed double the size of the young man I knew to be Mathias. He was so bloated that his features were unrecognizable, his body was rigid and convulsed rhythmically, shaking the bed, his eyes stared unseeing, and he was hooked to an array of machines monitoring his breathing and heartbeat. I have to admit that I was frightened and didn't know what to do. Should I try to comfort him? Would he know that I was there? Could he hear me? I stood by his bedside and waited, listening to the sound of the monitors and watching his heartbeat on the screen. Gradually life ebbed away, the beeps slowed to a stop, and a straight line showed that his heart no longer pumped. He had expired. In the space of a heartbeat he had gone from being a person to a mere body. Age-old questions flooded me. What had just happened to define this moment? What happened to the essence of the person I knew? I reached to old teachings about life after death and hoped that Mathias was in a better place.

Struggling with anger and sadness, I looked over the city from the window of the Intensive Care Unit which afforded an incredible view of the rising sun, and thought about how illogically our system works. Barely a couple of blocks away, homeless people live under the bridges and in cemeteries because we cannot afford to house them, while large sums are spent to prolong lives already lost. The resident physician who attended Mathias in his last hours was visibly touched by his story and said that his tragedy illustrated the drama of the power relationship between developed and underdeveloped countries. She talked about Western medicine's obsession with technology at the expense of more humane treatments. I thought of his peasant parents who would never comprehend what killed their son, where and why he had died, of the postcolonial legacy of oppression and the political system which controlled their lives. I could not help but worry about my own 20-year-old daughter on a five-week trek in the Himalayas, away from telephones, and hoped that another mother would be there for her too if she became ill.

Mathias was enmeshed in a network that he was never to understand, a victim of political bickering, lust for power, insensitive bureaucracies, class and ethnic hierarchies which reached far beyond his family, his village, and his country. Political oppression, a callous bureaucracy, and medical neglect killed Mathias but medical technology and early intervention could have saved his life. Like a child he had put his unconditional trust into the US – Americans had rescued his boat, fed and housed him in a detention camp, received him into their country to save him from political tyranny, given him medicine, and taken him to their hospital when he became ill. He believed in a benevolent, caring system which rescued poor Haitians and adopted them into its wealthy, advanced, generous, and free society. Although he did not understand their language and their curing methods, their technology was powerful. Even though he was scared he accepted the MRIs, dialyses, ultra-sounds, tubes, and catheters because the "blan"[9] knew better and would not let him die. Mathias was too innocent and unsophisticated to grasp the naked reality of prejudiced bureaucracies. This experience shook my complacency. Searching for explanations, I battled with many "ifs": Mathias might have survived if he had stayed home; if he did not have to support his family; if his reaction to the Isoniazid had been monitored; if the system had been more sensitive; if Haiti was free and wealthy and Haitians did not have to leave home.

The times I spent with Mathias were not always sad. I had learned a great deal about Mathias and life in Pillate in the weeks I went with him for tests and procedures. Since he could not receive pain killers (his liver would not process the drugs), I kept him talking to distract him. He would laugh when he talked about his childhood and the games he used to play with his friends. He remembered going to market with his mother as a young boy. She would buy him sweets and let him ride the donkey while she walked behind. Like other boys in his village he had walked barefooted on mountain paths, cooked over a charcoal fire, fished and worked the land.

Mathias was a keen observer and had a great sense of humor. Americans puzzled him. He liked to sit by the door of his room to watch the activity of the ward. When I visited he would update me on the goings-on of his fellow patients and the medical staff. He had nicknames for the nurses and physicians and his own interpretations of the interactions he observed. He found it very funny that all the doctors who visited him asked the same questions – do you hurt, where, how much, is it different from yesterday – and always nodded their heads wisely. One day my husband and I took him for a walk in the sun in his wheelchair but he became restless after a short time and asked to go back to his room. He had seen a security guard carrying a gun and asked me if I had noticed this *milite*.[10] Despite my assurances about his protecting patients, Mathias remained skeptical; he did not trust men in uniform.

Mathias was a handsome and strong young man of average height. He spoke in a gentle voice, had an engaging smile and soft dark brown eyes. He often looked bewildered, which gave him a childlike innocence. His eyes lit up the day I brought him a mango which, unfortunately, he was unable to eat. He loved above all to talk about the ocean and sunrises. He was polite and reserved, yet would pout if I arrived late or skipped a visit: "Where have you been, I've been waiting for days." He was not thrilled to have tubes and needles and fought being strapped to his bed at night.[11] To humor him I would promise that "tomorrow" they would remove the tubes or not poke him. After a while he stopped believing me. We did arrange a telephone conversation between Mathias and his sister, who had remained in Florida, and offered to bring her to Rochester. Virginie declined the invitation. I suppose she could not understand the tragedy that had befallen her brother. Their conversation was simple and strangely distant. Was it fear? Was there too much to tell in a short time? Too much for words? Shortly after, Mathias looked troubled and finally asked me if he was going to die. "I have never hurt anyone," he said, "I have not even started to live, who will help my mother?" I had no answers for him.

Mathias touched many lives in these three weeks. His story was published in the local paper and attracted the attention of several people. A retired man offered to send his mother $165.00, the same amount that Mathias had saved for his family. The lawyer who fought so valiantly on his behalf named his son after Mathias and went back to practicing immigration law. Over 200 people attended a funeral mass in his memory at my parish church (for the occasion, his picture and a ripe mango adorned the altar). For them, he became an icon for the hundreds of other boat people who lost their lives in search of freedom and a better future.

Over the years I have come to appreciate that anthropology is as much an avocation as a vocation and that one need not be "doing research" to gather data or search for explanations. It has been a challenge to try to maintain "objectivity" and keep "myself" out of my work as both participant and observer. This experience taught me some valuable lessons.

As a human being I was a participant in Mathias's drama; as an anthropologist I observed this drama unfold as on a stage. As a participant I was drawn into Mathias's struggles and built ties with him and his relatives. I communicated with his sister in Florida and acted on her behalf. On the cassette I received after his death, his parents say that my name is now included with family members during prayers and when they remember relatives who have left. There is an intimate quality in the recording which overwhelms me, takes me home. I am called "daughter," "sister"; in the background I can hear roosters crowing and the noise of cicadas. In rural Haiti people say that one can only get better among family, "*ou pa ka gueri ak etranje*" (you can't heal among strangers), and that dying alone is dying like a dog, without witnesses, without ties.[12] It must have brought comfort to his family to know that Mathias had his kin around him when he died.

For me, watching this young man die uselessly was awful. I had never seen anyone die before. In the short three weeks that I knew him, I had grown to love Mathias as one of my kin. Losing him was a personal tragedy. He had survived the trauma of being uprooted and endured detention. Now I watched helplessly as his opportunities narrowed beyond hope. One of my deep regrets is that I never felt free enough to hug Mathias when he was scared. Was I inhibited by the social distance between us? Did I feel self-conscious? Or was I too afraid of his pain? This is something I often grapple with; I am still sorry that I was not able to comfort him until it was too late.

Mathias also took me to the edge of the global ethnoscape I mentioned earlier. I experienced through him the devastating effects of marginality, racism, rejection, and bureaucratic anonymity. The language of exclusion is very powerful; it uses phrases like "interdiction at sea," "detention camps," "the poorest country in the western hemisphere," and concepts like exclusion and fear of differences. In the US, Haitian immigrants are often viewed as disease ridden and dangerous and are ostracized. Mathias was a nobody in this system, lacking place and identity.

Throughout this very painful experience I also remained a trained observer. I watched the health care system in action while reflecting on the meaning of suffering as Mathias slipped into death. I differentiated physicians who were dedicated healers from the strictly superb technicians. I also observed interactions between Mathias and his caregivers. Some stopped at his door to talk to him and handled him with utter detachment as if they feared becoming polluted by touching him. I also met nurses and social workers who showed immense patience trying to commun-icate with him and alleviate his pain and fears. It was also interesting to observe how my interactions with the medical team changed as my status shifted from "translator" to anthropologist. As "translator" I was almost invisible and could have no opinion or original thought. The dynamics changed when my status of "anthropologist" and my ties to the academic and Rochester communities became known. My friend's daughter, a res-ident at the time, recognized me on the floor and called me Dr. Chierici, sending the staff into utter confusion. What kind of doctor was the trans-lator? I did not try to clarify. As I took a more active part in Mathias's care I was invited to join in discussions about his case and offer my com-ments. There was much speculation about my involvement in Mathias's care. Was I a kin? If so, why was he black and I light skinned? Why would an educated person become involved in caring for a peasant?

As I write this essay I am troubled by the level of emotion this experi-ence still evokes in me and the overwhelming presence of my "ethnographic I." Nancy Scheper-Hughes (1992) suggests that "Anthropological work if it is to be in the nature of an ethical and a radical project, is one that is transformative of the self but not (and here is the rub) transformative of the other" (p. 24), i.e., does not seek to exploit or alter the other for its own ends. Fieldwork is an encounter, a relationship, which involves the par-ticipation and work of both parties (Gudeman and Rivera 1995). Writing about her experience as an anthropologist with physical disabilities, Colligan suggests that being open to others is a way of inviting them to share themselves with us. "In addition to my body becoming enabling, it became 'other-abling', generating a dialogue about self and others" (1994:8). I shared Mathias's last days and participated in his dying. My presence at his bedside, I hope, eased his suffering, while he in turn enhanced my understanding of human relationships. I have come to value human relationships above career, wealth, and even health.

This essay bears witness to Mathias's passing and the gifts he left me. One is the encouragement to return to Haiti for extensive fieldwork. Since 1995 I have been working in Borgne, a region on the northern coast of Haiti, collaborating with grassroots organizations on community develop-ment projects. As I drive to Borgne from Cap Haitian, I pass the turnoff to Pillate. I have not gone to visit the family that adopted me for taking care of their son but did manage to get a package to them. It contained a picture of Mathias and of the lawyer's son named after him as well as letters and some small gifts. Most importantly, I have refocused my gaze as an anthropologist. I resist averting my eyes from uncomfortable social issues, choosing instead to draw attention to the effects of gender, race, or economic inequality and call for social justice wherever they appear.

Mathias's misfortune is also the tragedy of Haiti; it symbolizes the predicament of all poor who are powerless to effect change – even when they try. The poor are disenfranchised and silenced in a globalized system that generates an ever-increasing gap between the rich and the destitute, strips their dignity, and robs them of the right to a fair share of the world's resources.

Mathias's short life represents a human tragedy more powerful than any analysis can do it justice. I have tried here to place it in a larger context to validate his stay among us and transform his story from a personal tragedy of a poor hopeful migrant to a wake-up call for all who stand in silence while great suffering takes place around us.

Notes

1 "Cheche lavi, detwi lavi" is a Haitian proverb which cautions that often desperate measures to find better opportunities end up tragically.

2 Kante is a creolized version of a Japanese brand name for powerful motors of speedboats. It is a pun on the reality that kante are all but luxurious or fast and rely only on the wind!

3 Using Wallerstein's world-systems theory, Patterson postulates a "West Atlantic System" that "emerged over the centuries as a single environment in which the dualistic United States center is asymmetrically linked to dualistic peripheral units . . . the West Atlantic system has a physical nexus in the metropolis at the tip of Florida" (cited in Farmer 1988:83–84).

4 Ambiguous figures mask the magnitude of the problem. Every life lost to political violence, every human being tortured or killed because of her or his race, ethnicity, or social circumstance, every individual stripped of human dignity for the benefit of another human being represents an incredible loss for humanity.

5 The Duvalier regime lasted 30y years (1957–87). Francois Duvalier ("Papa Doc") proclaimed himself President for life. He passed the reins to his son, Baby Doc, at his death. Both ruled ruthlessly and plundered the state coffers.

6 Cited in Farmer (1988:96).

7 "Parolee" is the status given to individuals who can prove to Immigration and Naturalization Services interrogators that they have just cause for leaving their homeland. Parolees are admitted conditionally into the US and must undergo an application process to receive permanent residence.

8 Farmer (personal communication) notes that Isoniazid (INH) is generally well tolerated and has been in use since 1952. The risk for Hepatitis among people using INH is 20.7/1000; of those with hepatitis, 4.6% of the cases were fatal. Mathias' reaction to the drug was therefore unusual. In Haiti INH is not

administered to PPD-positive people since it is assumed that most of them have been exposed to TB. The use of INH for PPD-positive patients is a standard public health practice in the US. See also Nachman (1993:231).

9 "Blan," a Haitian Creole term meaning white, is commonly used to refer to white people and, by extension, all foreigners.

10 Haitians often use the term *milité* to refer to police or military; both have acquired a bad reputation for oppressing and exploiting the poor and powerless.

11 Toward the end of his illness Mathias often had to be restrained to his bed at night. On a few occasions he woke up disoriented and scared, got out of bed and fell.

12 Steven Nachman's informants "indicated that only the family can create an environment suitable for recovery. A sick person does not recover among strangers" (p. 244).

References

Appadurai, Arjun
　　1991 Global Ethnoscapes: Notes and Queries for a Transnational Anthropology. *In* Recapturing Anthropology. R. Fox, ed. Pp. 191–210. Santa Fe, NM: School of American Research Press.
Basch, Linda, Nina Glick Schiller, and Christina Szanton Blanc
　　1994 Nations Unbound. Langhorne: Gordon and Breach.
Behar, Ruth
　　1996 The Vulnerable Observer: Anthropology That Breaks Your Heart. Boston: Beacon Press.
Colligan, Sumi Elaine
　　1994 The Ethnographer's Body as Text: When Disability Becomes "Other"-Abling. Anthropology of Work Review 15(2&3):5–9.
Farmer, Paul
　　1988 Blood, Sweat, and Baseball: Haiti in the West Atlantic System. Dialectical Anthropology 13:83–99.
Farmer, Paul
　　1991 AIDS and Accusation: Haiti and the Geography of Blame. Berkeley: University of California Press.
Farmer, Paul
　　2003 Pathologies of Power: Health, Human Rights, and the New War on the Poor. Berkeley: University of California Press.
Gudeman, Stephan, and Alberto Rivera
　　1995 From Car to House (Del coche a la casa). American Anthropologist 97(2):242–250.
Levine, Barry
　　1982 Surplus Populations: Economic Migrants and Political Refugees. Caribbean Review 21(1).

Nachman, Steven R.
   1993   Wasted Lives: Tuberculosis and Other Health Risks of Being Haitian in a US Detention Camp. Medical Anthropology Quarterly 7(3):227–259.
Scheper-Hughes, Nancy
   1992   Death Without Weeping. Berkeley: University of California Press.
Trouillot, Michel-Rolf
   1986   Les Racines Historiques de l'Etat Duvalierien. Port-au-Prince: Editions Deschamps.
Wallerstein, Immanuel
   1974   The Modern World-System: Capitalist Agriculture and the Origins of the European World-Economy in the Sixteenth Century. San Diego, CA: Academic Press.

Part V

Blurred Borders in the Ethnographic Encounter of Self and Other

Chapter 10

Field Research on the Run: One More (~~from~~) for the Road[1]

Dimitris Papageorgiou

Introduction

Field research is generally depicted, particularly by methodological "bibles" or guides, as an organized enterprise, marked by phases of involvement and withdrawal from "critical" data, as well as phases of "rethinking" the "knowledge" acquired after a (more or less) intense field experience. These phases consist of: entrance to the field and exploratory contacts; intensive data collection; withdrawal and rethinking of findings; return to field activities; and retrenchment and final data analysis. In this linear schema, ambitions for understanding are balanced with ambiguities of interpretation. Data provide a path to "knowledge" by understanding behavioral codes of persons forming ethnic, social, and cultural groups under various contexts and conditions. "Interpreting" involves a difficult, sometimes ambiguous, dialectical process, involving ongoing evaluation of objective "data" with personal "experiences" of the researcher as he or she engages with research "subjects" and the data.

Key to this process is dissociation from the data and their collection process. Researchers are encouraged to "objectify" their experience from the field, in moving toward their "scientific" conclusions. They are obliged to pack these experiences with "knowledge" extracted from all the other research findings using specific scientific paradigms.[2] This encourages reductions, subordinating the researcher's experience to already formulated theoretical abstractions. Under these conditions, subtle tones of "experience" rarely reach publications of the research.

This problematic has both distracted and attracted theorists from various disciplines, focusing attention on certain methodological aspects of "knowledge" and "experience."[3] Many social scientists have long questioned the basic structural elements of such standard research approaches (e.g., Aguilar 1981; Messerschmidt 1981a, 1981b; Watson and Watson-Franke

1985; Marcus and Fischer 1986; Lutz 1986; Asad 1987; Brenneis 1987; Johnson 1987). Still, problems of "interpretation" seem to tantalize epistemological traditions of anthropology and more generally, of the humanities.[4] Moreover, this interpretive problematic has questioned both theoretical and practical aspects of standard research processes (e.g., Phillipson and Roche 1974; Bertaux 1981; Ferrarotti 1981; Rodwin and Hollister 1984; White and Kirkpatrick 1985; Seremetakis 1990, 1991).

Working within this broad framework, I use an approach to problems of data analysis and retrospection in field research, focused on "understanding" and "interpreting" by extracting "noema" from "raw" field data. "Noema"[5] involves a dialectical binding of "objective" meaning and "subjective" experience, in an effort to overcome the division between "objects of observation" and "objectified observers" (Hastrup 1987), and to achieve a critical understanding of particular social strata where researchers and researched are integrated, not as (ontological) factums, but as complexes of actors and activities (Popper 1995 [1945], 1968). This continuum of interpretation involves an ongoing process of balancing between the poles of "knowledge" about the observed and "experience" by the observers. Pulling from two field examples – urban subcultures of extremist football fans ("hooligans") in Athens and Thessaloniki, and rural and semi-urban cultures of folk musicians of the North Aegean region of Greece (Lesvos, Chios, Lemnos, Psara), I utilize this approach, pointing out discontinuities and misjudgments that may occur in the process of knowledge construction.

The first case study addresses a "youth culture" (participants ranging from adolescents to the mid-30s) of football fans from economically depressed urban neighborhoods of Greece. The fans project their personal "manliness" into athletic terrains as a process of identity construction climaxing in individual "honor." This is achieved by "distinctions" gained in violent encounters with "opponent fans" and the police.

Folk musicians from the North Aegean also adopt a "sense of honor" as part of their personal and group identities. For them, however, "honor" is gained through the appreciation of their performance by *meraklides*[6] music enthusiasts ("revelers") and fellow musicians, as determined by their applause *and* amounts of money they ultimately spend for the entertainment.

Getting into the Field: the "Magic Carpet"[7] Takes Off

An indescribable ghost haunts the interpretations of every researcher: first impressions play an overwhelmingly *decisive* role in the formation of their conceptual framework and the result of their work. Theoretical and methodological "armory," however, often proves inadequate to soften the edge off the original "punch in the stomach" to the ethnographer from the observed and the overflow of information he or she may encounter. Under these terms, patterns of interaction that organize the initial communication between observers and observed may culminate in mutual preoccupations and misunderstandings. In these cases, temporary moods play a crucial role and initial contacts leave deep impacts on both sides, with judgments of the other based on instant "enlightment" of "sentiments" (Fajans 1983:116) rather than the progressive evaluation of each other's intentions.

In this context, the researchers and the researched emphasize ephemeral "survival" tactics over strategic options. These tactics elevate discontinuities and misjudgments that typically are not addressed by most methodological approaches. A supposed lack of affect by the *researcher* vis-à-vis the *"researched"* is no longer sustainable under these conditions. In fact, the *affect* generated in researchers faced with the general mentality of the researched predisposes them toward gradual entry into a field that might otherwise remain impenetrable.

Hastrup (1987) has addressed this issue using a dialectical methodological schema based on a triangular dialogue among "subjects of observation," "participant ego of the observers," and "dissociated ego of the observers." Her schema is *objectified* under theoretical reductions encapsulating "images of the researched" as "objects of observation," "images of the participant researchers" as "objectified observers," and "images of the dissociated observers" as "theoretical catalysts," using hermeneutical procedures which piece together a "holistic" view of "knowledge" *and* "experience" about the field.

Hastrup's approach, however, underestimates the problem, as personal feelings of the observers feed their "participant ego" into a "greedy beast," threatening their "dissociated ego." If we want to pinpoint this problem, it is *ex-citement*. The researchers feel *ex-cited*, cut off from their previous experiential environment toward new critical choices, which will transform forever their "view of the world." Crapanzano (1990:300) deems successful researchers those who suffer everlasting loss after leaving the field, recognizing that part of their experiences will always be bound with subjects of observation, who "stay behind." My view points to an even deeper and more "dangerous" feeling.

Field research resembles bungee-jumping: you get near the edge and you have to decide what to do. If you can take a step forward you taste the intermingled feelings of terror and almost limitless freedom in a flash; this experience marks you forever, but it is a very difficult sensation to convey, even to those who are close to you. The point is that agitation and upheaval are present in every entrance into field research, even for trained researchers who are better adept at gradually acquiring familiarity with particularities of the field.

Let me draw some examples from my research among extremist football fans ("hooligans"). When I first met hooligans they did not impress me as terribly different from others their age. I was wandering in a central plaza of Athens, known as the *steki* (meeting place) for fans of the city's three leading football teams. At the time, I was very much at the beginning of my research and I was in a process of "lurking" in the field (Blanchard and Cheska 1985:81–82). A gang of 40–50 young men wearing athletic shoes or ex-army boots, T-shirts and jeans, and flying bombers' jackets, decorated with emblems from their favorite team, moved into the plaza. They didn't look more threatening than others in the plaza, but impressively, most of the others left, leaving these youngsters alone. Some of them stopped near me, circling around an "orator," who was boasting about his fight with opponent fans from a rival team. I moved closer to better listen and perhaps talk to them, when an acquaintance from one of my earlier visits quickly stopped me: "Don't go there, these youngsters are really mad!" I ignored his warning, but by the time I returned, the circle was broken and the youngsters disappeared as silently and slowly as they had come.

My next "meeting" with hooligans changed my impressions dramatically. As a spectator of a game, I witnessed their extremely violent attack against opponent fans at the stadium. After an exchange of insults and rival chants, hundreds of them broke down the wired fence enclosing the stadium and crossed the whole length of the field to attack their "enemies," launching stones, wood, and pieces of iron from the destroyed fence. The police force charged with keeping the peace closed in, and the scene was filled with wounded fans and policemen and people chasing and fighting each other.

Following a brief period of intense bibliographic research in Oxford, I returned to Athens to begin the "real" research into the everyday life of the hooligans, but this time, I was cautious. After a few weeks of participant observation I witnessed another violent attack by over twenty hooligans against two opponent fans in a pub. My instinctive reaction was to protect the defenseless "enemies" and – somehow – I managed to complete this task.

I didn't realize that some elder fans who themselves did not take action were looking at me, evaluating my intentions.[8] Later, one of them explained that they had been questioning my identity, suspecting that I was working as an undercover cop. Since my actions challenged that view, they reassessed me a like-minded ally who valued and evinced "bravery"

– the highest measure of "manliness." This accidental encounter boosted my acceptance into the circle of the highly esteemed fans and I was able to make friends and explain the purpose of my research. Under the light of this experience, I gained a new understanding of the behavioral codes I had incorrectly assessed during my failed initial contact with fans in the central plaza of Athens one and a half years earlier.

As my new friends[9] explained to me, fans I had met would probably have judged me as an unwanted witness, but as I didn't provoke any reaction from their side, they probably decided to ignore me as an outsider who didn't deserve their attention. As I understood, their purpose was focused on spotting and fighting "opponent" fans who would be brave enough to show themselves in the central plaza, so my presence was bypassed as an ignorant nuisance interrupting their "hunt." In any case, my initial expectations of getting to talk with them by lurking around were probably wrong, as these youngsters would have likely denounced any contact with me without the approval of their leaders.

I faced a totally different problem when I conducted field research among folk musicians in the Northern Aegean islands. As an amateur player of Ud,[10] I was readily accepted into the professional musicians' inner circle and was thereby "trapped" from the beginning into perceiving "their world" according to their "inner" images. I thus uncritically accepted their evaluation of *meraki* and *meraklides'* attitudes. As a result, when I witnessed disputes among musicians or with revelers, I tended to respond more as a participant member of this community than as a researcher analyzing its practices.

In this context, when a reveler shouted at an elderly (70-year-old) musician, and close friend of mine, because he ignored an "order"[11] for a specific song, I felt personally insulted because this musician had been one of my teachers. To my surprise, my friend later acknowledged that the reveler was right, as he had paid some money for his "order," even though the amount was too low to honor his request.

This event helped me to understand the "subtle tones" of identity management among professional musicians. Before that, I had organized my perceptions of the folk musicians' world strictly in terms of meanings they attributed to ideological concepts like "professional pride" and "art perfection." This experience exposed me to economic concerns that shade these abstractions. Since folk musicians also must live from their profession, their "sense of honor" must be carefully balanced between necessity and pretenses of self-esteem. Under this new light I also could better understand internal considerations organizing their relationships with revelers and each other. For example, it became clear to me that characterizations disregarding other musicians' performance abilities were not necessarily unbiased, since they were colored by competition for employment opportunities.

This experience cut me free from *my own prejudices*: I was able to think and speak about folk musicians as ordinary men rather than the semi-gods fabricated in my "imaginary" of their "world." Moreover, I was more able to appreciate spontaneous expressions of their generosity. Two or three months later, I participated in a private tavern feast organized by this same elderly musician for his birthday. He and his friends played wonderful music nonstop for five or six hours, and at the end he insisted on paying every penny of the bill. When I jokingly asked if the rest of us would have to pay for the music, he turned serious: "You have never paid the last year we have known each other, and you will not ever do so when we have fun together as long as we are friends. But if you attend a public feast where I am performing, then I would like you to pay me, and pay me well, to affirm your esteem for me and my art!"

As I learned, there is no magic formula for introducing researchers to the field. Good theoretical training, familiarity with related research, improvisation and luck are important, but the main emphasis should be on subjective *interaction* with interlocutors in the field. This lacking, the research will inevitably fall short of its goals.

Intensive Data Collection: Turbulences and Rectifications

After some time in the field, researchers are better positioned to accumulate data. They gain information about people and practices, and learn to distinguish "leaders" or focal personas from ordinary members of a culture or a community. They observe and participate more fully in a larger range of activities and start building ongoing relationships with members of the community being studied. They may (or may not) choose to disguise negative reactions to particular people or practices; in general they relax and respond more easily to life in the "new" environment, having overcome the initial "shock" of immersion. By this point, many researchers feel they are moving toward completion of their data collection.

Still, the key for understanding does not end there. Objective data about social or cultural systems can never substitute for direct experience of them. Some researchers miss this crucial distinction, identifying knowledge with data. Others acknowledge the difference but they still privilege objective data over subjective experience.

Intensive data collection, however, can be seductive, and the overflow of "hard" evidence tends to obscure the absence of experiential aspects of the research process. This is common with researchers who aim to collect comprehensive sets of information about kinship relationships, social stratifications, leading personalities, and practices organizing communal life, and their "meanings" – and who feel satisfied *not testing them personally*. To paraphrase Turner's definition of performance (1987), interpretation enters the process of data collection as a synthesis of "information" and "experience" *squeezing for expression*. In this context, repression of sentiments that are developed and shared with subjects of observation is like "putting down (researchers') fire with gasoline."[12]

Drawing again from my field experience, I will describe some aspects of this progressive synthesis. As an amateur Ud player, I was already experienced in performing, mainly in urban intellectual circles. So, when I received an invitation to participate in a concert for a village audience, I felt prepared. On the night of the concert I was a bit nervous since I would be playing with professionals and semi-professionals trained as musicians. The audience filled the auditorium to capacity, and was interspersed with cameras from local TV channels. Our large group was arranged in a double row, facing the audience; I sat in the second row given my lower status in the band.

It was an extremely hot summer night, and the audience were nearly suffocating. (I had a full view of them from my position.) In the beginning they were just sitting listening to the music. After a time, there was a polite, quiet applause. Then the singer began performing some very old, rarely played songs from the local tradition. Several women began crying and accompanying the lyrics. The whole audience burst out in applause and the positive "vibes" became almost tangible, as waves of energy penetrated the auditorium. The cameras trembled on their bases, as cameramen were trying to protect them from the enthused crowd. I stopped playing and stared speechless as the people gathered close to the band. I learned that night (and later confirmed) that appreciation of folk traditions among urban intellectuals and local villagers connected to the tradition differ radically. The former experience the performances as a *pleasure*; for villagers, the music recalls painful *memories* of loved ones who have departed as such and a nostalgic melancholic recognition of a rapidly fading world. This experience enlightened me far more than had hundreds of interviews I had conducted with musicians and revelers until then.

Some years earlier, during my research with football fans, I joined a group of fans who were traveling from Athens to Thessaloniki to support "our team" against supporters of a Thessaloniki team, the group's "traditional enemies." During the trip several hundred fans in a dozen buses shouted, chanted, and drank heavily, like "soldiers" preparing for battle. These preparations proved useful, because trouble started immediately after we arrived. Outside the stadium the police overreacted to some provocative chants from "our side" and violence erupted around the entire perimeter of the stadium. Eventually, pushing and being pushed, we found ourselves in the stadium.

I remember nothing about the game, except that it ended in a draw. As I started participating in the "chants" though, I entered a trance-like state of mind and was lost in the mass of fans, facing the "opponents" who had come close enough to exchange face-to-face insults, ready to charge on us. Yet I felt invulnerable and fearless. I spotted some marks on the sky I thought were birds and I laughed, imagining their pleasure, looking down the masses of people ready to fight. I shared this with a friend who jokingly retorted, "These are missiles from the opponents, you moron." The very next moment, some stones and pieces of wood hit us, knocking down and injuring several among our ranks. Still, I felt invulnerable standing there waiting for a storming attack that never came.

As we waited for police permission to move to the buses, we knew the fight was not over, as the opponents would be waiting for us and the police would be less patient and more willing to use violent tactics after a long tiring day. I was standing in a circle with some close friends and we started a phony fight, laughing and pushing each other. My friend turned to me and said: "Man, I feel like an eagle now; I am flying." The very next thing I remember is that we were pushed out of the stadium by the police. Some people were running to the buses; others were struggling with opponents or the police. I was all alone, as I had lost my friends in the middle of the commotion. My feelings at this dangerous moment were hard to describe. It was as if I were "Sergeant Elias" in Oliver Stone's movie, *Platoon*, where he hunts enemies in the jungle, alive and free and unbound by commitment.

I eventually found my way to a bus returning to Athens. Many fans were wounded and all of us had suffered scratches and bruises, but morale was high and "we" were proud of our performance. When the bus arrived in Athens early the next morning, I didn't want to go home, so I paid a visit to an old friend who was still sleeping. I woke him up and he opened the door with surprise. As I entered his apartment, he asked, puzzled, "What is happening here, are you okay?" I stood there speechless, unable to transform my experience into words; I asked to take a shower instead. Later on, when I was ready to sleep on his sofa, emptiness overwhelmed my body and spirit; I knew that my "batteries" were dying out. I also knew that my research had been completed. For the first time since I had entered the research process, I felt confident there was nothing more to know.

Rethinking: Touch Down or Calling Off "Experience"

Preliminary reports of findings often require rethinking the data to evaluate and correct mistaken assessments and misunderstandings in the research. This helps prepare the researcher to return to the field to resolve doubts, fill gaps, and restore some cohesion in preparation for eventual publication. In this process theoretical constructs conceal insecurities and ambiguities; experience inevitably fades as it is obliterated by the artificial assurances and closure guaranteed by academic "knowledge" and discourse.[13] In this context, the theoretical ghost haunting interpretation returns triumphant. Researchers are typically torn by two opposing tendencies: experiences from the field research *squeezing to be expressed* versus professional *obligations and expectations* restricting their expression. Some fragments of their experiences may "slip" into their publications, but most are forgotten or suspended for possible examination later.

Every time I have returned from the field, I have felt disoriented. When I came back from research with the football fans, I had considerable difficulty organizing my thoughts as the theories I intended to examine appeared vague and disconnected from my research data. In addition, I didn't have enough time to adjust myself to the academic environment after returning from the field environment, so I was even less prepared to transform my experience into an organized "text"[14] from which *noema* could be extracted. My mentors were asking for descriptions about the internal hierarchies and everyday practices of "hooligans" and the symbolic boundaries discriminating them from other "urban youth subcultures." My interests, in contrast, were in experiences connected with esteemed "practices of manliness" among fans. I tended to view extensive Geertzian "thick" descriptions (1973) about the hooligans' subculture as extremely limited, and possibly misleading, in apprehending *noema* of their practices.

At a seminar in my department, I was asked to present my initial findings from my research among the hooligans. I had planned to discuss the extraction of noema from my data, but my mentors discouraged such methodological and theoretical experimentations, judging it premature and fearing it would interfere with my process of rethinking the collected data. They insisted that I stick to descriptive aspects of my work; analyzing *noema*, they feared, might obscure the "real evidence" in my research.[15] Thus I focused on differentiating the football fans from other "urban youth cultures" in their verbal and bodily expressions, and in redistribution of power and authority within their group. Yet something was missing.

Some years later, I was working with folk musicians from the Northern Aegean to create a series of CDs of the traditional music of Lesvos, when we entered an extensive debate over some recordings of amateur folk singers. I insisted that they should be excluded from the series as the sound was not clear enough, and the singers were overly sentimental in their expression, given the informal context of its production with fellow musicians.[16] One expert of the local musical tradition challenged me: "You are totally wrong, this is the essence of Lesvian folk music tradition, not the music performed by professionals in your 'sterilized' studio recordings! 'Real' music is 'dirty' and these recordings are as 'dirty' as they need to be in order to be persuasive of their authenticity."

At that point I remembered my disagreement with my mentors over my presentation several years earlier. I remained reluctant – as had my instructors at the time – but finally I (unlike my mentors) agreed with him. Despite mixed reviews from critics, I have not regretted our choice. These "dirty" recordings recall images of private feasts in coffee shops and homes, as musical "texts" transmitting *noema* about traditional life in Lesvos *and* research experience, more richly than the polished recordings by professional musicians that we included, or the written texts by researchers accompanying the series.

"Experience" Revisited? Consistencies and Asymmetries

After the process of "rethinking" data, researchers returning to the field often lose their initial enthusiasm. More pragmatic research pressures divert their attention to acquiring data, rather than making, or even reviving, existing friendships. The search for consistencies impede spontaneous and fluid interactions with interlocutors as the researchers become too busy to examine provocative ideas or practices that might open new, possibly competing, paths to knowledge and experience. Under these conditions, asymmetries calling into question the researcher's theoretical perspectives and assumptions are likely to be ignored.

In my own periods of return to fieldwork, I too have preferred to "stay on the beaten track." I typically felt detached from the environment, remembering that my long "rite of passage" would lead back to the academic world. Given this realization, I would concentrate on improving my "knowledge" by filling gaps in already conceptualized descriptive and interpretive frameworks. Fun and pleasure were largely missing in these processes. Images of my "friends" were gradually transforming into images of research subjects. My theoretical abstractions and

methodological exercises during this period of "rethinking" were erod-
ing our relationships. My memories and shared sentiments were also
fading. As one poet observed, "people are strange when you are (or feel
like) a stranger . . ."[17]

When I returned to my research with the football fans, I was consumed
with collecting statistics about their social origins, family relationships,
and educational and working prospects. I was seeking support for my
hypothesis that hooligans' subculture included young people from
mainly lower social strata, who were balancing social inequalities they had
to suffer in daily life with their performances in the "field of honor."

Some of my old friends, caught up in everyday life, questioned the value
of these statistics and discouraged my efforts to collect them. Others also
resisted my collection efforts, fearing the authorities would use my published findings against them. Finally, a highly regarded group leader
stepped in on my behalf: "I think that a book about us and our activities
will not do any harm to anybody. After all, we should have published it
ourselves, before meeting you . . ." After that, I was able to collect my
statistics and complete my research. And of course, I never disclosed their
identities.

Still, this "collection of statistics" marked my exclusion from the field,
as it detached me from my friends and repositioned me as mainly a researcher
rather than a friend. My formal "knowledge" about the research data
overshadowed my "experience" of the field. At this point I reached a melancholic conclusion: balancing experiential knowledge and concrete knowledge is very hard to do; there is no perfect theoretical or methodological
blend. Despite the prescriptions offered by my mentors, I concluded that
researchers must follow their own routes to ethnographic knowledge. It
is pursuing this process, while engaging fully with informants, rather than
obtaining any "final" knowledge, that assures success.

I tested this conclusion while revisiting my research with folk musicians
of the Northern Aegean. There, I met no resistance to publish. In fact, I faced
tremendous pressure, even from amateur musicians, to include information about them in my publications, and their recordings in my CDs; these
were their "tickets" for acknowledgment within the Greek folk music
"scene." Under these pressures, I was forced to reconsider what data I should
include (and exclude). I succeeded in negotiating with the musicians, despite
my agonies in recognizing the ambiguities within any "essence" of the
folk tradition that would be embedded in the presented results.

The last months of my return to this work, I was fully occupied with
finding old photos, conducting final recordings, and completing some life
histories. As people learned of my work and anticipated my publications,
they responded enthusiastically with documents and information far beyond

both my interest and capacity to process. After six months of revisiting the field, I politely renounced further offers of data and recordings and tried to concentrate on already collected material.

Here I faced a reversed version of the dilemmas I confronted some years before when revisiting the hooligans: difficulties in acquiring additional data were replaced by difficulties in being overwhelmed with additional data. Structural similarities were exaggerated in this inversion. In both cases, revisiting marked my dissociation from the field since asymmetries threatened to transform my relations with those I researched. At the same time, the need to acquire material knowledge threatened my experiential knowledge of the field. I was simply not able to counterbalance intimate relationships with my friends with the demands of the data collection. Gradually most of these relationships ended, as I was obliged to place emphasis on collecting data instead of experiencing everyday life. As years are passing by, I have reevaluated my choices with regret.

Data Evaluation: Conclusions (or Back to the Line of Duty)

There comes a moment when field research has been completed and final reports must be presented. At this point, strengths and limitations related to the research process play a crucial role in the final form of presentations, as *noema* adjusted to the presented data reflects a balance of knowledge *about* the field with experience *of* the field in every preceding stage of the research process. This balance is tied to the dialectical process organizing the dialogue between observers and observed as a series of practices in which data are mutually interpreted and knowledge is mutually constructed. In this conceptual process, *noema* comes to light as the *synthesis* of different conscious *and* subconscious perceptions of both observer and observed as inscribed in performances, narrations, memories, and sometimes even fantasies about the field. Both researchers and the research subjects struggle to control this dialectical process to determine results to be presented. The ambivalent outcome of this struggle is reflected over the entire process of evaluating data. In this context, critiques about the presented findings from the research subjects are extremely valuable, as they document multiple perspectives contributing to an ongoing *synthesis* of the results.

Soon after I completed my research with football fans in Athens, I moved to Mytilini, so I lost contact with most of them. However, I did maintain contact with my friend who had supported me against the other fans during my revisit to the field. Some years later, about the time my book was published, we unexpectedly met while vacationing on an island. We discussed the "good old days" and I informed him about the book and promised to send him a copy. A couple weeks later, he called to express approval: "I knew you were okay; the book is fine." Then, he more hesitantly added, "But, you know . . . it' s not exactly the type of book our colleagues would like very much . . . it's very – how can I say it – intellectual for our taste . . . But I liked very much the part where you speak about us and you present chants and practices of rivalry with opponent fans . . ." This laconic critique richly captures the ambivalence over the synthesis of concepts and understandings of observers and observed in the research field.

In the following years I continued to receive critiques of my presentations from those whom I studied. After completing a book about folk music in the Northern Aegean area, I participated in a conference in Athens with other researchers, followed by a musical performance. Much to the disappointment of the audience, the performers were denied adequate time to finish. The lead singer, however, decided to remain on the stage even though technicians were preparing for the following event. He resumed his singing, evoking enthusiastic applause from the audience, before he left. Several days later he explained his actions: "You (the researchers) were so confident and arrogant in speaking about us and our tradition. You went first and we had to wait for you to finish before we could proceed. But as you saw, the audience responded to our contribution more favorably than yours . . . you need to remember this and learn in the future . . ."

The process of data evaluation by researchers and research subjects continues long after "final results" are presented; the "dialogue" continues in different venues. In this context of ongoing engagement, expressive forms adopted by both researchers and researched may point out gaps in the research process, or deficiencies in the data. This process of continuous evaluation is fruitful both for the knowledge produced, as well as for the field experience. Researchers must continuously process such commentary as they dialectically engage with their informants. Only by such serious intersubjective engagements may they acquire *noema* in their research as they continue to construct, deconstruct, and reconstruct their interpretations of findings in their eternal analytic quest for knowledge.

Notes

1 In memory of Paul McCartney and the Band, and – especially – to Lynard Skynard, one of the best American rock bands ever. Their lyrics, music, and general performances reflect aspects of American cultural life in a profound way, sometimes keener and deeper than any scientific analysis published.

2   Following Thomas Kuhn's definition, the term refers to structured and stratified bodies of knowledge, which map out different scientific fields. Kuhn criticizes "scientific paradigms" as dogmatic structures, which restrict scientific innovations (Kuhn 1962).

3   These issues are strongly interconnected with philosophical questions about the "world of being and the world of becoming" as E. Husserl defined them, or distinctions of "phenomenon" or "state" from act as presented in J. P. Sartre's work (Grossmann R. 1984). J. B. Thompson deals with these issues in a systematic presentation of methodological aspects of interpretation, focusing on authors who have been (more or less) neglected in the English-speaking world, like Cornelious Castoriadis, Claude Lefort, Pierre Bourdieu, Michel Pecheux, Jean Pierre Faye, Paul Ricoeur (Thompson J. 1984).

4   In this context, Ricoeur's contribution was crucial for the construction of (new) "models of interpretation." Ricoeur introduced a methodological schema for interpretation of action, following analysis applied in speech-act. According to him, action-event develops a similar dialectic (with speech-act) between its temporal status as an appearing and disappearing event, and its logical status of identifiable meaning or "sense-content." Ricoeur points out that, "the propositional content of action . . . gives a basis to a dialectic of *event* and *meaning* similar to that of the speech-act . . . the noematic structure of action . . . may be fixed and detached from the process of inter-action and become an object to interpret." (Ricoeur P. 1979:82).

5   "Noema" is bound with intensive and extensive encounter of senses in a series of action in a certain historical, social, and cultural context. Abrahams points out that experience is not defined as an analytical term because its "meaning" is taken for granted (Abrahams 1986). Bruner (1984) underscores the differences between *representations* of social actions and *experiences* of social actions, in emphasizing sentiments provoking noema *only* for participant actors. For Csordas (1994) experience is substantiated as noema in subconscious schemata, determining "objectified" perceptions both of the acts experienced as such as the roles played by the actors. In this sense, noema extracted from experiences is rather embodied in the *habitus* or *ethos* of the participants, than transformed into analytical "knowledge" about the experience itself (Bourdieu P. 1977; Papagaroufali E. 1999).

6   The concept of *meraki* (adjectives, *meraklis* or *meraklides* [in plural]) refers to an attitude related to V. Turner's notion of "flow" – an experiential state in which participants in rituals follow the "voice of their hearts" defying "common logic" and interests of "everyday life" (Turner V. 1969, 1975). I use this term to refer to music enthusiasts or "revelers."

7   In memory of Steppenwolf, another "Skeleton from the Closet" haunting the "incredible and traumatic" sixties.

8   These elder (about 25–35 years old) fans were up in the internal hierarchy of the fans' subculture, as members of the leading team. As veterans of hundreds of encounters, they were directing their standards of esteem more on personal attitudes and "qualities" than on "victories" over opponent fans, especially when the latest were conquered under unequal terms.

9   This term also refers rather to an experiential state than a categorization characterizing relationships with "observational subjects" in the field. "Friendships" of (participant or non-participant) observers with "observational subjects" flourish as unique roses admired by both sides, as they understand their fragile character enforced by different cultural and – usually – social backgrounds. This "fatal" imprint rises up their "taste" almost to the point of unbearable, but still exceptional experience.

10   A musical instrument incorporated in general Eastern Mediterranean folk musical tradition.

11   Habitually, Northern Aegean folk bands, playing in private feasts or public festivals, are paid by "orders": revelers come to the musicians and they get a "number," thus forming a series of applicants, who wait their turn to perform their dancing and feasting abilities, after a call by the band leader. Revelers selected "order" the band to play their favorite music as far as they can spend enough money to "justify" their demands. In this context, the folk bands and especially the band leaders have to maintain a critical balance between demands put on by each bunch of revelers and time spent for their satisfactory fulfillment, as there are others waiting for their turn. The criteria for their decisions are focused mainly on (economical) "investments" made up by the revelers, but they have also to keep in mind social statuses of performing revelers, as such as (social and economical) expectations which correspond with people waiting for their turn.

12   In memory of David Bowie.

13   As Malinowski stated, there is no field description cleared of theoretical inscriptions. Every argument is (or has to be) connected with (preexisting) theoretical concepts (Malinowski B. 1960).

14   In the "Ricoeurian" sense of the term.

15   Later on, in the process of completion of my Ph.D. thesis, they proved very helpful with the problems I would like to deal with. I want to make a special reference to the head supervisor, Alexandra Bakalaki, now teaching in the University of Thessaloniki; she instructed me patiently in topics of current academic dialogue and helped me to discover my personal style of writing in order to present my conclusions without denouncing my experiences from the field.

16   Most of the musical archives had been recorded in private feasts organized by companies of friends with poor technical equipment.

17   In memory of Jim Morrison and the Doors.

References

Abrahams, R.
   1986 Ordinary and Extraordinary Experience. *In* The Anthropology of Experience. V. Turner and E. Bruner, eds. Pp. 45–72. Urbana: University of Illinois Press.

Aguilar, L. J.
  1981   Insider Research: Ethnography of a Debate. *In* Anthropologists at Home in North America: Methods and Issues in the Study of One's Own Society. D. A. Messerschmidt, ed. Pp. 15–26. Cambridge: Cambridge University Press.
Asad, T.
  1987   Are there Histories of Peoples Without Europe? Comparative Studies in Society and History 29(3):615–625.
Bertaux, D., ed.
  1981   Biography and Society. The Life History Approach in Social Sciences, London: Sage Publications Inc.
Blanchard, K., and T. Cheska
  1985   The Anthropology of Sport, South Hadley, MA: Bergin & Garvey Publications.
Bourdieu, P.
  1977   Outline of a Theory of Practice. Cambridge: Cambridge University Press.
Brenneis, D.
  1987   Performing Passions: Aesthetics and Politics in an Occasionally Egalitarian Community. American Ethnologist 14(2):236–250.
Bruner, E.
  1984   Text, Play and Story: The Construction and Reconstruction of Self and Society, Prospect Heights, IL: Waveland Press.
Crapanzano, V.
  1990   Afterword. *In* Modernist Anthropology: From Fieldwork to Text. M. Manganaro, ed. Pp. 300–308. Princeton: Princeton University Press.
Csordas, T.
  1994   Embodiment and Experience. Cambridge: Cambridge University Press.
Fajans, J.
  1983   Shame, Social Action and the Person among the Baining. Ethos 11(3): 166–180.
Ferrarotti, F.
  1981   On the Autonomy of the Biographical Method. *In* Biography and Society. The Life History Approach in Social Sciences. D. Bertaux, ed. Pp. 19–27. London: Sage Publications Inc.
Geertz, C.
  1973   Thick Description: Toward an Interpretive Theory of Culture. *In* The Interpretation of Cultures. Pp. 3–30. New York: Basic Books.
Grossmann, R.
  1984   Phenomenology and Existentialism. An Introduction. London: Routledge and Kegan Paul.
Hastrup, K.
  1987   Fieldwork among Friends. *In* Anthropology at Home. A. Jackson, ed. Pp. 94–108. London: Tavistock.
Johnson, M.
  1987   The Body in the Mind: The Bodily Basis of Meaning, Imagination and Reason. Chicago: University of Chicago Press.

Kuhn, T.
  1962 The Structure of Scientific Revolutions, Chicago: University of
  Chicago Press.
Lutz, C.
  1986 Emotion, Thought and Estrangement: Emotion as a Cultural Category,
  Cultural Anthropology 1(3):287–309.
Malinowski, B.
  1960 A Scientific Theory of Culture and Other Essays. New York: Oxford
  University Press.
Marcus, G. E., and M. J. Fischer
  1986 Anthropology as Cultural Critique. Chicago: University of Chicago
  Press.
Messerschmidt, D. A.
  1981a On Indigenous Anthropology: Some Observations. Current Anthro-
  pology 22(2):97–198.
Messerschmidt, D. A.
  1981b Anthropologists at Home in North America: Methods and Issues in
  the Study of One's Own Society. Cambridge: Cambridge University Press.
Papagaroufali, E.
  1999 Donation of Human Organs or Bodies After Death: A Cultural
  Phenomenology of "Flesh" in the Greek Context. Ethos 27:283–314.
Phillipson, M., and M. Roche
  1974 Phenomenology, Sociology and the Study of Deviance. *In* Deviance
  and Social Control. P. Rock and M. McIntosh, eds. Pp. 125–162. London:
  Tavistock.
Popper, K.
  1995 [1945] The Open Society and Its Enemies. London: Routledge and Kegan
  Paul. (Golden Jubilee Edition, Single volume version).
Popper, K.
  1968 The Logic of Scientific Discovery. New York: Harper Torchbooks.
Ricoeur, P.
  1979 The Model of the Text: Meaningful Action Considered as a Text.
  In Interpretive Social Science: A Reader. P. Rabinow and W. Sullivan, eds.
  Pp. 73–101. Berkeley: University of California Press.
Rodwin, L., and R. M. Hollister, eds.
  1984 Cities of the Mind. Images and Themes of the City in Social Sciences,
  New York: Plenum Press.
Seremetakis, N.
  1990 The Ethics of Antiphony: The Social Construction of Pain, Gender and
  Power in the Southern Peloponnese. Ethos 18(4):481–511.
Seremetakis, N.
  1991 The Last Word: Women, Death and Divination in Inner Mani.
  Chicago: University of Chicago Press.
Thompson, J.
  1984 Studies in the Theory of Ideology. Cambridge, Polity Press.

Turner, V.
  1969   The Ritual Process. Structure and Antistructure. Chicago: Aldine.
Turner, V.
  1975   Dramas, Fields and Metaphors: Symbolic Action in Human Society.
  London: Cornell University Press.
Turner, V.
  1987   The Anthropology of Performance. New York: PAJ Publications.
Watson, L. C., and M. B. Watson-Franke
  1985   Interpreting Life Histories. An Anthropological Inquiry. New
  Brunswick: Rutgers University Press.
White, G. M., and J. Kirkpatrick, eds.
  1985   Person, Self and Experience: Exploring Pacific Ethnopsychologies.
  Berkeley: University of California Press.

Chapter 11

Personal Travels through Otherness

Ellen Corin

The "Shadow Side" of Fieldwork

Calling upon the "shadow side" of fieldwork will likely shift the way ethnographic data is regarded. The data can no longer pretend to stand by themselves. What was once considered at the margins of description – at its borders or belonging to a contingent framework – increasingly appears to form the very core of description, influencing its articulation. This reflects the illusory nature of an objective, unmediated relationship with reality. More profoundly, it destroys any pretensions of the transparency of description and language. It reminds us that the words we use and images we form are always "haunted" by other words, voices, and visions – by sensations, shapes, and colors that depend intimately on the particular personal, social, and cultural histories that make up who we are, often without our knowledge. While we speak with others, still other figures insert themselves into the exchange; the discussion we think we are engaged in actually takes place simultaneously on several levels and extends to other interlocutors, partners or adversaries, and periods of time.

In approaching the essential diversity that permeates the way we understand and represent the world, I will place myself under a double horizon, both external and internal to the fieldwork experience: external in stemming from other activities, interests, and encounters which occur in other spheres of our lives; internal in arising from who we are – from the desires, avoidances, and refusals that move us from within. The shadow side of fieldwork therefore forms a two-dimensional space in which the horizontal network of outside effects is infused with the vertical nature of personal history, and with inner fears and desires.

The guiding thread that gradually came to organize this thought process is the idea that ethnographic descriptions might contain something unseen, not only to readers but also to the ethnographer; something that opens up a space of strangeness. This idea expresses my particular way of understanding the term "shadow" in "the shadow side of fieldwork." This perspective is likely influenced by my psychoanalytic training and a clinical practice that has taken on increasing importance in recent years. The two strands of my life – psychoanalytical and anthropological – have developed according to their respective logic, but I have come to realize that psychoanalysis has profoundly changed my view of reality and my approach to language. It has made me particularly sensitive to the connotation of "otherness" implicit in the term "shadow." I should also say that for me, ethnographic and clinical practices are as clearly divided as they are woven together, through complex networks of resonance that invite one to walk around the edges of each approach and discipline, exploring their shadowy borders (Corin 1998b).

It may also be that this particular "in-between" stance has prolonged and expanded previous dilemmas that have been like the curves of an ever-turning spiral constantly pulling me between disciplines (psychology and anthropology), countries,[1] and, more deeply, two names (Ellen and Élizabeth), a practice by the women in my mother's family in recent generations.

These reflections follow a personal journey through the trajectory of my fieldwork, looking back and searching for the undulations, bumps, and folds of a landscape. Ideas of otherness or estrangement which emerge ever more clearly from that quest are difficult to approach in anthropology; it is as if these ideas were parts of an alien, increasingly inaccessible, landscape, where it is difficult to think and put things into words.

The Paradox of the Anthropological Stance

A critique of the consistency between words, representations, and "reality" is inherent to modernity, even if that critique has been more particularly developed in the social sciences and humanities (Lyotard 1988; Foucault 1966). This has taken a particular form in ethnographers' awareness that it may be ultimately impossible to account for others' worlds in terms of our own words, images, and metaphors. In recent decades, ethnographic descriptions have been highly criticized for their implicit involvement in the process of colonization; the legitimacy of classical anthropology has been questioned for its participation in the construction of an objectified image of non-Western peoples. In this context, "cultural differences" have become highly suspect, and the very notion of culture has come under sharp attack (Clifford and Marcus 1986; Abu-Lughod 1991).

Another factor that has played an important role in reframing how anthropology views itself has been the modern world's transnational, globalized character and the fact that it is less and less possible to see cultures as separate, objective entities (Appadurai 1997); this has led to the realization that the image of well-defined, well-bounded societies is illusory (Gupta and Ferguson 1992; Clifford 1997). In this context, along with the emergence of postcolonial perspectives, other voices have entered academic debates, both deeply destabilizing and greatly enriching the academic environment. For Spivak, the colonial subject's detachment from the position of Native informant is in the process of being recoded by a certain postcolonial subject that reappropriates the Native informant's position (Spivak 1999:ix); however, the use of telecommunications informatics, which allows us to tap directly into indigenous knowledge, threatens to allow everybody to call upon indigenous signifiers and to integrate these signifiers within their own discourse.

More broadly, postcolonial writers have challenged conventional anthropological knowledge. The rapid diffusion of their ideas and perspectives has opened the way to a challenging dialogue between actors speaking from different positions and different epistemological horizons (Ashcroft, Griffiths, and Tiffin 1995; Young 2001). But these postcolonial authors have also mastered the approaches and perspectives of the most influential Western thinkers extremely well. This has allowed us to completely assimilate them as "one of us," despite the challenging intellectual perspectives they have introduced. I wonder whether their rapid integration into the Western academic scene, however necessary, has not further contributed to erasing the significance of the notion of cultural differences.

It appears that the idea of "difference" is becoming increasingly taboo in anthropology: it is as though differences necessarily imply objectification or domination – as though differences have lost their power to question and destabilize, leaving room only for the overriding idea of a common humanity. But could this position also be the guise of a new Western hegemony? Are "cultural differences" to be confined to the notion of "identity," with all the promises and traps associated with such a concept? Is it reasonable to think that ideas based on the work of the preeminent Western thinkers are the best frameworks for analyzing what is "really at stake" in other societies? From an interesting counter-perspective, Homi Bhabha (1994) draws attention to the latent figures of "otherness" that inhabit the inner margins of the Western world. He also argues for the need to articulate cultural differences in a way that acknowledges the "other" without reducing it to a homogeneous otherness or celebrating mere cultural relativism. He discusses the promises and pitfalls of a call for "human togetherness" in that context.

Theoretical schools throughout the history of anthropology introduced order and coherence in the others' worlds and may have contributed to minimizing that which resists our own schemes of understanding. They integrated cultural differences into frames of reference that allowed us to recognize ourselves but that also erased anything that did not fit with the intellectual spirit of the day. From that perspective, it did not really matter whether the coherence was perceived as inherent to the notion of culture, as in the interpretative posture; whether it responded to processes that transcend cultural boundaries, as in some versions of functionalism or in the interpretation of everything in terms of power differentials in current critical anthropology; or whether it depended, as in French structuralism, on meta-cultural modes of analysis that fragment the apparent unity of institutions, myths, or rituals and unveil universal sets of oppositions and contrasts that cut across cultures and societies.

While each of these perspectives may shed light on particular aspects of the reality and obscure others, they have colored the development of anthropology and have set important landmarks. They may also have served to defend against the feeling of estrangement evoked by the others' "otherness." But is it possible to have a dialogue that places as much weight on "otherness" as it does on "sameness" in the encounter with the others, one that remains sensitive to the irreducible difference attached to "otherness"?

This forces us once again to face a particular aspect of the original goal of anthropology: the desire to demonstrate how that which is considered natural in our own world (cultural, social, and scientific) appears under different lights in other societies. But this goal has a dark side: the risk of succumbing to the opposite tendency of projecting our own repressed imagination onto others, thereby emphasizing the differences between "us" and "them." Examples occur in Obeyesekere's analysis of the imaginary dimension of Captain Cook's travels (Obeyesekere 1992) and in the Western discourse on the Orient, which Said (1978) termed "Orientalism" – two critiques formulated from the edges of the Western paradigm. This tension in approaching other societies and cultures parallels the dilemma we confront as individuals. On the one hand, confrontations with different perspectives, epistemologies, and values allow us to glimpse that which infuses our own thoughts and perceptions from the outside looking in, and to approach what may be called the "work of otherness" within ourselves and in our relationships with others. On the other hand, there is the risk that we merely project our personal fantasies onto the screen provided by others. How, then, do we navigate these turbulent, paradoxical waters?

I propose that the shift experienced in any encounter does not have to be viewed as an irritant to be removed or overcome. Instead it can be seen as providing an analytical space from which we may question the manifest coherence of our own narratives and our pretense of control over what happens to us during fieldwork.

Itineraries of a Landscape

Based on my own field experience, I submit that knowledge is neither purely about the other nor purely about ourselves. However, we must explore what this means, examine its forms, and discuss its epistemological and methodological implications – not to attack the position of possibly knowing, but to better understand the constraints within which we work and to attempt to transform these constraints into tools of knowledge. To do this, the first step is to agree, at least from an epistemological standpoint, to dismantle the coherence of our own narratives and to explore what we bring to the field, so that the forces permeating our own descriptions rise to surface and become explicit – in other words, to explore their landscape and get an idea of their topography.

Here, I will take three successive vantage points. From the first, I draw some hidden contours of my fieldwork experience as they appear in hindsight. This approach reveals the intricate network of threads and motives that link research interests, questions, and findings to issues and positions anchored in an intimate, personal history. Here, influences must be perceived as two-directional: in the realm of "resonance," not "causality." From a second vantage point, I identify a few key signifiers that persist but progressively change as I move from one site to the other. These themes appear to have a subconscious influence on me rather than corresponding to an intentional intellectual focus. They refer to positions or perspectives that permeate the way we situate ourselves in regard to reality, and help fashion ethnographies. Finally, from the third vantage point, I explore debates and ideas from psychoanalysis to see if they add depth to anthropological explorations. I discuss the heuristic value of psychoanalytic insights in regard to the approach of "otherness" through fieldwork.

These three vantage points serve as anchor points for a self-reflective journey. They are my way of integrating myself into the current anthropological ethos.

Explorations along a Timeline

When I consider the landscape of my research journey, a few peaks rise above a broader plain, corresponding to specific themes and perspectives that have been especially significant in orienting my intellectual and personal history. At a manifest level, the choice of these topics appears to have been dictated by particular life circumstances. When considered from a certain distance, however, they interweave to form a textured fabric in which who we are plays an active role.

My first fieldwork took place in Congo, Central Africa, among the matrilineal Yansi. My Ph.D. thesis director was a psychoanalyst interested in exploring the maternal and paternal dimensions of the image of God. I decided to concentrate instead on the cultural development of the father figure in a matrilineal society. Utilizing my observation of infancy rituals and French structuralist theory, I identified the differential features culturally associated with various kinship relationships (Corin 1995).

A professorship at the National University of Zaire, during a period marked by the ideology of "authenticity" that argued for a return to African traditional values and ideas, allowed me to work closely with students to enrich and culturally anchor my courses in ethnopsychology and psychopathology. My memory of a dramatic encounter with a spirit-possessed woman pushed me to focus on spirit possession rituals. I was fortunate to develop meaningful fieldwork collaborations with healers and patients from three main spirit-possession rituals that differed in degree of traditionalism, region of origin, and importance of trance as a public manifestation of spirit possession: the Zebola, the Mpombo, and the Mizuka respectively, the last closely associated with Islam (Corin 1995, 1998a).

When I came to Canada, I was hired as a research director at a university psychiatric hospital. I developed a series of studies with psychotic patients and tried to access their subjective world. This led me to later explore how culture contributes to the articulation of psychotic experience (Corin 1990).

Now, in retrospect, I also see more personal motives underlying each of these choices, converging on the interface between culture and personal experience. My discoveries in one field also focused my attention in a certain direction and echoed my understanding of reality in different areas. I gradually developed an approach to reality that is at least partly independent of "facts" alone.

Among the Yansi, rituals during the first two years of life introduce the child to three main figures: the maternal uncle, the father, and the father's father. The rituals also impart the cultural significance of these figures to both the child and the society. The respective characteristics of these figures are amplified or complemented through later rituals associated with puberty, marriage, and, in particular, funerals. They are also further expressed in the long palavers, where illness and misfortune are discussed and latent fears and suspicions shared.

Within a complex web of references the maternal uncle is culturally positioned as the key figure of authority and identification, a formal source of protection and defense in social conflicts, and the one who represents the deceased of the lineage. Maternal uncles are part of a chain of asymmetrical relationships dominated by the lineage's elders, themselves dependent on deceased and ancestors, with whom authority ultimately rests. At the same time, maternal uncles are characterized by an immediate presence based on blood-kinship and on the uncles' "maternal quality" (they are called *Ngobeal*, or male mother). The maternal uncles' authority is marked by a power over life and death that is both concrete and symbolic (magical), and is always suspected as favoring the uncles' egoistical ends. The father is first ritually introduced to the child as the mother's husband and sexual partner, the child's guardian, and the person accountable to the uncle for the child's well-being. He is the one who introduces the male child to the world of men and adulthood, and later transmits his important fetishes of fecundity and hunting. Palavers indicate that the father is the only one who can interpose between a person and his or her maternal uncles' witchcraft. The grandfather is ritually introduced as a figure of identification for a person's singular characteristics. Grandfather/grandson relationships are part of a broader system of alternate generations marked by joking relationships and are structurally opposed to the lineage links. Alternate generations also mediate the relationships between the living and the dead. They play key roles in transmitting the lineage's objects and functions and during transitional rituals like funerals, where their casual and aggressive behaviors directly challenge lineage members and negate the event of death.

I determined two lines of identification framed by the Yansi culture and engaging different dimensions: a collective manifest dimension controlled by the maternal lineage, and an implicit individualized dimension that unfolds in grandfather/father/son relationships. I emphasized the all-powerful and threatening quality of the maternal line of descent, and the mediating, protecting, and individualizing function along the paternal line of transmission.

The conclusions of that first research were undoubtedly based on rigorous data analysis. However, my findings also closely paralleled dilemmas and questions intimately connected to my personal life, like the powerful and ambiguous character of my mother's figure in the absence of a father deceased a few weeks after my birth. I cannot avoid feeling perplexed by such an unintentional convergence. Would somebody with a different life trajectory have drawn similar conclusions? If not, were my own conclusions merely a projection of my psyche, or was I simply attentive to the duplicity of descent and the vital importance of mediating figures?

My research into spirit-possession groups also began with an interest in the inner structure of spirit-possession rituals and idioms. This gradually shifted to the personal experiences of women initiated into the ritual. In Congo, spirit possession manifests itself through physical and mental health problems, and initiation has a crucial therapeutic dimension. Spirit possession unfolds along a timeline, deeply reorganizing the person's life, health, and sense of self. I was also interested in how particular spirit-possession idioms provide a framework for reading a woman's discomfort or distress and in how idioms interweave ideas of election and protection, fault and attack, fragility and transgression, and in how people conceive of the relationship between the spirit and human worlds.

Through my work with several types of spirit-possession rituals and close relationships with healers and women engaged in the long initiation process, I was able to deconstruct the apparent unity of the term "spirit possession" to identify the differential features opposing these various rituals, particularly dramatized during the great dances ending an initiation.

As I continued to reflect on my material, I later explored the flexibility of each ritual (Corin 1979) and its appropriation by individual women in the context of their lives. Ricoeur's work on imagination and history exposed me to new ways of understanding the work of spirit possession on the sense of self and on rewriting personal history (Corin 1998a).

From where I stand now, I can see how later contacts with psychotic people and my own introduction to psychoanalysis guided my re-reading of my spirit-possession data. This new context sensitized me to infrarational levels of the action of the ritual. On one hand, it directed my attention to comments about beauty and desire, to the sensorial quality of daily anointing with the spirits' oil, to the pleasure of dancing for the spirits, and to how initiation helps deconstruct an initial, normative, and coherent self-narrative to reveal its more ambiguous and richer texture, and modifies the initiate's position in regard to the Law. On the other hand, this new context also sensitized me to signs that not everything can be bound by cultural symbols and representations. My previous work on spirit-possession rituals stressed how cultural signifiers are used to tame and articulate resistant physical and mental health problems and how they express and remodel social tensions between genders, within the family, and between the individual and culture. This emphasis on logic and coherence left out another aspect of spirit possession that is more obscure given its marginality to the Western ethos. This led me to India with new questions about how to access societies' differential awareness and tolerance of what escapes the order of common life. Would this awareness and tolerance, I wondered, significantly affect someone engulfed in an experience as radically self-altering as psychosis?

When one reworks past fieldwork data from a new perspective nourished by subsequent questions and discoveries, does the fieldwork merely act as a screen on which to project the confirmation, expansion, and legitimization of one's new personal interests? Or does intellectual and personal evolution open one up to latent aspects of that fieldwork that one was initially unable to perceive or develop?

In working with psychotic patients in Montreal, I wanted to understand the factors that allow some of these people to avoid rehospitalization and the significance they attach to "social integration." The people I interviewed impressed me with their unconventional ways of moving within culture and society. Contrary to my expectations, I discovered the protective value of "positive withdrawal." I tried to describe the intimate texture and progressive development of this position through an idiosyncratic *bricolage* of cultural signifiers. I noticed how patients often confer a spiritual quality onto positive withdrawal, and was struck by the solitary and fragile character of this construction and its profound cultural marginality.

Researchers have repeatedly documented the better prognoses of schizophrenia in India, compared with Western countries. My research observations in Montreal led me to wonder whether some parallel might be drawn between positive withdrawal and aspects of the ascetic quest in India. More specifically, I asked whether people facing the terrifying experience of psychosis might be able to borrow aspects of the ascetic figure in attempting to cope with it. I hypothesized that asceticism serves as a kind of myth model (Obeyesekere 1992) for people engaged in a range of limit experiences, including psychosis.

At a more personal level, I came to recognize a personal and previously unknown affinity with the "positive withdrawal" I had described in my research. I began to pay attention to it, to leave room for it in my life, and to find ways to inhabit that space in a richer way. The web of influences that weave together personal life and fieldwork seemed to spread from the outside inward. However, I also suspect that my implicit longing for such detachment pre-dated my findings and may have influenced the significance I attributed to particular words and postures in psychotic people.

These examples show how fieldwork experiences can leave traces seen as "shadows" that haunt a researcher's later fieldwork; they also permit a retrospective view of previously unseen dimensions of past fieldwork. Research trajectories are driven by a range of explicit and implicit motives that help to shape one's choice of research topics but that also inflect what one notices or emphasizes and how one interprets data. They form a shadowy fabric of interlaced motives.

From Margins to "Otherness"

At another, deeper, level I realize that whatever the area, my approach to collective and personal phenomena reflects a basic intellectual and personal position that pervades my work in various guises. This position developed and took shape throughout my life as a researcher and gradually changed. The notion of "margin," which I came to use as a central analytical device, was later reconfigured more radically as "otherness." I suspect that this transformation responded to a double logic from my fieldwork observations and my clinical practice. It illustrates my personal dialogue with my data and reflects a personal stance toward the world.

The notion of "margin" asserted itself explicitly during my work with people diagnosed as psychotic. It is an implicit correlative of "positive withdrawal" and offers a means of considering the social and cultural positions of people who explore ways of moving along the edges of society and culture – being "inside and outside" simultaneously. I was struck by the paucity of avenues available to psychotic people for exploring their profound questions about reality and life and suffering, and for sharing their experiences of alienation and strangeness. They exist at the edges of society largely unnoticed, erased, so to speak, and without power to question the "center." Expert jargon and prevalent modes of practice are instrumental in this process of "erasure." Their "abnormality" triggers two main types of reactions: either indifference or an attempt to normalize, particularly by family members and professionals. Patients may experience the de-dramatizing and "banalizing" of normalization (suffering psychosis is like having a flu) as negating or disqualifying their sense of deep alteration. Whatever its humanitarian dimension, normalization is dominated by neurobiological explanations, psycho-education, and the cognitive reen-gineering of troubled minds. Madness no longer leads to questions; now beyond our collective gaze, differences challenge nothing.

In North America, I worked with "consumer"-controlled mental health groups, which offered alternatives to the conventional mental health system (Corin 2000a). My research with the "consumers" further sensitized me to the mechanisms of exclusion in Western societies, economically, socially, and most importantly, in knowledge and "expertise." This forced me to reconceptualize how "positive withdrawal" develops through a person's attempts to deal both with an elusive experience and with marginalizing social forces.

According to Michel Foucault, societies can be defined by their limits – what they exclude at an epistemological level. Depending on the society or era, some phenomena may fall outside the realm of what can be known.

Regarding Western societies, Foucault wrote: "Perhaps one day we will no longer truly comprehend what madness once was. Its figure will have turned inward on itself, preventing us from deciphering the traces it has left behind – and to the uninitiated, such traces will seem nothing more than black marks" (Foucault 1994 [1964]:412; personal translation). One may wonder whether other societies allow for spaces that contain, or even encourage, the exploration of such limit-zones where meaning and culture appear to vanish, whether some cultures permit and frame that very act of vanishing.

Guided by this interest for margins and their dynamic place within society, I revisited my work in African cultures and designed a new set of studies in India. My African data suggested that the societies I worked with in Congo possess cultural mechanisms and a structural heterogeneity that affords dialectic interplay between centers and margins (Corin 1995).

In Yans society, the matrilineal line of descent is clearly posited as culturally prominent. But my research also revealed the reversibility, under special circumstances, of the relative importance of dominant and dominated cultural codes within the society. At funerals particularly, ritual inversions favor the preeminence of the patrilineal over matrilineal lines of descent. This provides flexibility and suspension of, or distancing from, the social order (Babcock 1978). It sets limits on the matrilineal principle and allows detachment from the rules of the dominant ideology, opening up means of escaping or balancing the imperative matrilineal power. At the level of the person, this enables individuation.

In therapeutic spirit-possession rituals, the marginal character of the spirits is manifested through a structural opposition to the society's male ancestral spirits, which are central to community life. The contrast between these two groups of spirits is expressed in ways that involve gender, cultural identity, the spirits' place of residence, and their relationships to the central cultural norm. In the Zebola ritual, female spirits protect women from the consequences of transgressing cultural norms or screen against malevolent influences due to jealousy or envy, and conflicts with family, kin, or neighbors. Complex processes of inversion during initiation contribute to healing by reframing the illness episode as a positive sign of having been chosen. The woman distances herself from the spirit while rebuilding a new alliance with it; she simultaneously distances herself and reintegrates into the family group, thus more deeply transforming her relationship with herself and the world. In the case of the *Mizuka* ritual, which requires obedience to Islamic laws, diversity among ritual spirits enables group members to express a range of positions of proximity and distance with respect to core Islamic values and dialectic relationships between Islamic and local African traditions. Initiates were able, by playing with the ritual's symbols, to engage in a dialectic of the relationship between central codes and values and their individual positions within the culture.

In these two cases – the Yans kinship system and the spirit-possession rituals – I argued that bringing the society's structural heterogeneity into play through ritual virtually opens up a space of freedom and individuation. It allows differences to be recognized, developed, and reintegrated into a shared societal space so that the margins of the culture remain in a productive tension with its center. I decided to explore as well how other cultures come to develop a range of "limit-experiences" locally seen as beyond common perceptions or behaviors. This triggered my work in India, in close collaboration with Gilles Bibeau, a medical anthropologist, and a local research team of clinical researchers from the Schizophrenia Research Foundation (SCARF). Together, we interviewed psychotic people in psychiatric wards but also in Hindu temples and Darghas (Muslim shrines).

The idea of margins gradually assumed autonomy, going from possibilities for inverting the preeminence of certain norms and codes, through the potential for articulation this affords individuals, to exploring how societies and cultures deal with limits. That notion of limits paved the way for my present interest in "otherness" – which also arose in my narratives from psychotic people. These narratives illustrate the limits of words for describing the existential drift associated with psychosis; they "say" more than they explicitly tell, evoking an unspeakable fear that barely finds its way to language. I expanded my question of the importance of margins in particular societies to the importance they place on a radical "otherness" that resists being "bound" by culture. Reexamining my African data led me to pay closer attention to the wildness of the spirit and to its resistance to being completely tamed by rituals. One might say that spirit-possession rituals acknowledge the existence of essential "otherness" in the culture and create a place for it (Corin 2000b).

The data from our work in India reveals that psychotic people, especially males, use various types of religious signifiers and religious places and symbols to enact, articulate, and legitimize a position of withdrawal. We hypothesized that in Hindu philosophy, the figure of the *Sadhu* – the emblematic embodiment of asceticism – provides a "myth model" that may be appropriated in a range of life circumstances and allows various limit-experiences to be integrated into the culture and the society (Corin et al. 2004). The Hindu ascetic position fosters a personal and collective exploration of the extreme limits of reality, and remains very popular in contemporary India for people of various social and educational backgrounds.

It seemed fair to ask if there are overlaps between asceticism and particular aspects of a psychotic quest, or whether people undergoing a range of limit-experiences are able to adopt asceticism. Gilles Bibeau,

Professor Ravi Kapur, of Bangalore, and I are currently conducting research among Sadhus we have encountered in various settings, from Ashrams to Himalayan pilgrimage sites. We explore the flexibility of the religious idiom of asceticism and its role and significance in the lives of individual ascetics who have found various ways of weaving together centrality and marginality within Hindu society.

I suspect that the particular way I have explored and understood psychotic patients' narratives, and my awakening to that which resists language and meaning, also echoes my intellectual and clinical journey through psychoanalysis. In fact, and by definition, the unconscious never appears clearly in the clinical encounter. It manifests itself only indirectly, through a particular texture of words, gaps and paradoxes, blanks, hesitations, and slips of the tongue. In addition, my sensitivity to "otherness" and the "work of culture" in other societies has influenced the way I listen to and understand people in the clinical setting. "Margins," "limits," and "otherness" are key signifiers that mark my research itinerary and likely express my stance toward the world as much as they reflect my fieldwork findings. In social science, knowledge of reality necessarily develops through successive approximations directed by both outside and inside influences. From this standpoint, the Saussurian notion of signifier must be complemented by a Lacanian perspective that defines signifiers as at once representing subjects and determining them. These are "signatures" that both identify the author and determine his or her approach to things, invisibly or subconsciously. They travel within and outside the frontiers of fieldwork, and serve as motors and beacons lighting the way. I should also say that they drive my explorations in psychoanalysis, and that psychoanalysis radicalizes their significance in my work. But I can only guess at their deep significance for me, since they work through me without my full awareness.

Deep Shadows: Explorations Based in Psychoanalysis

The shadow side of fieldwork is more than merely the contributions of other fieldwork experiences in framing and reframing what we observe and interpret. It is also made up of dialogues we have with authors and colleagues in our discipline (Crapanzano 1992) and of the epistemological horizons that dominate the spirit of the age. Current theories are perceived as sharpening the ethnographers' gaze, focusing their attention on what really counts. In this respect, one could say that fieldwork functions as something "real" that supports the truth of the narrative; however, references to the fieldwork erase the contribution of that very narrative in shaping what is presented as reality. But does our approach to field-work not also fall under the horizon of debates and advances in other disciplines?

Current anthropological debates and perspectives evoke for me ideas and perspectives in psychoanalysis. How legitimate is this perception? Does it distort the picture, or does it enrich anthropological questions and issues by inserting them into another framework, thereby revealing additional parts of the picture?

Here, I explore three possible areas of convergence between anthropology and psychoanalysis and discuss how I see them as a source of inspiration.

The first area concerns a theory of representation and questions the clarity of language to its speakers. On the side of psychoanalysis, access to what animates one's speech, behaviors, and feelings is directed by a technique that entails a particular treatment of speech. The double rule of free association by patients and free-floating attention by the therapist leads to a deconstruction of the coherence of narratives and to a loosening of the connection between words and meaning. Jean Imbeault (1997) com-ments that free association is in fact a technique of dissociation based on the fragmentation and recomposition of elements of discourse. It relates to the idea that the psyche works to distort unconscious representations and to transform them through displacements and condensations along a chain of signifiers. For Laurence Kahn (2001), the subversion of the theory of reference explored by psychoanalysis is its most important and disturbing contribution to contemporary anthropology. She speaks of an irreversible schism that dislodges us from our pretensions of mastery over reality and over what we think; it destabilizes our relationship with internal and external realities.

In Senegal, an interdisciplinary research team involving anthropologists and psychoanalysts (Ortigues and Zempleni 1968) explored the conver-gences between French structuralism and Lacanian psychoanalysis. Both led to breaks in the apparent consistency of symbols, rituals, and cultural representations. The authors also argue that case histories cannot be seen as exemplifying broader collective processes. People cannot be summed up as embodiments of the collective; their individuality appears negatively, through their own way of distancing themselves from cultural signifiers. For the ethnographer, the task is to trace the chains of meanings that crystallize within particular cultural elements and make connections with broader dimensions of the culture. It is also to examine particular asso-ciative chains employed by specific individuals and groups in response to the particular situations or dilemmas they face. This perspective echoes Crapanzano's idea (1977) that different people use cultural idioms in particular ways depending on their social and personal positions within the society and the culture. In my analysis of narratives, I first try to locate key nodes or recurrent signifiers and identify the associative chains in which they are embedded, both within the narrative itself and within the culture. I also examine how they are employed in particular cases. One might say that this practice approaches culture centrifugally, based on the signifiers employed in the narratives. It allows for a more flexible approach to the polysemy of cultural references, and opens one up to their diversity and to their true significance for the individual people who occupy unique positions in our transnational world.

For example, the interviews we collected in India of people with psychosis and their relatives indicate that they make use of different aspects of the religious sphere. This reflects the different dilemmas faced by patients and their relatives: the patients' attempt to tame and express a radical experience of alienation and "otherness," and the relatives' attempt to minimize patients' differences and reintegrate them into the normative social fabric. This contrast is in tune with the heterogeneity of the religious sphere within Hinduism. It extends and embodies a continuous tension that exists between a ritual path dominated by the Brahmins and the ascetic quest embodied in the Sadhus (Madan 1987).

In Montreal, research I am conducting with Cécile Rousseau among psychotic patients from different cultures, their relatives, and their practitioners illustrates the different ways each of these actors understands cultural differences and employs cultural references in their own narratives of the psychoses' histories. We examine how the signifier "culture" circulates in the clinical setting among patients, families, and practitioners; how they appropriate and subvert this signifier; and what seems to be at stake in each particular case.

The second area where anthropology and psychoanalysis converge is in the ethnographic encounter. It is now common in anthropology to criticize the asymmetrical divide often established between ethnographers and their subjects and to call for a more dialogical perspective. In psychoanalysis, the clinical encounter is seen as exacerbating the way all human encounters are haunted by ghosts, shadows, and demands that go far beyond the manifest content of the exchange. Speech is always directed; it is addressed to someone and animated by forces and desires that subvert the explicit content of the exchange. Patients gradually move from a position in which the psychoanalyst is supposed to have what they want – including an intimate knowledge of their inner selves – to an acknowledgment of the unfulfillable lack that makes up the Subject (Lacan, 1975).

Vincent Crapanzano's (1994) retrospective comments on *Tuhami: a Portrait of a Moroccan* illustrate the particular play of desires and expectations that motivated both partners – Tuhami, the ethnographic subject, and Crapanzano, the ethnographer. These desires both preexisted and were produced by the encounter. "Data" were created and circulated between the ethnographer and his subject as symbolic terms of unspoken underlying exchanges.

This play of reciprocal transferences unfolds in parallel to counter-transference that evokes the unconscious reactions that transference from the patient elicits in the psychoanalyst. Counter-transference engages the psychoanalyst's own psychic life in the effort to gain access to what lies behind the manifest discourse and to construct a representation of the patient's psychic reality (Kahn 2001). It reflects a "pathic" (as opposed to empathic) condition of reception to the patient's psychic movements and involves sensorial and affective components.

From this perspective, exploring others' "otherness" requires that one opens one's mind to the "work of otherness" within oneself; that one allows the "shadows of otherness" to echo within one's own zones of uncertainty and anguish. And if one's own words and representations may mask the continuing search for words or prematurely shape what lies at the borders of representation, is this not a risk inherent to all human encounters? Such a risk can only be limited by an intentional reach toward the unknown, by a reflexive and critical attention to the shadowy play of latent currents and slopes within ourselves.

The formative role of the ethnographic encounter also stems from the fact that each player's gaze acts as a mirror for the other and becomes part of what makes them who they are. Lacan's approach to the mirror stage (1966) clarifies the ambiguous implications of this process. The mirror stage refers to a developmental period when infants still experience themselves as parceled out and fragmented; the image in the mirror allows them to anticipate a unified self-image. It is therefore as another person that a child first experiences himself as a whole, through a form that he embodies and in which he alienates himself. The imaginary constitution of the self is both alienating and necessary. The person can remain trapped in the reflected image (the mirror or the other person's eyes) or go beyond this imaginary perspective to enter into the symbolic and develop his or her own individuality.

Through the ethnographic encounter, both participants tend to produce unified self-images for themselves and the other person. Such images may be particularly significant for people who experience themselves as parceled out, either personally or collectively. This may be the case for psychotic people or for people or groups who have experienced extreme trauma. This adds a particular nuance to ethnographers' responsibility toward their ethnographic subjects and should also call their attention to their own role in constructing the human reality they are trying to describe; this role may be alienating, formative, or liberating. This mirroring function also affects the ethnographer. Seeing oneself reflected in the other's gaze has significant implications for one's professional and personal identity. We all know the subjective impact of the perceived success or failure of field-work and how finding the clue that allows us to give coherence and logic to what we have observed is crucial to constructing our own coherence, at both personal and academic levels. The idea here is not to deny any "objective" basis to what we observe and interpret, but to reflect on the specific kind of truth that is in question in fieldwork.

A third area where psychoanalysis has enriched my ethnographic work – thereby participating in its shadowy texture – is in my exploration of the limits of words and meaning. And the overlap has given this explora-tion a particular spin and guided it through various cultures.

In his conclusion to *Les mots et les choses*, Michel Foucault (1966) argues that, along with ethnology, psychoanalysis occupies a special place among the humanities. Both push the exploration of the relativity of what is taken for granted to its extreme; both explore the radical finitude of the repres-entations we use to approach the realms of life, needs and work, and lan-guage. Psychoanalysis does so by examining that which necessarily slips away, reminding us in the process that the expectation for an ultimate unveil-ing of "truth" is futile. Beyond life's forms and functions, psychoana-lysis points to death; beyond the meanings and systems that form particular languages, to the Law; beyond needs and conflicts, to naked desire (that which remains unthought at the core of thought). Ethnology, by high-lighting synchronic correlations among cultures, helps us transcend the chronological framework by which we reflect upon our own culture within its very boundaries. Ethnology sets apart the particularities, differences, and limits of cultures against the backdrop of life, needs, and language and their organization within particular cultures. Both psychoanalysis and ethnology bypass the representations that, in any society, people form of themselves, and of life, their needs and meanings lodged within language. Both are thus "counter-sciences" taking sciences upstream and bringing them back to their epistemological base.

Working with psychotic people has confronted me with the limits of words to express the profound alteration of self and the world that these people experience. Here, the limits of language reflect not that there is nothing to say, but the fact that what can be said appears overwhelming, chaotic, and infused with fear and anguish. Philosophers and psychiatrists inspired by German phenomenology argue that psychosis is characterized by a defect in the "void" that allows people to detach themselves from the world and which forms the basis of language and speech. From this perspective, psychotic people suffer from an overall density of being, from an inability to create a space of play where they can move and exist as individual beings (Maldiney, 1986). I wonder whether this might shed additional light on the "positive withdrawal," which I found associated with self-healing or recovery in people diagnosed with schizophrenia.

In my psychoanalytical clinical work, I have been struck by the therapeutic significance of particular moments of some individual treatments. At these times, the power of words and images to give shape to inner desires or fears seems to fail; language appears to fade away or fall into pieces. The quality of the encounter, or its ambiance, suddenly changes and seems infused with a palpable feeling of anguish that resists any representation. In several such cases, the white color of my office walls became a central signifier that, for the patient, embodied a threatening dissolution of representations. Such transformations happen in exceptional moments in the clinical encounter with non-psychotic patients when they approach very deep zones of conflict or situations that reveal their traumatic power, and when they reach zones where speech seems to collide with pre-linguistic affects and impressions that merge and threaten to engulf them. In these moments, the "blank spaces" that permit the symbolic construction of reality appear transformed and absorbed into an abyssal void; the important role of negation in the constitution of language becomes a pure negative.

I have learned that if one is able to remain at that very limit and to contain the threatening quality of these moments within the transference–counter-transference space, without trying too rapidly to reduce its enigmatic character through interpretations, such moments can mark important turning points in the healing process. I see these moments mobilizing both the analyst and the patient, or rather the space formed by their encounter, in order to create a kind of embodied negative that may later be employed in the formation of proto-representations and symbols.

André Green (1995), a French psychoanalyst, has explored what he calls the "work of the negative" in its various forms. He distinguishes a destructive effect of the negative, which attacks the ability to distinguish and to name affects and emotions and the capacity to think and explain, from a constructive function of the negative in language that allows the creation of symbols and metaphors. My clinical work suggests a third form of the negative, whereby an embodied void constitutes a first step into the world of representations, preventing the patient's engulfment, while accessing words and meaning.

The experience of psychosis may appear dominated by the destructive work of the negative. Could the "positive withdrawal" that emerged from our research be an attempt to contain this type of negative and allow for the creation of embodied voids where representations can begin to form?

Foucault observed that madness was once considered a manifestation of the finitude within language; through psychology and psychiatry, however, madness has been transformed into a mere mental disorder. For a time, Foucault felt that literature was the new area where the finitude of language could be explored to its limits; later he became more skeptical.

Foucault called attention to what societies exclude and situate outside their borders. This "outside" has no niche in common language and images. Considering the forms and roles of the negative in psychosis, and the marginal, fragile place of positive withdrawal that emerged from my data, could it be that other societies provide culturally acceptable and more central ways to form, protect, and transcend such a marginal position, and might these ways be accessible, even indirectly, to people suffering from psychosis?

Hindu thinkers have described a form of epistemology that differs deeply from our familiar way of distinguishing inside from outside, in which notions that appear diametrically opposed are perceived as intimately related (Ramanujan 1989). Similarly, Hindu philosophical texts such as the Upanishads and the Yoga Sutra discuss techniques that permit detachment from the realm of manifest reality through work on perception, memory, dream, and dreamless sleep to reach a state of illumination in which the Atman and Brahman merge. The symbolic function of the negative seems to transcend and be integrated into a more radical process of detachment from the illusory character of self and the sensory and cognitive aspects of reality. But the question of possible parallel with the forms of retreat that psychotic people seem to actively employ remains open. This is what drives our current research with Indian ascetics and the observations and interviews we conduct in Himalayan pilgrimage sites.

Our preliminary findings confirm our impression that the "work of culture," through which private dynamics appear to merge with culturally developed processes, needs to be further refined in the case of people who suffer from psychosis. Psychotic people appear not to insert themselves directly into a culture's central signifiers; rather, they appropriate, transform, and subvert signifiers in their own ways. Ascetics radically distinguish their own quest – built on a long and extremely taxing work on the self – from the psychotic experience. But findings suggest that there are in fact zones of overlap that warrant clarification.

We have also had discussions with Hindu philosophers and scientists to explore how they read and interpret Hindu classical texts in light of today's reality. The "work of the negative" may provide a bridge between Hindu epistemology and some of my questions. Are there parallels, convergences, and/or radical differences between the position of detachment promoted in Hinduism and what Lacan says about the subject's need to free himself from the illusions of the dominating imaginary? Are Agamben's (1997) or Blanchot's (1955) explorations about language and death relevant here? Or, on another level, are there resemblances and/or radical differences between what Lacan terms "das Ding" and the "formless" referred to in the Upanishad? How do each of us approach the limits of reality? How do we approach the realm of death and finiteness? How can we try to say something about the unspeakable and its significance to being human? More generally, how can we use fieldwork to further explore and reframe areas of knowledge that we are exploring from a Western standpoint, not only in anthropology but also in the human sciences? Should that broader epistemological framework also be considered as part of fieldwork?

Conclusions

I have argued here that the shadow side of fieldwork emerges indirectly, as a multidimensional texture that can only be seen from the distance of hindsight. It is woven of a complex network of links that form between research themes and settings. These links move and shift as we evolve intellectually and personally. They also reflect and orient our discourse with various authors, both within and outside our discipline. They are driven by subconscious forces, desires, and expectations that often affect us without our knowledge, and that are steeped in our own particular life histories. And like our fieldwork decisions, our theoretical preferences also have a subjective dimension. They develop at the interface between external influences, debates, and fashions, and affective choices that extend well beyond the rational justifications we form.

Up to what point does this type of resonance contribute to shedding light on the phenomena under study and to uncovering aspects that might otherwise remain concealed or unseen? How far might it bias our observations and lead us to confuse reality with projection? What is our role as an "incubator" that transforms the tissue of reality or lets appear particular forms that were intertwined with other figures in a complex design that always resists full grasp? What are the driving forces behind our thirst for knowledge, other than the rational or overt motives we admit?

If subjectivity acts as a screen in the production of knowledge, what kind of screen is it? Is it an opaque screen that conceals reality and stands between ourselves and the people we work with? Is it a projection screen upon which we recognize only our own fantasies and hopes, or dark sides? Is it a defensive screen that protects us from the differences, the resistance of the other to our own ways of thinking? Or is it a screen that reveals, a "magic mirror" in which the "othernesses" within the other and ourselves resonate together, opening into a new dimension of reality?

Note

1 Today, it is Canada and Belgium; as a child, it was Belgium (my late father's country and where I grew up) and Switzerland (my mother's country and where we holidayed). This also leads to questions such as where do I belong, what does it mean to belong, and, concerning my fieldwork, why did I choose to move from Africa to South Asia, and how do these contrasting worlds interweave within who I am now?

References

Abu-Lughod, L.
   1991 Writing against Culture. *In* Recapturing Anthropology. Working in the Present. R. G. Fox, ed. Pp. 137–162. Santa Fe, New Mexico: School of American Research Press.
Agamben, G.
   1997 Le langage et la mort. Paris: Christian Bourgois Éditeur.
Appadurai, A.
   1997 Modernity at Large. Cultural Dimensions of Globalization. Minneapolis: University of Minnesota Press.
Ashcroft, B., G. Griffiths, and H. Tiffin, eds.
   1995 The Post-Colonial Studies Reader. London: Routledge.
Babcock, B. A., ed.
   1978 The Reversible World. Symbolic Inversion in Art and Society. Ithaca: Cornell University Press.
Bhabha, H. K.
   1994 The Location of Culture. London: Routledge.
Blanchot, M.
   1955 L'espace littéraire. Paris: Galimard, Folio/Essai.
Clifford, J.
   1997 Routes. Travel and Translation in the Late Twentieth Century. Cambridge: Harvard University Press.
Clifford, J., and G. Marcus, eds.
   1986 Writing Culture: The Poetics and Politics of Ethnography. Berkeley: University of California Press.
Corin, E.
   1979 A Possession Psychotherapy in an Urban Setting: Zebola in Kinshasa. Social Sciences and Medicine, 13B:327–338.

Corin, E.
  1990   Facts and Meaning in Psychiatry: An Anthropological Approach to the Lifeworld of Schizophrenics. Culture, Medicine and Psychiatry 14(2):153–188.
Corin, E.
  1995   Meaning Games at the Margins: The Cultural Centrality of Subordinated Cultures. *In* Beyond Textuality. Asceticism and Violence in Anthropological Interpretation. G. Bibeau and E. Corin, eds. Pp. 173–192. Berlin: Mouton de Gruyter Publishing.
Corin, E.
  1998a   Refiguring the Person: The Dynamics of Affects and Symbols in an African Spirit Possession Cult. *In* Bodies and Persons. Comparative Perspectives from Africa and Melanesia. M. Lambek and A. Strathern, eds. Pp. 80–102. Cambridge: Cambridge University Press.
Corin, E.
  1998b   Le rapport à l'autre. Psychanalyse et anthropologie. S. Harel, ed. *In* Résonances. Dialogues avec la psychanalyse. Pp. 11–58. Montreal: Liber.
Corin, E.
  2000a   Le paysage de l'alternatif dans le champ des thérapies. *In* Les ressources alternatives de traitement. Y. Lecomte and J. Gagné, eds. Montreal: Santé mentale au Québec.
Corin, E.
  2000b   L'étrange(r) dans les tracés de la mémoire. *In* L'infigurable. A. Nouss, S. Harel, and M. La Chance, eds. Cap-Saint-Ignace, Québec: Liber: 21–41.
Corin. E., R. Thara, and R. Padmavati
  2004   Living through a Staggering World: The Play of Signifiers in Early Psychosis in South India. *In* Schizophrenia, Culture and Subjectivity: The Edge of Experience. J. Jenkins and R. Barrett, eds. Pp. 110–145. Cambridge: Cambridge University Press.
Crapanzano, V.
  1977   Introduction. *In* Case Studies in Spirit Possession. V. Crapanzano and V. Garrison, eds. Pp. 1–40. New York: John Wiley & Sons.
Crapanzano, V.
  1992   Hermes' Dilemma and Hamlet's Desire. Cambridge: Harvard University Press.
Crapanzano, V.
  1994   Rethinking Psychological Anthropology: A Critical View. *In* The Making of Psychological Anthropology II. M. M. Suarez-Orozco and G. and L. Spindler, eds. Pp. 223–243. Fort Worth: Harcourt Brace College Publishers.
Foucault, M.
  1966   Les mots et les choses. Une archéologie des sciences humaines. Paris: NRF, Gallimard.
Foucault, M.
  1994 [1964]   Dits et écrits 1954–1988. I 1954–1969. Paris: NRF, Gallimard.

Green, A.
1995 Instances du négatif: transfert, tiercéité, temps. *In* Le négatif. A. Green, B. Favarel-Garrigues, J. P. Fédida et al., eds. Pp. 15–56. Paris: L'esprit du temps.
Gupta, A., and J. Ferguson
1992 Beyond "Culture": Space, Identity and the Politics of Difference. Cultural Anthropology 7(1):6–23.
Imbeault, J.
1997 Mouvements. Paris: NRF, Gallimard.
Kahn, L.
2001 L'hallucinatoire, la forme, la référence. Revue Française de Psychanalyse 65(4):1057–1074.
Lacan, J.
1966 Le stade du miroir comme formateur de la fonction du Je telle qu'elle nous est révélée dans l'expérience psychanalytique. *In* Les Écrits: 93–100. Paris: Le Seuil.
Lacan, J.
1975 Le séminaire, livre I: Les écrits techniques de Freud. Paris: Le Seuil.
Lyotard, J. F.
1988 Le Postmoderne expliqué aux enfants. Paris: Galilée.
Madan, T. N.
1987 Non-Renunciation. Delhi: Oxford University Press.
Maldiney, H.
1986 Daseinsanalyse: phénoménologie de l'existant? In Phénoménologie, Psychiatrie, Psychanalyse. P. Fédida, ed. Pp. 9–26. Paris: Ed. G.R.E.U.P.P., Echos-Centurion.
Obeyesekere, G.
1992 The Apotheosis of Captain Cook. European Mythmaking in the Pacific. Princeton: Princeton University Press.
Ortigues, E., M.-C. Ortigues, A. Zempleni, and J. Zempleni
1968 Psychologie clinique et ethnologie (Sénégal). Bulletin de Psychologie, 21(15–19):950–958.
Ramanujan, A. K.
1989 Is There an Indian Way of Thinking? An Informal Essay. Contributions to Indian Sociology (n.s.), 23(1):41–58.
Said, E.
1978 Orientalism. New York: Pantheon.
Spivak, G. C.
1999 A Critique of Postcolonial Reason. Towards a History of the Vanishing Present. Cambridge, MA: Harvard University Press.
Young, R. J. C.
2001 Postcolonialism. An Historical Introduction. Oxford: Blackwell.

Chapter 12

When the Borders of Research and Personal Life Become Blurred:
Thorny Issues in Conducting Dementia Research

Athena McLean

As I walked toward the social room of the special care unit,[1] I noticed a new resident sitting in a geri-chair.[2] Her head tilted to one side, she seemed to be nodding in and out. She was poorly wrapped in a hospital gown and appeared to be less well functioning than the other residents. I was looking for my mother who usually sat in this room that time of day. On closer inspection, I realized this "new resident" *was* my mother! I was not alone in my misrecognition; in the background, a nursing assistant asked, "Who's that new lady in the social room?" I went up to my mother and she smiled with an uncharacteristic lack of recognition – much to my alarm – before nodding off again. My alarm intensified when I discovered dark bruises on her forearms.

This was one of few field notes I would write during my mother's three-year stay at this nursing home. I wrote it several months after she moved there from an assisted living facility where she had lived several months before. Her tenure at both facilities overlapped with mine as Research Ethnographer of dementia care at a different nursing home.

The change I observed in my mother that day was sparked by events that led her to lose trust in the nursing home staff. Her subsequent trajectory of decline only confirmed the staff's grim expectations, despite several occasions of less remarkable recovery. Still, hers was a dramatic illustration of the poor resiliency of elders with dementia subjected to forcible pharmacological and physical interventions to suppress their disturbed behaviors. The details of my mother's decline painfully substantiated conclusions I was reaching independently in my own research.

My personal immersion into my mother's world and the unfortunate practices to which she was subjected there penetrated my very being, challenging my sensibilities and senses of justice and injustice. These lurked in the shadows of my research, piquing my interests, directing my attention to particular questions and persons, inciting or reinforcing insights, and driving me indefatigably to learn how key actors (staff, families, and elders) engaged with dementia and the persons it affected. Their intensity propelled me to unravel the differential conditions and ideologies that had contributed to decline like my mother's – or in happier cases, to more positive outcomes; they were thus instrumental in shaping my knowledge. At the same time, I wondered how much they might have affected my perceptions of what I was studying and whether revealing their influence might affect the credibility of my findings.

In this chapter, by referring to this unique set of overlapping circumstances, I examine how independent experiences and emotions can inflect ethnographic research and shape the ethnographer's motivations, insights, and interpretations, as well as future praxis. The overlap was uncanny in my case, leading to a more immediate view of the personal, and lending an uncommon intimacy to my research. Personal experiences and emotions are inevitably part of all ethnographic practice. However, the exceptional circumstances that conjoined my life and work in this case provided a unique opportunity for confronting issues – personal, methodological, epistemological, political, and moral/ethical – rarely dealt with so openly in ethnographies. I shall touch on each of these, but will draw particular attention to a few concerns.

First, ethnographic research is distinguished by its dependence on subjective engagement by the ethnographer as the very instrument for conducting research and filtering findings (Ortner 1995). At any point during the research, the ever-changing interface of the ethnographer's history, past research experiences, values, and life circumstances define her ongoing, ever-shifting relation to the "field" and immersion in it. These are the personal *shadows* that inevitably bear on the research process and its findings. While not negating the possibility of evaluating findings, they demand a self-critical reading of them (Crapanzano 2004:11). Here, by referring to my own particular circumstances, I hope to use the close proximity of my personal life (the private personal world of the "self") with my research life (the formal public world of the "other") to bring to the fore some of these typically hidden workings.

Second, emotions are an inevitable part of experience that color our perceptions and shade our engagement in the phenomenological world and with those we encounter in it. Given the poignancy of emotions associated with my experiences in my mother's nursing home, I hope to elucidate how these affected my perceptions of phenomena at the research site and my pursuit of research there.

Third, although the divide between the subjective private space of the "self" and the objective public space of the "other" (in the "field") has long been problematized as the artificial product of a positivist science, its resolution has hardly been achieved (Keane 2003:22). These distinctions came into play as I became immersed into two distinct spaces – the nursing home of my private world and that of my research world – each evoking distinctive thoughts and feelings, engaging my various selves and implicating me in different relations of power. As these worlds gradually blended into a single seamless "field," the distinction self/other blurred, and my impressions and feelings merged and intensified, subconsciously driving my research in various ways. Pulling from my own data, I hope to illustrate some of these typically hidden processes.

Fourth, the ethnographer's identity serves to locate him or her vis-à-vis others within the field, and can work to facilitate or impede access to institutional knowledge and the subjective worlds of others. Here, I consider how my eventual position as a kind of "halfie" (Abu-Lughod 1991) during the course of my research afforded me greater access to some "others" (elders and their families) while disrupting and confounding my position with regard to other "others" (some of the staff) (cf. Telfer 2004). My identity as a halfie and my experiences at my mother's home independently colored my negotiation of self and position as I engaged with those at the research site. This raised questions about positionality, its impact on knowledge, and the ethics and politics of conducting research.

Finally, the messiness that occurs in research is often hidden by deceptively finished ethnographies. Based on my experiences striding two interrelated nursing home worlds, I briefly address some of this messiness.

Dementia and the Study

Senile dementia is a syndrome affecting elderly persons, and involving cognitive, behavioral, verbal, and functional impairments generally attributed to Alzheimer's disease, vascular dementia, or their mixture (Norrgard, Mateis-Kraft, and Rigler 2000:465; Richter and Richter 2000). My research was concerned with disturbed behaviors (BDs), like repetitiveness, agitation, crying, swearing, and fighting, that often occur in dementia, and that upset the lives of elders, their families, and institutional caregivers. Dementia, earlier termed "senility," had once been regarded a "natural" condition of aging. After senility became reframed as a biomedical disorder in the 1970s, BDs became viewed as random pathological events resulting from progressive incurable disease (see McLean 2007:35). My research explored conditions unrelated to the dementia itself (e.g., pain, discomfort, hunger, loneliness, or dissatisfaction) that helped to explain the BDs as possibly meaningful acts (Shomaker 1987; Cottrell and Schulz 1993:207) given their context (cf. Fabian 2001:51) of expression. Thus it acknowledged the *agency* of elders despite their dementia, something the biomedical view had minimized or denied.[3]

The research was conducted sequentially in two nursing home units – each with very different approaches to dementia care – during 1992–94. I spent at least nine months in each, examining elders' behaviors and outcomes in relation to caregiving approaches, interactions with others in the unit, and interventions to their BDs. My discussion here focuses on my study of the first unit.

The Shadow Side of Fieldwork

Six months before my study began, my mother moved in with me, my husband and children after living independently for years. Her memory was worsening and she occasionally became confused, but otherwise she was functioning well.[4] A couple of months after my research began, however, she developed a pattern of sleep reversal that kept her pacing all night long, disrupting the sleep of others in my family. She was diagnosed with early dementia and her doctor suggested she move to an assisted living facility, where she could retain some freedom and receive help without disturbing the family. Although she agreed, the move was difficult for both of us. She disliked living with strangers; I felt a sense of filial betrayal for breaking an implicit family covenant to care for her myself. This situation heightened my sensitivity to what I encountered at both her nursing home and my study site. It also shaped my view of elder care as a moral enterprise charged with preserving not only the body, but the biographical *person* with dementia (McLean 2007:254–257).

Traces of institutional life

At the assisted living facility, my mother's reversed sleep pattern corrected itself, but due to lapses of memory, she began to worry about the whereabouts of her family. The physician at the facility prescribed a small dosage of a major tranquilizer to help her feel "more comfortable." I consented until I found her groggy and unable to recognize me or my children, over whom she had always doted. When I asked him to withdraw the medication, he refused, claiming that "it was unfair to the facility." I had placed my trust in him and, out of naïveté or denial, was shocked to find his allegiances with the institution over his patient. He later substituted a milder anti-anxiety medication PRN (as needed), but its liberal administration by one staff member left my mother inebriated and vulnerable to falling, and I feared for her safety.

From my previous research with psychiatric consumers/survivors (McLean 1995), I recalled stories of others similarly subjected to medication excesses for purposes of control. But this seemed different. My mother was elderly and had no psychiatric history. Her behaviors were not psychotic, but were due to lapses of memory and the anxiety these stimulated. Furthermore, this small home-like facility barely approached the total institution (Goffman 1962) that characterized larger facilities, like psychiatric hospitals or nursing homes. While it lacked the institutional wrappings, however, the mentality of order and control were certainly there and helped to socialize me about what was yet to come.

The ensuing crisis

A bit later, after my mother wandered unnoticed from the facility, I felt it was time to find a setting with more responsible staff. By this point, I had already spent several months studying the first nursing unit at my research site. That unit had adopted a rigid biomedical approach to dementia care that prioritized medical and standard maintenance care over attention to personal needs and foibles. Given my mother's previous experiences, I knew this approach would not satisfy her need for social interaction and personal reinforcement. I looked instead for a non-medicalized nursing home that specialized in person-oriented dementia care. Together my mother and I visited several facilities and agreed on a unit headed by a social worker who ran an impressive social program.

My mother settled in happily at this home. However, after a few months, it was taken over by a for-profit chain[5] that ushered in significant changes. The corporate office made drastic cuts to the social program and eliminated the positions of the social worker and most of her staff. Gone were the dependable caregivers who knew my mother's history, idiosyncrasies, and needs, and who had helped her grow comfortable in her new home. The new, much-reduced staff were overworked and experienced continual turnover. They showed little interest in the residents as people, focusing instead on managing their behaviors. Soon afterwards, my mother underwent the crisis.

Returning to that critical event, my notes say:

> I swiftly sought out the nurse in charge to find out what had transpired
> since the day before when my mother and I had enjoyed a pleasant outing.
> The nurse, who was new, explained that my mother had endured a "rough"
> night. She had become "agitated" late in the day and her oral tranquilizers
> did little to calm her. The nurse called her physician, who ordered an injectable
> medication, to be repeated if she did not settle down within thirty minutes.
> My tiny mother, slim and under five feet, was surrounded by four large
> aides who forcibly held her down as the nurse injected her. This intimidating
> experience served to intensify her agitation, necessitating the second equally
> forced dosage.

Trying to suppress both rage and tears, I reminded the nurse of the 24-
hour standing order to call me so I could attempt to calm my mother down
first;[6] this had invariably worked in the past. Being new to the unit, the nurse
did not notice the order until after midnight, when she presumed it was
too late to bother me. She instead called the physician, who deliberately
bypassed the order, taking the "medically logical" route to the problem.

Experiencing medicalization and institutional control

Despite promises from the administration to honor my future requests as
the legally responsible party, unanticipated problems regularly occurred,
partly because of staff turnover, partly because of refusals by some to
cooperate. In addition, the staff's excessive reliance on medication to
chemically control behaviors that were medically designated "symptoms"
resulted in vertigo, which they then controlled through physical restraints.
Sometimes my mother would be too groggy to talk until the medicine
wore off.[7] This led to a relational distancing from me that was yet another
consequence of the side effects. While the nursing home staff were intent
on controlling my mother's behavior, my goal was to maintain meaningful
relational contact with her – which the medications impeded. These were
incommensurable goals that did not lend themselves to easy resolution.

Our differing goals stemmed from differences in our attributions of her
agitation. They accepted it as an artifact of a dementing disease process
(which, in fact, no medication could "treat"). I understood it contextu-
ally – the product of insecurity from being in an unfamiliar setting among
strangers, worrying about her family; memory loss only exacerbated this.
It made greater sense to me to correct the source of her anxiety directly
using memory cues, reinforcement, or the desired social contact, than to
suppress the agitation with medication. The staff could not understand,
or refused to consider, this less efficient approach.

When I asked her doctor to consider less intrusive social interventions, he accused me of "not letting us treat" her. The consulting psychiatrist refused to answer questions about the medications he recommended: "It's technical; I don't know how much you'd understand," and then accused me of trying to "dictate treatment." Each of us felt the other was violating something precious: they, their medical terrain and authority; I, my mother's body and person.

As a medical anthropologist, I understood the doctors' desire to protect their position of expertise; their few years of practice, as fairly young physicians, probably exaggerated this. I also understood how chronic conditions like dementia can be frustrating to physicians, since there is little they can do for them. I could thus further understand how prescribing medications that reduce undesirable behaviors might make them feel they could control the situation, even though the dementia remained unchanged and the side effects were undesirable. However, their rigidity and insensitivity to the effects of their interventions and to my mother's subjective losses truly infuriated me. They also refused to consider my concerns or avail themselves of my knowledge as daughter or professional. The violence that they imposed on my mother through forced treatment was subtly extended to me by their aggressive accusations and refusal to negotiate her care. I had seen similar strategies used with "difficult" family members in my research, but had never before understood their impact.

Despite these problems, I decided not to move my mother from the home for fear of exacerbating her confusion – a frequent consequence of moving persons with dementia. Instead, I found a sympathetic physician who understood the politics of the nursing home and could successfully negotiate her care with the staff. We stayed in close contact and he remained a strong advocate for my mother.

The Power of Emotions in Fieldwork

My mother's experiences at both facilities taught me how quickly decline (which each staff predicted), but also recovery (which surprised them both) can occur in dementia. I learned how disturbed behaviors can express reasonable needs and should not be uncritically dismissed. I became familiar with particular contexts in which disturbed behaviors occur and may be resolved or prolonged. And I discovered all too well the power of clinical decisions in shaping lives and of critical events that can disrupt trust and, often, hasten decline of elders. These were lessons I was beginning to learn independently in my research, but with less acute attention to subtleties or the sentient appreciation of their moral urgency.

These experiences undoubtedly figured into the ways I perceived the phenomena in my fieldwork and engaged with those I encountered. It was impossible to filter out their emotional impact on the way I conducted my research and focused my attention. Equally, emotions played a part, whether or not obvious to me at the time, in the ways in which I became involved with others in the field (cf. Hume and Mulcock 2004:xxiii). Only time and distance enabled me to see this.

Emotions and empathy

The emotional impact of these experiences sensitized me to ideologies, practices, and policies that seemed to precipitate decline or impede optimal functioning. I was drawn to attentive staff and families who devised creative solutions to problematic conditions. My struggles with my mother's physicians attuned me to the elements of both productive and noxious doctor/family relationships.[8] Significantly, the challenge to preserve my mother's *relational* life (her personhood), in contrast to the *instrumental* control over her behaviors/"symptoms" emphasized at her home, became competing themes of my research (McLean 2007:200–202).

The impact of iatrogenic and institutionally induced impairment on my own mother heightened my empathy with elders and families in similar situations and my understanding of their lived experiences (Ellis 1991:126). I felt frustrated by staff who rebuffed families' concerns or offers to share relevant information to improve their elder's care,[9] and I experienced satisfaction, even relief, when their offers were accepted. I was especially saddened by a family's disappointments with their relative's care, understanding all too well the emotional losses they were already suffering over their failing relative; I also found myself angered if the staff ignored or trivialized these feelings of loss. However, although my emotions sensitized me to negative encounters and outcomes, I have wondered if they blinded me from recognizing more positive ones.

I did not set out deliberately to apply my personal experiences or insights to my research. They made an impression nonetheless, due to the poignancy of my encounters, charged with emotion and frustration. Still, I was too engrossed in my research to be conscious of their impact on my thinking or acting at the time.

The intelligence of emotions

Neuroscientists have found that emotions are tightly bound to reason, sometimes manifested in poorly reasoned decisions, at other times, in well-thought-out ones (Hume and Mulcock 2004; cf. Damasio 1999). Martha

Nussbaum (2001) questions the view of emotions as mindless energies "that simply push the person around," understanding them instead as evaluative "judgments" that ascribe great importance to particular persons and things and that impact our ability to flourish. They derive from our experiential history and personal vulnerability, which connect us to others in particular ways. This connectedness (or in some cases, fracture) intrinsically links emotions to our sense of compassion, morality, and justice, or reminds us of their absence.

The intensity of my emotional experiences served to amplify my sensitivity to similar situations I had encountered in the field by connecting me empathetically with persons experiencing them. These served as important "sources of information" and provided insights that would not otherwise have been available to me (cf. Ellis 1991:126–127). The power of experience is significant in ethnographic research because it raises epistemological questions about "how we know what we know" while providing embodied clues toward "new disclosures, revelations and insights" in answering these questions (Poewe 1996:179).

The energy of emotions

While my mother remained at the nursing home – throughout the entire tenure of my research – I always felt unsettled. The uncertainty of who would be in charge and which aide would be caring for her (and how) only intensified my distress. Although her new physician was very supportive, he was not on the regular staff, and high turnover made it difficult to find anyone else on whom I could depend. These conditions made visiting my mother's home an emotional ordeal. Sometimes I would sit in my car for over 30 minutes before I could overcome my crippling inertia and enter her unit.

In contrast, at the research site I felt curiously energized, almost pushed to get started,[10] like many fieldworkers (Fadzillah 2004). I felt the urge to take everything in, a kind of embodied "imbibing" of it all (cf. Fabian 2001:32). I also felt pulled in many directions, uncommonly attuned to everything around me. The environment seemed wondrously rich with its various actors with competing agendas, together with the compelling reality of multiple lives at stake. I spent my time observing the unit and its various occupants, or talking with a staff member, family visitor, or resident. I was eager to learn yet additional perspectives about life on the unit, dementia, and the needs of affected elders, as well as requisite caregiving practices. And I felt obliged to examine why some staff and relatives ignored elders' utterings as if they were nonsense, while others were committed to trying to understand and respond to them.

This was more than intellectual curiosity. The moral implications of what I studied became profound for me through my intimate exposure to institutional violence and my inclination to resist it. The empowered position I assumed at the research site, where I had access to information and people, was an energizing stimulus, when countered by my frustrated access to both at my mother's home. The combination, I believe, drove my curiosity, propelling me to learn more. My heightened senses and passion at the research units contrasted sharply with my blunted energy at my mother's home and marked their emotional distinctiveness for me.

I began to understand the reason for this difference from a colleague who had provided hospice care to her mother. Every day she would write prolific notes about her experience; every detail mattered. Such vigorous journaling, and the "systematic introspection" (Ellis 1991:128) it afforded, was "liberating" because it allowed her to dissociate from the experience. Perhaps my fieldwork and elaborate note-taking provided equivalent release from the frustration and uncertain predicaments of my private life and an outlet through which to explore vital questions that I could not explore there. The research and writing offered havens of escape that may well have been therapeutic.

My mother's foray into long-term care familiarized me with the realities of institutional life, and the multiple dissatisfactions and sufferings that can result from imposed discipline. These painful memories lurked in the shadows, surfacing as I encountered similar situations in the field, and variously stimulating pathos, outrage, and the impracticable urge to intervene (McLean 2001; Hume and Mulcock 2004:xxii) – sentiments demanding greater understanding and strategic praxis. As Jackson observes, "lived experience . . . encompasses both the rage for order and the impulse that drives to unsettle or confound the fixed order of things" (1989).[11]

Merging of Worlds, Knowledges, Selves, and "Others"

Merging field sites: the fatuousness of boundaries

My mother's nursing home and the research facility shared many features – similar staff structures, caregiving practices, and institutional constraints on their operations. Despite some differences in their caregiving ideologies, values, and practices, their standards of care were shared, borne out of common professional discourses and bureaucratic conditions of institutional life, the added constraints of government regulatory impositions, and the political economy of commoditized nursing-home care. Thus their residents, caregivers, and family members also faced similar issues.

Gradually the distinct physical boundaries of my mother's world and that which I studied blurred into a seamless field for me. My perceptions and ethnographic imaginings did not cease when I left the research site. Nor did the "field" remain confined to the physically bounded space of either site; it was located instead in my "moral relation" (Turner 1989:19) or intellectual stance (Fox 1991:96; cf. Crapanzano 1987) to both worlds. As I penetrated nursing home life at each site, I became highly attuned to compelling moral issues that traversed them both.

By engaging in these interpenetrating life-worlds, I acquired insights about institutional living that moved beyond either site, encompassing a larger moral terrain that aroused shared moral concerns. They were the common products of larger structures, (e.g., legal traditions, standards of practice, government regulations), similar societal values, and invisible actors (local administrators and board of directors, state regulators, and federal legislators) whose bureaucratic decisions had profound implications for those behind every locked unit.

Merging/identifying with subjects/"others"

In trying to see my mother's world as she might see it, my subject identification with her and my appreciation of constraints on her life (both cognitive and institutional) provided me with a vantage point from which to speculate about the nature of her disturbed behaviors (cf. Crapanzano 1987:181; Fabian 2001:25). As a family member, I was familiar with her history and sensitivities and attuned to the meaning content of her complaints (Bruner 1993:7), so I interpreted her behaviors not as objective facts, but within my past and continuing knowledge of her. By interpreting her interactions with others within a shared meaning framework, I moved toward defying the distinction subjectivity/objectivity that had been the source of considerable personal, epistemological, and methodological unease for me (cf. Rabinow and Sullivan 1987:6).

This subject identification reduced the subject/object distance between my mother and myself. It also drew me closer to the elders in my study and compelled me to examine my own interactions with them within a similar meaning framework. Hastrup has observed that as ethnographers, we can never know individuals as subjects; we can know only "the space that they are prepared to share with us" (Hastrup 1995:156–157). The wide space my mother extended to me imparted deeper understanding of her world – and the world she shared with elders I studied – than what I could glean from the smaller spaces to which most elders in my study could or would admit me.

When I first visited the research unit, I was struck by the visual exoticism of those who were locked behind the gate, neatly demarcated from the rest of humanity. My field notes read:

> The unit was a concentration of the bizarre – the extremes of ancient beings collectively united – and separated – by their differences from a humdrum humanity. True, there were folks here who needed special nursing care – whose bodies needed to be moved, toileted, bathed, fed, dressed, and nursed. But they too were here for clearly other reasons.

Later, after my mother's ordeal, there were times when she too appeared bizarre. Her distrust of strangers in an unfamiliar environment led her to panic and to become so distraught that she would forget proprieties; the staff's responses only worsened matters. Even though she would recover quickly upon seeing me, to strangers she must have appeared like all the other "others"; indeed, even I did not immediately recognize her after her initial crisis.

Identifying my mother with the "others" at my research site was deeply unsettling to me. But as I realized that they too had been affected by their social circumstances (cf. Turner 1989:25) and as I became more fully absorbed into their world, their visible "otherness" became denaturalized and gradually dissolved. Bowman has observed that "the other is not fundamentally different from us – is not Other – but shares with us the need to construct its subjectivity out of the elements provided for it by its concourse with others in the social world" (1997:45). Similarly, the apparent Otherness of these elders was not intrinsic to them, but was produced from the circumstances in which they, like my mother, found themselves.

Some time later, a nurse who watched me conversing with a resident, raised her eyebrows and teasingly offered, "She's awfully demented!" Although stated in a seemingly light-hearted manner, the comment invalidated the elder, and me by association. It also made me wonder how the staff at my mother's home talked about her. At that moment, I found myself personally embarrassed for the woman. Not only did I identify my mother with her; I identified with her myself by imagining a shared subject position and vulnerability in a like context (Bowman 1997:45; cf. Turner 1989:25). This exceeded empathy (cf. Fabian 2001:32); my very personhood felt violated.

Merging with "others" as a means to moral knowledge

My shared vulnerability aroused my alarm at the injustices to which the vulnerable might be subject; my own mother's experiences only intensified that alarm. As Gadamer notes of the moral realm, "the knower is not standing over against a situation that he merely observes, but . . . *is directly affected by what he sees* (1986:280) (emphasis, mine).[12] I saw how the medicalized label "dementia" afforded an institutional othering that sanctioned the exercise of power over these others in various ways – ignoring or silencing them, denying their validity as persons, depriving their basic rights (e.g., to participate in intimate relationships [McLean 1994] or to obtain help to get to a bathroom), and forcibly restraining or medicating them. Although I was not directly subjected to this power, imagining its effects proved painfully sentient. By gaining a glimpse of these everyday violences (Scheper-Hughes 2002) imposed on elders as "others," the elders ceased to exist as "other" for me. What became foreign and "other" instead were the experts and the controlling technologies they dispensed.

Having become sensitized to the violence of categorizing elders as "others" and of the disciplinary technologies of the nursing home (cf. Katz 1996), I did not want to subject them to further injustice through my research, tainted by its own history of "disciplinary practices" (Turner 1989:24; Fox 1991:10). Yet I could not deny my own imbalance of power with the elders, captive as they were to my researcher's gaze. And while I was free to enter and leave their space at will, they were confined to locked units that they did not choose. But I was not a detached observer. In fact, my growing awareness of this muddied moral "field" bred a skepticism and resistance (Turner 1989:16) that challenged the very violences that they/we confronted (see also Scheper-Hughes, this volume).

Self-Positioning and Positioning by Others

Negotiating self and position at the research site

The research units had many actors, several with a history of contentious relations. Families of elders at this nursing home were quite vocal about their concerns. Clinical and administrative staff sometimes disagreed about residents' care needs and the appropriate placement unit. And clinicians did not always share values or agree on goals and how to achieve them. Relations between administrative staff and nursing assistants had been contentious for some time, as were relations among different ranks of nurses, and sometimes between physicians and nurses. In addition, personal disagreements sometimes led staff to change their allegiances.

Since the environment fostered distrust, I had to carefully maneuver among its actors without appearing to be allied with any one group or point of view. Some of the staff and families voiced their fear that I would disclose their remarks to others, despite my assurances of confidentiality.

In addition, the units were intentionally designed to afford visibility of every resident, so I had little privacy or hope of escaping notice as I moved about, talking with different people. If the head nurse tried to steer me away from certain relatives or staff, for example, she could see, and be slightly put off, that I ignored her advice, even though I had often explained my need to talk with people having a variety of viewpoints.

Negotiating the research world as a "halfie"

To this environment I brought my own experiences, perspectives, and values. These subtly shaped my interactions with those whom I encountered, and my interpretations. After my mother moved to the first caregiving facility, about halfway into my research on the unit, I acquired the additional identity as family member; this further impacted my research. As a kind of halfie (Abu-Lughod 1991)[13] striding both the worlds of insider (as family member) and outsider (as researcher), I was afforded two separate vantage points from which to process my perceptions. My mother's life-world afforded a hidden point of comparison with those of elders in my study. My family self remained in the shadows as I strategically engaged with different persons in my research. It emerged now and then as I empathized with a family member or elder or privately revolted against practices I had seen hurt my mother. It submerged again as I tried to remain open to caregivers whose practices I had come to question. At times I was touched by compassion a clinician would show an elder. At other times, when elders' complaints were ignored or family members were criticized for voicing their concerns, I felt I was on enemy territory. I continually traversed between an "epistemology of intimacy," absorbed by my experiential insights, and an "epistemology of estrangement" (Keane 2003:240), which provided the distance to critically reflect on what I saw and experienced.

My relations with others in the field were shaded by my developing views about dementia care and my ongoing personal experiences at my mother's facilities. These no doubt affected our mutual politics of withholding and disclosing information and views. Later when my mother entered the nursing home, I did not hide this fact from the research staff or family members. Sharing this was part of the ordinary give-and-take that occurred during our daily chats. Although I *was* curious about reactions to this new piece of information about me, I did not deliberate set out to weigh these reactions. At the same time, my mother's move (and my revelation of it) occurred close to the end of my tenure on this unit, and I was well aware that my study might have been jeopardized – and that I might not have shared this fact – had it occurred earlier.

Being repositioned by staff and families

Initially, my new status seemed to bring me closer to everyone in my research. The nurses would inquire about my mother, offering bits of advice. Family members seemed more receptive to me. The better functioning residents also asked about my mother, expressing empathy. However, being a family member, even of a resident at a separate facility, variously redefined my relations to families and the staff. With families, it provided a leveling status that afforded me greater access to them. But to staff, especially some of the nurses who had been my major informants, identifying me with families rekindled distrust,[14] given their history of adversarial relations with many families. Now I too became subject to the challenges of my new label.

This marked a significant shift in my relations at the research site, as it prompted both staff and families to reposition themselves toward me and affected their continued willingness (or refusal) to admit me into their worlds. Some families now went out of their way to help me learn more about their elder's history. One brother of a resident showed me a questionnaire his sister had filled out 40 years earlier, identifying what she most valued; he hoped this would impart insight about her difficulties. Another family member invited me to her mother's funeral so I could hear her eulogy, which documented her rich life history. However, nurses who had familiarized me with operations of the unit and had previously apprised me of important events began to withdraw from me. For example, I was not made privy to an important "surprise" visit by the Director of Nursing (DON) (Mclean 2001:236–243), even though it was relevant to my research.

As demanded by the study, I regularly asked nurses about nonmedical factors (e.g., hearing difficulties, noise, physical discomforts, fears, and dissatisfactions) that might be contributing to residents' problems. The head nurse had always been very cooperative in responding, even though she personally believed these had very little to do with dementia behaviors. Under my new identity as "family," however, my questions took on a new flavor and pushed me into the camp of "unrealistic" families. Mild sarcasm sometimes surfaced as she would remark, "Now *you* sound like an unrealistic family member!"

Repositioning myself with regard to staff and families

The head nurse's classification of families (as "realistic" versus "unrealistic") stemmed from her view of dementia as an incurable disease that diminished the awareness of its victims; body maintenance and symptom control thus became the target of her care. Her instrumental approach thus focused on completing care tasks and eliminating undesirable behaviors, with minimal concern about their impact on the person and family. Personal needs and nonstandard requests were seen as superfluous, since they interfered with more essential (instrumental) tasks. "Realistic" families accepted her view of dementia and resigned themselves to the limitations of standard custodial care. "Unrealistic" families persisted in trying to improve their relative's condition by asking her staff to find such things as lost hearing aids[15] or shoes that "would only be lost again" – requests she regarded as "pointless."

During my stay on the unit I had witnessed how unreasonable some of the families' demands indeed seemed,[16] so I could understand the head nurse's impatience with some requests, and at times, even her reluctance to respond to reasonable ones; the many competing demands on her staff's time required that she be very selective in responding to requests.

Gradually, however, I came to appreciate the perspectives of families more fully. My mother's negative experiences with instrumental caregiving helped me further understand the families whom she regarded "unrealistic." Earlier in my research, I had avoided aligning myself with any one group, focusing strictly on understanding their positions. My own experiences dealing with a stalwart staff at my mother's home, and her unfortunate experiences there, later served to realign me more closely to the perspectives of families. I empathized, for example, with one woman's appeals to her husband's psychiatrist to reduce his sedative so she could converse with him again. Since he was large and difficult to "manage," I understood why the staff had sedated him. But I bolted against the psychiatrist's judgment of her request as "narcissistic" and evidence of an "exaggerated sense of entitlement." Quietly, I positioned myself with the woman and with several other "unrealistic" family members whom he had similarly pathologized. While I maintained my apparent neutrality as a researcher "observer", my embodied knowledge (Okeley 1992; cf. Csordas 1990) of the impact of nonnegotiable expert control positioned me to resist it.

The Messiness of Ethnographic Praxis

Striding positions/being disingenuous

Ethnographers must stride many positions in their research (cf. Forsey 2004). As both researcher and later, family member, I privately came to ally myself with the positions and interests of most patients and family members against the disciplinary technologies and control of caregivers on the unit. I never told the nurse, however, of my objections to what I concluded were her nihilistic view of dementia and instrumental approach to care (even though my research project clearly hinted at alternative possibilities) because I genuinely wanted to learn more about her perspective, and did not want to inhibit her sharing. Also, while I was aware that being more forthright about my views might have fostered a more equivalent dialogic relation (cf. Turner 1989:31), I felt at the time that it was not within my privilege as researcher (especially a nonclinically trained one) to directly question her views. Yet I felt somewhat disingenuous about not revealing my impressions, and in retrospect have wondered what directions my research might have taken had I done so.

Despite my developing objections to instrumental approaches, I nonetheless tried to gain fuller access to the head nurse's perspectives about dementia and the affected elders, as well as the structural conditions that further shaped her care priorities and interventions. Her answers helped me to appreciate the "intelligibility" of her own situation (cf. Turner 1989:25), which helped me comprehend why, as an otherwise apparently sensitive clinician, she would adopt an approach that frequently only precipitated decline.

Our ethnographic selves and identifications are not fixed, but "multiple, fragmented, and open to shifts and negotiations" (Coffey 1999:35–36). The anthropological field itself is social, calling on multiple relationships, interests, and identifications (Hume and Mulcock 2004:xxii). As I proceeded in my work as researcher I created a "field identity" (Coffey 1999:23), negotiating my existing selves and identifications – of family member with elders and their families, of working mother with the head nurse and nursing aides. These provided points of commonality with the various persons with whom I engaged. These identifications protected me from engaging in a totalizing othering of staff and also from feeling disingenuous about relating with staff members whose clinical practices I sometimes found disturbing. I could identify with their subject positions (Bowman 1997:47) at least in some areas; these afforded me access to their perspectives, and helped extend my effort to try to understand them, in areas where our identifications and perspectives departed.

With the overlapping sites I traversed throughout the research, and the confounded and diverse roles and positions I occupied at each, my research might challenge the limits of acceptability to diehard methodologists. Yet some researchers argue that working within tension or messiness produced by a situation is far more fruitful than attempting to separate out the complicating factors (Gubrium and Holstein 1999:561). For them, such complications enhance ethnographic work, rather than invalidate its findings. Coffey also argues that at her best the ethnographer *must* engage in a range of "position, place and identity" (Coffey 1999:36).

Biases in ethnographic research

I did not set out to criticize this unit or its approach to care. It was only gradually that I grew skeptical, and then quite critical, of it. By the time my mother had entered a nursing home, I had already developed a negative assessment about instrumental caregiving. I saw how ignoring elders' complaints or requests only intensified their behavioral problems, prolonging their discomfort and suffering and sometimes hastening their decline (McLean 2007:121–123).[17] I also saw how instrumental interventions (like medicating an agitated person) that proved ineffective would typically be augmented – often leaving elders even more functionally impaired – rather than abandoned for alternative strategies.

Since the medical staff and most of the nursing staff regarded BDs (behavioral disturbances) as disease symptoms, they resorted to pharmacological and other forced interventions (e.g., physical restraints) to control them. By focusing on the behavior as if it were disembodied from the person, these strategies bypassed the elder herself, effectively *silencing* her from communicating possible problems the BD had signaled. Witnessing such exercises of power over elders ill disposed me to this approach. My mother's and my own lesser sufferings at the hands of similarly instrumentally oriented practitioners only fueled my mounting criticism. What's more, the forced silencing of elders, which prevented their communicating actual sources of suffering (e.g., pain or sadness), raised serious ethical questions for me.

My developing criticism of instrumental approaches in favor of person-oriented ones was shaped by my concurrent experiences at my mother's home as well as preexisting perspectives that I, like any ethnographer, had brought with me to the field. But it introduced a bias into my research which my own involvement as a halfie intensified. Like ethnographic representations (Abu-Lughod 1991:143), research practices are also inevitably "positioned." As Abu-Lughod observes, "every view is a view from somewhere and every act of speaking is a speaking from somewhere . . ." (1991:141); one can say the same for every feeling, which also offers a clue to self-positioning (Ellis 1991:126). My intimate penetration into my mother's life-world afforded me an emotional vantage point that directed me to examine instrumental control and depersonalizing interventions over other aspects of institutional care.

All research has a subjective underside, however unacknowledged. This is most apparent for ethnographers, who must use themselves as research instruments. What is important is to be brutally honest in acknowledging this "shadow side" or bias (an "ethnocentrism") (Turner 1989) as one continues in field research (Dimitriadis 2001:280) or writing (Suleiman 1994:2).[18] Recognizing this is significant for knowledge production since, as Crapanzano observes, "our texts – our teachings, our commentary – issue from there" (1987:189).

Ethnography as political praxis

The morally engaged researcher does not simply hope the community does well, but actively seeks to improve its condition through "responsible *criticism*" (Walzer 1987[19]; cf. Dimitriadis 2001:581). Within a contested community such as that of the nursing home,[20] with its various actors and their competing assumptions, values, and agendas, the critic's engagement becomes even more complex.

A truly connected critic does not eliminate her or his biases, but uses readings of the moral field to locate the "intelligibility" of the behaviors of its various actors within the contexts of their circumstances (Turner 1989:25). It is through a "mindful" ethnocentrism (Turner 1989:21) that the researcher can clarify his or her own relation to the moral field shared with community members, and more responsibly critique the actions of those who inhabit it. The critic must measure the consequences of various actors' actions for others in the community. Insofar as the nursing home community is invested in caring for vulnerable elders, narratives and actions directed at caring become the principle focus of critical study. Whenever dominant narratives and practices are damaging to vulnerable members of the community, they need to be questioned. Critical inquiries thus provide a place from which to resist an oppressive life-world" (Turner 1989:20–1) and extend our research to political praxis.

Nearly two years of intensive immersion into the life-worlds of elders with dementia sensitized me to the potential abuses to which this population is vulnerable. It also exposed me to the repeated damage wrought by standard technological interventions that deny subjectivities and silence suffering. The power of my subjective encounter with these interventions through my mother and as a family member intensified my urgency to challenge them. This sensitized me to the political and moral demands of ethnographic praxis. To begin challenging potentially damaging practices, we ethnographers must strive to minimize the subject distance with those whose existential plights we can imagine sharing. Through this imagination of shared vulnerabilities, a common moral understanding and compassion can be achieved, and the perpetuation of such practices will no longer seem tenable. The need to realize humane alternatives will then become compelling. To be effective, our ethnographies must connect our own subjectivities and the subjectivities of those whom we study with those of our readers. Once identity is established, we must work to unsettle, disturb, and disrupt public sensibilities and unleash the social and moral imagination against violences that intensify needless suffering, often under the unselfconscious guise of helping.

Conclusion: The Place of Autobiography in Ethnography

Johannes Fabian has argued that worthwhile knowledge must be mediated by experience; hence "all ethno-graphy is connected to (auto)bio-graphy" (Fabian 2001:12). Far from being an impediment however, this is a strength as it requires that the researcher's history and involvement be taken seriously. Only by giving way to our passions, he insists further, can we be fair to those we study who have been brutally wronged. Our charge as ethnographers, however, is not to get caught up in these experiences, but rather to consider their implications for the knowledge that we produce.

Others have similarly foregrounded subjective experience in ethnographic research, arguing that our response to the phenomenological world should be "not in things themselves, but in our experience" of them (Hastrup 1995:178). This experience is necessarily tied to autobiographical associations and meanings from our past. Since the researcher's autobiography is integral to the ethnographic account, everything he or she does and experiences during fieldwork should be seen as relevant data (Ryang 2000:308). To separate the personal from the formal ethnographic study is to set up a "false dichotomy" (Bruner 1993:4).

Acknowledging the autobiographical and its hidden workings in our research – as I have tried to do in this essay – is not only an exercise in brutal honesty; it is a means for subjecting ethnographic research to rigorous standards that increase trust in the knowledge we produce. Such an exercise goes far beyond the cautious reflexivity (Watson 1987) that has too often stopped with self-absorbed reflections that cannot advance broader knowledge or theoretical understandings. Coffey acknowledges the epistemological value of our deep contextual engagement and its effect on our fieldwork, but she also reminds us that the "ethnographic imperative" is to make sense of the social worlds and experiences of others, and that the self should not become the focus of the fieldwork experience (1999:37). In fact, as Crapanzano notes, a focus on the "existential condition or malaise of the fieldworker" detracts from the effects or significance of these for anthropological practice and theory (1987:180).

In this essay I included considerable autobiographical material to show the ways in which my research was shaded by my private life. But I attempted to exercise discretion in doing so (see also Lovell, this volume). Using the case study of my research in dementia care, I brought forth personal data only insofar as was needed to illuminate the processes and circumstances under which my ethnographic knowledge was produced and informed. The extreme overlap between my private and research worlds also illustrated the artificial boundaries between them – boundaries we too often draw in any research; the unique circumstances of my research allowed me to explore their artificiality. I examined, for example, how my experiential engagement in separate physical spaces (my mother's unit and the research unit) began to blur those boundaries for me, and the epistemological significance of that blurring. And I examined the impact of emotion on my research, my own blurred identities as family member and researcher, and my messy negotiations of selves and positions, all of which inflected my research. Doing so revealed the complex, typically hidden processes always at play in ethnographic work, but blatantly apparent in my case, given the coincidental circumstances under which my research was conducted. Their blatancy lifted them from the shadows and demanded that they be examined.

In dealing with heart-rending life predicaments like those of the elders in my study, researchers cannot afford to be frivolous with their ethnographies. Ethnographers must be judicious in using autobiographical accounts only to expand knowledge of others' lives and the conditions that affect them, not to draw attention to their own. As Ryang argues, glorifying one's own personal history or personality is "not what anthropology is about and not what it should be about" (Ryang 2000:316). Drawing attention to one's self diverts critically needed attention from the sufferings of disempowered persons,[21] who, like the elders in my study, have been denied validation already; it also diverts us from exploring the conditions that have shaped their suffering. Oppressive disciplinary practices and the discourses and institutions that support and legitimate them must increasingly be the focus of anthropological analysis; insofar as personal experiences illuminate this, they should also inform the research. Only then can anthropologists promote alternative discourses and practices which hopefully will valorize, not violate, vulnerable subjectivities.

Acknowledgments

This research was conducted with the support of Grant # 11RG-92-076 from the Alzheimer's Association. The author wishes to thank all the people who kindly shared their time and perspectives with me so I could conduct my ethnographic research. Thanks also go to Robert Rubinstein for the opportunity to conduct the research. Finally, I appreciate the critical comments from Anne Lovell, Thea McLean, and Annette Leibing in helping me rethink this chapter.

Notes

1   A special care unit is a nursing home unit that provides care to persons with dementia who may display agitation, confusion, repetitive requests or calling out, or aggressive behaviors in connection with their dementia. See Maslow 1994.

2   A geri-chair is a large chair on wheels, with a large tray that closes in front of the person seated on it, and serves as a restraining device.

3   Persons with dementia, because of their cognitive disturbances, are generally seen as lacking the moral agency needed to make responsible decisions. This attributional view adopted by many biomedical ethicists relies strictly on reason as the determinant of agency. Alternative views, such as that of the situated embodied agent (Hughes 2001), rely on understanding a person's actions in light of the context and her history.

4   On one rare occasion though, she wandered around her apartment looking for her grandchildren she thought were with her. This prompted my family to invite her to move with us.

5   Many private nursing homes that tried to serve their residents well, but struggled to survive, were absorbed by for-profits that cut costs by trimming services. Like this facility, they eliminated positions and reduced salaries and benefits by using a temporary, if unstable, workforce.

6   This request puzzled the staff. One administrator, for example, asked, "Why must you be your mother's Ativan (an anti-anxiety medication)?" While well intended, the question dramatically revealed a powerful inversion of biomedicine over intersubjective contact as the more reasonable source of human comfort.

7   Psychiatrists at the research facility observed that some damage brought on by psychotropic medications on the elderly was actually irreversible.

8   See chapter 6, case study 3 in McLean 2007 for an example of an especially positive doctor/family relationship.

9   One woman, for example, noticed how her aunt's adverse reaction to getting water in her ears at bath-time triggered agitation. She asked the head nurse to use a rubber water bonnet that might solve the problem. It was never tried; her aunt's condition subsequently deteriorated. See McLean 2007, chapter 5, case study 2.

10 While a researcher's relation to the field can serve to propel her work, it can also serve to reduce her steam. See, for example, Mulcock 2004.

11 Cited in Ellis 1991, p. 125.

12 Cited in Turner 1989, p. 18.

13   However, unlike Abu-Lughod, who was a permanent "halfie" – an anthropologist studying non-Western cultures and a member of a non-Western culture – my status as a halfie was not part of my permanent ethnic identity, but rather, part of my current status as the family member of a nursing home resident.

14   Early in the study, many nursing assistants and some of the nurses thought I was a spy for the administration. I had worked hard to achieve their trust, so this new status provided a new challenge.

15   Hearing aids, however, could calm elders because they allowed them to hear and respond to others and thus feel more in control in their environment. This alone helped to minimize their BDs.

16   One relative, for example, held the head nurse "accountable" for pieces of candy that were missed from her mother's drawer. Another called her "personally responsible" for keeping her husband's shoes in the same location of his closet, and complained if they were not.

17   See, for example, McLean 2007, chapter 5, case study 2.

18   Cited in Mattingly 1998, p. vii.

19   See Turner 1989, p. 21.

20   For a discussion of the problems with the term "community" regarding nursing home settings, see McLean 2006.

21   Unless, as in many confessional autoethnographies (particularly of the emotional sociology variety), the ethnographer has been the primary victim. But even then, I would argue, that we need to move beyond confession, to a deconstructing and active political challenging of those victimizing practices.

References

Abu-Lughod, Lila
   1991   Writing Against Culture. *In* Recapturing Anthropology. Richard Fox, ed. Pp. 137–162. Santa Fe, NM: School of American Research Press.
Bowman, Glenn
   1997   Identifying versus Identifying with "the Other": Reflections on the Citing of the Subject in Anthropological Discourse. *In* After Writing Culture: Epistemology and Praxis. Allison James, Jenny Hockey, and Andrew Dawson, eds. Pp. 34–50. London and New York: Routledge.
Bruner, Edward
   1993   Introduction: The Ethnographic Self and the Personal Self. *In* Anthropology and Literature. Paul Benson, ed. Pp. 1–26. Urbana: the University of Illinois Press.
Coffey, Amanda
   1999   The Ethnographic Self. London: Sage.
Cottrell, Victoria, and Richard Schulz
   1993   The Perspective of the Patient with Alzheimer's Disease: A Neglected Dimension of Dementia Research. The Gerontologist 33(2):205–211.

Crapanzano, Vincent
  1987 Editorial. Current Anthropology 2(2):179–189.
Crapanzano, Vincent
  2004 Imaginative Horizons. Chicago: University of Chicago Press.
Csordas, Thomas
  1990 Embodiment as a Paradigm for Anthropology. Ethos 18(1):5–47.
Damasio, Antonio
  1990 The Feeling of What Happens: Body and Emotion in the Making of
  Consciousness. Antonio R. Damasio. New York: Harcourt Brace.
Dimitriadis, Greg
  2001 Coming Clean at the Hyphen: Ethics and Dialogue at a Local Com-
  munity Center. Qualitative Inquiry 7(5):578–597.
Ellis, Carolyn
  1991 Emotional Sociology. Studies in Symbolic Interaction 12:123–145.
Fabian, Johannes
  2001 Anthropology with an Attitude: Critical Essays. Stanford, CA: Stanford
  University Press.
Fadzillah, Ida
  2004 Going Beyond "The West" and "The Rest": Conducting Non-Western,
  Non-native Ethnography in Northern Thailand. *In* Anthropologists in the Field.
  Lynne Hume and Jane Mulcock, eds. Pp. 32–45. New York: Columbia
  University Press.
Forsey, Martin
  2004 "He's Not a Spy; He's One of Us": Ethnographic Positioning in a Middle-
  Class Setting. *In* Anthropologists in the Field. Lynne Hume and Jane Mulcock,
  eds. Pp. 59–70. New York: Columbia University Press.
Fox, Richard
  1991 Introduction. *In* Recapturing Anthropology. Richard Fox, ed. Pp. 1–16.
  Santa Fe, NM: School of American Research Press.
Gadamer, Hans-Georg
  1986 Truth and Method. New York: Crossroad.
Goffman, Erving
  1962 (1961) Asylums; Essays on The Social Situation of Mental Patients and
  Other Inmates. Chicago: Aldine Publishing Company.
Gubrium, Jaber, and James Holstein
  1999 At the Border of Narrative and Ethnography. Journal of Contemporary
  Ethnography 28(5):561–573.
Hastrup, Kirsten
  1995 A Passage to Anthropology. London: Routledge.
Hughes, Julian
  2001 Views of the Person with Dementia. Journal of Medical Ethics 27(2):86–91.
Hume, Lynne, and Jane Mulcock
  2004 Introduction: Awkward Spaces, Productive Places. *In* Anthropologists
  in the Field. Lynne Hume and Jane Mulcock, eds. Pp. xi–xxvii. New York:
  Columbia University Press.

Jackson, Michael
  1989   Paths Toward a Clearing: Radical Empiricism and Ethnographic Inquiry. Bloomington: Indiana University Press.
Katz, Stephen
  1996   Disciplining Old Age: The Formation of Gerontological Knowledge. Charlottesville: University Press of Virginia.
Keane, Webb
  2003   Self-Interpretation, Agency, and the Objects of Anthropology: Reflections on a Genealogy. Comparative Studies in Society and History 45(2):222–248.
Maslow, Katie
  1994   Special Care Units for Persons with Dementia. Alzheimer Disease and Associated Disorders 8 Suppl. 3:122–137.
Mattingly, Cheryl
  1998   Healing Dramas and Clinical Plots. Cambridge: Cambridge University Press.
McLean, Athena
  1994   What Kind of Love is This? The Sciences 34(5):36–40.
McLean, Athena
  1995   Empowerment and the Psychiatric Consumer/Ex-Patient Movement in the United States: Contradictions, Crisis and Change. Social Science and Medicine 40(8):1053–1071.
McLean, Athena
  2001   Power in the Nursing Home: The Case of a Special Care Unit. Medical Anthropology 19:223–257.
McLean, Athena
  2006   From Commodity to Community in Nursing Homes: An Impossibility? Ageing and Society 26:925–937.
McLean, Athena
  2007   The Person in Dementia: A Study of Nursing Home Care In the U.S. Peterborough, ON: Broadview Press.
Norrgard, Carolyn, Carol Matheis-Kraft, and Sally Rigler
  2000   Dementia. Clinical Reference Systems. Annual Review 2000:465.
Nussbaum, Martha
  2001   Upheavals of Thought: The Intelligence of Emotions. Cambridge: Cambridge University Press.
Okeley, Judith
  1992   Anthropology and Ethnography: Participatory Experience and Embodied Knowledge. *In* Anthropology and Autobiography. Judith Okeley and Helen Callaway, eds. Pp. 1–25. London: Routledge Press.
Ortner, Shery B.
  1995   Resistance and the Problem of Ethnographic Refusal. Comparative Studies in Society and History 37:173–193.
Poewe, Karla
  1996   Writing Culture and Writing Fieldwork: The Proliferation of Experimental and Experiential Ethnographies. Ethnos 61:3–4.

Rabinow, Paul, and William Sullivan
   1987   The Interpretive Turn: A Second Look. *In* Interpretive Social Science: A Second Look. Paul Rabinow and William Sullivan, eds. Pp. 1–30. Berkeley: University of California Press.
Richter, Ralph W., and Brigitte Zoeller Richter
   2002   Alzheimer's Disease. London: Mosby.
Ryang, Sonia
   2000   Ethnography or Self-Cultural Anthropology? Reflections on Writing About Ourselves. Dialectical Anthropology 25:297–320.
Scheper-Hughes, Nancy
   2002   The Genocidal Continuum: Peace-Time Crimes. *In* Power and the Self. Jeannette Mageo, ed. Pp. 29–47. Cambridge: Cambridge University Press.
Shomaker, Dianna
   1987   Problematic Behavior and the Alzheimer Patient: Retrospection as a Method of Counseling. The Gerontologist 27(3):370–375.
Suleiman, Susan
   1994   Risking Who One Is: Encounters with Contemporary Art and Literature. Cambridge, MA: Harvard University Press.
Telfer, Jonathan
   2004   Dissent and Consent: Negotiating the Adoption Triangle. *In* Anthropologists in the Field. Lynne Hume and Jane Mulcock, eds. Pp. 71–81. New York: Columbia University Press.
Turner, Roy
   1989   Deconstructing the Field. *In* The Politics of Field Research. Jaber Gubrium and David Silverman, eds. Pp. 13–29. London: Sage.
Walzer, Michael
   1987   Interpretations and Social Criticism. Cambridge, MA: Harvard University Press.
Watson, Graham
   1987   Make me Reflexive – But Not Yet: Strategies for Managing Essential Reflexivity in Ethnographic Discourse. Journal of Anthropological Research 43(1):29–41.

Index